OS JCL
AND UTILITIES

OS JCL
AND UTILITIES:
A COMPREHENSIVE TREATMENT

MICHAEL TROMBETTA

Queensborough Community College

SUE CAROLYN FINKELSTEIN

IBM Corporation

ADDISON-WESLEY PUBLISHING COMPANY

Reading, Massachusetts • Menlo Park, California
London • Amsterdam • Don Mills, Ontario • Sydney

Library of Congress Cataloging in Publication Data

Trombetta, Michael.
  OS JCL and utilities.

  Bibliography: p.
  Includes index.
  1. Operating systems (Computers)   I. Finkelstein, Sue Carolyn.   II. Title.
III. Title: O.S. J.C.L. and utilities
QA76.6.T76   1984   001.64′2   83-6333
ISBN 0-201-07970-4

Reprinted with corrections, May 1985

ISBN 0-201-07970-4

GHIJ-DO-89876

To Angela
If they asked me I could write a different book

MT

To my mother Yetta Klieger, who made this book possible,
and my daughter Marla Rose Diamond, who made it necessary

SCF

PREFACE

The principles and techniques of JCL (Job Control Language) are among the simplest in the field of computer programming, yet students dread studying them and many professionals never learn to use them properly. We assert that JCL is simple because there is almost no logic involved. You can understand someone's having trouble coding a sequential update or a control break problem, because those programs involve complex logic. In contrast, JCL is all a matter of getting the commas in the right places.

Not everyone agrees that JCL involves almost no logic. When a colleague of ours marks JCL tests, he deducts two points for syntax errors and five points for logic errors. He calls coding a disposition of NEW for an existing data set or specifying a volume serial number for a cataloged data set a logic error. You could call those logic errors, but the logic they involve is about as complex as the logic involved in coming in out of the rain.

If JCL is so simple, why does it strike terror into the hearts of students and professionals alike? We believe the reason is that JCL is not taught as a programming language. Two principles guide the teaching of programming languages: first, students must see statements used in the context of complete programs; and second, students must execute solutions to programming assignments.

When JCL is taught, neither of these principles is followed. Parameters are presented in isolation. Students do not see a complete job stream (i.e., a

PREFACE

program) until late in their studies. Homework assignments follow the same pattern: "Code a JOB statement to request three minutes of CPU time," or "Code a DD statement to direct output to the punch." Students need homework assignments that require them to code and execute a job stream to perform some specified processing.

But how can students see complete job streams and execute solutions to programming assignments early in their study of JCL? If a JCL assignment requires the students to write a program in assembler or COBOL or PL/I, the program must be compiled and executed, which means that from the beginning of their studies students must use complex procedures. Furthermore, substantial effort must be applied to debugging the program, and the JCL principles the assignment was meant to illustrate may be obscured.

It was after we had been teaching JCL for several years that we arrived at the happy solution of using IBM utilities to illustrate JCL principles. This procedure has the extra benefit that students learn how to use the utilities while they are learning JCL. This book is based on that idea.

After some preliminaries in Chapter 1, in Chapter 2 the student sees a complete job stream which uses IEBGENER to list a card deck. The programming assignment in Chapter 2 requires the student to code and execute a similar job stream. Chapter 3 introduces tape and disk data sets, and Chapter 4 introduces a two-step job stream. In each chapter the programming assignment requires the student to code and execute a job stream similar to those presented in the chapter.

The succeeding chapters follow the same pattern: complications are gradually introduced, always with the assistance of complete job streams; when appropriate, new utilities are introduced; the student is required to code and execute job streams similar to the ones in the chapter. This pattern is broken only in Chapter 11, in which so many keywords are explained that illustrating them all with complete job streams would have been impractical. We hope that by the time students get to Chapter 11, they can supply the missing job streams.

When appropriate, particularly in the early chapters, we show and explain the output produced when a job stream is executed. Included are some job streams that did not execute properly, because they contain errors. This will help students to understand their output and in particular to understand error messages and how to correct their errors.

We believe that by teaching JCL as a programming language, this book will permit students to learn JCL more easily than they now learn COBOL or assembler or PL/I. To further help students we begin every chapter with a statement of learning objectives and a list of terms that will be defined in the chapter. When a term is defined in the chapter, it is printed in boldface

PREFACE

type. All the terms are also defined in the glossary. Every chapter contains an extensive set of exercises. These exercises test whether the students remember what was said in the chapter, whether they understand what was said, and whether they can apply what was said. Every chapter after Chapter 1 contains one or more programming assignments. The solutions to the exercises and programming assignments are contained in an Instructor's Guide which is available from the publisher: Addison-Wesley Publishing Company, Reading, MA 01867.

Our experience has been that students have difficulty understanding the relationship between JCL and COBOL, assembler, and PL/I programs. Therefore, we have emphasized this relationship whenever we could. Chapter 2 shows how ddnames and return codes are specified in programs. Chapter 3 shows how record format and blocksize are specified, and Chapter 4 illustrates how user completion codes are specified. Chapter 8 shows how programs receive PARM values. Chapter 12 discusses how COBOL and PL/I programs access ISAM data sets, and Chapter 13 talks about how they access VSAM data sets.

Although most students who study from this book will have had some exposure to computers, we assume no previous knowledge. For example, in Chapter 1 we explain the functions of input and output units, the CPU, and main and secondary storage. Chapter 3 discusses the characteristics of magnetic tape and disk. Chapter 10 explains sorting on major and minor keys. Although we begin at the beginning and try to move slowly enough that students are never lost, we nevertheless cover some advanced topics. For example, Chapter 5 discusses mass storage devices and Chapter 7 the 3800 Printing Subsystem. Chapter 8 shows how to link subroutines written in different languages, and Chapter 10 shows how to modify the collating sequence for a sort. Chapter 12 demonstrates how to exit from IEBISAM to a user-written routine. Chapter 13 discusses how to use an alternate index with a VSAM data set.

We have tried to live up to the subtitle, "A Comprehensive Treatment," by including everything an application programmer is likely to have to know about JCL and utilities. As a result the book contains more material than can be covered in the usual course. To decide what to omit, the instructor has to know what material must be covered if later chapters are to be understandable. Chapter 1 should be covered completely, with the possible exception of the section on data storage. Chapters 2, 3, and 4 also contain fundamental material which should be covered completely. However, the instructor may choose to omit some of the material on utility control statements.

In the remaining chapters the material is more or less independent, and the instructor may select material according to the needs and interests of the students and the dictates of time. For example, it is not necessary to learn all the utilities that process libraries or all the control statements of the utilities that are studied. The material on generation data groups in Chapter 6, mass storage in Chapter 7, and the linkage editor in Chapter 8 is not required for an understanding of later chapters. It is not necessary to cover throughly both Chapter 12 on ISAM and Chapter 13 on VSAM. The discussions of the advanced JCL features in Chapter 11 and the various utilities in Chapter 14 are completely independent, so the instructor may choose whatever seems most valuable to his or her class. The Instructor's Guide contains a suggested course outline.

We have tried to keep the discussion understandable to a reader who is not enrolled in a course, so that students can read on their own any topics that are omitted. We expect that professionals reading the book on their own will be able to understand the discussion of any topic to which their interests or needs lead them.

If students are to execute the programming assignments, they will need some information about their computer center. They must know their account number, the job class they must use, the serial numbers of the volumes they may use, etc. The inside front cover has been designed to help the instructor give the students this information. The instructor may choose to give the students the information at the appropriate time and have them enter it on the inside front cover; alternatively the inside front cover may be copied, the information entered, and copies of the completed form distributed to students at the start of the course.

It is a pleasure to acknowledge the assistance we received while writing this book. When Michael Trombetta was first learning JCL, John Zipfel was already a master; he was always ready to share his experience and knowledge. It is unfortunate that other commitments prevented him from joining us as a coauthor. Mel LaSala suggested a number of topics to be included, for which we thank him. Michael DelFranco made a particularly valuable contribution, for which we are grateful. We also thank our reviewers, particularly Larry Egan, for their exceptionally thorough and thoughtful reviews. Mike Merritt, Stanley Monsowitz, Larry Nelson, and Vincent Quintano each offered help when needed, and we are grateful to them all. Judy Perna typed the manuscript with commitment and skill, which was greatly appreciated.

Manhasset, New York   M.T.
October, 1983   S.C.F.

CONTENTS

CONTENTS

CHAPTER 3

CREATING SEQUENTIAL DATA SETS ON TAPE AND DISK   57

CHAPTER 4

ACCESSING SEQUENTIAL DATA SETS   91

CONTENTS

CHAPTER 5

LIBRARIES 145

CHAPTER 6

GENERATION DATA GROUPS 187

CONTENTS

CHAPTER 7

MASS STORAGE   203

CHAPTER 8

USING SYSTEM PROCEDURES   211

CONTENTS

CHAPTER 9

CHAPTER 10

CHAPTER 11

CONTENTS

CONTENTS

CHAPTER 14

UTILITIES 485

OS JCL
AND UTILITIES

CHAPTER 1

INTRODUCTION

CHAPTER 1 / INTRODUCTION

LEARNING OBJECTIVES

IN THIS CHAPTER YOU WILL LEARN

- what job control language (JCL) is
- what an operating system is
- what the components of a computer system are
- what the components of an operating system are
- what versions of the operating system have been and are currently available
- how a job is processed by the operating system
- how data are represented in storage
- the notation used to describe the syntax of JCL statements

YOU WILL ALSO LEARN THE MEANINGS OF THE FOLLOWING TERMS:

- access method
- auxiliary storage
- bit
- byte
- central processor unit (CPU)
- data set
- direct access
- direct access storage device (DASD)
- EBCDIC

3

- hexadecimal number system
- indexed sequential access method (ISAM)
- input work queue
- I/O
- job
- job control language (JCL)
- job entry subsystem (JES, JES2, JES3)
- job step
- job stream
- main storage
- MFT
- multiple virtual storage (MVS)
- multiprogramming
- MVT
- operating system
- output work queue
- packed format
- page
- paging
- partition
- queue
- real storage
- remote job entry (RJE)

- sequential access method (SAM)

- spooling

- syntax

- sysgen

- task

- terminal

- time sharing

- transparent

- unit record device

- unpacking

- utility program

- virtual storage

- virtual storage access method (VSAM)

- virtual storage operating system (VS1)

- workstation

One objective of this book is to teach you **JCL**, so you might well ask, "What is JCL and why do I need it?" JCL stands for **job control language**, which is the language you use to communicate with the computer's operating system. That answer just raises another question: "What is an operating system and why do I want to communicate with it?" An **operating system** is a collection of programs that control a computer system. To have the computer execute your program you use JCL to tell the operating system which computer resources the program requires. Before we can discuss the resources your program requires, you have to learn more about computer systems and operating systems.

5

COMPONENTS OF A COMPUTER SYSTEM

A modern computer system consists of several interconnected units. At the heart of the computer system is the **central processor unit**, or **CPU**. Instructions are executed in the CPU. Another unit is the **main storage** unit, where programs and data are stored while they are being processed. Main storage is temporary in the sense that after processing is complete, the programs and data are replaced by the next set of programs and data to be processed. Programs and data are permanently stored in **auxiliary storage** such as magnetic tape, disk, and mass storage. For reasons that will be explained later in this chapter, magnetic disks are called **direct access storage devices**, abbreviated **DASD**. You will learn more about magnetic tape and disk in Chapter 3 and about mass storage in Chapter 7.

Card readers may be used to enter programs and data into the computer. Printers and card punches are used to obtain results. Card readers, punches, and printers are called **unit record devices**. Frequently unit record devices miles from the central computer are connected to a small computer, which in turn is connected to the central computer by communication lines, often supplied by the telephone company. These remote unit record devices and their computer constitute a **remote job entry (RJE)** station. It is possible to enter programs and data and receive results at an RJE station just as though the unit record devices were at the central site.

There is a movement to eliminate cards and to have users enter programs and data into the computer by typing at terminals. Such **terminals** usually consist of a typewriter-like keyboard and a TV-like display screen. Like an RJE station, terminals may be miles from the central site and connected by telephone or other communication lines. Many terminals may be in use at the same time. Using terminals in this way is known as **time sharing**.

A device, such as an RJE station or a terminal, from which it is possible to submit programs and data and receive results is called a **workstation**.

Supervising the whole computer system is the computer operator. The operator's console includes a keyboard and a display screen which are used to enter commands to the computer and receive messages from the computer. You might think that the operator, who runs the whole computer system, would be very busy. Sometimes he or she is, but one of the main functions of the operating system is to increase the efficiency of a computer system by automating the operation of the computer and relieving the operator of many routine tasks.

COMPONENTS OF AN OPERATING SYSTEM

The programs that make up the operating system may be classified into two categories: control programs and processing programs. Control programs schedule and supervise work done by the computer. Users do not communicate directly with control programs. Instead the user codes JCL statements indicating the computer resources the program requires. The control programs interpret the JCL statements and make those resources available.

You might be wondering what kind of resources your programs will need. At this point in your studies it is impossible to describe completely the resources you will request. In fact, one of the things you will learn from this book is what resources you need and how to request them. Perhaps two simple examples will give you an idea of what is meant by resources. Suppose your program needs five minutes of computer time to execute: you must request those five minutes. Suppose your program prints a report: you must request that a printer be made available to your program.

The second category of operating system programs consists of processing programs. There are three categories of processing programs: language translators; service programs; and utility programs. In contrast to the situation with control programs, when you want to use one of the processing programs you must explicitly ask for it. Let us briefly describe the three categories.

The language translators are used to translate programs into machine language. They include the assemblers, which translate programs written in assembler language, and the compilers, which translate programs written in higher-level languages such as COBOL, FORTRAN, and PL/I. Computers only understand machine language, and before a program written in one of these other languages can be executed it must be translated into machine language. You will learn how to use the language translators in Chapter 8.

The service programs include the linkage editor, the loader, and the sort/merge program. The linkage editor and the loader are used with the language translators: you will learn how to use them in Chapter 8. The sort/merge program is used to sort or merge records; its use is explained in Chapter 10.

Utility programs perform commonly required tasks such as copying data from one storage device to another. Teaching you how to use utility programs is a major objective of this book. In all, 21 utility programs are discussed. Throughout the book utility programs are used to illustrate the elements of JCL. In addition, Chapter 14 is devoted to utility programs.

VERSIONS OF OPERATING SYSTEMS

The operating systems we will be studying are those that have been developed by IBM and that have the family name of OS, which stands for "operating system."* OS is used on the System/360, System/370, 303X, 308X, and 43XX series of computers.

The MFT and MVT Operating Systems

There have been a number of operating systems in the OS family. One of the first was **MFT**, which stands for multiprogramming with a fixed number of tasks. **Multiprogramming** means that a computer executes two or more programs simultaneously. Actually, the control unit can execute only one instruction at a time. Multiprogramming works as follows. Input and output (**I/O**) instructions are thousands of times slower than instructions that are executed internally, such as arithmetic instructions. In a multiprogramming system several programs are stored in the main storage unit and one of them is executed. When the currently executing program executes an I/O instruction, it is put into a "wait" state, and another program is executed. This means that instead of waiting until the slow I/O instruction is executed, the CPU can keep busy.

In an MFT system a portion of main storage is reserved for the operating system programs, and the rest is divided into a fixed number of partitions. A **partition** is simply a region of main storage in which a program is executed. The number and sizes of the partitions are decided when the operating system is installed on the computer (the operator may modify them during execution). Installing the operating system is called generating the system or, more commonly, **sysgen**. Using this term, you could say that the number of partitions is established at sysgen time.

An MFT system may sometimes be inefficient because a partition may be available but too small to hold any of the programs waiting to be executed. That partition will not be used until a program that it can hold is sub-

---

* IBM also has a series of operating systems that have the family name DOS, which stands for disk operating system, designed to be used on their smaller computers. The JCL for DOS is entirely different from the JCL for OS, and we will not discuss it in this book.

mitted for execution. To eliminate this source of inefficiency, IBM introduced the **MVT** operating system. MVT stands for multiprogramming with a variable number of tasks. In an MVT operating system, a portion of main storage is reserved for operating system programs, and the rest is available in one large pool to be used by jobs. The user specifies how much main storage a program needs, and a region of storage is allocated to that program.

Both MFT and MVT were early operating systems and are no longer supported by IBM, although many computer centers still use them. They have both been replaced by virtual storage operating systems.

Virtual Storage Operating Systems

Virtual storage operating systems permit a program to use more main storage than is actually available. This sounds impossible, but it is done by treating auxiliary storage as an extension of main storage. When virtual systems are discussed, it is customary to call main storage **real storage**, to distinguish it from **virtual**—that is, auxiliary—**storage**. To understand how it is possible to use more storage than is actually available, you must realize that it is necessary to keep in main storage only the instructions that are currently being executed and the data that are currently being processed. The rest of the program and data are kept on auxiliary storage. A virtual operating system divides a program into small sections called **pages**, some of which are in real storage and the rest of which are on auxiliary storage. When instructions or data that are not in real storage are needed, a page of the program is written to auxiliary storage, and the required page is read into real storage. This process is called **paging**. Because paging must be done quickly, the auxiliary storage used must be DASD.

The programmer does not have to be concerned with the fact that the program will be divided into pages and that these pages will be paged between real and auxiliary storage. We describe this situation by saying that paging is **transparent** to the user.

There are two versions of virtual operating systems: VS1 and VS2. The latter is more commonly known as MVS, which stands for multiple virtual system. VS1 is a virtual version of MFT, and MVS is a virtual version of MVT.

Although operating systems have changed, the JCL that is used to communicate with them has not changed very much. Most of the JCL that you will be studying is vital for all versions of the operating systems. You will be told when a feature that is being discussed is not valid for all versions of the operating systems.

EXECUTING A JOB

It may seem to you that an operating system is extremely complicated, and indeed it is. Fortunately to learn how to use an operating system you do not need a detailed understanding of how it works. A general understanding, however, will make your study of JCL more meaningful.

When a programmer wants to use a computer, he or she prepares a job stream. A job stream consists of one or more jobs. A **job** is a unit of work the computer is to perform. A job stream may consist of punched cards; or, if a terminal is used, it may consist of a file of card images. A **job stream** consists of JCL statements, programs that are to be executed, and data that are to be processed. The system is able to distinguish JCL statements from the other statements in the job stream because JCL statements have two slashes, //, or a slash and an asterisk, /*, in columns 1 and 2. A job stream is shown in Figure 1.1.

The first statement in a job stream must be a JOB statement. The main function of the JOB statement is to identify the job to the system. The JOB statement is usually followed by an EXEC (execute) statement. The EXEC statement names the program or the procedure that is to be executed. (Procedures are discussed in Chapter 8, so for now assume that you will only execute programs.) Following the EXEC statement are the DD (data definition) statements. The DD statements describe the data used by the program. An EXEC statement and its DD statements make up a **job step**. A job may consist of any number of job steps. Figure 1.1 shows a job stream that contains a three-step job followed by a one-step job.

The JOB, EXEC, and DD statements are the most important JCL statements. The others are the delimiter, null, and comment statements, which you will study in Chapter 2, and the PROC and PEND statements, which you will study in Chapters 8 and 9.

Figure 1.2 uses standard system flowchart symbols (which are explained in Appendix A) to illustrate a job being processed by a computer system. The job stream is entered into the computer by being read by a card reader or by being submitted from a terminal. The first part of the operating system the job encounters is the **job entry subsystem**. The job entry subsystem reads jobs into the system, schedules jobs for execution, and handles the output produced by jobs. VS1 uses a job entry system named **JES**, and MVS uses either **JES2** or **JES3**.*

* The job entry subsystems used with MFT and MVT were ASP and HASP.

FIGURE 1.1

A job stream on cards

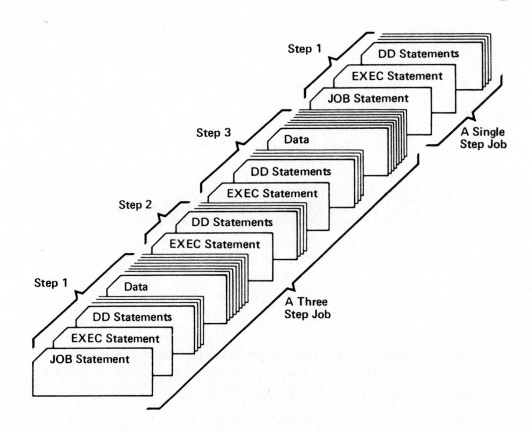

Reprinted by permission from *IBM System/360 Operating System* (GC 28-6534-4). © 1964 by International Business Machines Corporation.

A portion of the job entry system known as the reader/interpreter, sometimes called the converter/interpreter, reads the job stream and checks the coding of the JCL statements. If it finds an error, it prints a message and then stops further processing of the job. If there are no errors, the job stream is written to a direct access device, where it joins other jobs waiting to be executed in what is known as the **input work queue**. A **queue** is just a waiting list.

FIGURE 1.2

Progress of a job through a computer system

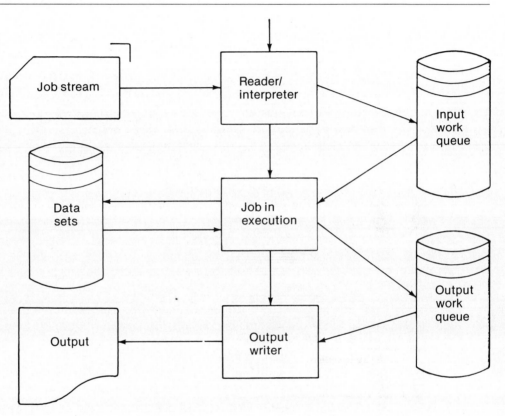

There are actually several input work queues. To balance the computer's workload, computer centers establish job classes. For example, one class might be for jobs that have high I/O requirements, while another might be for jobs that require a lot of time. The programmer is told to which class to assign his or her job. You will learn how jobs are assigned to classes in Chapter 2. A separate input work queue is established for each job class.

Writing the job stream to a direct access device is known as **spooling**. Spooling is also done on output. When a program creates output that is to be printed or punched, it is not usually sent directly to a printer or punch. Rather, it is written to the **output work queue** on a disk. After a job terminates, a part of the job entry subsystem named the output writer sends the output to a printer or punch. The purpose of spooling is to isolate the CPU from the relatively slow card readers, punches, and printers. Spooling is transparent to the programmer, so that programs may be written as though they read card data and write to a printer, when actually they are reading and writing spooled files.

The job waits in the input work queue for its turn to be executed. Jobs may be assigned priorities, so the order in which they are executed is not necessarily the order in which they entered the system. When it's a job's turn to be executed, execution is started by a program named the initiator. Job steps within a job are executed separately in the order in which they appear in the job stream. Before the initiator starts a job step, it makes sure that any input and output devices required by the job step are available. A program in executable form and the data it needs are called a **task.**

Although we have been following one job through the system, keep in mind that several jobs are executed concurrently.

DATA SETS

You may be familiar with the concept of a file, which is defined as a collection of related records. In JCL terminology a file is called a **data set.** Data sets can be classified according to the way their records are organized, as follows: sequential data sets (discussed in Chapters 2, 3, and 4); partitioned data sets (also called libraries and discussed in Chapter 5); direct data sets (briefly discussed in Chapter 12); indexed sequential data sets (discussed in Chapter 12); **virtual storage access method (VSAM)** data sets (discussed in Chapter 13).

Sequential data sets may be stored on either magnetic tape, magnetic disk, or mass storage devices. The other organizations must be stored on magnetic disk or mass storage devices.

No matter how a data set is organized, it may be accessed sequentially. Sequential access means that records are processed in the order in which they physically occur in the data set. Direct, indexed sequential, and VSAM data sets may also be accessed directly. **Direct access** means that the computer can process a desired record without having to process all the preceding records. Because magnetic disks permit direct access, they are called direct access storage devices, or DASD.

The programs that actually transfer data between main storage and the input/output devices are called **access methods**. Different access methods are used depending on the organization of the data set and whether it is being accessed sequentially or randomly. Sometimes the type of data set is indicated by using the name of the access method used to access it. We have already seen an example of this in VSAM data sets. Similarly, indexed sequential data sets are frequently called **ISAM (indexed sequential access method)** data sets, and sequential data sets are sometimes called **SAM (sequential access method)** data sets.

DATA STORAGE

You can understand about 95 percent of the following chapters without knowing how data are stored in main and auxiliary storage. But to understand the remaining 5 percent, you must know a little about data storage.

Main storage is made up of several million electronic components called **bits.** Bits may be in one of two states: they are either on or off. These two states are represented by the digits 0 and 1. On auxiliary storage, magnetic spots are used to represent the 0 and 1 states. A group of eight bits is called a **byte**. If you want to specify the contents of a byte, you must specify the states of the eight bits. For example, you might say that a byte contains 11010100.

Writing all those zeros and ones is time consuming and error prone, so a code was developed to permit the contents of a byte to be specified with only two characters. The code is the hexadecimal number system. The **hexadecimal number system** is a real number system in which it is possible to do arithmetic, but for your purposes you can consider it to be just a code which represents the state of four bits with one character. The code is shown in Table 1.1.

To use this code to represent the contents of a byte, you separate the eight bits into two groups of four bits each and use a hexadecimal digit to represent each set of four bits. For example, to find the hexadecimal representation for the byte that contains 11010100, you separate it into 1101 and 0100. Using the table, you find that 1101 is represented by D and 0100 by 4, so the contents of the byte may be written as D4.

CHAPTER 1 / INTRODUCTION

TABLE 1.1

The hexadecimal number system

Bits	Hexadecimal Digit	Bits	Hexadecimal Digit
0000	0	1000	8
0001	1	1001	9
0010	2	1010	A
0011	3	1011	B
0100	4	1100	C
0101	5	1101	D
0110	6	1110	E
0111	7	1111	F

The EBCDIC Code

The code used in IBM computers to represent characters is called the **EBCDIC code**. In the EBCDIC code a character occupies a byte. Starting from 00 and going through FF, there are 256 different values that may be stored in a byte. So the EBCDIC code could represent 256 characters, but not all the values are used to represent characters. The code for commonly used characters is shown in Table 1.2. As you can see, both uppercase and lowercase letters, digits, and special characters are represented.

If the letters CAT are entered on a data card or on a terminal and those data are read into main or auxiliary storage, they will occupy three consecutive bytes, which will contain C3 C1 E3. Similarly, if three consecutive bytes containing C4 D6 C7 are sent to a printer, the printer will print DOG.

Numeric Data

Numeric data may be stored in several different forms. When numbers are stored in character form, the EBCDIC code is used. So the number 724 would appear in storage as F7 F2 F4. The left digit of the rightmost byte is used to represent the sign of the number. If the number is unsigned, as in our

DATA STORAGE

TABLE 1.2

The EBCDIC code

Hexadecimal Code	Character	Hexadecimal Code	Character	Hexadecimal Code	Character
40	space	84	d	C8	H
4A	¢	85	e	C9	I
4B	.	86	f	D1	J
4C	<	87	g	D2	K
4D	(	88	h	D3	L
4E	+	89	i	D4	M
4F	|	91	j	D5	N
50	&	92	k	D6	O
5A	!	93	l	D7	P
5B	$	94	m	D8	Q
5C	*	95	n	D9	R
5D	)	96	o	E2	S
5E	;	97	p	E3	T
5F	¬	98	q	E4	U
60	–	99	r	E5	V
61	/	A2	s	E6	W
6B	,	A3	t	E7	X
6C	%	A4	u	E8	Y
6D	—	A5	v	E9	Z
6E	>	A6	w	F0	0
6F	?	A7	x	F1	1
7A	:	A8	y	F2	2
7B	#	A9	z	F3	3
7C	@	C1	A	F4	4
7D	'	C2	B	F5	5
7E	=	C3	C	F6	6
7F	"	C4	D	F7	7
81	a	C5	E	F8	8
82	b	C6	F	F9	9
83	c	C7	G		

example, that digit is an F. If the number has a positive sign, the left digit of the rightmost byte is C. So +628 would appear as F6 F2 C8. If the number has a negative sign, the left digit of the rightmost byte is a D. So −459 would appear as F4 F5 D9.

Numeric data may also be represented in packed format. In **packed format** two decimal digits are stored in each byte except for the rightmost byte, which contains one decimal digit and the sign of the number. The sign of the number is represented by the right digit of the rightmost byte (recall that it is the left digit of the rightmost byte that represents the sign when the number is stored in character form). So +628 would appear as 62 8C, and −459 would appear as 45 9D.

Notice what would happen if you tried to print the packed number 62 8C. Table 1.2 shows that neither 62 nor 8C represents a printable character. When presented with a byte that does not represent a printable character, most printers don't print anything. Either nothing or meaningless characters would be printed if you tried to print a packed number. Before a packed number may be printed, it must be converted to character form by a process known as **unpacking**.

Numeric data may also be stored in binary form and in floating point form, a discussion of which would take us too far afield. It is important to know, however, that, like numbers in packed form, numbers in binary and floating point form must be converted to character form before they may be printed.

NOTATION USED TO DESCRIBE SYNTAX

The basic references for JCL are two IBM manuals: *OS/VS1 JCL Reference* (GC24-5099) for VS1 systems and *MVS JCL* (GC28-1300) for MVS systems. These manuals explain how to code JCL statements.

The basic references for utilities are also two IBM manuals: *OS/VS1 Utilities* (GC26-3901) for VS1 systems and *OS/VS2 MVS Utilities* (GC26-3902) for MVS systems. These manuals describe the functions of the various utilities and explain how to code utility control statements which govern the processing done by the utilities.

These manuals, and others that will be mentioned later on, use an excellent notation which clearly and succinctly shows the rules you must follow when you code a statement. These rules are known as the **syntax** of the statement. Since this notation is so useful, it is used in this book. Ap-

NOTATION USED TO DESCRIBE SYNTAX

pendix B shows the syntax of JCL statements for both VS1 systems and MVS systems using this notation.

In this notation you code uppercase letters and words exactly as they appear, and you substitute values for lowercase letters and words. For example, the format for the CLASS parameter, which you will study in Chapter 2, is

```
CLASS=jobclass
```

This means that you must code the word CLASS, but that you substitute a value for jobclass.

Braces ({ }) are used to group related items and to indicate that you must code one of the items. Two methods are used to list the items from which you must choose. Since one purpose of this book is to prepare you to read the IBM manuals on your own, both methods are illustrated. In the JCL manuals the items from which you must select are listed in a column. For example, part of the format of the SPACE parameter, which you will study in Chapter 3, is

```
⎧ TRK       ⎫
⎨ CYL       ⎬
⎩ blocksize ⎭
```

This means that you must code either TRK or CYL or you must substitute a value for blocksize.

In the utilities manuals the items from which you must select are written in a row, separated by a vertical line. For example, part of the format of the FIELD parameter for IEBGENER, which you will study in Chapter 4, is

```
{input-location|'literal'}
```

In this case you would substitute a value for either input-location or literal.

Brackets ([ ]) are used to enclose an optional item or items. As in the case of braces, if you may choose one of several items, they will be listed either in a column or in a row separated by a vertical line. Sometimes showing both braces and brackets can make the description confusing. In this book the text will specify that the items are "optional" and the brackets will not be shown.

Ellipses (...), three consecutive periods, indicate that the preceding item may be repeated. For example, the format of the COND parameter, which you will study in Chapter 4, is

```
COND=((code,operator),...)
```

The ellipses mean that (code,operator) may be repeated.

DIFFERENCES BETWEEN COMPUTER CENTERS

In your study of JCL you will occasionally have to code values that depend on conventions established at your computer center. For example, as previously mentioned, each computer center establishes its own job classes. Similarly, tape reels and disk packs are given serial numbers which are chosen by each computer center. Since these values are different in different computer centers, someone familiar with your computer center will have to tell you what values to code. If you are studying this book as part of a course, your instructor will give you this information. If you are studying this book on your own, your supervisor or perhaps a coworker will give you this information. Throughout this book the person who will give you this information is called your advisor.

When one of these variable values is discussed, you will have to ask your advisor what value to use at your computer center. The inside front cover of this book has been designed to permit you to enter these values, so they will be available in one convenient place. You can start now by asking your advisor the names of the operating system and of the job entry subsystem used at your computer center. Enter these names in the place provided on the inside front cover.

EXERCISES

1. What is an operating system?

2. What is JCL used for?

3. What are the functions of the CPU, main storage, auxiliary storage, and the operator's console?

4. What devices are used for auxiliary storage?

EXERCISES

5. What are the three unit record devices?

6. What is a workstation?

7. What is a language translator?

8. What is a utility program?

9. What is multiprogramming?

10. What is a virtual operating system?

11. What are the names of the virtual operating systems?

12. What is a job stream?

13. What is a job step?

14. What are the names of the JCL statements?

15. Describe briefly the functions of the JOB, EXEC, and DD statements.

16. What are the functions of the job entry subsystem? What are the names of the job entry subsystems used by VS1 and MVS?

17. What is spooling and why is it done?

18. What does it mean to say that spooling is transparent to the programmer?

19. What are the ways in which a data set may be organized?

20. What are the ways in which a data set may be accessed?

21. What kind of data set organization does magnetic tape support?

22. What is the meaning of DASD? Give an example of DASD.

23. What is an access method?

24. What is a bit?

25. What is a byte?

26. Suppose a byte contains 10011110. Express the contents in hexadecimal form.

27. Three consecutive bytes of storage contain the characters JCL. Express the contents in hexadecimal form.

28. How would the number + 505 appear if it were stored in packed format? What would be printed if this value were sent to a printer without being unpacked?

29. The syntax of the MSGCLASS parameter is

    [MSGCLASS=output-class]

    Explain.

30. The syntax of the BURST parameter is

    [BURST=$\left\{ \begin{matrix} Y \\ N \end{matrix} \right\}$]

    Explain.

SUMMARY

In this chapter you have learned

- what job control language (JCL) is and what it is used for

- what an operating system is

- the functions of the CPU, main storage, auxiliary storage, and operator's console

- in what ways the MFT, MVT, VS1, and MVS operating systems are similar and in what ways they are different

- how virtual storage operating systems permit programmers to use more storage than is really available

- the functions of the JOB, EXEC, and DD statements

- the functions of the reader/interpreter, initiator, and output writer

- how and why spooling is done

- how data sets may be organized and accessed

- how data are stored in main and auxiliary storage

- how the contents of storage may be represented using the hexadecimal number system

- the notation used to describe the syntax of JCL and utility control statements

CHAPTER 2

LISTING A CARD DECK

LEARNING OBJECTIVES

IN THIS CHAPTER YOU WILL LEARN

- how to use the utility program IEBGENER to list a card deck
- how to code simple versions of the JOB, EXEC, and DD statements
- how to code the comment, delimiter, and null statements
- how to read the system messages produced when a job is executed

YOU WILL ALSO LEARN THE MEANINGS OF THE FOLLOWING TERMS:

- abend
- alphameric characters
- comments field
- condition code
- ddname
- default values
- input stream data
- jobname
- K
- keyword parameter
- logic error
- name field
- national characters
- operand field
- operation field

- parameter

- positional parameter

- return code

- special characters

- stepname

- syntax error

In this chapter you will see your first examples of JCL statements. The problem posed will be to list a card deck on a high-speed printer. This problem will be solved by developing all the JCL statements required to use the IBM utility progam IEBGENER to list the card deck.

USING IEBGENER TO LIST A CARD DECK

The processing we want to do is shown in the system flowchart in Figure 2.1. System flowcharts are useful because they clearly show the relationships between the data sets and the programs that are used to process them. Figure 2.1 shows that a card deck is the input data set, that the program named IEBGENER will be executed, and that a listing of the card deck is the

FIGURE 2.1

System flowchart to list a card deck

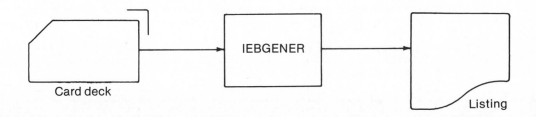

Card deck   IEBGENER   Listing

FIGURE 2.2

Job stream to list a card deck

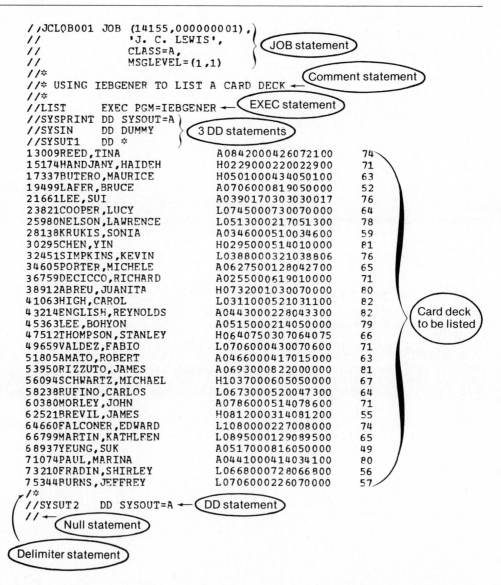

```
//JCLQB001 JOB (14155,000000001),
//              'J. C. LEWIS',          } JOB statement
//              CLASS=A,
//              MSGLEVEL=(1,1)
//*                                        Comment statement
//* USING IEBGENER TO LIST A CARD DECK
//*
//LIST      EXEC PGM=IEBGENER           EXEC statement
//SYSPRINT DD SYSOUT=A
//SYSIN     DD DUMMY                    } 3 DD statements
//SYSUT1    DD *
13009REED,TINA              A0842000426072100      74
15174HANDJANY,HAIDEH       H0229000220022900      71
17337BUTERO,MAURICE        H0501000434050100      63
19499LAFER,BRUCE           A0706000819050000      52
21661LEE,SUI               A0390170303030017      76
23821COOPER,LUCY           L0745000730070000      64
25980NELSON,LAWRENCE       L0513000217051300      78
28138KRUKIS,SONIA          A0346000510034600      59
30295CHEN,YIN              H0295000514010000      81
32451SIMPKINS,KEVIN        L0388000321038806      76
34605PORTER,MICHELE        A0627500128042700      65
36759DECICCO,RICHARD       A0255000619010000      71
38912ABREU,JUANITA         H0732001030070000      80
41063HIGH,CAROL            L0311000521031100      82
43214ENGLISH,REYNOLDS      A0443000228043300      82
45363LEE,BOHYON            A0515000214050000      79
47512THOMPSON,STANLEY      H0640750307064075      66
49659VALDEZ,FABIO          L0706000430070600      71
51805AMATO,ROBERT          A0466000417015000      63
53950RIZZUTO,JAMES         A0693000822000000      81
56094SCHWARTZ,MICHAEL      H1037000605050000      67
58238RUFINO,CARLOS         L0673000520047300      64
60380MORLEY,JOHN           A0786000514078600      71
62521BREVIL,JAMES          H0812000314081200      55
64660FALCONER,EDWARD       L1080000227008000      74
66799MARTIN,KATHLEEN       L0895000129089500      65
68937YEUNG,SUK             A0517000816050000      49
71074PAUL,MARINA           A0441000414034100      80
73210FRADIN,SHIRLEY        L0668000728066800      56
75344BURNS,JEFFREY         L0706000226070000      57
/*
//SYSUT2    DD SYSOUT=A                 DD statement
//                                       Null statement
                                         Delimiter statement
```

Card deck to be listed

output data set. (This statement of the problem assumes you are using a card system. If you are using a terminal system, you may assume that the data we want to list are in the form of 80-column card images instead of a card deck.) IEBGENER is an IBM utility program that is used to copy sequential data sets. In this problem we are using IEBGENER to copy the card deck to the printer listing.

Figure 2.2 shows the job stream to list a card deck. The job stream consists of a JOB statement, three comment statements, an EXEC statement, four DD statements, a delimiter statement, a null statement, and the card deck we want to list. The same card deck will be used in examples throughout the text. Although you can understand everything in this chapter without knowing the meaning of the various fields on the cards, if you would like to know what they mean you can find them explained in Appendix C. Let us now examine the job stream in detail.

FORMAT OF THE JOB, EXEC, AND DD STATEMENTS

The JOB, EXEC, and DD statements have a common format which is shown below:

```
//name operation operand comments
```

The two slashes must be in columns 1 and 2. They are followed by the **name field**, which must start in column 3. The name field is the only field that must start in a specific column. Notice that there must not be a blank between the second slash and the name.

The name may consist of from one to eight characters. The permitted characters are the letters A through Z, the digits 0 through 9, and the three characters #, @, and $, which are called **national characters**. The first character of the name must be a letter or a national character. The letters and digits together are called the **alphameric characters**. Any characters other than alphameric and national characters used in coding JCL statements are known as **special characters**. The comma, period, and blank, for example, are special characters.

The name field is followed by the **operation field**. In the operation field you specify the kind of statement you are coding, either JOB, EXEC, or DD. There must be at least one blank between the name field and the operation

CHAPTER 2 / LISTING A CARD DECK

field, although you can have as many blanks as you want. Not much more need be said about the name and operation fields; the rest of this book is mostly devoted to discussing the operand field.

The **operand field** follows the operation field. There must be at least one blank between the operation field and the operand field, and, again, you can have as many blanks as you want. The operand field consists of a single parameter or a series of parameters. The **parameters** provide detailed information about the job, the program being executed, and the data sets being used. The parameters are separated by commas; there may not be blanks within the operand field.

The operand field may not extend beyond column 71. If all the parameters will not fit within the first 71 columns, the statement must be continued onto the next line. Even if the parameters would fit in the first 71 columns, the programmer may choose to interrupt a statement before column 71 and continue on the next line.

When a JCL statement is continued, these rules must be followed:

INTERRUPT THE STATEMENT AFTER A PARAMETER OR SUBPARAMETER AND THE COMMA THAT FOLLOWS IT ANYWHERE YOU LIKE BEFORE COLUMN 71.

BEGIN THE NEXT LINE WITH A // IN COLUMNS 1 AND 2 AND A BLANK IN COLUMN 3.

START CODING THE PARAMETER ON THE NEW LINE ANYWHERE BETWEEN COLUMNS 4 AND 16.

You will see applications of these rules shortly.

The operand field is followed by the **comments field**. Again, one or more blanks must separate the operand field and the comments field. The comments field is optional: it is more common to use the comment statement to include comments in a job stream than to use the comments field. None of the statements in Figure 2.2 uses the comments field.

Although the operand field may not extend beyond column 71, the comments field may extend out through column 80. There are special rules to follow if you want to continue a comments field, but instead of remembering the special rules, the easiest thing to do is to make the next line a comment statement. If you do that, the statement is technically not being continued, so you do not have to follow any special rules.

THE JOB STATEMENT

CODING CONVENTIONS

This book uses conventions similar to those many businesses have adopted for coding JCL statements. If these conventions are followed, the JCL rules are automatically obeyed, and in addition the JCL will be easy to read. Having JCL that is easy to read is a big advantage because it means that you will be able to find and correct errors more readily.

The first convention is to begin the operation fields, JOB, EXEC, and DD, in column 12. This ensures that even with a name that contains eight characters there will be one space between the name and the operation. (In Chapter 8 you will learn that the name on a DD statement may be longer than eight characters. In those cases it will be necessary to begin DD in a later column.)

Leave one space after the operation field and then start the first parameter of the operand field. Code only one parameter on a line. When a line is continued, start the parameter on the next line in column 16.

These are useful conventions for you to follow; you should realize, however, that they are only conventions and are not required by the rules of JCL.

THE JOB STATEMENT

Let us now examine the JOB statement in detail. For convenience the JOB statement in Figure 2.2 is repeated here:

```
//JCLQB001 JOB (14155,000000001),
//              'J. C. LEWIS',
//              CLASS=A,
//              MSGLEVEL=(1,1)
```

The main functions of the JOB statement are to indicate the beginning of a job and to assign a name to the job.

The Jobname

The name that is coded on the JOB statement is known as the **jobname**, and is usually printed in large block letters on the first page of the output produced by the job. When you invent a jobname, you must, of course, follow the rules for names we discussed earlier—one to eight characters consisting of alphameric and national characters with the first character a letter or a national character. However, jobs that are submitted at the same time should have different jobnames. You can imagine that several users might choose the same name, for example TEST, for their jobname and submit their jobs at the same time. To prevent this, computer centers often impose additional rules on which jobnames may be used.

At the City University of New York (CUNY) Computer Center, where the programs in this book were run, it is suggested that a jobname consist of three initials to identify the user, two letters to identify the user's school, and three digits to number the job. For the purposes of this book, a user whose name is J. C. Lewis (and whose initials just happen to be JCL) and whose school identification is QB (which stands for Queensborough Community College) was created. The job shown in Figure 2.2 is the first job that student ran, so the three-digit number 001 was added to the user's initials and the school identification to create the jobname JCLQB001. Your computer center may or may not have rules for forming jobnames. If it does, your advisor will tell you what they are, and you should write them in the space provided on the inside front cover.

Positional and Keyword Parameters

As required, a space is left after the jobname, followed by the operation (JOB), then another space, and then the operand field is begun. There are two kinds of parameters in the operand field: **positional parameters** and **keyword parameters**. The operating system recognizes positional parameters by their position in the operand field. They must be coded in a specific order before any keyword parameters. In the example, the first two parameters

    (14155,000000001)

and

    'J. C. LEWIS'

are positional parameters which will be discussed in detail shortly. The other parameters, CLASS and MSGLEVEL, are keyword parameters. The keyword—for example, CLASS or MSGLEVEL—is followed by an equal sign and the value you want to assign to that keyword parameter. In the example we assign the value A to the keyword parameter CLASS and the value (1,1) to the

THE JOB STATEMENT

keyword parameter MSGLEVEL. (What this all means will be explained shortly.) In contrast to positional parameters, which must be coded in a specified order, keyword parameters may be coded in any order.

THE ACCOUNTING INFORMATION PARAMETER.   The first parameter in the operand field is the accounting information parameter, which in Figure 2.2 is (14155,000000001). The accounting information parameter is a positional parameter, and it must be the first parameter in the operand field if it is coded. The accounting information parameter, however, is optional; some computer centers do not require accounting information, while others obtain it from a job entry subsystem statement. Your advisor will tell you if accounting information is required at your computer center and, if it is, how it is specified and what your account number is. You should write this information in the place provided on the inside front cover.

The form that the accounting information parameter takes is determined by the computer center. At the CUNY Computer Center it consists of two subparameters: a five-digit number and a nine-digit number. Notice how the two subparameters are separated by a comma and how the whole accounting information parameter is enclosed in parentheses. That is a general rule for all parameters:

> IF A PARAMETER CONSISTS OF A SERIES OF SUBPARAMETERS, THE SUB-PARAMETERS ARE SEPARATED BY COMMAS, AND THE WHOLE PARAMETER IS ENCLOSED IN PARENTHESES.

A second general rule is the following:

> IF THE PARAMETER CONSISTS OF JUST ONE SUBPARAMETER, THE ENCLOSING PARENTHESES MAY BE OMITTED.

This means that if the accounting information parameter consists of a single subparameter—say XHB4702—then it would be legal to code it as

```
//JCLQB001 JOB XHB4702,
```

without the parentheses.

Because it is so variable, the accounting information parameter tends to be somewhat confusing. As you will see, the other parameters are not as variable or as confusing.

THE PROGRAMMER'S NAME PARAMETER. Following the conventions discussed earlier, we code a comma after the accounting information, and continue the JOB statement onto the next line. On the next line we code a // in columns 1 and 2 and begin the programmer's name parameter in column 16. In Figure 2.2, the programmer's name parameter is 'J. C. LEWIS'. It is the first apostrophe (not the J) that is coded in column 16.

Like the accounting information parameter, the programmer's name parameter is a positional parameter and is optional. If it is coded, it must immediately follow the accounting information parameter. A programmer's name must consist of no more than 20 characters. It may contain any characters you like, but if it contains special characters (and remember a blank is a special character), it must be enclosed in apostrophes. (Under special circumstances a programmer's name may contain special characters and not require the apostrophes, but it is easier to type the apostrophes than to remember the special circumstances.)

If a programmer's name contains an apostrophe, you must code two consecutive apostrophes to stand for it. So if a programmer's name were O'Neill, you would code it as 'O''NEILL'.

OMITTING POSITIONAL PARAMETERS. As you know, positional parameters must be coded in the specified order. On the JOB statement this means that the accounting information must precede the programmer's name. But that raises a question: Suppose you want to omit the accounting information. How can accounting information precede the programmer's name if you do not code the accounting information? The general rule is as follows:

IF A POSITIONAL PARAMETER IS OMITTED, YOU MUST CODE A COMMA IN ITS PLACE.

Suppose we wanted to omit the accounting information from the JOB statement in Figure 2.2. The first line of the JOB statement could be written as

```
//JCLQB001 JOB ,'J. C. LEWIS',
```

When the system encounters the comma before 'J. C. LEWIS', it realizes that accounting information has been omitted.

THE JOB STATEMENT

Suppose we wanted to include accounting information, but omit the programmer's name. Following the rule we could write the first two lines of the JOB statement as

```
//JCLQB001 JOB (14151,000000001),,
//              CLASS=A
```

Notice that we code two consecutive commas. One comma stands for the missing programmer's name, while the second comma is the usual comma that separates parameters.

This coding is correct, but another rule permits us to simplify it. This rule is as follows:

> IF THE OMITTED POSITIONAL PARAMETER IS THE LAST ONE, OR IF ALL THE LATER POSITIONAL PARAMETERS ARE ALSO OMITTED, YOU DO NOT HAVE TO CODE REPLACING COMMAS.

This rule means that the last example could also be coded as

```
//JCLQB001 JOB (14151,000000001),
//              CLASS=A
```

Notice that the comma that stood for the missing programmer's name is gone, but the comma that follows the accounting information remains, because that comma separates the accounting information and CLASS parameters.

Finally, consider what happens if both positional parameters are omitted. Following the rule we could write

```
//JCLQB001 JOB ,,CLASS=A
```

However, a third rule allows us to simplify this statement:

> IF ALL THE POSITIONAL PARAMETERS ARE OMITTED, YOU DO NOT HAVE TO CODE THE REPLACING COMMAS.

This rule means that the last example could also be coded as

```
//JCLQB001 JOB CLASS=A
```

Although these three rules have been illustrated by the accounting information and programmer's name parameters, they apply to all positional parameters and also to positional subparameters, which we will encounter shortly.

THE CLASS PARAMETER.   The third parameter

```
CLASS=A
```

is a keyword parameter that specifies the class of the job. In Chapter 1 you learned that computer centers establish a number of job classes to indicate the resources the job requires. Your advisor will tell you the class you must use on your jobs, which you should write in the place provided on the inside front cover.

DEFAULT VALUES.   The CLASS parameter is optional, and if you do not code it, the class for your job will be assigned a **default value**. What is a default value? It is the value that is automatically assigned to a parameter. For example, a computer center may decide that any job that does not have a CLASS parameter coded on the JOB statement will be assigned a job class of P. For that computer center P is the default job class. If your job should be run under class P, you do not have to code the CLASS parameter; you get it automatically. Your advisor will tell you the default value for the CLASS parameter at your computer center. If the default value is the value you should use, you do not have to code the CLASS parameter.

Default values are widely used in JCL. Sometimes, as in the case of the CLASS parameter, the default value is assigned by the computer center, and in other cases the default value is assigned by the operating system. In both cases the purpose of default values is to save programming effort. Making the commonly used values the default values saves the programmer the trouble of coding them. You will meet many examples of default values as you continue to study JCL.

THE MSGLEVEL PARAMETER.   The fourth parameter

```
MSGLEVEL=(1,1)
```

specifies which JCL statements and system messages you want printed when the job is executed. MSGLEVEL is a keyword parameter that consists of

THE JOB STATEMENT

two positional subparameters. The two positional subparameters have the following meanings:

```
MSGLEVEL=(statements,messages)
```

The `statements` subparameter may be assigned the value 0, 1, or 2. The meaning of these values is shown below:

Value	Meaning
0	Print only the JOB statement
1	Print all the input JCL and the JCL from cataloged procedures*
2	Print only the input JCL

*Cataloged procedures will be discussed in Chapter 8.

A value of 1 for the `statements` subparameter says essentially, "Print everything." Since you want everything printed during testing, all the examples in this book use a value of 1 for the `statements` subparameter.

The `messages` subparameter controls the printing of allocation messages. Allocation messages show which physical devices are allocated to the data sets used in a job and what the system did with the data sets at the end of the job. The `messages` subparameter may be assigned the value 0 or 1. The meaning of these values is shown below:

Value	Meaning
0	Do not print allocation messages unless the job abnormally terminates
1	Print all allocation messages

Notice that if you code 0 for the messages subparameter, the allocation messages are printed only if the job abnormally terminates. Abnormal termination occurs when an error condition for which no provision is made in the program causes the program to stop executing. When a program abnormally terminates, it is said to **abend**, which is the abbreviation for abnormal end. We shall see several examples of programs that abend. As in the case of the JCL statements, during testing you want everything printed, so the examples in this book use a value of 1 for the messages subparameter.

If you do not code the MSGLEVEL parameter or if you code only one subparameter, default values are supplied. The default values are determined by the computer center, so your advisor will have to tell you what they are at your computer center. You should write them in the place provided on the inside front cover. If the default values for the MSGLEVEL parameter are (1,1), then you do not have to code it.

OMITTING POSITIONAL PARAMETERS—A REVIEW. The MSGLEVEL parameter provides a convenient example to review what you have learned about the use of parentheses and commas with positional parameters or subparameters. Suppose you were willing to accept the default value for the statements subparameter, but wanted to specify a value of 1 for the messages subparameter. You would code

```
MSGLEVEL=(,1)
```

Notice that you must include the comma to indicate the missing first positional subparameter.

If the situation were reversed and you wanted to specify a 1 for the statements subparameter and accept the default value for the messages subparameter, you would code

```
MSGLEVEL=(1,)
```

Using the rule that when the last positional parameter is omitted the comma is not required, you could write this as

```
MSGLEVEL=(1)
```

Finally, using the rule that if only one subparameter is coded the enclosing parentheses may be omitted, this could be written as

```
MSGLEVEL=1
```

ORDER OF KEYWORD PARAMETERS.   Since CLASS and MSGLEVEL are keyword parameters that may be coded in any order, you might wonder which order to use. In general, the order does not matter. (I coded CLASS before MSGLEVEL because I wanted to discuss the CLASS parameter before I discussed the MSGLEVEL parameter.) Sometimes for one reason or another, one order seems preferable. In Chapter 3 you will see the order I use on complex DD statements and why I prefer that order. However, you should understand that that will be only a personal preference and that keyword parameters may be coded in any order.

ADDITIONAL PARAMETERS.   Several other parameters may be coded on the JOB statement. However, we do not need any of the additional parameters to solve the current problem and to discuss them now would just be confusing. The complete format of all the JCL statements is shown in Appendix B. As you proceed through this book, you will be shown only what you need to know to solve the current problem. This will allow complications to be introduced gradually. If your curiosity gets the better of you, remember you can always find the full format of any JCL statement in Appendix B.

THE COMMENT STATEMENT

For convenience, the comment statements in Figure 2.2 are repeated here.

```
//*
//* USING IEBGENER TO LIST A CARD DECK
//*
```

Two blank comment statements are used so that the real comment stands out. The comment statement must start with the characters //* in columns 1, 2, and 3. The comment itself may start in column 4, may extend through column 80, and may contain any character you can type at your keyboard.

To avoid accidental confusion with JES statements, column 4 should be left blank. You may have as many comment statements as you want, and you may place them anywhere you want after the JOB statement. If a comment won't fit on one comment statement, don't continue the comment statement; simply use additional comment statements. The JCL in Figure 2.2 might have included the following comment statements:

```
//*
//* THIS IS AN EXAMPLE OF A JOB STREAM WHICH SHOWS HOW
//* TO USE IEBGENER TO LIST A CARD DECK
//*
```

You should use comment statements to document your JCL statements for the same reason you would document any program you write—so that anyone who has to read your coding can understand what you have done.

THE EXEC STATEMENT

For convenience the EXEC statement in Figure 2.2 is repeated here.

```
//LIST     EXEC PGM=IEBGENER
```

The EXEC statement names the program that is to be executed.*

The Stepname

The name that is coded on the EXEC statement is called the **stepname**. It is optional, but you should code it. When you invent a stepname, you must, of course, follow the rules for forming names we have already discussed, but in addition you should invent names that are meaningful. Since the purpose of the job stream in Figure 2.2 is to list a card deck, LIST was chosen as the stepname. There are rarely any computer center restrictions on permissible stepnames, the way there are on permissible jobnames.

---

* In Chapter 8 you will learn that procedures may also be executed.

The PGM Parameter

There are several parameters that may be coded on the EXEC statement, but for now all we need is the PGM parameter. The PGM parameter is a positional parameter that identifies the program to be executed. In Figure 2.2 the name of the program to be executed is IEBGENER.

The PGM parameter and the PROC parameter, which we will study in Chapter 8, are the only two positional parameters that use an equal sign. When you see an equal sign used with any other parameter, you know that parameter is a keyword parameter.

THE DD STATEMENT

Figure 2.2 contains four DD statements, which are repeated here.

```
//SYSPRINT DD SYSOUT=A
//SYSIN    DD DUMMY
//SYSUT1   DD *
//SYSUT2   DD SYSOUT=A
```

The DD statements describe the data sets used by the program, and there must be a DD statement for each one. Since Figure 2.2 contains four DD statements, you know that the program IEBGENER uses four data sets. The DD statements may be in any order, but when I use IEBGENER, I usually code the DD statements in the order shown in Figure 2.2.

The name on a DD statement is called the **ddname**. The rules for ddnames are the same as the rules for jobnames and stepnames which we discussed above.

The IEBGENER DD Statements

SYSPRINT is the ddname of the data set that IEBGENER uses to write messages to you. For example, it might write a message that an error occurred during execution or, more optimistically, that your job ran successfully. SYSIN is the ddname of the data set that contains the control statements to tell IEBGENER how the input data set should be modified while it is being copied.

SYSUT1 is the ddname of the input data set that IEBGENER is to copy, and SYSUT2 is the ddname of the output data set that is to be created.

Let us study the parameters coded on these four DD statements.

The SYSOUT Parameter

Both the SYSPRINT and SYSUT2 DD statements have as their only parameter

```
SYSOUT=A
```

SYSOUT is a keyword parameter which assigns a data set to an output class. In this example the output class is A. The output classes are defined by the computer center, but most computer centers use class A to mean that the data set should be printed on a high-speed printer and class B to mean the data set should be punched on cards. Other letters and numbers are used by computing centers to define output classes that meet their needs. For example, one class may designate low-priority output and another class high-priority output. Other classes may indicate special printer forms.

Recall that SYSPRINT is the ddname of the data set that IEBGENER uses to write messages to you. By coding SYSOUT=A on that DD statement, we specify that we want those messages printed. Similarly, recall that SYSUT2 is the ddname of the data set that IEBGENER creates. By coding SYSOUT=A on that DD statement, we specify that we want that data set printed.

It is important to understand that coding SYSOUT=A directs a data set to the printer and that this has nothing to do with the program that is being executed. It happens that in Figure 2.2 the program being executed is IEBGENER, but you would code SYSOUT=A to direct a data set to the printer if you were executing a COBOL, PL/I, FORTRAN, or assembler program, or a different utility program.

The DUMMY Parameter

The SYSIN DD statement in Figure 2.2 contains the parameter DUMMY. DUMMY is a positional parameter that indicates that the data set is not to be processed. DUMMY may be coded on DD statements for both input and output data sets. When DUMMY is specified for an input data set, the first read of that data set causes an end-of-file to be recognized. When DUMMY is specified for an output data set, write statements to the data set are executed, but no data are actually transmitted. That is a convenient way to suppress output which you do not wish to have produced. Suppose, for example, a program produces

39

THE DD STATEMENT

several reports and for a particular execution of that program you do not want one of the reports printed. You can suppress printing of that report by coding DUMMY on the DD statement for that report, without affecting the rest of the program.

Why was DUMMY coded for the SYSIN DD statement in Figure 2.2? Recall that the SYSIN data set (strictly speaking "the data set whose ddname is SYSIN" is proper, but "the SYSIN data set" is more convenient and just as clear, so generally the shorter expression is used) contains the control statements which tell IEBGENER how the input data set is to be modified while it is being copied. In this program we do not want to make any modifications to the input data set, and therefore we do not need any control statements. But we may not simply omit the SYSIN DD statement! IEBGENER expects to find a SYSIN DD statement, and if we leave it out the program will not run. One way to include a SYSIN DD statement, but to have the data set empty, is to DUMMY the DD statement.

The * Parameter

The SYSUT1 DD statement in Figure 2.2 contains the positional parameter *. The * parameter indicates that data follow immediately after the DD statement. Such data are called **input stream data**. As you can see in Figure 2.2, the card deck to be listed is placed immediately behind the SYSUT1 DD statement.

Specifying Ddnames in a Program

The ddnames are selected by the person who wrote the program. The method used within a program to specify a ddname varies depending on the language in which the program is written. For example, in an assembler program the ddname is specified in the DCB instruction.

```
SALEFILE DCB DDNAME=SALES, ...
```

In a COBOL program the ddname is specified in the ASSIGN clause.*

```
SELECT SALEFILE
       ASSIGN TO UT-S-SALES.
```

* VSAM data sets follow different rules. VSAM data sets are discussed in Chapter 13.

CHAPTER 2 / LISTING A CARD DECK

In a PL/I program the ddname is specified in a DECLARE statement.

```
DECLARE SALES FILE ...
```

These three programs would use the same ddname,

```
//SALES    DD ...
```

In a FORTRAN program the ddname is selected differently; the file number specified in a READ or WRITE statement is used to construct the ddname. For example, the statement

```
WRITE (6,1000) ...
```

results in the ddname FT06F001, so that the DD statement would be

```
//FT06F001 DD ...
```

If you are going to use a program written by someone else, the author of the program must supply documentation that specifies the ddnames that must be used and their meanings. In the case of IEBGENER the IBM utilities manual specifies the four ddnames: SYSPRINT, SYSIN, SYSUT1, and SYSUT2.

THE DELIMITER (/*) STATEMENT

The delimiter statement, which has /* in columns 1 and 2, indicates the end of input stream data. In Figure 2.2, the SYSUT1 DD statement marks the beginning of the input data set, and the /* statement marks its end.

Strictly speaking the delimiter statement in Figure 2.2 is not required because the end of input stream data may be marked not only by a delimiter statement, but also by any other JCL statement. In Figure 2.2, if the delimiter statement were omitted, the system would realize it had come to the end of the input stream data when it encountered the SYSUT2 DD statement, which is the next JCL statement. Nevertheless, it is good practice to include a delimiter statement to mark the end of all input stream data, and all the examples in this book will use it.

SYNTAX ERRORS

FIGURE 2.4

Execution of a job stream that contains syntax errors

```
IAT6140 JOB ORIGIN FROM GROUP=LOCAL    , DSP=IJP, DEVICE=INTRDR   , 000  First page
16:46:31 IAT4204  JOB FAILED WITH CONVERTER/INTERPRETER JCL ERROR ←────(A)
16:46:31 IAT4801 JOB JCLQB002 (9268) EXPRESS CANCELED BY INTERPRETER DSP
```

```
//JCLQB002 JOB (14155,000000001),                              ✻Second page
// 'J. C. LEWIS',                                              ✻
// CLASS=A,                                                    ✻
// MSGLEVL=(1,1)
//✻
//✻ USING IEBGENER TO LIST A CARD DECK
//✻
//LISTEXEC PGM=IEBGENER
//SYSPRINT DD SYSOT=A
//SYSIN    DD DUMMY
//SYSUT1   DD ✻
/✻
//SYSUT2   DD SYSOUT=A
//
     1      //JCLQB002 JOB (14155,000000001),                        ✻
            // 'J. C. LEWIS',                                        ✻
            // CLASS=A,                                              ✻
            // MSGLEVL=(1,1)
            ✻✻✻
            ✻✻✻ USING IEBGENER TO LIST A CARD DECK
            ✻✻✻
     2      //LISTEXEC PGM=IEBGENER
     3      //SYSPRINT DD SYSOT=A
     4      //SYSIN    DD DUMMY
     5      //SYSUT1   DD ✻,DCB=BLKSIZE=80
     6      //SYSUT2   DD SYSOUT=A
            //
```

STMT NO. MESSAGE   Third page

```
     1      IEF630I UNIDENTIFIED KEYWORD IN THE CLASS FIELD
     2      IEF605I UNIDENTIFIED OPERATION FIELD
     3      IEF630I UNIDENTIFIED KEYWORD ON THE DD STATEMENT
     6      IEF607I JOB HAS NO STEPS
```

where MSGLEVEL is misspelled. You will find that often the error messages are not as clear as you would like and it takes experience and imagination to interpret them properly.

The second error message says that statement 2 contains an UNIDENTI-FIED OPERATION FIELD. Here is another error message whose meaning is not immediately clear. What happened in statement 2 was that because the required space between the stepname, LIST, and the operation field, EXEC, was left out, the system took the stepname to be LISTEXEC. Then it tried to interpret PGM=IEBGENER as the operation field, but this obviously doesn't make sense as an operation field, so it gave up on the statement and printed the message UNIDENTIFIED OPERATION FIELD. The way to correct that statement is to insert the required space between LIST and EXEC.

The third error message refers to statement 3. That is a much easier error to fix, so it is left to you. The last error message refers to statement 6 and says JOB HAS NO STEPS. What happened here was that because of the error in statement 2, the system did not find the EXEC statement. A job stream without an EXEC statement has no steps, makes no sense, and is illegal. The error message was associated with statement 6 because that is the last numbered statement in the job stream; there is nothing wrong with statement 6. When we correct statement 2, this error message will disappear.

LOGIC ERRORS

Unfortunately, syntax errors are not the only kind of errors you can make. A second kind of error you can (and will!) make is a **logic error**. A job stream contains a logic error when it executes but gives incorrect results. An example of a job stream that contains a logic error is shown in Figure 2.5. Notice that there are no JCL syntax errors, that the condition code is 0, and that the message from IEBGENER says PROCESSING ENDED AT EOD. All that sounds good, but no output was produced!

The clue to what happened here can be found on the second page. There you can see that an extra SYSIN DD statement has been added to the job stream. The extra statement has the word JES3GEN in columns 73 through 79. JES3GEN indicates that this statement was generated by JES3; it was not part of the original job stream.

To understand why JES3 generated this statement you have to realize that a job stream consists of only two kinds of statements: JCL statements and data statements. Any statement that has a // or a /* in columns 1 and 2 is a JCL statement. All the other statements are data statements. If you are used to writing programs, this definition of data statements may be surprising. It includes not only those statements that contain the data your program will process, which you usually think of as data statements, but even the program statements themselves. The assembler, COBOL, FORTRAN,

FIGURE 2.5

Execution of a job stream that contains a logic error

```
IAT6140 JOB ORIGIN FROM GROUP=LOCAL     , DSP=IJP, DEVICE=INTRDR     , 000        First page
17:00:16 IAT2000 JOB 9770 JCLQB003 SELECTED M1          GRP=BATCH
17:00:22 M1 R= JCLQB003 IEF403I JCLQB003 - STARTED
17:00:58 M1 R= JCLQB003 IEF404I JCLQB003 - ENDED

//JCLQB003 JOB (14155,000000001),                                         *   *  Second page
// 'J. C. LEWIS',                                                         *   *
// CLASS=A,
// MSGLEVEL=(1,1)
//*
//* USING IEBGENER TO LIST A CARD DECK
//*
//LIST     EXEC PGM=IEBGENER
//SYSPRINT DD SYSOUT=A
//SYSIN    DD DUMMY
//SYSUT1   DD *
//*
//SYSIN DD *                                                JES3GEN
//SYSUT2 DD SYSOUT=A
//
     1      //JCLQB003 JOB (14155,000000001),                            *   *
            // 'J. C. LEWIS',                                            *   *
            // CLASS=A,
            // MSGLEVEL=(1,1)
            *** USING IEBGENER TO LIST A CARD DECK
            ***
     2      //LIST     EXEC PGM=IEBGENER
     3      //SYSPRINT DD SYSOUT=A
     4      //SYSIN    DD DUMMY
     5      //SYSUT1   DD *,DCB=BLKSIZE=80
     6      //SYSIN DD *,DCB=BLKSIZE=80
     7      //SYSUT2   DD SYSOUT=A                                       JES3GEN
            //
```

(cont.)

49

```
IEF236I ALLOC. FOR JCLQB003 LIST
IEF237I JES3 ALLOCATED TO SYSPRINT
IEF237I DMY  ALLOCATED TO SYSIN
IEF237I JES3 ALLOCATED TO SYSUT1
IEF237I JES3 ALLOCATED TO SYSIN
IEF237I JES3 ALLOCATED TO SYSUT2
IEF142I JCLQB003 LIST - STEP WAS EXECUTED - COND CODE 0000
IEF285I   LIST.SYSPRINT                         SYSOUT
IEF285I   JESI0001                              SYSIN
IEF285I   JESI0002                              SYSIN
IEF285I   LIST.SYSUT2                           SYSOUT

** START - STEP=LIST  JOB=JCLQB003 DATE=10/26/81 CLOCK=17.00.03  PGM=IEBGENER REGION USED= 36K OF 192K **
** END -                           DATE=10/26/81 CLOCK=17.00.39  CPU TIME = 0 MIN 0.08 SEC     CC=    0 **
** I/O COUNTS - DISK=     0,  SPOOL/OTHER=    4,  TAPE=    0,  VIO=    0; TOTAL=     4 **

** START - JOB=JCLQB003     DATE=10/26/81   CLOCK=17.00.03
** END   -                  DATE=10/26/81   CLOCK=17.00.39   CPU TIME =    0 MIN   0.08 SEC  **
```

```
DATA SET UTILITY - GENERATE

IEB352I WARNING : OUTPUT RECFM/LRECL/BLKSIZE COPIED FROM INPUT

PROCESSING ENDED AT EOD
```

and PL/I statements are considered data statements for the simple reason that they don't contain either a // or a /* in columns 1 and 2.

So a job stream contains only JCL statements and data statements. Furthermore, the data statements can only occur immediately behind a DD * statement. If the operating system scans your job stream and finds any data statements that are not immediately behind a DD * statement, it inserts a SYSIN DD * statement just in front of those data statements. So that you will know that a statement was inserted, the inserted statement contains the word JES3GEN (in your system it might be a different but similar word) starting in column 73.

What error caused the system to insert the SYSIN DD statement? The data deck was put behind the delimiter statement, instead of in front of it. Since these misplaced data statements were not immediately behind a DD * statement, the system inserted a SYSIN DD * statement just in front of them. Remember that as far as IEBGENER is concerned, the input data set consists of all those statements between the SYSUT1 DD statement and the delimiter statement. There were no statements between the SYSUT1 DD statement and the delimiter statement, so the input data set was empty. That is why IEBGENER produced no output. IEBGENER does not consider an empty input data set an error, so it did not print any error message.

EXERCISES

1. Name, in order, the four fields on the JOB, EXEC, and DD statements.

2. Which are the national characters?

3. Which are the special characters?

4. Which of the following are valid names?
    a. VALIDNAME
    b. GOODNAME
    c. BADNAME
    d. TEST-JOB
    e. JOB#1
    f. #1JOB
    g. STEP ONE
    h. 123JOB

5. Which of the following are legal? Which of the following are equivalent to each other?

    a.   `MSGLEVEL=(0,0)`

    b.   `MSGLEVEL=(1)`

    c.   `MSGLEVEL=(1,)`

    d.   `MSGLEVEL=(,2)`

    e.   `MSGLEVEL=(,1)`

    f.   `MSGLEVEL=2`

6. How many blanks may there be between the name field and the operation field?

7. What are the two categories of parameters?

8. What are the rules for continuing a JCL statement?

9. What must you do if you omit a positional parameter?

10. What must you do if you omit a keyword parameter?

11. Why are parentheses required when you code `MSGLEVEL=(1,1)` but not when you code `MSGLEVEL=1`?

12. What is a default value? What is the purpose of default values?

13. What is the default value for `CLASS` at your computer center?

14. What are the functions of the two subparameters of the `MSGLEVEL` parameter?

15. Correct any errors you find in the following `JOB` statements. (Assume that there are no computer center restrictions on jobnames and that 12345 is a valid account number.)

```
a.    //MYJOB     JOB 12345
      //              'SNOOPY',
      //              CLASS=A,
                      MSGLEVEL=(1,1)
b.    //YOURJOB   JOB MSGLEVEL=(2,2)
      //              CLASS=P
c.    //HISJOB    JOB CLASS=F,
      //              'WOODSTOCK'
```

EXERCISES

```
d.    // HERJOB   JOB 12345,
      //              'LUCY',
      //              CLASS=B,
      //              MSGLEVEL=(0,1),
```

16. a. Code a JOB statement which uses default values for the CLASS and MSGLEVEL parameters and omits accounting information. Use your name for the programmer's name.

   b. Code a JOB statement which omits accounting information and the programmer's name, assigns the job to class W, and requests that only the job card be printed and system messages be suppressed.

17. What is an abend?

18. How many comment statements may a job contain?

19. The name on a JOB statement is called the jobname, and the name on a DD statement is called the ddname. What is the name on an EXEC statement called?

20. Code the EXEC statement to execute the program named BLUE. The stepname should be COLOR.

21. What are the names and purposes of the four DD statements used by IEBGENER?

22. In what order must you code the DD statements?

23. How do you direct a data set to the printer?

24. What is input stream data? How do you include input stream data in a job stream?

25. What is the function of the delimiter statement?

26. What is the function of the null statement?

27. Show how you would change the job stream in Figure 2.2 if:
   a. you wanted to suppress the IEBGENER messages.
   b. you wanted to punch the card deck rather than list it.

28. Correct the error in statement 3 in Figure 2.4.

29. Correct the errors in the following job stream. (Assume that there are no computer center restrictions on jobnames and that 12345 is a valid account number.)

```
//THEIRJOB JOB 12345,
//              'CHARLIE BROWN',
//              CLASS=A,
//              MSGLEVEL=1,
//PRINT    EXEC IEBGENER
//SYSOUT   DD SYSPRINT=A
//SYSIN    DD DUMMY,
//SYS1     DD *
/*
//SYS2     DD SYSPRINT=A
```

30. What is a return code? What does a return code of 0 usually mean?

31. Assume your computer center has just purchased a program named COPY which is supposed to replace IEBGENER. COPY writes its messages to a data set whose ddname is MESSAGES, it gets its input from a data set whose ddname is INPUT, and it writes its output to a data set whose ddname is OUTPUT. COPY does not use control statements. Code the job stream to use COPY to list a card deck.

PROGRAMMING ASSIGNMENT

Write and execute a job stream to use IEBGENER to list a card deck. You may use the data listed in Appendix D or any other data your advisor suggests.

SUMMARY

In this chapter you have learned

- how to use IEBGENER to list a card deck
- the format of the JOB, EXEC, and DD statements
- how to code the comment, delimiter, and null statements
- the rules for forming jobnames, stepnames, and ddnames
- the rules for coding positional and keyword parameters

SUMMARY

- the rules for continuing JCL statements

- how to read the system messages produced when a job is executed

- how to read the error messages produced when a job that contains a JCL syntax error is executed

- how to code the accounting information, programmer's name, CLASS, MSGLEVEL, DUMMY, *, and SYSOUT parameters

CHAPTER 3

CREATING SEQUENTIAL DATA SETS ON TAPE AND DISK

LEARNING OBJECTIVES

IN THIS CHAPTER YOU WILL LEARN

- the characteristics of magnetic tape and magnetic disk
- how to create a sequential data set on tape and disk
- how to use the parameters

```
DSN (DSNAME)     VOL (VOLUME)
DISP             REGION
UNIT             SPACE
                 DCB
```

YOU WILL ALSO LEARN THE MEANINGS OF THE FOLLOWING TERMS:

- allocation, primary and secondary
- block
- blocking factor
- blocksize
- contiguous
- cylinder
- data set name, qualified and unqualified
- extent
- interblock gap
- label records
- logical record length
- off-line
- on-line

- recording density
- serial number
- track
- volume
- volume label
- VTOC

Magnetic tape and disk are widely used for auxiliary storage, so it is important that you understand how to use them. In this chapter you will study the characteristics of tape and disk and learn how to create a sequential data set and store it on a tape or a disk.

CHARACTERISTICS OF MAGNETIC TAPE*

Magnetic tape used with computers is ½-inch wide and comes in reels that usually contain 2,400 feet of tape. Each reel is called a **volume**. When a new reel is received at a computer center, it is assigned a unique **serial number** which is used to identify that reel. A paper label containing the serial number is pasted to the outside of the reel. In addition, an IBM utility program, which you will study in Chapter 14, may be used to write the serial number magnetically on the tape in an area of the tape known as the **volume label**. The tape is then stored in a tape library with the computer center's other tapes. Tapes stored in the tape library are said to be **off-line**, meaning that they are not immediately available to be processed by a computer.

When a job is to be run, the tapes it requires are retrieved from the tape library and mounted on tape drives. The system reads the volume labels to verify that the correct volumes are mounted.

* This section discusses the basic principles of magnetic tape. If you are familiar with magnetic tape, you may skip this section.

When data are stored on tape or disk, the area occupied by the data is called a **block**. Each block is separated from its neighbors by a gap called the **interblock gap**. The length of the gap depends on the model tape or disk drive used. On many tape drives it is 0.6 inch.

Record Formats

Records may be stored on tape and disk in several formats. Two record formats used with sequential data sets are shown in Figure 3.1. (The term RECFM, which appears in Figure 3.1, means record format and is explained later in this chapter.) Additional record formats used with sequential data sets and with ISAM data sets are discussed in Appendix E.

FIXED LENGTH RECORDS.   Figure 3.1a shows the simplest format, which is called fixed length. All the records are the same size, and each block consists of one record.

As you learned in Chapter 1, when data are stored in the computer's storage unit or recorded on tape or disk, each letter or special character occupies one byte. When numbers are stored in character form, each digit requires a byte. When numbers are stored in packed form, each byte contains

FIGURE 3.1

Record formats used with sequential data sets on tape and disk

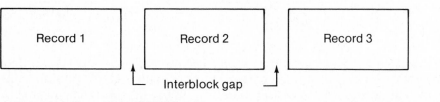

a. Fixed-length records (RECFM = F)

b. Fixed-length blocked records (blocking factor 3, RECFM = FB)

two digits except for the last byte which contains one digit and the sign of the number. The number of bytes of data in a record is called the **logical record length**. The number of bytes of data in a block is called the **blocksize**. For fixed length records, since each block contains one record, the logical record length and blocksize are equal. So if the records were created by copying 80-column cards to tape, the logical record length and the blocksize would both be 80 bytes.

The length of a block on tape depends on the blocksize and the recording density. The **recording density** is the number of bytes recorded per inch of tape, and the value depends on the particular model tape drive used. Common values of recording density are 800, 1600, and 6250 bytes per inch. Some tape drives, called dual-density drives, can record and read at two densities; for example, 800 and 1600 or 1600 and 6250 bytes per inch.

Suppose records with a logical record length and blocksize of 80 bytes are recorded at a density of 800 bytes per inch. The length of a block is 80 bytes/800 bytes per inch = 0.1 inch. Since the interblock gap is 0.6 inch, six times as much tape is wasted as is used. Similar considerations apply to disk.

BLOCKING.   To use tape and disk more efficiently, records are frequently blocked. Figure 3.1b shows how fixed length records look when they are blocked. When records are blocked, a number of records are stored together in one block. The number of records in a block is called the **blocking factor**. Suppose the 80-byte records in the previous example were blocked using a blocking factor of 10. The blocksize would be $10 \times 80 = 800$ bytes. The length of a block is 800 bytes/800 bytes per inch = 1 inch. The gap remains the same size it was before, 0.6 inch. So you see that now almost twice as much tape is used as is wasted, while without blocking six times as much tape was wasted as was used.

Besides increasing the efficiency with which data are stored, blocking also reduces the time required to read or write a data set. The time is reduced because the tape drive reads (or writes) a complete block and then stops the tape. When the next block is required, the drive starts the tape again and the next block is read (or written). When the data set is blocked, there are fewer gaps and fewer stops and starts, and therefore less time is required to process the data set. Blocking also reduces processing time for data sets on disk.

If we repeated our previous analysis using a blocking factor of 100 instead of 10, we would find that the data set occupied less space and was processed faster with a blocking factor of 100 than with a blocking factor of 10. In general, the larger the blocking factor, the less space the data set occupies and the faster it can be processed. So, you might wonder, why stop? Why not increase the blocking factor until the whole data set is one giant block! One reason is that the maximum blocksize is 32,760 bytes, but there is a second reason. Since a whole block is read at one time, there has to be enough room in main storage to accommodate it. If the blocking factor is too large, there may not be enough space in main storage to accept a block.

Selecting the best blocking factor in any particular case involves a trade-off between the efficient use of tape and disk and faster processing speed (which are improved by large blocking factors) and the demand on main storage (which is reduced by low blocking factors). As main storage has become less expensive, there has been a tendency to use larger blocking factors. Usually, a systems analyst selects the blocking factor.

We have discussed how large a block may be; we must also consider how small a block may be. The minimum blocksize is 18 bytes. Blocks smaller than 18 bytes may be confused with background noise and not read.

Label Records

When a data set is stored on a tape, you can have the system automatically write header label records in front of the data set and trailer label records in back of it. These **label records** are similar to the volume header record we discussed earlier, but these records contain information about the data set, such as the logical record length, the blocksize, the recording density, and the number of blocks the data set contains.

Data sets that have system-written header and trailer label records are said to have standard labels. Data sets may also have user-written label records or no label records at all. If a data set has no labels, it is called, naturally enough, an unlabeled data set.

CHARACTERISTICS OF MAGNETIC DISK*

There are a number of different models of disks available which have different storage capacities, data retrieval speeds, and costs. Because the IBM 3330 Disk Storage Facility is widely used, it will serve as an example. The 3330 Disk Storage Facility uses a disk pack called the 3336 Disk Pack.

* This section discusses the basic principles of magnetic disk. If you are familiar with magnetic disk, you may skip this section.

CHARACTERISTICS OF MAGNETIC DISK

The 3336 Disk Pack consists of 11 metallic coated disks mounted on a common shaft, as shown in Figure 3.2. Data are recorded on these disk surfaces. The exterior surfaces are not used for recording data, and one interior surface is used by the disk drive for system functions, so each pack·contains 19 surfaces which may be used by the programmer to record data. Each recording surface is divided into 808 concentric circles, called **tracks**, on which data are recorded. In addition there are several alternate tracks which may be used if any of the 808 tracks become unusable. Although the tracks

FIGURE 3.2

A 3336 Disk Pack

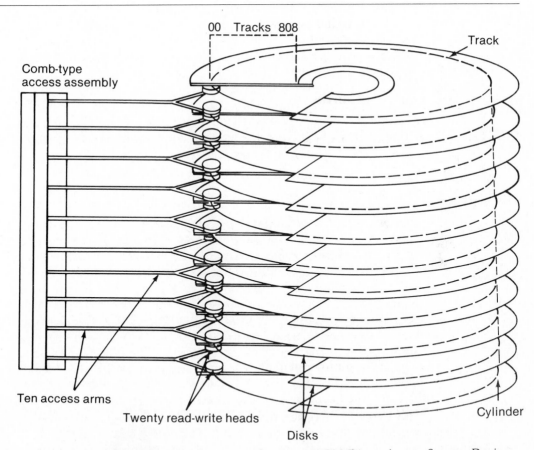

Reprinted by permission from *Introduction to IBM Direct-Access Storage Devices and Organization Methods.* © 1974 by International Business Machines Corporation.

get smaller toward the center of the disk, all the tracks can hold the same amount of data.

As Figure 3.2 shows, each recording surface has its own read/write head. All the read/write heads move together. So, for example, if you wanted to read data on track 158 of the sixth recording surface, the access mechanism would position all 20 read/write heads over track 158 of their respective surfaces. This leads to the important concept of a cylinder. A **cylinder** is all the data that can be read (or written) without moving the read/write heads. The reason the cylinder concept is important is that it takes a (relatively) long time to move the read/write heads. Since all the data in a cylinder can be accessed without moving the read/write heads, a cylinder of data can be accessed quickly.

A disk pack is called a **volume**. Like a tape reel, a new disk pack is assigned a serial number when it is received at a computer center. A paper label containing the serial number is pasted to the plastic housing of the disk pack, and an IBM utility program, which you will study in Chapter 14, is used to write the serial number magnetically on the volume label.

Unlike tapes, many disk packs remain permanently mounted in a disk drive; they are **on-line.** When a job requests a disk volume that is on-line, the computer can begin processing immediately without waiting for the requested disk volume to be retrieved and mounted.

The VTOC

A disk pack usually contains many data sets. To make it possible to keep track of where each data set is and where the unused tracks are, each disk contains a volume table of contents (**VTOC**) that is automatically maintained by the system. The VTOC is stored on the disk and contains the name of each data set stored on the disk (how a data set gets a name is explained later in this chapter) and where the data set is. For example, a disk pack might contain a data set named PAYROLL which starts at track 764, surface 6. That information would be stored in the VTOC. The VTOC contains additional information about the data sets stored on the disk pack, such as logical record length and blocksize, similar to the data stored in header and trailer labels on tape.

Besides information on the data sets on the disk pack, the VTOC also contains information on the unused tracks. Usually, the unused tracks are not all together in one place but scattered throughout the pack. Tracks that are in the same cylinder and cylinders that are next to each other are said to be **contiguous**. A group of contiguous tracks make up an **extent**. The VTOC contains information on the location and size of the unused extents. It is not necessary that a data set occupy only one extent. A data set can be spread out over as many as 16 extents. The system does all the work, remembering where on the disk pack each portion of a data set is stored. Generally, the user is not even aware that the data set is not stored in one extent.

Additional information about magnetic disks is in Appendix E.

CREATING A SEQUENTIAL DATA SET ON A DISK

Assume you have a card deck that you want to use as input to create a sequential data set and store it on a disk. The system flowchart in Figure 3.3 shows the processing you want to do. The ddnames SYSUT1 and SYSUT2 are shown in Figure 3.3. (Based on the discussion in Chapter 2 you know that IEBGENER requires two additional data sets with the ddnames SYSIN and SYSPRINT. However, these two data sets are not important to the processing being done and are therefore not shown in Figure 3.3.) Throughout this book illustrations will always show the ddnames on the flowlines connecting the data set and the program symbols.

Figure 3.4 shows a job stream to use IEBGENER to create a sequential data set and store it on a disk. Some changes have been made to the JOB statement, and the SYSUT2 DD statement contains some new entries, but the other statements should be familiar to you from Chapter 2.

FIGURE 3.3

System flowchart to create a sequential data set on disk

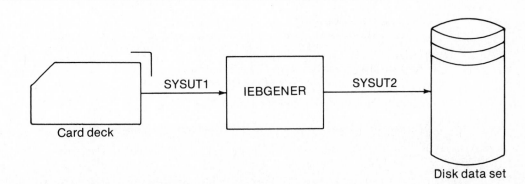

Card deck   SYSUT1   IEBGENER   SYSUT2   Disk data set

FIGURE 3.4

Job stream to create a sequential data set on disk

```
//JCLOB010 JOB ,'J. C. LEWIS',
//          REGION=40K
//*
//* USING IEBGENER TO CREATE A SEQUENTIAL DATA SET ON A DISK
//*
//CREATE EXEC PGM=IEBGENER
//SYSPRINT DD SYSOUT=A
//SYSIN    DD DUMMY
//SYSUT1   DD *
13009REED,TINA              A0842000426072100     74
15174HANDJANY,HAIDEH        H0229000220022900     71
17337BUTERO,MAURICE         H0501000434050100     63
19499LAFER,BRUCE            A0706000819050000     52
21661LEE,SUI               A0390170303030017     76
23821COOPER,LUCY           L0745000730070000     64
25980NELSON,LAWRENCE       L0513000217051300     78
28138KRUKIS,SONIA          A0346000510034600     59
30295CHEN,YIN              H0295000514010000     81
32451SIMPKINS,KEVIN        L0388000321038606     76
34605PORTER,MICHELE        A0627500128042700     65
36759DECICCO,RICHARD       A0255000619010000     71
38912ABREU,JUANITA         H0732001030070000     80
41063HIGH,CAROL            L0311000521031100     82
43214ENGLISH,REYNOLDS      A0443000228043300     82
45363LEE,BOHYON            A0515000214050000     79
47512THOMPSON,STANLEY      H0640750307064075     66
49659VALDEZ,FABIO          L0706000430070600     71
51805AMATO,ROBERT          A0466000417015000     63
53950RIZZUTO,JAMES         A0693000822000000     81
56094SCHWARTZ,MICHAEL      H1037000605050000     67
58238RUFINO,CARLOS         L0673000520047300     64
60380MORLEY,JOHN           A0786000514078600     71
62521BREVIL,JAMES          H0812000314081200     55
64660FALCONER,EDWARD       L1080000227008000     74
66799MARTIN,KATHLEEN       L0895000129089500     65
68937YEUNG,SUK            A0517000816050000     49
71074PAUL,MARINA          A0441000414034100     80
73210FRADIN,SHIRLEY       L0668000728066800     56
75344BURNS,JEFFREY        L0706000226070000     57
/*
//SYSUT2   DD DSN=WYL.QB.JCL.POLYFILE,
//            DISP=(NEW,KEEP,DELETE),
//            UNIT=DISK,
//            VOL=SER=WYL002,
//            SPACE=(TRK,5),
//            DCB=(RECFM=FB,LRECL=80,BLKSIZE=800)
//
```

CREATING A SEQUENTIAL DATA SET ON A DISK

The JOB Statement

The accounting information and the CLASS and MSGLEVEL parameters have been eliminated from the JOB statement and the REGION parameter added. The CUNY computer system obtains accounting information from a JES3 accounting statement, so it is not necessary to specify accounting information on the JOB statement. At the CUNY computer center the default values for CLASS and MSGLEVEL are CLASS=A and MSGLEVEL=(1,1). Since these are the values desired, they need not be coded on the JOB statement. They were included in the examples in Chapter 2 to show you how they are coded.

THE REGION PARAMETER.   REGION is used in MVT and MVS systems to request main storage. REGION has no meaning in MFT systems and has meaning in VS1 systems only under the unusual condition when you request that your program not be paged.

The REGION parameter

```
REGION=40K
```

was added to the JOB statement to request 40K bytes of main storage. If REGION is not coded, the job is allocated the default amount of storage. As you saw in Chapter 2, at the CUNY computer center the default value for REGION is 192K, but only 36K are required to execute IEBGENER. (Examine the output produced by your solution to the Programming Assignment in Chapter 2 to determine the default value of REGION at your computer center.) This JCL requests 40K instead of 36K because the actual amount of main storage required depends on the characteristics of the data sets being processed, and it is good practice to request a little extra space as a safety margin. The value you code on the REGION parameter should be an even number; if you code an odd number, the system rounds up to the next even number.

You should always code the REGION parameter unless your job requires the default amount of main storage. If your job requires more than the default amount of main storage and you don't request the amount you need, your job may not run. On the other hand, if your job requires less than the default amount of main storage and you don't request the amount you need, your job may not run as quickly as it could. This is because the operating system will not start executing your job until the default amount of storage is available, while the smaller amount of storage that your job actually requires might be available earlier. Since virtual systems usually have a large amount of main storage, competition between jobs is not as important as in nonvirtual systems.

The SYSUT2 DD Statement

The SYSUT2 DD statement directs the output from IEBGENER to a disk. It is important to understand that the SYSUT2 DD statement in Figure 3.4 shows how to create a sequential data set on disk. It happens that the program that is executed in Figure 3.4 is IEBGENER, but you would code the same DD parameters if you were executing a COBOL, PL/I, FORTRAN, or assembler program or a different utility program to create a sequential data set on disk. Only the ddname would be different, since it would have to be changed to the ddname the program required.

Let us now discuss the parameters on the SYSUT2 DD statement in turn.

NAMING THE DATA SET—THE DSN PARAMETER. The first parameter

```
DSN=WYL.QB.JCL.POLYFILE
```

assigns a name to the data set. DSN, which is an abbreviation for DSNAME, is a keyword parameter and stands for data set name. The name assigned by this entry, WYL.QB.JCL.POLYFILE, is the name entered into the VTOC of the disk pack. If later we want to use this data set, we must use the name WYL.QB.JCL.POLYFILE to refer to it.

Qualified and Unqualified Names. The rules you must follow when you invent a data set name are a little complicated. **Data set names** may be either **unqualified** or **qualified**. The rules for an unqualified data set name are similar to the rules you learned in Chapter 2 for jobnames, stepnames, and ddnames. You recall that jobnames and stepnames must consist of from 1 to 8 characters, that the first character must be alphabetic or national, and that the remaining characters must be alphameric or national. In addition to these characters, a data set name may contain a hyphen after the first character.

Now that you know what an unqualified data set name is, understanding what a qualified data set name is is easy. A qualified data set name consists of two or more unqualified data set names connected by periods. The only new rule is that the total length of a qualified data set name, including

FIGURE 3.5

Output produced by executing the job stream in Figure 3.4

```
IAT6140 JOB ORIGIN FROM GROUP=LOCAL      , DSP=IJP, DEVICE=INTRDR  , 000    First page
15:56:17 IAT5110 JOB 6476 (JCLQB010) USES D WYL002 WYL.QB.JCL.POLYFILE
15:56:20 IAT5200 JOB 6476 (JCLQB010) IN SETUP ON MAIN=M1
15:56:20 IAT5210 SYSUT2  USING D WYL002 ON 377   WYL.QB.JCL.POLYFILE
15:56:23 IATXXXX JOB 6476 (JCLQB010) SETUP COMPLETED ON MAIN=M1
15:56:27 IAT2000 JOB 6476 JCLQB010 SELECTED M1    GRP=BATCH
15:56:35 M1 R= JCLQB010 IEF403I JCLQB010 - STARTED
15:57:14 M1 R= JCLQB010 IEF404I JCLQB010 - ENDED
15:57:23 IAT5400 JOB 6476 (JCLQB010) IN BREAKDOWN

                                                                *          Second page

//JCLQB010 JOB ,'J. C. LEWIS',
//       REGION=40K
//*
//* USING IEBGENER TO CREATE A SEQUENTIAL DATA SET ON A DISK
//*
//CREATE EXEC PGM=IEBGENER
//SYSPRINT DD SYSOUT=A
//SYSIN    DD DUMMY
//SYSUT1   DD *
//*
//SYSUT2   DD DSN=WYL.QB.JCL.POLYFILE,
//            DISP=(NEW,KEEP,DELETE),
//            UNIT=DISK,
//            VOL=SER=WYL002,
//            SPACE=(TRK,5),
//            DCB=(RECFM=FB,LRECL=80,BLKSIZE=800)
//
//
//
```

(cont.)

79

```
1       //JCLQB010 JOB ,'J. C. LEWIS',
        // REGION=40K
        *** USING IEBGENER TO CREATE A SEQUENTIAL DATA SET ON A DISK
        ***
2       //CREATE EXEC PGM=IEBGENER
3       //SYSPRINT DD SYSOUT=A
4       //SYSIN    DD DUMMY
5       //SYSUT1   DD *,DCB=BLKSIZE=80
6       //SYSUT2   DD DSN=WYL.QB.JCL.POLYFILE,
        //            DISP=(NEW,KEEP,DELETE),
        //            UNIT=DISK,
        //            VOL=SER=WYL002,
        //            SPACE=(TRK,5),
        //            DCB=(RECFM=FB,LRECL=80,BLKSIZE=800)
```

Third page

```
IEF236I ALLOC. FOR JCLQB010 CREATE
IEF237I JES3 ALLOCATED TO SYSPRINT
IEF237I DMY  ALLOCATED TO SYSIN
IEF237I JES3 ALLOCATED TO SYSUT1
IEF237I 377  ALLOCATED TO SYSUT2
IEF142I JCLQB010 CREATE - STEP WAS EXECUTED  - COND CODE 0000
IEF285I    CREATE.SYSPRINT                              SYSOUT
IEF285I    JESI0001                                     SYSIN
IEF285I    WYL.QB.JCL.POLYFILE          KEPT
IEF285I    VOL SER NOS= WYL002.
```

The data set is on WYL002.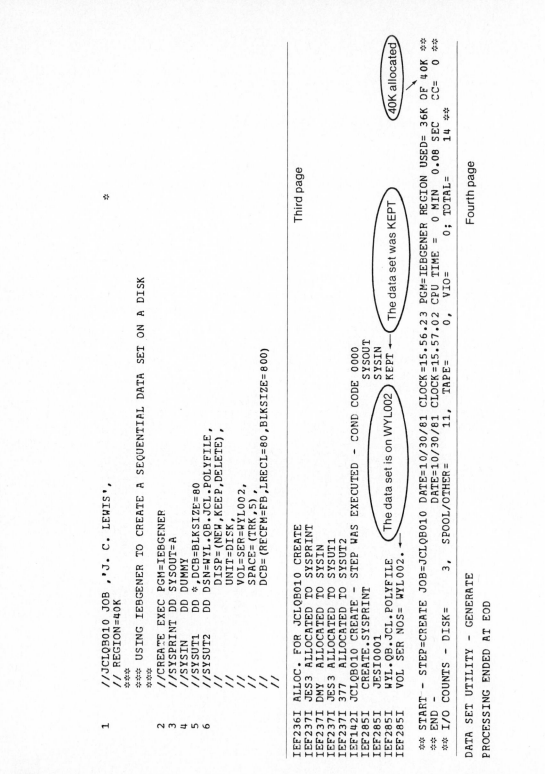

The data set was KEPT

40K allocated

```
** START - STEP=CREATE JOB=JCLQB010 DATE=10/30/81 CLOCK=15.56.23  PGM=IEBGENER REGION USED= 36K OF 40K **
** END -                            DATE=10/30/81 CLOCK=15.57.02  CPU TIME =  0 MIN  0.08 SEC  CC=  0 **
** I/O COUNTS - DISK=    3,  SPOOL/OTHER=    11, TAPE=    0,  VIO=    0; TOTAL=   14 **
```

Fourth page

```
DATA SET UTILITY - GENERATE
PROCESSING ENDED AT EOD
```

80

CREATING A SEQUENTIAL DATA SET ON TAPE

Figure 3.6 shows the output produced when a job stream that uses IEBGENER to create a sequential data set on tape is executed. The output was originally on four pages. The original job stream is shown on the second page. The only changes required from Figure 3.4 are to the SYSUT2 DD statement. First, the UNIT parameter must specify a tape drive rather than a disk drive. Second, the VOL parameter is not coded. The reason for not specifying a tape volume is that the particular volume may already be in use, or it might have been in such poor condition that it was replaced. When you are using tape, it is better to let the operator mount any available tape. The allocation message on the third page tells you the tape serial number actually used was QBT010. Third, the SPACE parameter is not coded. The SPACE parameter is not specified for tape; it is only specified for direct access devices such as disks.

The DEN Subparameter

Finally, the DEN subparameter of the DCB parameter is coded. DEN specifies the recording density to be used for the data set and is sometimes coded when data sets are created on tape using a dual-density tape drive. The values that DEN may have and the recording densities they correspond to are shown in Table 3.2.

TABLE 3.2

Values of DEN and
corresponding recording densities

Value of DEN	Recording Density (bytes per inch)
0	200
1	556
2	800
3	1600
4	6250

FIGURE 3.6

Output produced by a job stream that creates a data set on tape

```
IAT6140 JOB ORIGIN FROM GROUP=LOCAL            ,DSP=IJP, DEVICE=INTRDR   ,000          First page
16:30:56 IAT5110 JOB 7357 (JCLQB015) GET T QBT010 ,SL WYL.QB.JCL.POLYFILE
16:30:56 IAT5200 JOB 7357 (JCLQB015) IN SETUP ON MAIN=M2
16:30:56 IAT5210 SYSUT2   MOUNT T QBT010 ON 48A   ,SL,RING    WYL.QB.JCL.POLYFILE
16:32:19 IATXXXX JOB 7357 (JCLQB015) SETUP COMPLETED ON MAIN=M2
16:32:19 IAT2000 JOB 7357 JCLQB015 SELECTED M1      GRP=BATCH
16:32:19 M1 R= JCLQB015 IEF403I JCLQB015 - STARTED
16:33:42 M1 R= JCLQB015 IEF234E K 68A,QBT010,PVT,JCLQB015,CREATE
16:33:43 M1 R= JCLQB015 IEF471E FOLLOWING VOLUMES NO LONGER NEEDED BY JCLQB015
16:33:43 M1 R= JCLQB015                QBT010.
16:33:43 M1 R= JCLQB015 IEF404I JCLQB015 - ENDED
16:33:44 IAT5410 KEEP    T QBT010 ON 48A,M2
16:33:45 IAT5400 JOB 7357 (JCLQB015) IN BREAKDOWN
```

```
//JCLQB015 JOB ,'J. C. LEWIS',                        *          Second page
// REGION=40K
//*
//* USING IEBGENER TO CREATE A DATA SET ON A TAPE
//*
//CREATE EXEC PGM=IEBGENER
//SYSPRINT DD SYSOUT=A
//SYSIN    DD DUMMY
//SYSUT1   DD *
//*
//SYSUT2   DD DSN=WYL.QB.JCL.POLYFILE,
//            DISP=(NEW,KEEP,DELETE),
//            UNIT=TAPE,
//            DCB=(RECFM=FB,LRECL=80,BLKSIZE=800,DEN=4)
//
```

```
1       //JCLQB015 JOB ,'J. C. LEWIS',
        // REGION=40K
        ***  USING IEBGENER TO CREATE A DATA SET ON A TAPE
        ***
2       //CREATE   EXEC PGM=IEBGENER
3       //SYSPRINT DD SYSOUT=A
4       //SYSIN    DD DUMMY
5       //SYSUT1   DD *,DCB=BLKSIZE=80
6       //SYSUT2   DD DSN=WYL.QB.JCL.POLYFILE,
        //            DISP=(NEW,KEEP,DELETE),
        //            UNIT=TAPE,
        //            DCB=(RECFM=FB,LRECL=80,BLKSIZE=800,DEN=4)
```

Third page

```
IEF236I ALLOC. FOR JCLQB015 CREATE
IEF237I JES3 ALLOCATED TO SYSPRINT
IEF237I DMY  ALLOCATED TO SYSIN
IEF237I JES3 ALLOCATED TO SYSUT1
IEF237I 68A  ALLOCATED TO SYSUT2
IEF142I JCLQB015 CREATE - STEP WAS EXECUTED - COND CODE 0000
IEF285I   CREATE.SYSPRINT                           SYSOUT
IEF285I   JESI0001                                  SYSIN
IEF285I   WYL.QB.JCL.POLYFILE          The data set is on QBT010.   KEPT
IEF285I   VOL SER NOS= QBT010.
```
(The data set is on QBT010)
(The data set was KEPT)

```
** START - STEP=CREATE JOB=JCLQB015 DATE=10/30/81 CLOCK=16.32.08  PGM=IEBGENER REGION USED= 36K OF 40K **
** END -                            DATE=10/30/81 CLOCK=16.33.30  CPU TIME = 0 MIN  0.10 SEC    CC= 0   **
** I/O COUNTS - DISK=    0,  SPOOL/OTHER=    52,  TAPE=    3,  VIO=    0;  TOTAL=    55 **
```

Fourth page

DATA SET UTILITY - GENERATE
PROCESSING ENDED AT EOD

83

However, if DEN is not coded, the recording density actually used will be the highest value the tape drive is capable of. Since recording at the highest possible density is generally desirable, it is customary to omit the DEN subparameter. The job stream in Figure 3.6 would execute with exactly the same results if the DEN subparameter had been omitted.

It is important to understand that the SYSUT2 DD statement in Figure 3.6 shows how a sequential data set on tape is created. Although the program that is executed in Figure 3.6 is IEBGENER, you would code the same DD parameters if you were using a COBOL, PL/I, FORTRAN, or assembler program to create a sequential data set on tape. Only the ddname would be different, since it would have to be changed to the ddname the program required.

The DISP Parameter for Tape

The DISP parameter works a little differently for tapes than it does for disks. When you code NEW for the status of your data set, the data are written on the tape; any data that were originally on the tape are simply erased. When you code KEEP for the disposition, at the end of the job the tape is rewound and unloaded from the tape drive. The system issues a message to the operator that the tape volume is to be kept. The operator sends the tape volume to the library. When you code DELETE for the disposition, at the end of the job the tape is rewound and unloaded, but this time the system issues a message to the operator that the tape volume may be used. The operator sends the tape volume to be stored with the other tapes that are available to be used by any job that needs a tape.

ERRORS

Figure 3.7 shows the output produced by a job stream that contains a syntax error. Although there are three error messages, there is only one error. The error is that the SPACE parameter begins in column 17. Recall that when a JCL statement is continued, the continuation statement must have two slashes in columns 1 and 2 and the coding must resume between columns 4 and 16.

Because of the comma after WYL002, the system expected the statement to be continued on the next line, but because SPACE begins in column 17, the SPACE line was not recognized as a continuation line. The system therefore

FIGURE 3.7

Execution of a job stream that contains a syntax error

```
IAT6140 JOB ORIGIN FROM GROUP=LOCAL    , DSP=IJP, DEVICE=INTRDR   , 000   First page
16:23:52 IAT4204  JOB FAILED WITH CONVERTER/INTERPRETER JCL ERROR
16:23:52 IAT4801 JOB JCLQB016 (7172) EXPRESS CANCELED BY INTERPRETER DSP
```

```
//JCLQB016 JOB ,'J. C. LEWIS',                            *Second page
// REGION=40K
//*
//* USING IEBGENER TO CREATE A SEQUENTIAL DATA SET ON A DISK
//*
//CREATE EXEC PGM=IEBGENER
//SYSPRINT DD SYSOUT=A
//SYSIN    DD DUMMY
//SYSUT1   DD *
/*
//SYSUT2   DD DSN=WYL.QB.JCL.POLYFILE,
//              DISP=(NEW,KEEP,DELETE),
//              UNIT=DISK,
//              VOL=SER=WYL002,
//               SPACE=(TRK,5),
//              DCB=(RECFM=FB,LRECL=80,BLKSIZE=800)
//
     1    //JCLQB016 JOB ,'J. C. LEWIS',                          *
          // REGION=40K
          ***
          *** USING IEBGENER TO CREATE A SEQUENTIAL DATA SET ON A DISK
          ***
     2    //CREATE EXEC PGM=IEBGENER
     3    //SYSPRINT DD SYSOUT=A
     4    //SYSIN    DD DUMMY
     5    //SYSUT1   DD *,DCB=BLKSIZE=80
     6    //SYSUT2   DD DSN=WYL.QB.JCL.POLYFILE,
          //              DISP=(NEW,KEEP,DELETE),
          //              UNIT=DISK,
          //              VOL=SER=WYL002,
     7    //*               SPACE=(TRK,5),
     8    //              DCB=(RECFM=FB,LRECL=80,BLKSIZE=800)
          //
```

```
STMT NO. MESSAGE                                          Third page

     6    IEF621I EXPECTED CONTINUATION NOT RECEIVED
     7    IEF605I UNIDENTIFIED OPERATION FIELD
     8    IEF605I UNIDENTIFIED OPERATION FIELD
```

printed the error message EXPECTED CONTINUATION NOT RECEIVED and printed an asterisk in column 3 of the SPACE line, treating that line as a comment. The system then tried to interpret the SPACE and DCB statements as independent JCL statements, but it couldn't recognize them, so it printed the error

FIGURE 3.8

Execution of a job stream that contains a logic error

```
IAT6140 JOB ORIGIN FROM GROUP=LOCAL    , DSP=IJP, DEVICE=INTRDR  , 000
16:42:35 IAT5110 JOB 7607 (JCLQB020) USES D WYL002 WYL.QB.JCL.POLYFILE
16:42:35 IAT5200 JOB 7607 (JCLQB020) IN SETUP ON MAIN=M1
16:42:35 IAT5210 SYSUT2  USING D WYL002 ON 377  WYL.QB.JCL.POLYFILE
16:42:35 IATXXXX JOB 7607 (JCLQB020) SETUP COMPLETED ON MAIN=M1
16:42:35 IAT2000 JOB 7607 JCLQB020 SELECTED M2     GRP=BATCH
16:42:36 M2 R= JCLQB020 IEF403I JCLQB020 - STARTED
16:42:37 M2 R= JCLQB020 IEF453I JCLQB020 - JOB FAILED -  JCL ERROR
16:42:38 IAT5400 JOB 7607 (JCLQB020) IN BREAKDOWN
```
First page

```
//JCLQB020 JOB ,'J. C. LEWIS',
//         REGION=40K
//*
//*  USING IEBGENER TO CREATE A SEQUENTIAL DATA SET ON A DISK
//*
//CREATE EXEC PGM=IEBGENER
//SYSPRINT DD SYSOUT=A
//SYSIN    DD DUMMY
//SYSUT1   DD *
//*
//SYSUT2   DD DSN=WYL.QB.JCL.POLYFILE,
//         DISP=(NEW,KEEP,DELETE),
//         UNIT=DISK,
//         VOL=SER=WYL002,
//         SPACE=(TRK,5),
//         DCB=(RECFM=FB,LRECL=80,BLKSIZE=800)
```
Second page

```
1      //JCLQB020 JOB ,'J. C. LEWIS',                                          *
       // REGION=40K
       ***
       *** USING IEBGENER TO CREATE A SEQUENTIAL DATA SET ON A DISK
       ***
2      //CREATE   EXEC PGM=IEBGENER
3      //SYSPRINT DD SYSOUT=A
4      //SYSIN    DD DUMMY
5      //SYSUT1   DD *,DCB=BLKSIZE=80
6      //SYSUT2   DD DSN=WYL.QB.JCL.POLYFILE,
       //            DISP=(NEW,KEEP,DELETE),
       //            UNIT=DISK,
       //            VOL=SER=WYL002,
       //            SPACE=(TRK,5),
       //            DCB=(RECFM=FB,LRECL=80,BLKSIZE=800)


IEF253I JCLQB020 CREATE SYSUT2 - DUPLICATE NAME ON DIRECT ACCESS VOLUME        Third page
IEF272I JCLQB020 CREATE - STEP WAS NOT EXECUTED.
IEF285I    CREATE.SYSPRINT                            SYSOUT
IEF285I    JESIO001                                   SYSIN

** START - JOB=JCLQB020      DATE=10/30/81    CLOCK=16.42.36
** END   -                   DATE=10/30/81    CLOCK=16.42.37    CPU TIME =    0 MIN    0.00 SEC  **
```

message UNIDENTIFIED OPERATION FIELD. To fix the error all you have to do is to retype the SPACE line, starting SPACE between columns 4 and 16.

An error people often make when creating a data set on a disk is illustrated in Figure 3.8. Typically, this error comes about in the following way. A job was executed but did not run perfectly. However, the space was allocated and the data set name was entered in the disk pack's VTOC. The allocation messages for the job show that the data set was kept. Unfortunately, the programmer often does not read the allocation messages, and therefore does not realize that the data set name has been entered into the VTOC. The programmer therefore corrects the program and reruns the job. The second job also fails, and the system prints the error message shown on the third page in Figure 3.8,

```
DUPLICATE NAME ON DIRECT ACCESS VOLUME
```

What this message means is that when the system saw the disposition NEW, it tried to enter the data set name in the VTOC. However, since the exact same name was already in the VTOC and data set names in the VTOC must be unique, the system printed the error message and the job was terminated.

The easiest way to correct this error is change the DISP parameter to

```
DISP=(OLD,KEEP,DELETE)
```

As the error message implies, this kind of error cannot occur with tape, since only direct access volumes have VTOCs.

EXERCISES

1. What is the purpose of assigning serial numbers to tape and disk volumes?

2. Suppose that when a particular tape drive writes fixed unblocked records it uses an interblock gap of 0.6 inch. What size would the gap be when that drive writes blocked records?

3. What is the purpose of blocking?

4. What are label records?

EXERCISES

5. What is a cylinder?

6. What is a VTOC?

7. What is an extent?

8. What parameters must be coded on a DD statement to create a permanent data set on a disk? Would the same parameters be used for tape?

9. When you use a COBOL program to create a data set on disk, the data set has three names: the file name used in the COBOL program, the ddname, and the data set name. Which of these names, if any, must be the same when you later access that data set?

10. What are the three subparameters of the DISP parameter?

11. What is the difference between coding OLD, SHR, and MOD as the status subparameter?

12. Suppose DISP is not coded. What is the default?

13. What is the advantage of using a group name when you code the UNIT parameter?

14. What is the meaning of SPACE=(300,(200,100))?

15. When will a secondary allocation be made? How many times will a secondary allocation be made?

16. How do you return unused space on a DASD to the system?

17. In what order must the keyword parameters DSN, DISP, UNIT, VOL, SPACE, and DCB be coded?

18. What does coding DEN=4 mean?

19. Write a DD statement to create a sequential data set on a disk. Use values for the DSN, UNIT, and VOL parameters which are valid at your computer center. The data set should be kept if the job terminates normally and deleted if it terminates abnormally. The record length is 120 bytes, and a blocking factor of 10 is used. Request space in blocks. There will be about 10,000 records in your data set. You should request a secondary allocation of 100 blocks, and you should release unused space.

20. Write a DD statement to create a sequential data set on tape. Use values for the DSN, UNIT, and VOL parameters which are valid at your computer center. The data set should be kept no matter how the job terminates. Do not code the DCB parameter.

21. Rewrite correctly any entry that is wrong.

    a.   `DSN=PAYROLLFILE`

    b.   `DISP=NEW,KEEP,KEEP`

    c.   `DISP=OLD`

    d.   `DISP=(OLD,OLD,OLD)`

    e.   `VOL=SER=DISK01`

    f.   `VOL=TAPE05`

    g.   `SPACE=(500,500)`

    h.   `SPACE=(TRK(10,4)RLSE)`

    i.   `DCB=(RECFM=FB,LRECL=100,BLOCKSIZE=550)`

    j.   `DCB=(RECFM=VB,LRECL=200,BLOCKSIZE=400)`

PROGRAMMING ASSIGNMENT

Execute a job to use `IEBGENER` to create a sequential data set on a disk. Use the data given in Appendix D or data suggested by your advisor.

SUMMARY

In this chapter you have learned

- the characteristics of magnetic tape and magnetic disk

- the parameters used to create a sequential data set on tape or disk:

    `DSN`—to assign a name to a data set

    `DISP`—to specify a status and disposition

    `UNIT`—to specify a physical device

    `VOL`—to specify a particular volume

    `SPACE`—to request space in terms of tracks, cylinders, or blocks on a disk volume

    `DCB`—to assign a data set characteristics of record format, logical record length, blocksize, and recording density

- the rules for forming qualified and unqualified data set names

CHAPTER 4

ACCESSING SEQUENTIAL DATA SETS

CHAPTER 4 / ACCESSING SEQUENTIAL DATA SETS

LEARNING OBJECTIVES

IN THIS CHAPTER YOU WILL LEARN

- how to add records to a data set

- how to catalog a data set

- how to code control statements for IEBGENER and IEBPTPCH

- how to code a job stream that contains more than one step

- how to read the system messages produced when a job abends

- how to use the parameters COND and TIME

YOU WILL ALSO LEARN THE MEANINGS OF THE FOLLOWING TERMS:

- backward reference

- cataloged

- completion code

- control statement

- dump

- SDS

Now that you have created a data set and stored it on a disk, the next thing you must learn is how to access that data set. Most job streams contain more than one step, and in this chapter you will also learn how to code multistep job streams. So far you have used IEBGENER in its simplest form. You are now ready to learn how to code control statements to modify the processing that IEBGENER does. In this chapter you will also learn how to use a second utility program, IEBPTPCH.

LISTING A DISK DATA SET

In Chapter 3 we created `WYL.QB.JCL.POLYFILE`. From now on when there is no chance for confusion, only the last part of the data set name, `POLYFILE`, will be used. The output produced by the job that created `POLYFILE` is shown in Figure 3.5. You may have noticed when you studied Figure 3.5 that there is no output showing the data records that were put on the disk. The system messages indicate that the job ran properly, and there is every reason to believe that all the records in the card deck were successfully put on the disk, but it would be nice if you could be sure. The way to be sure is to list `POLYFILE`. The system flowchart for listing `POLYFILE` is shown in Figure 4.1.

Listing `POLYFILE` should be easy, since back in Chapter 2 we listed a card deck using the job stream in Figure 2.2. All we have to do is to change the `SYSUT1` DD statement in Figure 2.2 so that it refers to `POLYFILE` instead of to a card deck. The DD statement shown in Figure 4.2 would work.

If you compare this DD statement with the `SYSUT2` DD statement in Figure 3.4, which was used to create the data set, you will notice several interesting

FIGURE 4.1

System flowchart to list POLYFILE

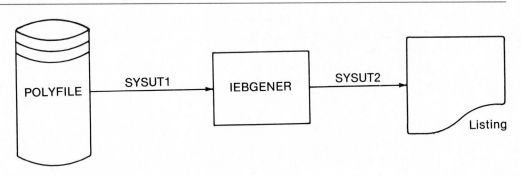

FIGURE 4.2

DD statement to access an existing data set

```
//SYSUT1    DD DSN=WYL.QB.JCL.POLYFILE,
//             DISP=(OLD,KEEP),
//             UNIT=DISK,
//             VOL=SER=WYL002
```

things. First, the same DSN that created the data set is used here. Remember the data set name is the permanent name of the data set, the name that is stored in the disk pack's VTOC. The ddname has no permanent association with the data set; when POLYFILE was created the ddname used was SYSUT2, and now to access it the ddname SYSUT1 is used.

The second thing to notice is the way we code the DISP parameter. Since the data set exists, we code the status as OLD, and since we want to retain the data set when this job is over, we code the normal disposition as KEEP. The abnormal-disposition subparameter is not coded since the default value is KEEP, which is what is desired.

The DISP parameter could just as well have been coded as

```
DISP=OLD
```

since for an existing data set the default value for the normal disposition is KEEP.

The third thing to notice is that we code the UNIT and VOL parameters exactly as we did when we created the data set. Finally, notice that we do not code the SPACE or DCB parameters. The only time the SPACE parameter is needed is when you are creating a data set on a disk. This is when the system needs to know how much space is required. Once the data set has been created, the space has already been obtained.

Similar considerations apply to the DCB parameter. The only time the DCB parameter is needed is when you are creating a data set and you want to assign values to RECFM, LRECL, BLKSIZE, DEN, and other subparameters you will learn about later. (As you will learn in Chapter 12, the DCB parameter is always required with ISAM data sets.) As mentioned in Chapter 3, when the data set is created, this DCB information is stored in the header labels. Since the system can get the information by reading the header labels, the DCB parameter need not be coded to access the data set.

To repeat: If we replace the SYSUT1 DD statement in Figure 2.2 by the DD statement in Figure 4.2, we can run the job and produce a listing of POLYFILE. But before we do that, let's discuss how to catalog a data set and how to include control statements for IEBGENER so that the output produced will be easier to read.

CATALOGING A DATA SET

Table 3.1 shows that the normal-disposition and abnormal-disposition subparameters could be assigned the value CATLG. Coding CATLG means you want the data set cataloged. When a data set is **cataloged**, its DSN, UNIT, and volume

FIGURE 4.3

DD statement to access an existing data set and catalog it

```
//SYSUT1    DD DSN=WYL.QB.JCL.POLYFILE,
//             DISP=(OLD,CATLG),
//             UNIT=DISK,
//             VOL=SER=WYL002
```

serial number are recorded in the system catalog. The system catalog is a data set that the system uses to determine the UNIT and volume serial number of a data set once its DSN is known. The benefit to the programmer is that once a data set has been cataloged, only the DSN and DISP parameters need be coded to access the data set. The system uses the system catalog to determine the UNIT and volume serial number. Both disk and tape data sets may be cataloged. POLYFILE could have been cataloged when it was created by simply coding the DISP parameter in Figure 3.4 as

```
DISP=(NEW,CATLG,DELETE)
```

The only reason I didn't catalog the data set then was because I didn't want the discussion in Chapter 3 to get too complicated.

It should be clear that no two cataloged data sets can have the same DSN, because if they did and you tried to access one, the system would have no way of knowing which of the two you wanted. So although you can have data sets with the same DSN on different disk packs and tape reels, only one of them may be cataloged.

To catalog WYL.QB.JCL.POLYFILE, we change the DD statement in Figure 4.2 to the version shown in Figure 4.3.

Notice that in Figure 4.3 we must specify the UNIT and VOL parameters. At this time, the data set is not yet cataloged; after this job is run the data set will be cataloged, and then we will be able to omit the UNIT and VOL parameters.

UTILITY CONTROL STATEMENTS

So far, we have used IEBGENER simply to copy a sequential data set. Chapter 2 mentioned that IEBGENER could edit a data set as it copied it. To have IEBGENER edit, you must include control statements in the SYSIN data set.

FIGURE 4.4

Editing to be performed by IEBGENER

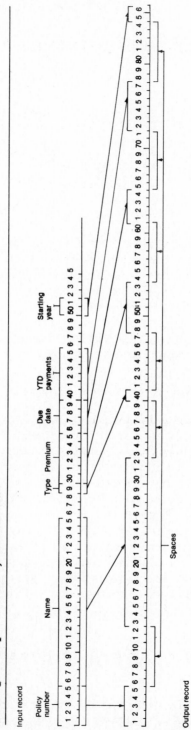

FIGURE 4.5

IEBGENER control statements to insert seven blanks between fields in POLYFILE

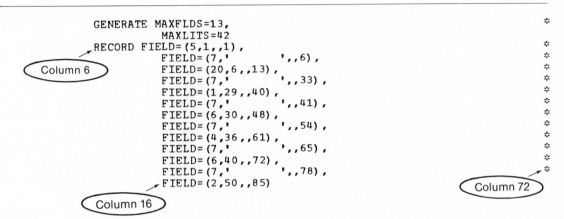

Control statements are used to describe exactly what you want the utility program to do. Since this is the first example, let us keep the editing simple and just have IEBGENER insert seven spaces between fields. Even this simple formatting will make the output much easier to read. The editing to be done is shown in Figure 4.4.

To have IEBGENER insert seven spaces between fields, we must use the two control statements shown in Figure 4.5.

Control Statement Format

Control statements for all the utilities you will study in this book have the same format (with the exception of IEBUPDTE, which you will study in Chapter 5, and IDCAMS, which you will study in Chapter 13). The control statements contain four fields, which are coded in the following order:

```
label operation operand comments
```

Control statements are coded in columns 1 through 71. Column 72 is used to indicate that the statement is being continued, as will be explained shortly, and columns 73 through 80 may be used for identification or sequence numbers.

The four fields must be separated by at least one space, but as in the case of JCL statements, you can use as many spaces as you like. The label field is optional, but if it is used, it must begin in column 1. The label field is usually omitted, and the statements in Figure 4.5 do not have one. If the label field is omitted, column 1 must be blank.

The operation field specifies the type of control statement. In Figure 4.5, the operation field of the first statement is GENERATE and of the second is RECORD. The operation field must be preceded by at least one blank, but other than that can start anywhere you like. In Figure 4.5 I arbitrarily stated the operation in column 6.

The next field is the operand field. The operand field consists of one or more keyword parameters, separated by commas. In Figure 4.5, the GENERATE statement contains two parameters, MAXFLDS and MAXLITS, and the RECORD statement contains thirteen FIELD parameters.

The operand field must be separated from the operation field by one or more blanks. By convention I usually separate them by one blank. To make the control statement easier to read, I usually code only one parameter on a line. If there is more than one parameter, as in both the GENERATE and RECORD statements in Figure 4.5, I continue the statement onto the next line.

As with JCL statements, to continue a control statement you interrupt it after the comma following a parameter. However, there are two additional rules for continuing control statements which are stricter than the rules for continuing JCL statements. First, you must put a nonblank character in column 72 of the statement that is being continued. In Figure 4.5, an asterisk is the nonblank character. Notice that there is no asterisk in column 72 of the MAXLITS line or in the last FIELD line in Figure 4.5; although these lines are continuations of the previous lines, they themselves are not continued, so they do not have an asterisk in column 72.

Second, continued control statements must begin in column 16. You remember that a continued JCL statement could begin anywhere between columns 4 and 16. Not so for continued control cards. (Some utilities relax these rules. IEBGENER, for example, does not require a nonblank character in column 72, and the continued statement may begin anywhere between columns 4 and 16. However, if you use these rules you'll never be wrong.)

IEBGENER Control Statements

The three most frequently used IEBGENER control statements are the GENERATE, MEMBER, and RECORD statements. When they are used, these statements must be coded in the order given above. These statements are described in Table 4.1. The MEMBER statement is used with libraries and is discussed in Chapter 5.

UTILITY CONTROL STATEMENTS

TABLE 4.1

The IEBGENER control statements

Control Statement	Parameter	Meaning
GENERATE	MAXFLDS=a	a is greater than or equal to the number of FIELD parameters in the following RECORD statements.
	MAXLITS=b	b is greater than or equal to the number of characters contained in the literal fields of the FIELD parameters in the following RECORD statements.
	MAXNAME=c	c is greater than or equal to the number of names and aliases in the following MEMBER statements.
	MAXGPS=d	d is greater than or equal to the number of IDENT parameters in the following RECORD statements.
RECORD	FIELD=(length, {input-location|'literal'}, conversion, output-location)	length is the length, in bytes, of the input field or literal to be processed. Default is 80.
		input-location is the starting byte of the input field to be processed. Default is 1.
		'literal' is the literal to be placed in the output location. It may not be longer than 40 bytes.
		conversion is the type of conversion to be done to the field. PZ causes packed data to be unpacked, ZP causes unpacked data to be packed, and HE causes BCD data to be converted to EBCDIC. If omitted, no conversion is done.
		output-location specifies the starting location of this field in the output record. Default is 1.

(cont.)

TABLE 4.1 (cont.)

The IEBGENER control statements

Control Statement	Parameter	Meaning

	IDENT=(length,
	     'name',
	     input-location)
		length is the length, in bytes, of the identifying name. Length must be less than 9.

		'name' is the literal that identifies the last input record of a record group.
		input-location specifies the starting location of the field that contains the 'name' in the input records.
MEMBER	NAME=(name[,alias] ...)	name is the name and alias the alias of the member of a partitioned data set which is being created.

THE GENERATE STATEMENT.   The four commonly used parameters of the GENERATE statement are MAXFLDS, MAXLITS, MAXNAME, and MAXGPS. The MAXFLDS parameter is used to specify the number of FIELD parameters that are coded on the following RECORD statements. In Figure 4.5, MAXFLDS=13 is coded, because there are 13 FIELD parameters coded on the following RECORD statement.

The MAXLITS parameter is used to specify the number of characters of literal data which appear in the literal fields of the FIELD parameters that are coded on the following RECORD statements. In Figure 4.5, MAXLITS=42 is coded. Exactly how this number was calculated will be explained shortly when the RECORD statement is discussed.

The MAXNAME and MAXGPS parameters will be discussed in Chapter 5, since they involve libraries.

THE RECORD STATEMENT.   The only RECORD statement parameters we will discuss are the FIELD and IDENT parameters. The IDENT parameter is discussed in Chapter 5, since it involves libraries. The FIELD parameter specifies the fields to be copied and where they are to be put in the output record.

UTILITY CONTROL STATEMENTS

Let us use the description of the FIELD parameter in Table 4.1 to understand the first FIELD parameter in Figure 4.5,

```
FIELD=(5,1,,1)
```

This parameter controls the printing of the policy number field, which as shown in Figure 4.4 occupies the first 5 bytes of the policy record. The values coded indicate that 5 bytes, starting at byte 1 in the input record, are to be moved to byte 1 in the output record. There is no conversion, so the conversion subparameter was omitted. However, since these are positional subparameters, a comma was coded to indicate that the conversion subparameter was omitted, just as when a positional subparameter is omitted from a JCL statement.

Because the second FIELD parameter is a little different, let's decipher it also.

```
FIELD=(7,'       ',,6)
```

This parameter moves 7 blanks to the output record starting in byte 6. The 7 specifies the length of the literal, and the literal is 7 blanks enclosed within apostrophes. Again no conversion was specified. The blanks are moved to byte 6 because the policy number occupies bytes 1 through 5.

You must move spaces to the output area when you use IEBGENER for the same reason you move spaces to the output area when you write assembler, COBOL, or PL/I programs—because if you did not, the output area could contain garbage left over from the previous program that used these storage locations. The remaining FIELD parameters were designed in the same way.

There are 6 FIELD parameters, each of which moves 7 blanks to the output record. The total number of characters of literal data is therefore $6 \times 7 = 42$. That is how the 42 that is specified for MAXLITS on the GENERATE statement was calculated.

Actually, MAXFLDS and MAXLITS specify the maximum number of FIELD parameters and characters of literal data which follow in RECORD statements. The job will execute properly as long as the number of FIELD parameters is not greater than the value specified for MAXFLDS, and the number of characters of literal data is not greater than the value specified for MAXLITS. So Figure 4.5 could have been coded

```
MAXFLDS=100,
 MAXLITS=100
```

and the job would have executed properly.

To convert data in a field from one form to another, you code a value for the `conversion` subparameter. When we created `POLYFILE`, we could have packed the numeric fields by using a `RECORD` statement with `ZP` coded for the `conversion` subparameter for the numeric fields. If we pack the numeric fields when the data set is created, those numeric fields have to be unpacked when they are printed. They can be unpacked by coding `PZ` for the `conversion` subparameter.

When you pack and unpack fields, you must remember that the length of the field changes. Suppose the length of an unpacked numeric field is n bytes. If n is an odd number, then when the field is packed it will occupy $(n - 1)/2 + 1$ bytes. For example, if $n = 7$, the packed field occupies 4 bytes. If n is an even number, then when the field is packed, it will occupy $n/2 + 1$ bytes. For example, if $n = 8$, the packed field occupies 5 bytes.

When you want to print a packed numeric field, you must unpack it and allow for the length increase. If the length of a packed numeric field is m bytes, then when the field is unpacked it will occupy $2m - 1$ bytes. For example, if $m = 4$, the unpacked field occupies 7 bytes.

Besides permitting you to insert spaces between fields, the `RECORD` statement allows you to rearrange and omit fields during copying. For example, suppose we wanted to print only the name, premium, and policy number fields of `POLYFILE` in that order and that we wanted 5 spaces between the first two fields and 10 spaces between the second and third fields. The following control statements could be used:

```
GENERATE MAXFLDS=5,                                         *
         MAXLITS=15
RECORD FIELD=(20,6,,1),                                     *
       FIELD=(5,'     ',,21),                               *
       FIELD=(6,30,,26),                                    *
       FIELD=(10,'          ',,32),                         *
       FIELD=(5,1,,42)
```

`MAXFLDS`, `MAXLITS`, and `MAXNAME` are keyword parameters and may be coded in any order. Also the `FIELD` parameters may be coded in any order.

THE COMPLETE JOB STREAM

The complete job stream to list and catalog `POLYFILE` is shown in Figure 4.6.

THE COMPLETE JOB STREAM

FIGURE 4.6

Job stream to list and catalog an existing data set

```
//JCLQB033 JOB ,'J.C.LEWIS',
//             REGION=40K,
//             TIME=(0,5) ← TIME parameter
//*
//* USING IEBGENER TO LIST A DISK DATA SET
//* WITH CONTROL CARDS TO FORMAT THE OUTPUT
//*
//LIST     EXEC PGM=IEBGENER
//SYSPRINT DD SYSOUT=A
//SYSIN DD *
     GENERATE MAXFLDS=13,                             *
              MAXLITS=42                              *
     RECORD FIELD=(5,1,,1),                           *
            FIELD=(7,'          ',,6),                *
            FIELD=(20,6,,13),                         *
            FIELD=(7,'          ',,33),               *
            FIELD=(1,29,,40),                         *
            FIELD=(7,'          ',,41),               *
            FIELD=(6,30,,48),                         *
            FIELD=(7,'          ',,54),               *
            FIELD=(4,36,,61),                         *
            FIELD=(7,'          ',,65),               *
            FIELD=(6,40,,72),                         *
            FIELD=(7,'          ',,78),               *
            FIELD=(2,50,,85)
/*
//SYSUT1   DD DSN=WYL.QB.JCL.POLYFILE,
//            DISP=(OLD,CATLG),
//            UNIT=DISK,
//            VOL=SER=WYL002
//SYSUT2   DD SYSOUT=A,DCB=(RECFM=FB,LRECL=86,BLKSIZE=860)
//
```

The TIME Parameter

A TIME parameter is coded on the JOB statement. The TIME parameter specifies the maximum amount of CPU time that a job may use. The format of the TIME parameter is

```
TIME=(minutes,seconds)
```

In Figure 4.6, a time limit of 0 minutes and 5 seconds is specified.

Do not confuse CPU time with clock time. CPU time is the time the job has exclusive control of the CPU. Because of multiprogramming the actual elapsed clock time may be much greater.

If you code

```
TIME=1440
```

it means that you want no time limit applied to your job. (Notice that 1440 is the number of minutes in 24 hours.) Never code TIME=1440 unless you have a working, fully tested program and are sure that much time is required.

If you don't code a TIME parameter, the time limit is the system default, which varies from one computer center to another. The actual time a job required is printed in the system messages. If your job requires more than the default time, you must code the TIME parameter; otherwise the job will use the default amount of time and then abnormally terminate. Even if your job requires less than the default time, it's a good idea to code the TIME parameter, using as the time limit a reasonable estimate of the time the job should require. That way if you make a mistake and your program goes into an endless loop, you'll avoid wasting a lot of CPU time. It is hard to imagine how IEBGENER could go into an endless loop, but the TIME parameter is coded in Figure 4.6 to ensure that there will be no problem.

The DD Statements

In Figure 4.6, to supply control statements to IEBGENER, we code an asterisk as the operand of the SYSIN DD statement and follow this statement with the control statements in Figure 4.5. To catalog POLYFILE we use the SYSUT1 DD statement in Figure 4.3.

To print the data set, we direct SYSUT2 to the printer by coding SYSOUT=A. In addition, however, we must also code a DCB parameter. To understand why we need the DCB parameter, recall that if DCB information is not specified for SYSUT2, IEBGENER will copy the DCB information from SYSUT1. In this case that means that SYSUT2 will have a logical record length of 80 bytes. But that is impossible, since our control statements specify that the last field is to be printed in byte positions 85 and 86. Therefore we must specify the logical record length of SYSUT2 to be at least 86 bytes.

For efficiency, the JCL specifies that SYSUT2 should be blocked. It may seem contradictory to block printer output, but remember that with spooling, output is first written on disk, for which blocking is useful, and is later sent to the printer.

```
DATA SET UTILITY - GENERATE
GENERATE MAXFLDS=13,
         MAXLITS=42
RECORD FIELD=(5,1,,1),
       FIELD=(7,' ',,6),
       FIELD=(20,6,,13),
       FIELD=(7,' ',,33),
       FIELD=(1,29,,40),
       FIELD=(7,' ',,41),
       FIELD=(6,30,,48),
       FIELD=(7,' ',,54),
       FIELD=(4,36,,61),
       FIELD=(7,' ',,65),
       FIELD=(6,40,,72),
       FIELD=(7,' ',,78),
       FIELD=(2,50,,85)
```

Listing of control statements

PROCESSING ENDED AT EOD

13009	REED,TINA	A	084200	0426	072100	74
15174	HANDJANY,HAIDEH	H	022900	0220	022900	71
17337	BUTERO,MAURICE	H	050100	0434	050100	63
19499	LAFER,BRUCE	A	070600	0819	050000	52
21661	LEE,SUI	A	039017	0303	030017	76
23821	COOPER,LUCY	L	074500	0730	070000	64
25980	NELSON,LAWRENCE	L	051300	0217	051300	78
28138	KRUKIS,SONIA	A	034600	0510	034600	59
30295	CHEN,YIN	H	029500	0514	010000	81
32451	SIMPKINS,KEVIN	L	038800	0321	038806	76
34605	PORTER,MICHELE	A	062750	0128	042700	65
36759	DECICCO,RICHARD	A	025500	0619	010000	71
38912	ABREU,JUANITA	H	073200	1030	070000	80
41063	HIGH,CAROL	L	031100	0521	031100	82
43214	ENGLISH,REYNOLDS	A	044300	0228	043300	82
45363	LEE,BOHYON	A	051500	0214	050000	79
47512	THOMPSON,STANLEY	H	064075	0307	064075	66
49659	VALDEZ,FABIO	L	070600	0430	070600	71
51805	AMATO,ROBERT	A	046600	0417	015000	63
53950	RIZZUTO,JAMES	A	069300	0822	000000	81
56094	SCHWARTZ,MICHAEL	H	103700	0605	050000	67
58238	RUFINO,CARLOS	L	067300	0520	047300	64
60380	MORLEY,JOHN	A	078600	0514	078600	71
62521	BREVIL,JAMES	H	081200	0314	081200	55
64660	FALCONER,EDWARD	L	108000	0227	008000	74
66799	MARTIN,KATHLEEN	L	089500	0129	089500	65
68937	YEUNG,SUK	A	051700	0816	050000	49
71074	PAUL,MARINA	A	044100	0414	034100	80
73210	FRADIN,SHIRLEY	L	066800	0728	066800	56
75344	BURNS,JEFFREY	L	070600	0226	070000	57

FIGURE 4.8

System flowchart to add records to POLYFILE and list it

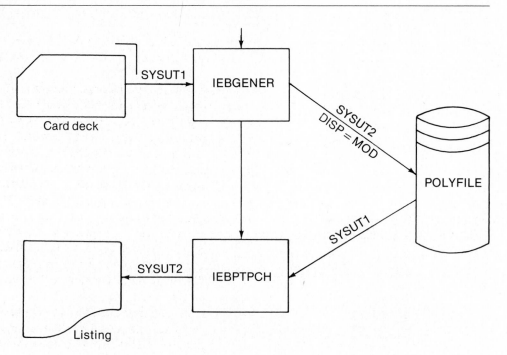

IEBPTPCH CONTROL STATEMENTS. Remember that when IEBGENER is used to make an unedited copy of a data set, no control statements are required. Unfortunately, IEBPTPCH always requires at least one control statement.

The control statements for IEBPTPCH are PRINT, PUNCH, TITLE, MEMBER, and RECORD. These statements are described in Tables 4.2 and 4.3. PRINT specifies that the data are to be printed and PUNCH that they are to be punched. TITLE specifies that a title is to be printed, MEMBER specifies that a member of a library is to be printed or punched (we will study libraries in Chapter 5), and RECORD specifies the editing that is to be performed.

Every execution of IEBPTPCH must include either a PRINT or a PUNCH control statement, and it must be the first statement. The other statements are optional, but if they are used they must be coded in the following order: TITLE, MEMBER, RECORD.

TABLE 4.2

Parameters for the IEBPTPCH PRINT and PUNCH control statements

| Parameter | Control Statement | | Meaning |
	PRINT	PUNCH	
PREFORM={A|M}	Yes	Yes	Specifies that the first character of each record is a control character. A means the control character is an ASA character, and M means it is a machine-code character. If PREFORM is coded, all other operands and control statements are ignored.
TYPORG={PS|PO}	Yes	Yes	Specifies the organization of the input data set. PS means sequential, and PO means partitioned. Default is PS.
TOTCONV={XE|PZ}	Yes	Yes	Specifies the data are to be converted before being printed or punched. XE means the data are to be converted to hexadecimal, and PZ means packed data are to be unpacked. If TOTCONV is omitted, no conversion is done.
CNTRL=a	Yes	Yes	For printing, specifies line spacing: a=1 is single spacing a=2 is double spacing a=3 is triple spacing For punching, specifies stacker, either 1 or 2. Default is 1.
STRTAFT=b	Yes	Yes	Skip b records before starting printing or punching.
STOPAFT=c	Yes	Yes	c is the number of records to be printed or punched.
SKIP=d	Yes	Yes	Print or punch every d record.
MAXNAME=e	Yes	Yes	e is greater than or equal to the number of MEMBER statements that follow.
MAXFLDS=f	Yes	Yes	f is greater than or equal to the number of FIELD parameters in the following RECORD statements. (cont.)

TABLE 4.2 (cont.)

Parameters for the IEBPTPCH PRINT and PUNCH control statements

| Parameter | Control Statement | | Meaning |
	PRINT	PUNCH	
INITPG=g	Yes	No	g is the initial page number.
MAXLINE=h	Yes	No	h is the maximum number of lines printed on a page. Default is 60.
CDSEQ=i	No	Yes	i is the initial sequence number punched in columns 73 through 80. If CDSEQ is not coded, the cards are not numbered.
CDINCR=j	No	Yes	j is the increment used to generate sequence numbers. Default is 10.

The PRINT Statement. You can print a data set by coding the PRINT statement with no parameters:

    PRINT

No other control statements are required. The format rules for control statements that you learned earlier apply to IEBPTPCH control statements. Therefore PRINT must not begin in the first column. IEBPTPCH does not require a nonblank character in column 72 of a continued statement.

If you print a data set using the simple PRINT control statement, the output is printed in groups of eight characters separated by two blanks. The first 15 records from POLYFILE printed in this format are shown in Figure 4.9. As you can see, the inserted blanks made the output difficult to read. To get output that is easier to read, you have to use the RECORD statement to edit the output. You will see how to do that later.

Notice the asterisks at the end of each line and the double asterisk at the end of the tenth line in Figure 4.9. If no editing is done, IEBPTPCH prints an asterisk at the end of each logical record and a double asterisk at the end of each block.

ADDING RECORDS TO A DATA SET AND LISTING IT

TABLE 4.3

The IEBPTPCH TITLE, MEMBER, and RECORD control statements

Control Statement	Parameter	Meaning
TITLE	ITEM=('title', output-location)	'title' is the title to be printed on each page. 'title' may not be longer than 40 bytes.
		output-location is the byte position in the output record where the title is to start. Default is 1.
MEMBER	NAME=name	name is the name of the member of a partitioned data set that is to be printed or punched.
RECORD	FIELD=(length, input-location, conversion, output-location)	length is the length, in bytes, of the input field to processed.
		input-location is the starting byte of the input field to be processed. Default is 1.
		conversion is the type of conversion to be done to the field. PZ causes packed data to be unpacked, and XE causes data to be converted to hexadecimal. If omitted, no conversion is done.
		output-location specifies the starting location of this field in the output record. Default is 1.

You should know about another nice feature of IEBPTPCH. When the input record length is greater than the printer line and no editing is done, IEBPTPCH prints the whole record, using as many lines as necessary. This is in contrast to IEBGENER, which prints whatever will fit on one line and discards the rest of the record.

The parameters that may be coded on a PRINT statement are shown in Table 4.2. You can have the data set printed in hexadecimal by using the following control statement:

```
PRINT TOTCONV=XE
```

FIGURE 4.9

The first fifteen records of POLYFILE printed by IEBPTPCH using a PRINT control statement

```
13009REE  D,TINA            A084  20004260  72100  74   *
15174HAN  DJANY,HA  IDEH    H022  90002200  22900  71   *
17337BUT  ERO,MAUR  ICE     H050  10004340  50100  63   *
19499LAF  ER,BRUCE          A070  60008190  50000  52   *
21661LEE  ,SUI              A039  01703030  30017  76   *
23821COO  PER,LUCY          L074  50007300  70000  64   *
25980NEL  SON,LAWR  ENCE    L051  30002170  51300  78   *
28138KRU  KIS,SONI  A       A034  60005100  34600  59   *
30295CHE  N,YIN             H029  50005140  10000  81   *
32451SIM  PKINS,KE  VIN     L038  80003210  38806  76   *
34605POR  TER,MICH  ELE     A062  75001280  42700  65   *
36759DEC  ICCO,RIC  HARD    A025  50006190  10000  71   *
38912ABR  EU,JUANI  TA      H073  20010300  70000  80   *
41063HIG  H,CAROL           L031  10005210  31100  82   *
43214ENG  LISH,REY  NOLDS   A044  30002280  43300  82   *
```

FIGURE 4.10

The first five records of POLYFILE printed by IEBPTPCH in hexadecimal

```
F1F3F0F0 F9D9C5C5 C46BE3C9 D5C14040 40404040 40404040 C1F0F8F4 F2F0F0F0 F4F2F6F0 F0404040
40F7F440 40404040 40404040 40404040 40404040 40404040 40404040 40404040 F7F2F1F0 F0404040
F1F5F1F7 F4C8C1D5 C4D1C1D5 E86BC8C1 C9C4C5C8 40404040 C8F0F2F2 F9F0F0F0 F2F2F0F0 F0404040
40F7F140 40404040 40404040 40404040 40404040 40404040 40404040 40404040 F2F2F9F0 F0404040
F1F7F3F3 F7C2E4E3 C5D9D66B D4C1E4D9 C9C3C540 40404040 C8F0F5F0 F1F0F0F0 F4F3F4F0 F0404040
40F6F340 40404040 40404040 40404040 40404040 40404040 40404040 40404040 F5F0F1F0 F0404040
F1F9F4F9 F9D3C1C6 C5D96BC2 D9E4C3C5 40404040 40404040 C1F0F7F0 F6F0F0F0 F8F1F9F0 F0404040
40F5F240 40404040 40404040 40404040 40404040 40404040 40404040 40404040 F5F0F0F0 F0404040
F2F1F6F6 F1D3C5C5 6BE2E4C9 40404040 40404040 40404040 C1F0F3F9 F0F1F7F0 F3F0F3F0 F0404040
40F7F640 40404040 40404040 40404040 40404040 40404040 40404040 40404040 F3F0F0F1 F7404040
```

ADDING RECORDS TO A DATA SET AND LISTING IT

Figure 4.10 shows the first five records of POLYFILE printed in hexadecimal. Since it takes two hexadecimal digits to represent one byte, a record could not fit on one line. If you use the EBCDIC code in Table 1.2, you can easily interpret Figure 4.10. You would print a data set in hexadecimal if the data set contained data that were not character data or if you had a data set and didn't know what it contained. Printing it in hexadecimal allows you to see exactly what's there.

The RECORD Statement. To eliminate the blanks that IEBPTPCH inserts after every eight characters, you have to edit the output, using the FIELD parameter of the RECORD statement. Fortunately, as Table 4.3 shows, the FIELD parameter for IEBPTPCH works very much like the FIELD parameter for IEBGENER, in which by now you are an expert. The only difference is that with IEBGENER you can move a literal to the output area, but with IEBPTPCH you are not permitted to.

To prevent IEBPTPCH from inserting blanks, you could use the following statement:

```
RECORD FIELD=(80,1,,1)
```

This RECORD statement instructs IEBPTPCH to treat the whole input record as one field, starting at input byte 1 for a length of 80 bytes, and to print it starting at output byte 1 with no conversion. Using default values for the starting bytes for the input and the output, this RECORD statement could be written in the simpler form

```
RECORD FIELD=(80)
```

(You might think that since this FIELD parameter contains only one positional subparameter, you could code this statement without the parentheses. However, omitting the parentheses when there is only one positional subparameter is a rule that applies to JCL statements, not utility control statements. The parentheses are required in utility control statements.)

The following control statements prevent IEBPTPCH from inserting blanks and show how the STRTAFT, SKIP, and STOPAFT parameters work:

```
PRINT MAXFLDS=1,                                              *
           STRTAFT=5,                                         *
           SKIP=2,                                            *
           STOPAFT=4
RECORD FIELD=(80)
```

FIGURE 4.11

Selected, edited records of POLYFILE printed by IEBPTPCH

```
25980NELSON,LAWRENCE        L0513000217051300     78
30295CHEN,YIN              H0295000514010000     81
34605PORTER,MICHELE        A0627500128042700     65
38912ABREU,JUANITA         H0732001030070000     80
```

Notice that the MAXFLDS parameter is coded on the PRINT statement. MAXFLDS is required because of the FIELD parameter on the RECORD statement. MAXFLDS for IEBPTPCH works exactly the same way it does for IEBGENER, specifying the number of FIELD parameters on the following RECORD statement.

The output produced when these control statements are applied to POLYFILE is shown in Figure 4.11. The STRTAFT=5 parameter causes the first 5 records to be skipped, the SKIP=2 parameter causes every second record to be printed starting with the seventh record, and the STOPAFT=4 parameter causes the printing to stop after 4 records have been printed. The STRTAFT, SKIP, and STOPAFT parameters are useful when you have a large data set and you want to print only a sample of the records.

The control statements which will print POLYFILE with seven spaces between the fields are shown in Figure 4.12. These statements also illustrate the use of the TITLE statement. The TITLE statement causes a title to be printed on each page of output. The title in each ITEM parameter may not be longer than 40 characters. Longer titles may be created by using more than one ITEM parameter. The number following the title is the position in the print line where the title starts printing. In this example, using 25 for this

FIGURE 4.12

IEBPTPCH control statements to insert seven blanks between fields in POLYFILE

```
PRINT MAXFLDS=7
TITLE ITEM=('LISTING OF POLYFILE WITH ADDED RECORDS',25)
RECORD FIELD=(5,1,,1),                                          *
           FIELD=(20,6,,13),                                    *
           FIELD=(1,29,,40),                                    *
           FIELD=(6,30,,48),                                    *
           FIELD=(4,36,,61),                                    *
           FIELD=(6,40,,72),                                    *
           FIELD=(2,50,,85)
```

number roughly centers the title. A maximum of two TITLE statements may be used to print a title and a subtitle.

The RECORD statement in Figure 4.12 is the same as the RECORD statement used with IEBGENER in Figure 4.6, except that the FIELD parameters which move spaces to the output record have been deleted; with IEBPTPCH you may not specify a literal as part of the FIELD parameter. Remember that when we used IEBGENER to print POLYFILE, we had to move spaces to the unused parts of the output record. With IEBPTPCH that is not necessary, because IEBPTPCH automatically moves spaces to the unused part of the output record. As a result, in Figure 4.12 we need only 7 FIELD parameters, while in Figure 4.6 we needed 13.

The PUNCH Statement. So far all these examples have involved printing a data set. To punch a data set, only two changes are required: the SYSUT2 data set must be directed to the punch, usually by coding SYSOUT=B; and the PRINT control statement must be replaced by the PUNCH control statement. When punching a data set, IEBPTPCH does not insert blanks, the way it does when printing. So a data set may be punched using the simple control statement

```
PUNCH
```

If desired, parameters may be coded on the PUNCH statement. As Table 4.2 shows, many of the same parameters may be coded for both the PRINT and PUNCH statements. In addition, when a data set is punched, sequence numbers can be punched in columns 73 through 80. (Of course, you would punch sequence numbers in columns 73 through 80 only if those columns didn't already contain data.) The initial sequence number is specified by coding CDSEQ=number, and the increment to be used between sequence numbers is specified by coding CDINCR=increment. So the control statement

```
PUNCH CDSEQ=1000,                                      *
          CDINCR=100
```

will punch a data set with sequence number 00001000 in columns 73 through 80 on the first card, sequence number 00001100 on the second card, and so on.

The statements listed in Table 4.3 have been covered except for the MEMBER statement, which will be discussed in Chapter 5.

COMPARING IEBGENER AND IEBPTPCH. Since you now know two IBM utilities which can be used to print or punch data sets, you might wonder which one you should use. The answer depends on what you want to do.

If you want a simple listing or punching of a data set, and if the logical record length of the data set is not greater than the length of the output device (typically 132 bytes for the printer and 80 bytes for the punch), then IEBGENER is easier to use since it does not require any control statements. However, if the logical record length of the data set does exceed the length of the output device, IEBGENER will truncate the record, while IEBPTPCH will use as many lines or cards as necessary to print or punch the whole record.

If you want to edit the record, IEBPTPCH is easier to use since you do not have to move spaces to unused portions of the output record. Finally, if you want to print a title, or control the number of lines printed per page, or print or punch selected records, or punch sequence numbers, or in general use any of the parameters listed in Table 4.2, then you must use IEBPTPCH.

Appendix F contains a listing of commonly required functions and the utilities that may be used to perform them. As Appendix F shows, it is common for several utilities to be able to perform similar functions.

THE COMPLETE JOB STREAM

Now that you understand how to use IEBPTPCH, we can get back to the original problem, which was to add records to POLYFILE and to list the whole data set (recall that the system flowchart for this problem was shown in Figure 4.8). We can both add records and list the data set in one job. The job stream is shown in Figure 4.13.

This job stream contains only one JOB statement, so you know that it contains only one job. However, it contains two EXEC statements, so that one job contains two job steps. The name of the first step is ADD, and the name of the second step is LIST. This is the first job stream you have seen that contains more than one job step, but in practice jobs that contain several steps are much more common than jobs that contain only one step.

Notice how the job stream is arranged. The JOB statement must always be the first statement. Following the JOB statement is the first EXEC statement, along with the DD statements which that EXEC statement requires. In Figure 4.13, the first EXEC statement causes IEBGENER to be executed, and following that EXEC statement you see the familiar SYSPRINT, SYSIN, SYSUT1, and SYSUT2 DD statements.

THE COMPLETE JOB STREAM

FIGURE 4.13

Job stream to add records to a disk data set and list it

```
//JCLQB057 JOB ,'J.C.LEWIS',
//             REGION=40K,
//             TIME=(0,5)
//*
//* A TWO STEP JOB TO ADD RECORDS TO A DATA SET
//* AND THEN TO LIST IT
//*
//* STEP 1 USING IEBGENER TO ADD RECORDS
//ADD      EXEC PGM=IEBGENER
//SYSPRINT DD SYSOUT=A
//SYSIN    DD DUMMY
//SYSUT1   DD *
77478KATZ,HAL            A0485000406038500    64
79610WRIGHT,DONNA        H0926000901092000    75
81742CUOMO,DONNA         L0900000313090000    69
83872LOPEZ,ANNA          A0679000716010000    80
86002ALEXANDER,LISA      A0402000623030200    73
88130GOLDBERG,LORI       H0987000524095000    67
92057HOFMANN,PATRICA     H0737000315040000    77
92384PUGH,CLIFFORD       A0750000423075000    80
94509FERRIS,LAURA        A0135000815013500    73
96633BERGIN,MICHAEL      L1608000116100000    74
//SYSUT2   DD DSN=WYL.QB.JCL.POLYFILE,
//             DISP=(MOD,PASS)
//*
//* STEP 2 USING IEBPTPCH TO LIST THE DATA SET
//*
//LIST     EXEC PGM=IEBPTPCH,
//             COND=(0,NE)
//SYSPRINT DD SYSOUT=A
//SYSIN    DD *
 PRINT MAXFLDS=7
 TITLE ITEM=('LISTING OF POLYFILE WITH ADDED RECORDS',25)
 RECORD FIELD=(5,1,,1),
             FIELD=(20,6,,13),
             FIELD=(1,29,,40),
             FIELD=(6,30,,48),
             FIELD=(4,36,,61),
             FIELD=(6,40,,72),
             FIELD=(2,50,,85)
//SYSUT1   DD DSN=WYL.QB.JCL.POLYFILE,
//             DISP=(OLD,KEEP)
//SYSUT2   DD SYSOUT=A
//
```

Records to be added

The second step has the same arrangement: an EXEC statement followed by the DD statements that the EXEC statement requires. In Figure 4.13, the second EXEC statement causes IEBPTPCH to be executed. It is just a coincidence that the four DD statements required by IEBPTPCH have the same ddnames as the four DD statements required by IEBGENER. If the job had additional steps, they would follow the same pattern.

Let's now examine some of the interesting parts of Figure 4.13 more closely.

Accessing a Cataloged Data Set

The ADD step is similar to the one in Figure 3.4 which was used to create POLYFILE. However, in this case the SYSUT2 DD statement is simpler, because now POLYFILE exists and is cataloged. To access a cataloged data set you need code only the DSN and DISP parameters. Notice that we don't have to do anything special to indicate that POLYFILE is cataloged. When the system notices that we have not coded the unit or the volume information, it assumes POLYFILE must be cataloged, so it automatically accesses the catalog to determine the unit and volume information.

Adding Records to a Data Set

The DISP parameter involves coding that is new to you:

```
DISP=(MOD,PASS)
```

A value of MOD coded for the status subparameter means that the data set exists and that new records are going to be added to the end of the data set. If we ran this job with the status subparameter equal to OLD, the new records would be written to the beginning of the data set and the original data would be lost.

Passing a Data Set

A value of PASS coded for the normal-disposition subparameter means that at the end of the current job step, the data set will be passed to a later step. If a data set will be used in a later step, it is better to code PASS rather than KEEP as the normal disposition. When a data set is passed, the system remembers the unit and volume information and that information is available when the data set is used in a later step. Therefore, when you refer to a "passed" data set, you do not have to code the UNIT or VOL parameters. On the other hand,

THE COMPLETE JOB STREAM

when you refer to a "kept" data set, unless it is cataloged you do have to code UNIT and VOL parameters. Even for cataloged data sets it is better to code PASS rather than KEEP. If you code KEEP for a cataloged data set and the data set is used in a later step, the system has to refer to the catalog to determine the unit and volume information. By coding PASS you can avoid that extra reference to the catalog.

There is an additional advantage to coding PASS when the data set resides on tape. As mentioned in Chapter 3, when KEEP is coded, the tape reel is rewound and unloaded. When the data set is used in a later step, the operator must load the tape again. When PASS is coded, the tape is rewound but not unloaded, so it is ready to be used by a later step.

POLYFILE, which is passed by the SYSUT2 DD statement in the first step, is received by the SYSUT1 DD statement in the second step. To receive a passed data set, you simply code the DSN and DISP parameters just as you do for a cataloged data set. For a received data set, the status is OLD, SHR, or MOD, all of which mean that the data set existed before the current job step began. Even if a data set is created in one job step and passed to a later step, by the time the data set is received in the later step it already exists, so in the later step the status is OLD, MOD, or SHR.

A data set may be passed through several job steps. In each step that uses the data set, you code PASS as the normal disposition. In the last step that uses the data set, you specify the final disposition of the data set, which could be DELETE, KEEP, CATLG, or UNCATLG. For POLYFILE a final disposition of KEEP is coded. Notice that it was not necessary to code CATLG. POLYFILE was cataloged in a previous job; it does not need to be cataloged every time it is used. It will remain cataloged until a disposition of UNCATLG or DELETE is coded.

No abnormal disposition is coded for POLYFILE, which means the default value is used. As discussed in Chapter 3, the default value for the abnormal disposition is the value coded for the normal disposition. If the first step were to abend, POLYFILE would be passed to the second step. However, if a step abends, the following steps are usually not executed. (The conditions under which the following steps *are* executed are discussed in the next section.) Therefore, if the first step abended, the second step would not be executed, and POLYFILE would be a passed data set that was never received. The final disposition of a passed data set that is never received depends on its original status. If the data set's original status is OLD, it is kept. That is POLYFILE's situation, so it would be kept. If the data set's original status is NEW and it is passed from step to step, it is deleted. However, if any step specifies KEEP or CATLG rather than PASS for the normal disposition and the data set is subsequently passed and not received, the data set is kept.

CHAPTER 4 / ACCESSING SEQUENTIAL DATA SETS

You should not be surprised that in Figure 4.13 the ddname of POLYFILE is different in the two steps. In the first step, POLYFILE is the output data set from IEBGENER, so its ddname is SYSUT2. In the second step, POLYFILE is the input data set to IEBPTPCH, so its ddname is SYSUT1. Both these names are shown in the system flowchart in Figure 4.8. As mentioned earlier, the only name permanently associated with a data set is the data set name.

Using IEBPTPCH to List a Data Set

The IEBPTPCH control statements in Figure 4.13 were shown in Figure 4.12 and were discussed earlier. Notice that we did not have to code a DCB parameter for the SYSUT2 DD statement in the LIST step, as we did in Figure 4.6 when we used IEBGENER to produce an edited listing of POLYFILE. Unlike IEBGENER, IEBPTPCH does not copy DCB information for SYSUT2 from SYSUT1. Instead IEBPTPCH uses LRECL default values of 121 for printing and 81 for punching. If you wanted to print more than 121 characters on a line (many printers allow lines of up to 133 characters), you would code a DCB on the SYSUT2 DD statement to override the default value. You must specify a LRECL at least one greater than the length of the record you want to print because IEBPTPCH adds one byte to the record for carriage control.

Controlling Step Execution—The COND Parameter

The EXEC statement for the LIST step is coded with a COND parameter,

    COND=(0,NE)

The COND parameter offers a method of controlling whether or not a step will be executed by testing the return codes issued by the previous steps. The format of a simplified version of the COND parameter is

    COND=(value,operator)

You replace value with a number between 0 and 4095. The symbols you may code for operator and their meanings are shown in Table 4.4.

The coding in Figure 4.13 is interpreted as follows: if 0 is not equal to the return code from the previous step, skip this step. Many people find the operation of the COND parameter confusing. The COND parameter causes the value you enter to be tested against the return code from the previous step,

THE COMPLETE JOB STREAM

TABLE 4.4

Operators that may be used with
the COND parameter

Operator	Meaning
GT	Greater than
GE	Greater than or equal to
EQ	Equal to
NE	Not equal to
LT	Less than
LE	Less than or equal to

using the operator you choose. If the test is true, the step is skipped. If the test is false, the step is executed.

One reason for coding a COND parameter is to avoid wasting computer time. In Figure 4.13, unless the ADD step had executed perfectly, there was no point in executing the LIST step.

Let us study another example.

COND=(612,EQ)

This is read as follows: if 612 is equal to the return code from a previous step, skip this step. The return codes issued by utilities and compilers are usually 0, 4, 8, 12, and 16, but you may recall from Chapter 2 that in your programs you can set the return code to any value between 0 and 4095.

If there is more than one previous step, the return code from each of the previous steps is separately tested. If any of the tests are true, the step is skipped.

You may code more than one test, up to a maximum of eight separate tests, for example,

COND=((8,LT),(2,EQ))

When more than one test is coded, all the tests must be enclosed in parentheses. If any of the tests are true, the step will be skipped. In this example, the step will be skipped if 8 is less than the return code or if 2 is equal to the return code. (This is the Boolean *or*.) That is, the step will be executed only if the return codes from the previous steps are 0, 1, 3, 4, 5, 6, 7, or 8.

You must be careful when you code more than one test, because it is easy to code incompatible tests so that the step is never executed. For example, coding

```
COND=((0,NE),(8,GT))
```

will never allow the step to execute.

A more elaborate version of the COND parameter allows us to specify a stepname. The format is

```
COND=(value,operator,stepname)
```

Suppose you have a six-step job, in which the steps are named STEP1, STEP2, STEP3, etc. Then on the STEP4 EXEC statement, you might code

```
COND=((0,NE,STEP1),(2000,EQ,STEP2),(8,GE,STEP3))
```

This means that if 0 is not equal to the return code from STEP1 or 2000 is equal to the return code from STEP2 or 8 is greater than or equal to the return code from STEP3, STEP4 will be skipped. Notice again that if any of the tests are true, the step is skipped; all the tests must be false for the step to be executed.

ABNORMAL TERMINATION—EVEN AND ONLY. Chapter 2 mentioned that some kinds of errors may cause a program to abnormally terminate, or abend. If one step of a multistep job abends, usually all the remaining steps are skipped. However, there are cases in which you want to execute a step even if a previous step abends. In other cases, you may want to execute a step only if a previous step abends. You can do this by coding EVEN or ONLY in the COND parameter as follows:

```
COND=EVEN
```

or

```
COND=ONLY
```

EVEN or ONLY counts as one of the eight possible tests in the COND parameter.

THE COMPLETE JOB STREAM

As the names imply, EVEN causes a step to be executed even if a previous step abends, and ONLY causes a step to be executed only if a previous step abends. You may not code both EVEN and ONLY in the same COND parameter. As an illustration of when you might want to code EVEN or ONLY, consider the case where STEP1 updates a file, STEP2 removes the changes (backs out) from the file, and STEP3 lists the file. In this case, you want STEP2 to execute only if STEP1 fails and STEP3 to execute no matter what happens. The job to accomplish this might appear as follows:

```
//          JOB
//STEP1     EXEC PGM=UPDATE
            .
            .
            .
//STEP2     EXEC PGM=BACKOUT,COND=ONLY
            .
            .
            .
//STEP3     EXEC PGM=LIST,COND=EVEN
            .
            .
            .
```

Consider again the six-step job discussed earlier. Suppose STEP5 is coded

```
COND=((0,EQ,STEP4),EVEN)
```

Even when EVEN and ONLY are coded, the rule still applies: if any of the other tests are true, the step is skipped. With this coding, STEP5 will be skipped if STEP4 issues a return code of 0; under all other circumstances, even an abend, STEP5 will be executed.

Suppose a step abends, causing later steps to be skipped. The skipped steps do not issue return codes, and any later tests that refer to a return code from a skipped step are ignored. For example, suppose STEP1 abends, and STEP2 is skipped, and STEP3 has the following COND:

```
COND=((0,EQ,STEP2),EVEN)
```

The test involving the return code from STEP2 is ignored, and the EVEN ensures that STEP3 will be executed. Neither EVEN nor ONLY may be coded with a stepname.

CHAPTER 4 / ACCESSING SEQUENTIAL DATA SETS

Executing the Job Stream

The job stream in Figure 4.13 was executed and produced the output shown in Figure 4.14. You can see that each step has its own messages, showing the region used, the disposition of the data sets, the return code, etc. (Recall that the terms return code and condition code are used interchangeably.) IEBP-TPCH used only 24K, and both steps issued return codes of 0000. In addition, there are START and END statements for the whole job which show total CPU time used by the job. This job required only 0.11 second, so our time limit of 5 seconds was certainly generous. You see that WYL.QB.JCL.POLYFILE was PASSED at the end of the ADD step and KEPT at the end of the LIST step.

You also see the familiar message from IEBGENER (PROCESSING ENDED AT EOD), the control statements for IEBPTPCH, and two messages from IEBPTPCH (EOF ON SYSIN, which means all the control statements were read, and END OF DATA FOR SDS OR MEMBER, which corresponds to IEBGENER's PROCESSING ENDED AT EOD and means that the complete input data set was processed). SDS stands for sequential data set. You'll learn what MEMBER means in Chapter 5. Finally, you see the edited listing of POLYFILE, including the title and the added records.

PARAMETERS COMMON TO THE JOB AND EXEC STATEMENTS

You have learned how to code the REGION and TIME parameters on the JOB statement and the COND parameters on the EXEC statement, but in fact all three parameters may be coded on either the JOB or EXEC statement.

You learned earlier that when TIME is coded on the JOB statement, it specifies the maximum time permitted for the job. When TIME is coded on an EXEC statement, it specifies the maximum time permitted for that step. If TIME is coded on both the JOB and EXEC statements, each step is limited to the time specified on its EXEC statement and the whole job is limited to the time specified on the JOB statement. If any step exceeds its limit, or if the job as a whole exceeds its limit, the job is abnormally terminated.

When REGION is coded on an EXEC statement, it requests main storage for that step. If a job consists of several steps which require substantially dif-

FIGURE 4.14

Output produced by executing the job stream in Figure 4.13

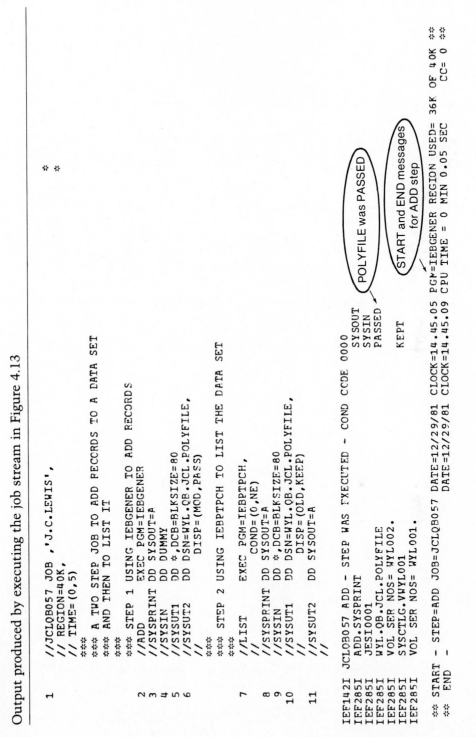

```
 1      //JCLQB057 JOB ,'J.C.LEWIS',                                    ** **
        // REGION=40K,
        // TIME=(0,5)
        ***  A TWO STEP JOB TO ADD RECORDS TO A DATA SET
        ***  AND THEN TO LIST IT
        ***
        ***  STEP 1 USING IEBGENER TO ADD RECORDS
 2      //ADD      EXEC PGM=IEBGENER
 3      //SYSPRINT DD SYSOUT=A
 4      //SYSIN    DD DUMMY
 5      //SYSUT1   DD *,DCB=BLKSIZE=80
 6      //SYSUT2   DD DSN=WYL.QB.JCL.POLYFILE,
        //            DISP=(MOD,PASS)
        ***
        ***  STEP 2 USING IEBPTPCH TO LIST THE DATA SET
        ***
 7      //LIST     EXEC PGM=IEBPTPCH,
        //            COND=(0,NE)
 8      //SYSPRINT DD SYSOUT=A
 9      //SYSIN    DD *,DCB=BLKSIZE=80
10      //SYSUT1   DD DSN=WYL.QB.JCL.POLYFILE,
        //            DISP=(OLD,KEEP)
11      //SYSUT2   DD SYSOUT=A

IEF142I JCLQB057 ADD - STEP WAS EXECUTED - COND CODE 0000
IEF285I   ADD.SYSPRINT                              SYSOUT
IEF285I   JESI0001                                  SYSIN
IEF285I   WYL.QB.JCL.POLYFILE                       PASSED
IEF285I   VOL SER NOS= WYL002.
IEF285I   SYSCTLG.VWYL001                           KEPT
IEF285I   VOL SER NOS= WYL001.

**  START - STEP=ADD JOB=JCLQB057 DATE=12/29/81 CLOCK=14.45.05  PGM=IEBGENER REGION USED=  36K  OF  40K **
**  END   -                       DATE=12/29/81 CLOCK=14.45.09  CPU TIME = 0 MIN 0.05 SEC     CC= 0     **
```

POLYFILE was PASSED

START and END messages
for ADD step

(cont.)

125

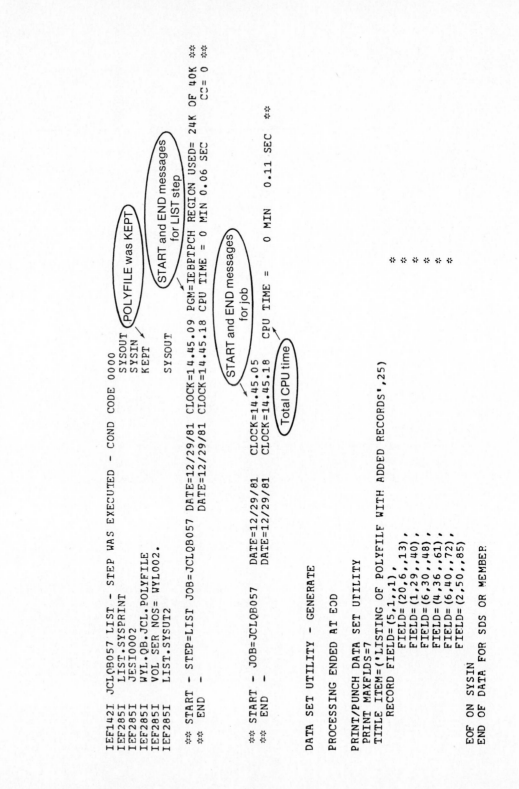

```
IEF142I JCLQB057 LIST - STEP WAS EXECUTED - COND CODE 0000
IEF285I    LIST.SYSPRINT                         SYSOUT
IEF285I    JESI0002                              SYSIN
IEF285I    WYL.QB.JCL.POLYFILE                   KEPT
IEF285I    VOL SER NOS= WYL002.
IEF285I    LIST.SYSUT2                           SYSOUT

**  START - STEP=LIST JOB=JCLQB057 DATE=12/29/81 CLOCK=14.45.09 PGM=IEBPTPCH REGION USED= 24K OF 40K  **
**  END   -                       DATE=12/29/81 CLOCK=14.45.18 CPU TIME = 0 MIN 0.06 SEC      CC= 0   **


**  START - JOB=JCLQB057    DATE=12/29/81    CLOCK=14.45.05
**  END   -                 DATE=12/29/81    CLOCK=14.45.18    CPU TIME =    0 MIN   0.11 SEC  **


DATA SET UTILITY - GENERATE

PROCESSING ENDED AT EOD

PRINT/PUNCH DATA SET UTILITY
PRINT MAXFLDS=7
TITLE ITEM=('LISTING OF POLYFILE WITH ADDED RECORDS',25)
       RECORD FIELD=(5,1,,1),
              FIELD=(20,6,,13),
              FIELD=(1,29,,40),
              FIELD=(6,30,,48),
              FIELD=(4,36,,61),
              FIELD=(6,40,,72),
              FIELD=(2,50,,85)

EOF ON SYSIN
END OF DATA FOR SDS OR MEMBER.
```

POLYFILE was KEPT

START and END messages for LIST step

START and END messages for job

Total CPU time

* * * * * *

126

Added records

ID	Name			Title		
13009	REED,TINA	A	084200	0426	072100	74
15174	HANDJANY,HAIDEH	H	022900	0220	022900	71
17337	BUTERO,MAURICE	H	050100	0434	050100	63
19499	LAFER,BRUCE	A	070600	0819	050100	52
21661	LEE,SUI	A	039017	0303	030017	76
23821	COOPER,LUCY	L	074500	0730	070000	64
25980	NELSON,LAWRENCE	L	051300	0217	051300	78
28138	KRUKIS,SONIA	A	034600	0510	034600	59
30295	CHEN,YIN	H	029500	0514	010000	81
32451	SIMPKINS,KEVIN	L	038800	0321	038806	76
34605	PORTER,MICHELE	A	062750	0128	042700	65
36759	DECICCO,RICHARD	A	025500	0619	010000	71
38912	ABREU,JUANITA	H	073200	1030	070000	80
41063	HIGH,CAROL	L	031100	0521	031100	82
43214	ENGLISH,REYNOLDS	A	044300	0228	043300	82
45363	LEE,BOHYON	A	051500	0214	050000	79
47512	THOMPSON,STANLEY	H	064075	0307	064075	66
49659	VALDEZ,FABIO	L	070600	0430	070600	71
51805	AMATO,ROBERT	A	046600	0417	015000	63
53950	RIZZUTO,JAMES	H	069300	0822	000000	81
56094	SCHWARTZ,MICHAEL	H	103700	0605	050000	67
58238	RUFINO,CARLOS	L	067300	0520	047300	64
60380	MORLEY,JOHN	A	078600	0514	078600	71
62521	BREVI,JAMES	H	081200	0314	081200	55
64660	FALCONER,EDWARD	L	108000	0227	008000	74
66799	MARTIN,KATHLEEN	L	089500	0129	089500	65
68937	YEUNG,SUK	A	051700	0816	050000	49
71074	PAUL,MARINA	A	044100	0414	034100	80
73210	FRADIN,SHIRLEY	L	066800	0728	066800	56
75344	BURNS,JEFFREY	A	070600	0226	070000	57
77478	KATZ,HAL	H	048500	0406	038500	64
79610	WRIGHT,DONNA	L	092600	0901	092000	75
81742	CUOMO,DONNA	A	090000	0313	090000	69
83872	LOPEZ,ANNA	A	067900	0716	010000	80
86002	ALEXANDER,LISA	H	040200	0623	030200	73
88130	GOLDBERG,LORI	H	098700	0524	095000	67
92057	HOFMANN,PATRICA	A	073700	0315	040000	77
92384	PUGH,CLIFFORD	A	075000	0423	075000	80
94509	FERRIS,LAURA	L	013500	0815	013500	73
96633	BERGIN,MICHAEL	L	160800	0116	100000	74

ferent amounts of main storage, it is desirable to code REGION on the EXEC statements, so each step gets the amount of main storage it requires. When REGION is coded on the JOB statement, the amount of main storage requested applies to the whole job. So if you code REGION on the JOB statement instead of on the EXEC statements, you must request the largest amount of space required by any of the steps. If you code REGION on both the JOB and EXEC statements, the REGION parameters on the EXEC statements are ignored.

When COND is coded on the JOB statement, it applies to every step in the job. If the test specified is true, then all the remaining steps are skipped. Suppose that in a five-step job you code

```
COND=(4,LE)
```

on the JOB statement. If the first step issues a return code of 8, then all the remaining steps are skipped.

If COND is coded on both the JOB and EXEC statements, then before a step is executed all tests are checked. If one of the tests coded on the JOB statement is true, then the current step and all the remaining steps are skipped. If none of the tests coded on the JOB statement is true, then the tests coded on the EXEC statement are checked. If any of these tests are true, the step is skipped.

Only the simple form of the COND parameter,

```
COND=(value,operator)
```

is legal on the JOB statement. You may not specify a stepname to restrict a test to the return code issued by a particular step, nor may you code EVEN or ONLY. You may, however, code up to eight tests.

BACKWARD REFERENCE

In Figure 4.13, when we wanted to refer to POLYFILE in the LIST step, we coded the DSN. That is not the only way we could have referred to POLYFILE; we could also have used a technique known as **backward reference**. When you use a backward reference, you copy information from an earlier DD statement.

BACKWARD REFERENCE

The SYSUT1 DD statement in the LIST step could have been coded

```
//SYSUT1    DD DSN=*.ADD.SYSUT2,
//              DISP=(OLD,KEEP)
```

This coding uses a backward reference to copy the DSN from the SYSUT2 DD statement in the ADD step. One general form of a backward reference is

```
DSN=*.stepname.ddname
```

Notice especially the asterisk and the period.

If you make a backward reference to an earlier DD statement in the same step, you do not have to code the stepname. You could write

```
DSN=*.ddname
```

Copying DCB Information

You can also use a backward reference to copy DCB information. You could code

```
DCB=*.ddname
```

or

```
DCB=*.stepname.ddname
```

depending on whether or not the earlier DD statement was in the same step. When you copy DCB information using a backward reference, you may at the same time add or change DCB subparameters by coding them. For example,

```
DCB=(*.STEP1.MASTER,BLKSIZE=1600)
```

copies DCB information from the MASTER DD statement in STEP1, but changes (or adds) the BLKSIZE subparameter. Notice that when you code a backward reference with one or more subparameters, it is necessary to enclose all the values in parentheses.

It is important to understand that when you make a backward reference to a DD statement, the DCB information is copied from the DD statement, not from the data set's header label. An example will make this clear. Suppose you have

```
//STEP1     EXEC PGM=PGM1
//MASTER    DD DSN=SALEFILE,
//              DISP=(NEW,KEEP),
//              VOL=SER=DISK01,
//              SPACE=(TRK,10),
//              DCB=(RECFM=FB,LRECL=80,BLKSIZE=800)
               .
               .
               .
//STEP2     EXEC PGM=PGM2
//COPY      DD DSN=COPYFILE,
//              DISP=(NEW,PASS),
//              VOL=SER=DISK02,
//              SPACE=(TRK,10),
//              DCB=(*.STEP1.MASTER,BLKSIZE=1600)
```

This coding works fine. The DCB for COPYFILE will be copied from the DCB on the MASTER DD statement, changing the BLKSIZE from 800 to 1600. But suppose SALEFILE is a cataloged data set. Then we might code the MASTER DD statement as follows:

```
//MASTER     DD DSN=SALEFILE,
//               DISP=OLD
```

In this case, the backward reference would not work, because the MASTER DD statement does not contain a DCB parameter. The system knows SALEFILE's DCB information, since it is contained in SALEFILE's header label, but for the backward reference the system does not examine the header label to obtain the DCB information; only the JCL is examined.

However, you can have the system copy DCB information from the header label of a cataloged data set. This is done by coding a reference to a data set name, rather than to a DD statement. For example, you could replace the backward reference for COPYFILE by coding

```
//               DCB=(SALEFILE,BLKSIZE=1600)
```

For a reference to a data set name to work, the referenced data set must be cataloged, it must reside on a direct access volume, and the volume must be mounted before the step begins execution.

It is not necessary for the referenced data set to be used in the job stream. Even if SALEFILE were not used in an earlier step, the reference to the data set would work. This is convenient because it permits a computer center to create cataloged data sets that may be used as DCB patterns. For example, programs frequently have to store 80-byte card images on a disk. Someone at the computer center can determine the optimal blocksize for such records. Then a data set can be cataloged which has a RECFM=FB, a LRECL=80, and a BLKSIZE equal to the optimal value. Suppose that data set is named CARDS. You can copy those DCB values simply by coding in your job stream

```
//              DCB=CARDS
```

Copying Volume Information

You may also use a backward reference to specify a volume serial number. Suppose, for example, that you are creating a new data set, and you want it to be placed on the same volume as an old data set. You could code

```
//OLD      DD DSN=WYL.QB.JCL.OLD,
//            DISP=OLD,
//            VOL=SER=USR012,
//            UNIT=DISK
//NEW      DD DSN=WYL.QB.JCL.NEW,
//            DISP=(NEW,KEEP),
//            VOL=REF=*.OLD,
//            SPACE=(TRK,10)
```

Notice that a backward reference for VOL requires that you code REF. This backward reference will cause WYL.QB.JCL.NEW to be put on disk pack USR012. When you use a backward reference to copy volume information, the system obtains unit information also, so it is not necessary to code the UNIT parameter.

If in the above example the OLD and NEW DD statements were not in the same step, the stepname would have to be included in the backward reference. So if the OLD DD statement were in a step named UPDATE, the backward reference would have to be

```
//          VOL=REF=*.UPDATE.OLD,
```

Just as for DCB information, you may also specify a volume serial number by coding a reference to a data set name. The referenced data set must be cataloged or passed. If ACCOUNTS is the name of a cataloged data set, you can have a new data set put on the same volume as ACCOUNTS by coding

```
//          VOL=REF=ACCOUNTS
```

Notice that REF is required when you refer to a data set name, just as it is when you refer back to a DD statement.

ERRORS

Skipping a Step

To illustrate how the COND parameter works, the SYSIN DD statement was eliminated from the ADD step in Figure 4.13, and the job rerun. The output produced is shown in Figure 4.15. The missing SYSIN DD statement prevented IEBGENER from executing properly, and it issued a return code of 12. The COND parameter coded on the LIST EXEC statement specifies that the LIST step should be skipped if 0 is not equal to the return code issued by the previous step. Since 0 is not equal to 12, the LIST step was skipped. Notice how clear the message is.

```
STEP WAS NOT RUN BECAUSE OF CONDITION CODES
```

For some reason, the system printed two almost identical messages about the LIST step being skipped.*

The system messages show that WYL.QB.JCL.POLYFILE was PASSED at the end of the ADD step. However, the LIST step that was supposed to receive it

---

* It could have been worse. The designers of the system could have followed the advice of the Bellman, who in Lewis Carroll's "The Hunting of the Snark" says, "What I tell you three times is true," and printed three messages.

ERRORS

sure that the DSN parameter is correct." Checking the DSN parameter in Figure 4.16 reveals that POLYFILE was misspelled.

In Figure 4.16, you see U0000 at (A) and USER=0000 at (C). Both of these messages refer to a user completion code of zero, which means that the user did not specify a completion code. It is possible for assembly language programmers to specify a user completion code by invoking the ABEND macro. Coding

```
ABEND     789
```

gives an abend with a user completion code of 789. COBOL programmers must define a working storage item with USAGE COMP:

```
01 COMP-CODE          PIC S999 USAGE COMP.
```

They may move a numerical value to that item and call module ILBOABNO, as follows:

```
MOVE 789 to COMP-CODE.
CALL 'ILBOABNO' USING COMP-CODE.
```

This coding will give an abend with a user completion code of 789. For some kinds of errors, COBOL itself (not the COBOL programmer) will abend with a user completion code. To find the cause of that abend, you must consult the *COBOL Programmer's Guide* (SC28-6483).

It is not possible for PL/I or FORTRAN programmers to specify a user completion code.

Some Special DD Statements

Sometimes, especially when a user-written program abends, the information in the *System Codes* and *System Messages* manuals is not sufficient to allow you to correct the error. In those cases it may be necessary to examine the contents of main storage at the time of the abend. The contents of main storage is called a **dump**. You can have a dump produced if you include either a SYSUDUMP, SYSABEND, or, for MVS systems only, SYSMDUMP DD statement in the step that abends. SYSUDUMP and SYSABEND produce a formatted dump, so

CHAPTER 4 / ACCESSING SEQUENTIAL DATA SETS

the data sets defined by these statements are usually directed to a printer. These statements would appear as

```
//SYSUDUMP DD SYSOUT=A
```

or

```
//SYSABEND DD SYSOUT=A
```

The difference between SYSUDUMP and SYSABEND is in how much of main storage is dumped. SYSUDUMP dumps the storage area used by the program. SYSABEND dumps the storage area used by the program plus certain system areas. The dump produced by SYSABEND is usually much larger than the dump produced by SYSUDUMP. In most cases the smaller dump provided by SYSUDUMP is all the user needs. These are the usual definitions of SYSUDUMP and SYSABEND, but computer centers may modify these definitions to suit their needs.

Since even a dump produced by SYSUDUMP can be quite large, many computer centers request that you assign dump output to a special class. For example, you might code

```
//SYSUDUMP DD SYSOUT=D
```

Class D output might be held. You can examine your output and determine if you need the dump to find the error. If you need the dump, it can be printed, but if you don't, it can be purged, saving printer time and paper.

SYSMDUMP produces an unformatted, machine-readable dump. SYSMDUMP output must be directed to magnetic tape or DASD. A SYSMDUMP DD statement might appear as

```
//SYSMDUMP DD DSN=DUMP,
//           DISP=(NEW,KEEP),
//           UNIT=2400
```

which directs the output to magnetic tape.

COBOL programmers can request that COBOL produce a formatted dump of their DATA DIVISION. The dump is written to a data set with the ddname SYSDBOUT. Similarly, PL/I programmers may obtain a dump formatted for their use by including a PLIDUMP DD statement.

EXERCISES

1. Answer true or false: The SPACE parameter is coded only when a data set is created on a DASD.

2. Usually you do not code the DCB parameter when you access an existing data set. Why?

3. Why would a programmer want to catalog a data set?

4. Why may you have data sets with the same DSN on different volumes, but be allowed to catalog only one of them?

5. a. A data set named EXAMPL is stored on disk pack DISK01. You want this data set to be input to IEBGENER. Code the required DD statement.

   b. Suppose the data set EXAMPL is cataloged. Code the required DD statement.

6. Name the four fields of utility control statements. Which fields are optional?

7. Answer true or false: If the label field is omitted, the operation field may begin in column 1.

8. What are the rules for continuing a utility control statement?

9. Explain how the value assigned to MAXFLDS is determined.

10. Explain how the value assigned to MAXLITS is determined.

11. What does the FIELD parameter FIELD=(4,26,PZ,35) do?

12. Code a TIME parameter to request 2.5 minutes of CPU time.

13. When you execute IEBPTPCH, you must supply at least one control statement. What is it?

14. Each line of output in Figure 4.9 ends with a single or double asterisk. What do they mean?

15. A data set has 80-byte records. Code the IEBPTPCH control statements to punch this data set and insert sequence numbers in columns 73 through 80. The first sequence number should be 100, and the increment should be 10.

16. Under what circumstances would you use IEBPTPCH instead of IEBGENER to print a data set?

17. A job stream contains five job steps. How many JOB, EXEC, DD, delimiter, and null statements does it contain?

18. In Figure 4.13, in the ADD step, MOD is coded as the status of POLYFILE. Why?

19. Suppose on a two-step job TIME=1 is coded three times: on the JOB statement and on both EXEC statements. What is the maximum CPU time the job may use?

20. Which parameters may be copied using a backward reference?

21. When you copy volume information using a backward reference, you may refer either to an earlier DD statement or to a cataloged data set. Code examples of both kinds of backward references.

22. What condition would cause an abend with a completion code of 322?

23. What is the reason for including a SYSUDUMP DD statement in a job step?

24. Use the COPY utility described in Exercise 31 in Chapter 2 to print a cataloged data set named INVENTRY.

25. The records in a data set contain a name in bytes 1 through 20, an address in bytes 21 through 50, and a phone number in bytes 60 through 69. You want to list this data set, with 5 spaces between the name and address and 10 spaces between the address and the phone number.

    a. Write the IEBGENER control statements required.

    b. Write the IEBPTPCH control statements required.

26. Consider the following job stream skeleton:

```
//EXAMPLE  JOB ,'MINNIE',
//              COND=(8,GE)
              .
              .
              .

//STEP1    EXEC PGM=PGM1,
//              COND=(0,EQ)
              .
              .
              .
```

EXERCISES

```
//STEP2     EXEC PGM=PGM2
                  .
                  .
                  .
//STEP3     EXEC PGM=PGM3,
//               COND=ONLY
                  .
                  .
                  .
//STEP4     EXEC PGM=PGM4,
//               COND=((2,GT,STEP1),(5,EQ,STEP2))
                  .
                  .
                  .
//STEP5     EXEC PGM=PGM5,
//               COND=EVEN
```

   a.   Under what circumstances will STEP1 be skipped? Comment on the COND parameter for STEP1.

   b.   Under what circumstances will STEP2 be skipped?

   c.   Under what circumstances will STEP3 be skipped?

   d.   Under what circumstances will STEP4 be skipped?

   e.   Simple Simon says that the EVEN coded for STEP5 ensures that STEP5 will be executed under all possible circumstances. Comment.

27. You have a four-step job in which the steps are named STEP1, STEP2, STEP3, and STEP4. Code the COND parameters to do the following:

   a.   If any step issues a return code of 8, 12, or 16, skip all the remaining steps.

   b.   Skip STEP2 unless STEP1 issues a return code of 0 or 4.

   c.   Skip STEP3 if STEP2 issues a return code of 500.

   d.   Skip STEP4 unless STEP3 abends.

28. Consider the following job stream:

```
//EX1         JOB ,'MICKEY',
//STEP1       EXEC PGM=PGM1
//DD1         DD DSN=DATASET1,
//               DISP=OLD
//DD2         DD DSN=DATASET2,                    (cont.)
```

```
//              DISP=(NEW,KEEP),
//              UNIT=DISK,
//              VOLUME=PACK07,
//              SPACE=(TRK,(5,2)),
//              DCB=(RECFM=VB,LRECL=150,BLKSIZE=900)
//STEP2    EXEC ?
//DD3      DD DSN=?
//              DISP=OLD
//DD4      DD DSN=DATASET4,
//              DISP=(NEW,KEEP),
//              ?
```

Where possible use backward references to complete the coding. You want:

a. STEP2 to execute the same program as STEP1.

b. the data set referenced in the DD3 DD statement to be DATASET1.

c. DATASET4 to be on the same volume as DATASET7. (DATASET7 is a cataloged data set.)

d. DATASET4 to have the same DCB as DATASET2.

e. DATASET4 to have the same space allocation as DATASET2.

PROGRAMMING ASSIGNMENTS

1. Execute a job to have IEBGENER list the data set you created in Chapter 3. Use control statements to insert 5 spaces between each field.

2. Execute a job to add the additional records in Appendix D to the data set you created in Chapter 3. In the same job use IEBPTPCH to produce an edited listing of the complete data set. Use the COND parameter to skip the listing step if the return code from the first step is greater than 4.

3. Misspell IEBGENER in the job stream you wrote for Programming Assignment 2 and execute the job. What completion code do you get? What return code accompanies the completion code? What explanations do you find in the *System Codes* and *System Messages* manuals?

SUMMARY

In this chapter you have learned

- how to code MOD, PASS, and CATLG for the DISP parameter to add records to a data set, pass a data set, and catalog a data set

- how to code control statements for IEBGENER and IEBPTPCH

- how to code a job stream that contains more than one job step

- how to code the COND parameter to control step execution

- how to code the TIME parameter

- how to code a backward reference to obtain DSN, DCB, and volume information

- how to read the system messages, including the completion code, produced when a job abends

- how to use the SYSUDUMP, SYSABEND, or SYSMDUMP DD statement to produce a dump when a job abends

CHAPTER 5

LIBRARIES

LEARNING OBJECTIVES

IN THIS CHAPTER YOU WILL LEARN

- what a library is

- how a library is used

- how to create, access, and modify libraries with the utility programs IEFBR14, IEBGENER, IEBPTPCH, IEBUPDTE, IEBCOPY, IEHPROGM, and IEHLIST

YOU WILL ALSO LEARN THE MEANINGS OF THE FOLLOWING TERMS:

- directory

- directory block

- library

- member

- partitioned data set (PDS)

WHAT IS A LIBRARY?

A **library** consists of groups of sequential records and a directory. Another name for a library is a **partitioned data set (PDS)**. The terms library and PDS are synonymous. The groups of sequential records are called **members** and may be treated as physical sequential data sets. All of the members must have the same DCB characteristics. If one member consists of 80-byte records blocked 1600, then all members must consist of 80-byte records blocked 1600. A library must reside on one DASD volume.

Figure 5.1 illustrates a PDS that contains three members named A, C, and E. The **directory** occupies the beginning of the PDS. It is made up of

WHAT IS A LIBRARY?

FIGURE 5.1

Structure of a PDS showing directory and members

Directory

A pointer	C pointer	E pointer	Free directory space	←

Member A

Member C ————→ ←———— Member E ————→

Available space

Available space

Available space

Available space

←———— Track ————→

256-byte blocks as shown in Figure 5.2a. The first two bytes indicate how many bytes of the block are in use. The lowest value that this field may contain is 2, which is the size of this field. The rest of the block consists of entries for members. As shown in Figure 5.2b, each entry for a member is from 12 to 74 bytes long. In Figure 5.2b, 8 bytes are shown as allocated for the member name. This means that the member name is limited to 8 characters. These 8 characters must be alphameric, except the first, which must be alphabetic or one of the three nationals (@, $, #). Basically, the same rules that apply to job names, which you learned in Chapter 2, also govern member names. The next three bytes contain the pointer, which indicates where the member is located on the DASD. When we access the member,

FIGURE 5.2

(a) Contents of a PDS directory block

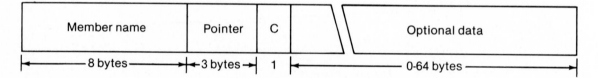

(b) Entry in a PDS directory block

The pointer is in the form TTR, where

TT is the track number
R is the block number relative to the start of the track
C contains control information

the pointer tells the system where the member is. We will not discuss the optional data which may be included in the directory entry for a member.

Figure 5.3 shows what happens when member B is added to the PDS shown in Figure 5.1. While the new member itself is added to the end of the data set, the entry is inserted in the directory in sort sequence. (The EBCDIC sort sequence is shown in Table 1.2.) The directory has entries for members A, B, C, and E in that order, but the members themselves are in the order in which they were added to the library.

Figure 5.4 shows what happens when member E is replaced with a larger version. The new version is shown as being added to the end of the data set. The entry in the directory for member E is changed to point to the

FIGURE 5.3

PDS with a new member

Directory

A pointer	B pointer	C pointer	E pointer	Free directory space	

Member A

Member C — Member E

Member B — Available space

Available space

Available space

Available space

Track

new member. The old version of member E is still there, but since there is no pointer to it, it cannot be accessed.

Figure 5.5 shows what happens when member A is deleted from the PDS illustrated in Figure 5.4. The entry for member A is removed from the directory, and member A is no longer accessible in the same way that the old version of member E is no longer available.

When members are replaced or deleted, the space is not recovered. Eventually the PDS becomes full so that it must be reorganized to reclaim the lost space. We will discuss how to reorganize a PDS later.

FIGURE 5.4

PDS with a replaced or changed member

Directory

A pointer	B pointer	C pointer	E pointer	Free directory space	

Member A

Member C — Not used (old Member E)

Member B — Member E

Available space

Available space

Available space

Track

LIBRARY USE

If each member of a library may be treated as a physical sequential data set, why bother using libraries at all? To answer this question, think back to the jobs run in previous chapters. The DD statements told the system where to find the input information and where to write the output data, but how did the system find the program to be executed? As standard procedure the system goes to a system library whose DSN is usually SYS1.LINKLIB. The executable forms of the utility programs are located in this library. Unless told otherwise, the system always searches the directory of SYS1.LINKLIB to find

FIGURE 5.5

PDS with a deleted member

Directory

B pointer	C pointer	E pointer	Free directory space	

Not used
(old Member A)

Member C — | Not used
(old Member E)

Member B — | Member E —

Available space

Available space

Available space

◄——————— Track ———————►

the program to be executed. (In Chapter 8 we will discuss how to access programs in other libraries.) If you have a group of programs in a library, only one data set need be searched to find a desired program. In most installations, source code for programs is kept in one library and executable code in another. One advantage of keeping source code in a library is that when a program must be changed, you know where to find it.

Another advantage of using a library is that the DASD space is used more efficiently. If you refer back to Figure 5.1, you will see that member C starts on the same track as member A. In fact, in Figure 5.1 the three members require two tracks. If they were independent physical sequential data sets, then three tracks would be needed.

JCL TO CREATE A LIBRARY

Using IEFBR14

Figure 5.6 illustrates a job that could be used to create a library named SOURCE.LIBRARY. The program used is IEFBR14. Strictly speaking IEFBR14 is not a utility program because in fact it does nothing. The name is derived from the fact that the entire program consists of one assembly language instruction; BR (branch) 14, which immediately returns control to the operating system. Since IEFBR14 does not do anything itself, you might wonder why it is needed. Sometimes, as in Figure 5.6, you merely want to process one or more DD statements. However, you may not submit a job that consists of just a JOB and DD statements; every job must have at least one EXEC statement. So executing IEFBR14 permits the disposition in the DD statement to occur. If, for example, DISP=(OLD,DELETE) is coded, the data set is deleted. If DISP=(,KEEP) is specified, a new, empty data set is created. In Figure 5.6, DISP=(,CATLG) is specified. This means that after the job ends, a new, empty data set is created and cataloged.

DD Statement Parameters

Let us now look at the DD statement in Figure 5.6. The first notable difference from what you have studied in earlier chapters is in the SPACE parameter. In addition to a primary and secondary space allocation, there is a third number specified. This number indicates the number of directory blocks to be allocated within the PDS. In Figure 5.6, 10 directory blocks are requested.

FIGURE 5.6

Allocating a library using IEFBR14

```
//JCLQB500 JOB ,'SLEEPY',
//             REGION=32K
//CREATE   EXEC PGM=IEFBR14
//DD1      DD DSN=WYL.QB.JCL.SOURCE.LIBRARY,
//             DISP=(,CATLG),
//             UNIT=SYSDA,
//             VOL=SER=WYL004,
//             SPACE=(TRK,(5,2,10)),
//             DCB=(RECFM=FB,LRECL=80,BLKSIZE=1680,
//             DSORG=PO)
//
```

ADDING A MEMBER WITH IEBGENER

Depending on how much optional data each entry includes, a directory block of 256 bytes can hold from 3 to 21 entries. With 10 directory blocks, the PDS can hold from 30 to 210 entries. Make sure that you specify enough space for the directory in the initial allocation. While the data set as a whole may expand by obtaining more space with the secondary allocation, the number of directory blocks is fixed. The space for the directory blocks is included in the primary allocation. Thus in the example shown in Figure 5.6, the primary allocation is five tracks. The directory will be in the beginning of the first of these five tracks. This means that slightly less than five tracks will initially be available for members.

Two tracks were specified as the secondary allocation. If we had chosen not to have a secondary allocation, then the SPACE parameter would have been coded as

```
//              SPACE=(TRK,(5,,10))
```

Note the double comma following the primary allocation. The second comma indicates the absence of a value for the secondary allocation.

The next difference to observe in the JCL in Figure 5.6 is the subparameter DSORG=PO in the DCB parameter. DSORG stands for Data Set ORGanization. DSORG=PO means that the data set organization is partitioned.

To summarize, the two differences in the JCL to create a PDS are (1) use of the third number in the SPACE parameter to request directory blocks and (2) specification of PO for the data set organization. Actually, the DCB subparameter DSORG=PO is optional. If a value for the number of directory blocks is coded in the SPACE parameter, a library will be created.

You will notice that there are no comment statements in Figure 5.6. Comment statements are important, and all the previous examples have contained them. However, since these examples are part of a book, they are discussed in the text, so comment statements are not really necessary. Therefore, from now on comment statements will be used sparingly. Your programs are not part of a book and must be understandable on their own, so you should continue to use comment statements in your programs.

ADDING A MEMBER WITH IEBGENER

You already know how to use IEBGENER in dealing with physical sequential data sets. In this section you will see how to use IEBGENER in dealing with libraries.

FIGURE 5.7

Adding one member to a library using IEBGENER

```
//JCLQB502 JOB ,'BASHFULL',
//            REGION=40K
//PDSCREAT EXEC PGM=IEBGENER
//SYSPRINT DD SYSOUT=A
//SYSUT1   DD DSN=WYL.QB.JCL.TAPEIN,
//            DISP=OLD
//SYSUT2   DD DSN=WYL.QB.JCL.SOURCE.LIBRARY,
//            DISP=OLD
//SYSIN    DD *
 GENERATE MAXNAME=1
 MEMBER NAME=COB1
/*
//
```

Figure 5.7 shows how IEBGENER can be used to add a member to the PDS created in Figure 5.6. The input defined by the SYSUT1 DD statement is a cataloged physical sequential data set on tape, named TAPEIN. The SYSUT2 DD statement defines the library to which a new member is to be added. Notice that the DISP coded on the SYSUT2 DD statement is OLD. The member we are adding to SOURCE.LIBRARY is new, but DISP refers to the whole PDS, which in this case already exists. Similarly, you cannot delete a member of a PDS by coding

```
//DD1      DD DSN=LIBRARY(MEMBER),
//            DISP=(OLD,DELETE)
```

This coding deletes the whole PDS named LIBRARY, not just the member named MEMBER. The way to delete members of a library is discussed later in this chapter.

Neither SYSUT DD statement in Figure 5.7 has explicit DCB information in it. The necessary information will be found by the system in the standard labels. When you add a member to a library, you must make sure that the physical sequential data set that is the input data set has the same logical record length as the library to which the new member is being added.

The MEMBER Statement

Let us look at the control statements in Figure 5.7. You are familiar with the GENERATE statement which was discussed in Chapter 4. The MAXNAME

ADDING A MEMBER WITH IEBGENER

parameter was listed in Table 4.1, but was not discussed in Chapter 4. MAX-
NAME is related to the MEMBER statement. How to determine the value to
assign to MAXNAME is explained later. The MEMBER statement indicates the
name of the member being created. In Figure 5.7, the name of the member
being created is COB1. If several members are being created, each member
must have its own MEMBER statement. We will study an example of multiple
MEMBER statements later.

Figure 5.7 shows the simplest version of the MEMBER statement. A
member in a PDS can have more than one name. The first name is the
member name. Any other name is an alias. If you wished the member to
have an alias, the MEMBER statement would be coded as follows:

```
MEMBER NAME=(COB1,UPDATE)
```

The result of this MEMBER statement is that a member named COB1 will be
created. It will have another name, or alias, which in this example is UPDATE.
The member may be referred to by using either its name or its alias. If you
wanted, for example, three aliases, the MEMBER statement would be coded as
follows:

```
MEMBER NAME=(COB1,UPDATE,PGM1,ASSIGN1)
```

If the idea of an alias confuses you, think of your friendly neighborhood
gangster. He has a name that appears on his birth certificate; this is
equivalent to COB1 in the example. He is also known to the police by other
names or aliases; these are equivalent to UPDATE, PGM1, and ASSIGN1 in the example. While it may be obvious why your friendly neighborhood gangster
might wish to use different names, why might you want a library member to
have more than one name? I have a member in a library whose name is
PRNTMEMB that contains JCL I use to print library members. Since I frequently
would get confused and refer to that member as MEMBPRNT, I solved the problem by giving member PRNTMEMB an alias of MEMBPRNT.

Let us return to the MAXNAME parameter in the GENERATE statement. The
value assigned to the MAXNAME parameter must be greater than or equal to the
number of names and aliases in the MEMBER statements that follow. Since in
Figure 5.7 there is only one name, MAXNAME is set equal to 1. Like the MAXFLDS
and MAXLITS parameters which we discussed in Chapter 4, if you set MAXNAME
equal to a higher value than needed, the job will execute properly. If, for example, there are a total of 6 names and aliases, MAXNAME must be set equal to
6 or more. A value of 7 will work, but 5 will not.

The IDENT Parameter

Figure 5.8 illustrates the creation of a library named GENERLIB with four members. If the SYSUT2 DD statement referenced an existing library instead of a new one, then this job would add four members to that library. The data to create the four members are contained in the cataloged data set named SEQIN.

Examining the first control card in Figure 5.8, the GENERATE statement, you see a new parameter, MAXGPS. MAXGPS indicates how many IDENT parameters will appear in the RECORD statements that follow. MAXGPS must be equal to or greater than the actual number of IDENT parameters in the following RECORD statements. If, in the example in Figure 5.8, we had specified 6 for MAXGPS, the job would work. If, on the other hand, we had specified 2, the job would not work.

Looking at the control statements in Figure 5.8, you see four MEMBER statements and three RECORD statements. The first MEMBER statement is followed by a RECORD statement, as are the second and third MEMBER statements.

FIGURE 5.8

Creating a library containing four members using IEBGENER

```
//JCLQB504 JOB ,'GRUMPY',
//              REGION=40K
//CREATPDS EXEC PGM=IEBGENER
//SYSPRINT DD SYSOUT=A
//SYSUT1   DD DSN=WYL.QB.JCL.SEQIN,
//              DISP=OLD
//SYSUT2   DD DSN=WYL.QB.JCL.GENERLIB,
//              UNIT=SYSDA,
//              VOL=SER=WYL002,
//              DISP=(,CATLG),
//              SPACE=(TRK,(10,2,5),RLSE),
//              DCB=(RECFM=FB,LRECL=100,BLKSIZE=2000,DSORG=PO)
//SYSIN    DD *
 GENERATE MAXNAME=4,MAXGPS=3
 MEMBER NAME=MEM1
 RECORD IDENT=(8,'11111111',1)
 MEMBER NAME=MEM2
 RECORD IDENT=(8,'22222222',1)
 MEMBER NAME=MEM3
 RECORD IDENT=(8,'33333333',1)
 MEMBER NAME=MEM4
/*
//
```

The first RECORD statement applies to the first MEMBER statement, the second to the second MEMBER statement, and the third to the third MEMBER statement. No RECORD statement applies to the last MEMBER statement.

The IDENT parameter in the RECORD statement is used to create multiple members from one physical sequential data set. In Figure 5.8, the IDENT parameter of the first RECORD statement specifies an 8-byte literal, 11111111, that starts in position 1 of the record. As each record is read, it is examined to determine if it contains the characters 11111111 starting in position 1. Once this literal is found, the first member, MEM1, is completed and the second member, MEM2, is built, followed by the building of the third member, MEM3. The last member, MEM4, consists of the remaining records in the input data set.

As Table 4.1 shows, the general format of the IDENT parameter is

```
IDENT=(length,'literal',starting position)
```

The IDENT parameter in the RECORD statement supplies a literal, its length (which has a maximum value of 8), and its position, to mark the end of the input for a member. Be aware that the record that includes this literal becomes part of the member.

ACCESSING A LIBRARY WITH IEBPTPCH

You have already studied how to use IEBPTPCH to print or punch a physical sequential data set. In the beginning of this chapter, you learned that members of a PDS may be treated as physical sequential data sets. In Figure 5.9a, the JCL to print a member of a PDS as a sequential data set is illustrated. If you compare this job with those shown in Chapter 4, the only significant difference you will find is in the DSN for the SYSUT1 DD statement. WYL.QB.-JCL.GENERLIB is the data set name of the library, and MEM1 is the member to be treated as a sequential data set. Specifying the DSN as WYL.QB.JCL.-GENRLIB(MEM1) results in a physical sequential data set.

To summarize: to treat a member of a library as a physical sequential data set, give the library name with the member name in parentheses, e.g., LIBRARY(MEMBER).

Figure 5.9b illustrates the JCL used to print MEM1, treating it as a member of the library GENERLIB. The DD statements are no different from those shown in Chapter 4. The SYSUT1 DD statement points to the library

FIGURE 5.9

(a) Printing a PDS member as a sequential data set

```
//JCLQB506 JOB ,'DOC',
//          REGION=32K
//PRNTSEQ  EXEC PGM=IEBPTPCH
//SYSPRINT DD SYSOUT=A
//SYSUT1   DD DSN=WYL.QB.JCL.GENERLIB(MEM1),
//            DISP=SHR
//SYSUT2   DD SYSOUT=A
//SYSIN    DD *
 PRINT MAXFLDS=1
 RECORD FIELD=(100)
/*
//
```

(b) Printing a PDS member as a PDS member

```
//JCLQB508 JOB ,'SNEEZY',
//          REGION=130K
//PRNTPDS  EXEC PGM=IEBPTPCH
//SYSPRINT DD SYSOUT=A
//SYSUT1   DD DSN=WYL.QB.JCL.GENERLIB,
//            DISP=SHR
//SYSUT2   DD SYSOUT=A
//SYSIN    DD *
 PRINT TYPORG=PO,MAXFLDS=1,MAXNAME=1
 MEMBER NAME=MEM1
 RECORD FIELD=(100)
/*
//
```

that has the members we wish to print. You will observe that just by looking at the DD statement, you cannot tell that WYL.QB.JCL.GENERLIB is a library. The rules for DD statements to access a partitioned data set are no different from the rules to access a physical sequential data set that resides on DASD. If you have any doubts about the rules to access a physical sequential data set on DASD, refer back to Chapter 4.

The Control Statements

Let us now look at the control statements for IEBPTPCH in Figure 5.9b. In the PRINT statement, you see the parameter TYPORG=PO. This means that the TYPe of ORGanization is Partitioned Organization. This parameter is how

THE IEBUPDTE UTILITY

TABLE 5.1

IEBUPDTE ADD, CHANGE, REPL, and REPRO parameters

Parameter	Definition
LIST=ALL	SYSPRINT data set to contain the entire update member.
SEQFLD=col	This parameter gives the column in which the sequence number is to start and the length of the sequence field. The default is 738, which means that the sequence field starts in column 73 and is 8 bytes long.
NEW=PO NEW=PS	This parameter is used only if the SYSUT1 and SYSUT2 data sets have different organizations. PO means that SYSUT2 will be partitioned and PS that it will be physical sequential.
NAME=memb	This parameter supplies the name of the member.
COLUMN=nn	This parameter applies only to the change operation. The default is 1. It specifies the starting column for the data.
UPDATE=INPLACE	This parameter specifies that the member is to be changed where it currently is. This means the member size must remain the same and the SYSUT2 DD statement is not required.

The only difference between the control statements used to add member JCL and those used for member COBOL is in the NUMBER statement. The first record of JCL will have a sequence number of 00000100, the second 00000110, and so forth.

The parameters used in the NUMBER detail statement are shown in Table 5.2.

Skipping to the end of Figure 5.11a, you come to the ENDUP statement, which marks the end of the control data set. If this control statement were omitted, the delimiter statement by itself would mark the end of the control data set.

TABLE 5.2

IEBUPDTE NUMBER and DELETE parameters

Parameter	DELETE	NUMBER	Definition
SEQ1=cccc	Yes	Yes	Specifies the sequence number of the first record to be deleted or renumbered.
SEQ2=cccc	Yes	Yes	Specifies the sequence number of the last record to be deleted or renumbered.
SEQ1=ALL	No	Yes	Specifies that the entire member is to be renumbered.
NEW1=cccc	No	Yes	Specifies the first number assigned to new or replacement data, or the first sequence number assigned in a renumbering operation.
INCR=cccc	No	Yes	Specifies an incremental value for the sequence numbers.

Figure 5.11b shows the output produced when the job stream in Figure 5.11a is executed. Since we coded LIST=ALL, the records in each member are printed. You can also see the sequence numbers which were added to each member as a result of our coding the NUMBER statement. These sequence numbers will be useful when we update the members.

Adding a Member to a PDS

Figure 5.12 illustrates the addition of a new member named BAL to CLASSLIB. Comparing Figure 5.11a and Figure 5.12, you see that the only difference between them is in the SYSUT2 DD statement. In Figure 5.11a the SYSUT2 DD statement defines a new PDS, while in Figure 5.12 it points to an existing PDS. In both examples, the PARM field is set equal to NEW. Remember that specifying NEW in the PARM field does not mean that the PDS is new. It means only that there is no SYSUT1 DD statement.

THE IEBUPDTE UTILITY

FIGURE 5.12

Adding a member to an existing PDS using IEBUPDTE

```
//JCLQB514 JOB ,'J.C.LEWIS',
//            REGION=38K
//STEPADD  EXEC PGM=IEBUPDTE,
//            PARM=NEW
//SYSPRINT DD SYSOUT=A
//SYSUT2   DD DSN=WYL.QB.JCL.CLASSLIB,
//            DISP=OLD
//SYSIN    DD *
./ ADD NAME=BAL,LIST=ALL
./ NUMBER NEW1=100,INCR=100
AMATO,ROBERT        403015422
ENKOWITZ,STEVE      557049836
HUYNH,CHAM          864524753
MORLEY,JOHN         465302116
PFLUGBEIL,MARIE     104523232
SCHWARTZ,MICHEAL    073671186
./ ENDUP
/*
//
```

Changing a Member in a Library

Figure 5.13a illustrates changing a member. In this example assume that two new students, Alexander and Osborn, have registered for the JCL class. Records for these students are to be inserted in their proper alphabetical position. Assume also that Falconer has dropped the course, so his record should be deleted. Finally, an error in Fradin's social security number must be corrected.

When you examine the JCL statements in Figure 5.13a, you will notice that PARM is not coded, so the default MOD applies. Therefore, we need both SYSUT1 and SYSUT2 DD statements. SYSUT1 defines the input PDS, and SYSUT2 defines the output PDS. The member to be changed is read from the input PDS defined by SYSUT1, changed, and then written to the output PDS defined by SYSUT2. In this example both SYSUT1 and SYSUT2 refer to CLASSLIB. So the system will read a member from CLASSLIB, change it, and then write it back to CLASSLIB. Later you will see an example in which the input and output PDS's are not the same.

Let us now examine the control statements following the SYSIN DD statement. The first one is the CHANGE statement. The NAME parameter specifies

FIGURE 5.13

(a) Changing a member using IEBUPDTE

```
//JCLJOB516 JOB ,'MARLA',
//          REGION=38K
//STEPCHNG EXEC PGM=IEBUPDTE
//SYSPRINT DD SYSOUT=A
//SYSUT1   DD DSN=WYL.QB.JCL.CLASSLIB,
//            DISP=OLD
//SYSUT2   DD DSN=WYL.QB.JCL.CLASSLIB,
//            DISP=OLD
//SYSIN    DD *
./ CHANGE NAME=JCL,LIST=ALL
./ NUMBER SEQ1=ALL,NEW1=100,INCR=100
ALEXANDER,LISA    71984306                          00000105
./ DELETE SEQ1=120,SEQ2=120
FRADIN,SHIRLEY    687965722                          00000130
OSBORN,BRIAN      136462732                          00000135
./ ENDUP
/*
//
```

(b) IEBUPDTE change messages

```
SYSIN                      NEW MASTER          IEBUPDTE LOG PAGE 0001
./ CHANGE NAME=JCL,LIST=ALL
./ NUMBER SEQ1=ALL,NEW1=100,INCR=100
   ABOLITZ,HANNA        015761231            00000100
   ALEXANDER,LISA       71984306             00000200      *   INSERTED*
./ DELETE SEQ1=120,SEQ2=120
   BURNS,JEFFREY        825494122            00000300          DELETED*
   FALCONER,EDWARD      205100235            00000120      *   REPLACED*
   FRADIN,SHIRLEY       687965722            00000130      *   REPLACEMENT*
   FRADIN,SHIRLEY       687965722            00000400      *   REPLACEMENT*
   OSBORN,BRIAN         136462732            00000500      *   INSERTED*
./ ENDUP
   SCHWARTZ,MICHAEL     073671186            00000600

IEB816I MEMBER NAME (JCL    ) FOUND IN NM DIRECTORY. TTR IS NOW ALTERED.
IEB818I HIGHEST CONDITION CODE WAS 00000000
IEB819I END OF JOB IEBUPDTE.
```

which member is to be changed. Additional parameters are defined in Table 5.1. In this case, all the defaults are acceptable except for LIST=ALL; it is a good idea to see what the changed member looks like.

The next control statement is the NUMBER statement. The NUMBER statement in Figure 5.13a differs from those shown in Figures 5.11a and 5.12 only in the presence of the SEQ1=ALL parameter. This parameter means that the entire member will be renumbered after the changes are made. The NEW1 and INCR parameters will work the same way here as with the NUMBER statement used with the ADD function.

Following the NUMBER statement are the data records and the DELETE statement. The data records have sequence numbers in columns 73 through 80. IEBUPDTE uses these sequence numbers to determine where these new data records should be put in member JCL. Figure 5.11b shows how member JCL looked when it was created. We want the new record for Alexander to be inserted in its proper alphabetical position between the records for Abolitz and Burns, which have sequence numbers of 100 and 110. So in Figure 5.13a we gave Alexander's data record a sequence number of 00000105. (The leading zeros are required.)

Skipping the DELETE statement for a second, you see that the data record for Fradin has a sequence number of 00000130. Since there is already a record in member JCL with a sequence number of 130, this new record will replace it. The new record has Fradin's correct social security number so this is exactly what we want to happen.

The data record for Osborn has a sequence number of 00000135. This sequence number will cause Osborn's record to be inserted between Fradin's (sequence number 130) and Schwartz's (sequence number 140), which is its proper alphabetical position.

Let us now return to the DELETE statement. The DELETE statement may be coded only with a CHANGE statement. The parameters for the DELETE statement are shown in Table 5.2. The DELETE statement in Figure 5.13a will cause the record whose sequence number is 00000120 to be deleted. The DELETE statement can also be used to delete several consecutive records. If we coded

```
./ DELETE SEQ1=110,SEQ2=130
```

then all the records with sequence numbers from 110 through and including 130 would be deleted.

The data records and DELETE statements must be coded in order by sequence number. We coded Alexander's record first because its sequence number is the lowest, 105. It is followed by the DELETE statement, because it deletes the record whose sequence number is 120. The DELETE statement is followed by the data records whose sequence numbers are 130 and 135. If we used a different order—for example, coding the DELETE statement before Alexander's record—the job would not run. If we wanted to delete Schwartz's record, we would include a second DELETE statement,

```
./ DELETE SEQ1=140,SEQ2=140
```

after Osborn's data record.

The output produced when the job in Figure 5.13a is executed is shown in Figure 5.13b. You can see that the output contains a clear record of the changes that were made. Notice that the NUMBER statement caused the entire member to be renumbered after the changes were made. We were able to change the numbering sequence by coding INCR=100 instead of INCR=10, which was used when member JCL was created.

In Place Member Change

Figure 5.14 illustrates the one and only time when the SYSUT2 DD statement is not required. In this example we want to replace two statements in member BAL because of an error in the social security number of record 300 and a misspelling of the name in record 500.

FIGURE 5.14

In place member change using IEBUPDTE

```
//JCLQB518 JOB ,'BENITO',
//          REGION=32K
//INPLACE   EXEC PGM=IEBUPDTE
//SYSPRINT DD SYSOUT=A
//SYSUT1    DD DSN=WYL.QB.JCL.CLASSLIB,
//             DISP=OLD
//SYSIN     DD *
./ CHANGE NAME=BAL,LIST=ALL,UPDATE=INPLACE
HUYNH,CHAM        864534753                      00000300
PFLUGBEIL,MARIA   104523232                      00000500
./ ENDUP
/*
//
```

THE IEBUPDTE UTILITY

Since the only action taken in this change will leave the member exactly the same size it was, we can make the change in place. This means that the member stays exactly where it is in the PDS; it is not moved to the end of the library as it was in the previous example. The only difference between the CHANGE control statement in this example and in Figure 5.13a is the UPDATE=INPLACE parameter.

Replacing a Member

The REPL control statement is used to replace a member in a library. The data records that follow the REPL statement will be used to replace the member named by the NAME parameter. Both SYSUT1 and SYSUT2 DD statements are required and point to the same PDS.

In Figure 5.15, assume that there are so many errors in member COBOL that it is easier to completely replace the member than to correct it. When you code REPL, the named member must exist in the library. Thus in Figure 5.15, unless COBOL is the name of a member in CLASSLIB, the job will fail. If COBOL is not in CLASSLIB, we should use the ADD statement to add it rather than the REPL statement.

FIGURE 5.15

Replacing a PDS member using IEBUPDTE

```
//JCLQB520 JOB ,'MELITA',
//           REGION=38K
//REPLACE  EXEC PGM=IEBUPDTE
//SYSPRINT DD SYSOUT=A
//SYSUT1   DD DSN=WYL.QB.JCL.CLASSLIB,
//           DISP=OLD
//SYSUT2   DD DSN=WYL.QB.JCL.CLASSLIB,
//           DISP=OLD
//SYSIN    DD *
./ REPL NAME=COBOL,LIST=ALL
./ NUMBER NEW1=100,INCR=100
BOTERO,MAURICE     526206289
CHAU,YIN           427476080
DESCOVICH,STEVEN   178050554
GOLD,STEPHEN       238340187
./ ENDUP
/*
//
```

FIGURE 5.16

Copying a member from one PDS to another using IEBUPDTE

```
//JCLOB522 JOB ,'J.C.LEWIS',
//              REGION=38K
//REPRODUC EXEC PGM=IEBUPDTE
//SYSPRINT DD SYSOUT=A
//SYSUT1    DD DSN=WYL.QB.JCL.SOURCE.LIBRARY,
//              DISP=OLD
//SYSUT2    DD DSN=WYL.QB.JCL.PGMLIB,
//              DISP=OLD
//SYSIN     DD *
./ REPRO NAME=COB1,LIST=ALL
./ REPRO NAME=COB2,LIST=ALL
./ CHANGE NAME=COB3,LIST=ALL
./ NUMBER SEQ1=ALL,NEW1=100,INCR=100
./ DELETE SEQ1=200,SEQ2=500
./ ENDUP
/*
//
```

Copying Members

Members may be copied from one library to another using the REPRO control statement. Figure 5.16 illustrates copying two members, COB1 and COB2, from SOURCE.LIBRARY to PGMLIB. After this job is executed, COB1 and COB2 will exist in both SOURCE.LIBRARY and PGMLIB. The parameters for the REPRO control statement are shown in Table 5.1.

Figure 5.16 shows how the CHANGE statement may be used to change a member while it is being copied from one library to another. Member COB3 is in SOURCE.LIBRARY. It will be changed and then stored in PGMLIB. After this job is executed, there will be two versions of COB3: the original version in SOURCE.LIBRARY and the changed one in PGMLIB.

You must remember that the maximum record size when you use IEBUPDTE is 80 bytes.

THE IEBCOPY UTILITY

IEBCOPY is a utility program that may be used to copy one or more members from an existing PDS to a new or existing PDS, to make a backup copy of a PDS, and to reorganize a PDS in order to reclaim the unused space, which is shown in Figure 5.5.

THE IEBCOPY UTILITY

Copying the Entire PDS

Figure 5.17 illustrates a job that copies all of the members of a PDS to a new PDS. We will examine this job in detail because it illustrates the basic function of IEBCOPY. Once you understand how this job works, you will have no difficulty with the rest of this section.

The EXEC statement invokes the program IEBCOPY, and the SYSPRINT DD statement provides the message data set. These two statements exist in all steps. The next two DD statements, SYSUT3 and SYSUT4, provide workspace used by the program IEBCOPY. There are complex formulas that may be used to calculate the amount of space needed. These formulas are usually unnecessary because most of the time one track is sufficient. These two DD statements are different from the DD statements you have studied earlier because they do not point to a particular data set. Rather, they make workspace available on a particular DASD volume. [If you are thinking that the SPACE parameter could be coded SPACE=(TRK,1), you are correct. The extra set of parentheses is not required. Since you will see examples of both forms in your work, both forms are included in this book.]

The INPUT DD statement defines an existing PDS, and OUTPUT defines a new PDS. The ddnames for the input and output PDS's are selected by the

FIGURE 5.17

Copying a library using IEBCOPY

```
//JCLQB524 JOB ,'JOE TINKER',
//             REGION=130K
//COPYLIB  EXEC PGM=IEBCOPY
//SYSPRINT DD SYSOUT=A
//SYSUT3   DD UNIT=SYSDA,
//             SPACE=(TRK,(1))
//SYSUT4   DD UNIT=SYSDA,
//             SPACE=(TRK,(1))
//INPUT    DD DSN=WYL.QB.JCL.GENERLIB,
//             DISP=OLD
//OUTPUT   DD DSN=WYL.QB.JCL.COPYLIB,
//             DISP=(,CATLG),
//             UNIT=SYSDA,
//             VOL=SER=WYL003,
//             SPACE=(TRK,(5,2,3)),
//             DCB=(RECFM=FB,LRECL=100,BLKSIZE=1600)
//SYSIN    DD *
 COPY INDD=INPUT,OUTDD=OUTPUT
/*
//
```

programmer. The names INPUT and OUTPUT were selected because those names reflect what is being done. Let us now examine these DD statements a little more carefully. The INPUT DD statement obviously points to the cataloged data set named GENERLIB which was created in Figure 5.8. The OUPUT DD statement points to a new data set named COPYLIB that is to be cataloged upon job end. You know that a library is being created because 3 directory blocks are specified in the SPACE parameter.

The DCB parameter is coded on the OUTPUT DD statement, although it is not required. If a DCB is not coded for the output PDS, the DCB information is copied from the input PDS. When you do code the DCB parameter for the output PDS, you must keep the logical record length the same as in the input PDS, but you may change the blocksize.

The control statements in the SYSIN data set tell IEBCOPY what is to be done. The control statement in Figure 5.17 is the simplest form of the statement. The operation is COPY and indicates the start of the copy operation. Since we invented the ddnames for the input and output PDS's, we must tell IEBCOPY the names we invented. The parameter INDD names the ddname of the input PDS, and OUTDD the ddname of the output PDS.

To summarize: when the job shown in Figure 5.17 is executed, a new PDS named COPYLIB is created that contains all the members that are in GENERLIB. The main difference between GENERLIB and COPYLIB is that all the free space is at the end of COPYLIB and, consequently, available for use.

Merging Libraries Together

Figure 5.18 illustrates a job that copies the members from two libraries into an existing library. Comparing this job with the one in Figure 5.17, you see one more DD statement and a slightly different control statement. Let us examine the control statement. As in the previous example, the operation is COPY. The OUTDD parameter points to the DD statement OUT, which in turn points to an existing PDS named MIXLIB. The INDD parameter points to two DD statements, IN1 and IN2, which point to existing PDS's, OLDLIB1 and OLDLIB2.

During this copy operation, IEBCOPY finds the first member in the PDS pointed to by the DD statement IN1. If a member with the same name is *not* in the output PDS, the member is added to the output PDS. If a member with the same name *is* in the output PDS, the member is not added to the output PDS. This continues until all the members in the PDS pointed to by the IN1 DD statement have been processed. Then IEBCOPY proceeds with the PDS referenced by DD statement IN2. In the control statement, IN2 is fol-

THE IEBCOPY UTILITY

FIGURE 5.18

Merging two libraries into an existing library using IEBCOPY

```
//JCLQB526 JOB ,'JOHN EVERS',
//              REGION=130K
//COPYMULT EXEC PGM=IEBCOPY
//SYSPRINT DD SYSOUT=A
//SYSUT3   DD UNIT=SYSDA,
//              SPACE=(TRK,(1))
//SYSUT4   DD UNIT=SYSDA,
//              SPACE=(TRK,(1))
//IN1      DD DSN=WYL.QB.JCL.OLDLIB1,
//              DISP=OLD
//IN2      DD DSN=WYL.QB.JCL.OLDLIB2,
//              DISP=OLD
//OUT      DD DSN=WYL.QB.JCL.MIXLIB,
//              DISP=OLD
//SYSIN    DD *
 COPY OUTDD=OUT,INDD=(IN1,(IN2,R)),LIST=NO
/*
//
```

lowed by R, which means replace. Thus, if there are members in the output PDS with the same names as members in the PDS pointed to by IN2, they will be replaced with those in the input PDS.

The last parameter in the control statement is LIST=NO. This means that the SYSPRINT data set will not include a list of the members copied. This parameter is not recommended, but is included to illustrate the coding.

Selectively Adding Members to a Library

You are more likely to wish to copy a few members of a library into a new or existing library than to want to copy the entire library. This procedure is illustrated in Figure 5.19. The principal difference between this job and the preceding one is in the control statements. The first control statement uses abbreviations: C is for COPY, I is for INDD, and O is for OUTDD. If you use this utility frequently, use of the abbreviations is recommended. If, on the other hand, you do not use it often, do not abbreviate, because if you don't use the abbreviations often, you will forget what they mean.

Immediately following the COPY control statement is a SELECT control statement. The SELECT control statement applies to the COPY statement preceding it and restricts the copy operation. The COPY statement alone

FIGURE 5.19

Selectively adding members to a PDS using IEBCOPY

```
//JCLQB528 JOB ,'FRANK CHANCE',
//            REGION=130K
//SELECOPY EXEC PGM=IEBCOPY
//SYSPRINT DD SYSOUT=A
//SYSUT3    DD UNIT=SYSDA,
//             SPACE=(TRK,(1))
//SYSUT4    DD UNIT=SYSDA,
//             SPACE=(TRK,(1))
//IN1       DD DSN=WYL.QB.JCL.OLDLIB1,
//             DISP=OLD
//IN2       DD DSN=WYL.QB.JCL.OLDLIB2,
//             DISP=OLD
//OUT       DD DSN=WYL.QB.JCL.MIXLIB,
//             DISP=OLD
//SYSIN     DD *
  C I=IN1,O=OUT
  SELECT MEMBER=(MEMB1,MEMB2,(MEMB3,,R),MEMB4)
  C I=IN2,O=OUT
  EXCLUDE MEMBER=(MEMB1,MEMB2,MEMB3,MEMB4)
/*
//
```

would cause all the members in the input PDS to be copied to the output PDS unless that particular member name were already in the output PDS. The SELECT control statement indicates that you want only those members named in this statement to be copied from the input PDS to the output PDS. In this case MEMB1, MEMB2, and MEMB4 will be copied from the input PDS to the output PDS if those member names are not already in the output PDS. MEMB3 will be copied to the output PDS even if a member with that name is already there because R is specified. This R coded on the SELECT statement has the same meaning as the R coded on the COPY statement in Figure 5.18.

Notice the extra comma coded for MEMB3:

(MEMB3,,R)

As you have probably guessed, these are positional parameters and the extra comma is coded to indicate that a positional parameter has been omitted. The positional parameter omitted is the new name which could be given to the member. That parameter will be discussed later when we study renaming members.

THE IEBCOPY UTILITY

The SELECT in the control statement could be abbreviated as S and the parameter MEMBER as M.

This job, unlike the preceding examples, includes a second copy operation, which is also restricted. The EXCLUDE statement that follows the COPY statement prevents a total copy. Here, the entire input PDS is to be copied with the exception of the four members MEMB1, MEMB2, MEMB3, and MEMB4. This is the purpose of the EXCLUDE statement.

The EXCLUDE could be abbreviated as E and the parameter MEMBER as M.

No one copy operation may have both a SELECT and EXCLUDE statement applied to it. Any copy operation may have more than one SELECT or EXCLUDE statement follow it. The subsequent statements are treated as continuation cards.

Renaming a Member

Figure 5.20 shows how to copy a member from one library to another, giving the member a new name in the process. The SELECT control statement is used to accomplish this purpose. In Figure 5.19, the SELECT statement selected the members to be copied from one PDS to another. In this example the SELECT statement does that as well as provides a new name. Studying the SELECT statement, you see that the first member to be processed is MEMB1.

FIGURE 5.20

Renaming a member as it is copied using IEBCOPY

```
//JCLQB530 JOB ,'J.C.LEWIS',
//              REGION=130K
//RENCOPY  EXEC PGM=IEBCOPY
//SYSPRINT DD SYSOUT=A
//SYSUT3   DD UNIT=SYSDA,
//            SPACE=(TRK,(1))
//SYSUT4   DD UNIT=SYSDA,
//            SPACE=(TRK,(1))
//IN     DD DSN=WYL.QB.JCL.OLDLIB1,
//           DISP=OLD
//OUT    DD DSN=WYL.QB.JCL.MIXLIB,
//           DISP=OLD
//SYSIN  DD *
 COPY INDD=IN,OUTDD=OUT
 SELECT MEMBER=((MEMB1,MEMBA),(MEMB2,MEMBB,R))
/*
//
```

The library referenced by the DD statement IN is searched for member MEMB1. If MEMB1 is not found, the SELECT statement is in error. If MEMB1 is found, then the library referenced by the DD statement OUT is searched for a member named MEMBA. If MEMBA is not found in the output library, then MEMB1 from the input library is copied to the output library and given the name MEMBA. If MEMBA is found in the output library, then MEMB1 is not copied.

The second member to be copied from the input PDS is MEMB2. In the output PDS, it will have the name MEMBB. Since R is specified, even if MEMBB already exists in the output library, MEMB2 will be copied and given the name MEMBB.

Later in this chapter we will discuss how to rename a member already in a library.

Reorganizing a Library

The reason you reorganize a library is to reclaim the unused space, which is shown in Figure 5.5. There are three main ways to reorganize a library: (1) create a backup and then compress it in place, (2) unload then load the PDS, and (3) copy the PDS, scratch the original, and then give the new PDS the old PDS name with the rename function. These three methods will be illustrated by reorganizing COPYLIB, which was created in Figure 5.17.

Figure 5.21 illustrates the first approach. The first step, which creates the backup tape, is run for safety's sake. If the system were to go down for any reason during the next step, which does the compress in place, the library would probably be destroyed. If we have created the backup tape, we can re-create the library with it. In most well-run installations, even if the library does not need to be reorganized, a backup tape will be created on a regular basis in case the library is destroyed in some manner. The backup tape is really an unloaded version of the PDS.

In the output (OUT) DD statement, only the data set name, unit, and disposition have been coded. For a backup tape, this is all that is required. IEBCOPY will supply the DCB information. Since volume has not been specified, the operator is free to use any available tape. When we receive the output, the deallocation message will tell us which volume was used.

The second step actually reorganizes the PDS. Because of the COND parameter coded on the second EXEC statement, the second step will not execute unless the backup tape has been successfully created. The COPY control statement points to the same PDS for both input and output. That is why this operation is called a "compress-in-place" operation. The PDS remains in the same DASD space that it was in before the operation began.

THE IEBCOPY UTILITY

FIGURE 5.21

Creating a PDS backup and compressing in place using IEBCOPY

```
//JCLQB532 JOB ,'M. HART',
//              REGION=130K
//BACKUP    EXEC PGM=IEBCOPY
//SYSPRINT  DD SYSOUT=A
//SYSUT3    DD UNIT=SYSDA,
//              SPACE=(TRK,(1))
//SYSUT4    DD UNIT=SYSDA,
//              SPACE=(TRK,(1))
//IN        DD DSN=WYL.QB.JCL.COPYLIB,
//              DISP=OLD
//OUT       DD DSN=WYL.QB.JCL.BACKUP,
//              DISP=(,KEEP),
//              UNIT=TAPE
//SYSIN     DD *
 COPY OUTDD=OUT,INDD=IN
/*
//COMPRESS EXEC PGM=IEBCOPY,COND=(0,NE)
//SYSPRINT  DD SYSOUT=A
//SYSUT3    DD UNIT=SYSDA,
//              SPACE=(TRK,(1))
//SYSUT4    DD UNIT=SYSDA,
//              SPACE=(TRK,(1))
//INOUT     DD DSN=WYL.QB.JCL.COPYLIB,
//              DISP=OLD
//SYSIN     DD *
 COPY OUTDD=INOUT,INDD=INOUT
/*
//
```

The second approach to reorganizing the library is illustrated in Figure 5.22. The first step in Figure 5.22 performs the same service as the first step in Figure 5.21. The only difference is in the disposition of the PDS and the tape. In Figure 5.21, the PDS is to be kept. In Figure 5.22, the PDS is to be deleted unless the step abends, in which case it will be kept. In Figure 5.21, the backup tape is kept, although it could have been cataloged. In Figure 5.22, it is passed. Since we have no way of knowing which volume will be used, we cannot possibly code the volume serial number in the second step, where this tape forms the input. By specifying PASS for the disposition, we eliminate the need to know the volume serial number.

In the LOAD step, a new library is created using the unloaded tape as input. The disposition of the tape in this step is specified as KEEP. We will wish to retain this tape for backup purposes until the next time this job is

FIGURE 5.22

Unloading then loading a PDS using IEBCOPY

```
//JCLQB534 JOB ,'S. RAND',
//           REGION=130K
//UNLOAD    EXEC PGM=IEBCOPY
//SYSPRINT  DD  SYSOUT=A
//SYSUT3    DD  UNIT=SYSDA,
//              SPACE=(TRK,(1))
//SYSUT4    DD  UNIT=SYSDA,
//              SPACE=(TRK,(1))
//IN        DD  DSN=WYL.QB.JCL.COPYLIB,
//              DISP=(OLD,DELETE,KEEP)
//OUT       DD  DSN=WYL.QB.JCL.UNLOAD,
//              DISP=(,PASS),
//              UNIT=TAPE
//SYSIN     DD  *
 COPY OUTDD=OUT,INDD=IN
/*
//LOAD      EXEC PGM=IEBCOPY,
//              COND=(0,NE)
//SYSPRINT  DD  SYSOUT=A
//SYSUT3    DD  UNIT=SYSDA,
//              SPACE=(TRK,(1))
//SYSUT4    DD  UNIT=SYSDA,
//              SPACE=(TRK,(1))
//INTAP     DD  DSN=WYL.QB.JCL.UNLOAD,
//              DISP=(OLD,KEEP)
//OUTDSK    DD  DSN=WYL.QB.JCL.COPYLIB,
//              UNIT=SYSDA,
//              VOL=SER=WYL004,
//              DISP=(,CATLG),
//              SPACE=(TRK,(5,2,3))
//SYSIN     DD  *
 COPY OUTDD=OUTDSK,INDD=INTAP
/*
//
```

run. If, for some reason, the library is destroyed, it may be re-created using this tape. Because we did not code a DCB parameter for the new PDS, it will have the same characteristics as the original PDS.

The third approach is shown in Figure 5.23. The two previous examples only used the IEBCOPY utility. This approach uses the utility IEHPROGM as well. The first step, which employs IEBCOPY, copies the existing PDS to a new PDS. The old PDS will be deleted unless the step abends, in which case it will be kept as indicated in the disposition parameter for the old PDS. The next step, which only executes if the first was successful, performs two

FIGURE 5.23

Copying a PDS using IEBCOPY and then renaming it

```
//JCLQB536 JOB ,'G. R. LEE'
//COPYLIB  EXEC PGM=IEBCOPY,
//             REGION=130K
//SYSPRINT DD SYSOUT=A
//SYSUT3   DD UNIT=SYSDA,
//             SPACE=(TRK,(1))
//SYSUT4   DD UNIT=SYSDA,
//             SPACE=(TRK,(1))
//OUT      DD DSN=WYL.QB.JCL.NEWLIB,
//             UNIT=SYSDA,
//             VOL=SER=WYL003,
//             DISP=(,KEEP),
//             SPACE=(TRK,(5,2,3))
//IN       DD DSN=WYL.QB.JCL.COPYLIB,
//             DISP=(OLD,DELETE,KEEP)
//SYSIN    DD *
 COPY OUTDD=OUT,INDD=IN
/*
//SCREN    EXEC PGM=IEHPROGM,
//             COND=(0,NE),
//             REGION=36K
//SYSPRINT DD SYSOUT=A
//ANYNAME  DD UNIT=SYSDA,
//             VOL=SER=WYL003,
//             DISP=OLD
//SYSIN    DD *
 RENAME DSNAME=WYL.QB.JCL.NEWLIB,VOL=SYSDA=WYL003,      *
            NEWNAME=WYL.QB.JCL.COPYLIB
 CATLG DSNAME=WYL.QB.JCL.COPYLIB,VOL=SYSDA=WYL003
/*
//
```

functions. The new PDS is given the name of the old PDS and then is cataloged. (Although the new PDS does not have to be cataloged, it was cataloged here because, as you can see from the manner in which the DD statement for the original PDS is coded, the original was cataloged.) The JCL and control cards in this step will be explained later in this chapter where other functions of IEHPROGM that relate to libraries are discussed.

Figure 5.23 differs from the first two examples in that the REGION parameter is coded on the EXEC statements. The reason for this is that storage requirements are so different. The first step requires 130K, while the second requires only 36K.

Of the three approaches discussed for reorganizing a library, either the first or second is recommended. Both of these methods provide backup tapes that may be used for recovery if the library is destroyed for some reason. The backup tape may also be used to transport the library from one system to another.

THE IEHMOVE UTILITY

The utility program IEHMOVE can perform functions similar to those of IEBCOPY. Discussion of IEHMOVE is deferred to Chapter 14. The decision to introduce IEBCOPY first was based on the fact that IEBCOPY is a little easier to understand and work with than IEHMOVE.

THE IEHLIST UTILITY—
LISTING LIBRARY MEMBER NAMES

To list the names of the members of a library, the IEHLIST utility program is used. IEHLIST can do more than just list the names of the members of a PDS, as will be discussed in Chapter 14. Now, however, let's concentrate on listing the names of members of a library.

Figure 5.24 illustrates the use of IEHLIST for this purpose. The EXEC statement invokes the utility IEHLIST, and the SYSPRINT DD statement provides the message data set. The next DD statement is a little unusual. The ddname ANYNAME is used in this example because it does not matter what name you use as long as it is a legal one. Also there is no data set name coded on this DD statement even though the disposition says OLD. Unlike most DD statements, this one does not reference a data set. Instead it makes a DASD volume available to the utility program.

The control statement has the LISTPDS operation. A label starting in column 1 could have been coded in the control statement, but there is no point in doing so. In the control statement, unlike the DD statement, the parameter DSNAME may *not* be abbreviated.

A listing of the names of members that are in the two libraries OLDLIB1 and OLDLIB2 is requested. More than two libraries could have been named in the control statement, provided that they all reside on the same DASD volume. The VOL parameter is used to indicate the unit type and DASD

THE IEHPROGM UTILITY

FIGURE 5.24

Listing members of a library with IEHLIST

```
//JCLQB538 JOB ,'J.C.LEWIS',
//              REGION=38K
//LISTPDS  EXEC PGM=IEHLIST
//SYSPRINT DD SYSOUT=A
//ANYNAME  DD UNIT=SYSDA,
//              VOL=SER=WYL004,
//              DISP=OLD
//SYSIN    DD *
 LISTPDS DSNAME=(WYL.QB.JCL.OLDLIB1,WYL.QB.JCL.OLDLIB2),          *
              VOL=SYSDA=WYL004
/*
//
```

volume upon which the library or libraries may be found. The volume named in the control statement must also be named in a DD statement. That is why the ANYNAME DD statement is included. The coding of the VOL parameter is quite different from what you would expect. It is

```
VOL=unit-type=volume-serial-number
```

For unit-type you code what is usually coded in the UNIT parameter of a DD statement: DISK, SYSDA, 3330, etc. In some installations only actual unit types such as 3330 are permitted. Check with your advisor for the correct coding of this parameter and write it in the place provided on the inside front cover. Make sure that you understand this parameter, because it is used in the same form with several other utility programs. The same format was used in Figure 5.23.

THE IEHPROGM UTILITY

Figure 5.25 shows how the utility program IEHPROGM may be used to delete and rename members. Using IEHPROGM requires JCL very similar to that required by IEHLIST. If you compare the JCL in Figure 5.25, which illustrates the use of IEHPROGM, with that in Figure 5.24, which illustrates the use of IEHLIST, you will see that the only difference is in the EXEC statements, which invoke IEHPROGM and IEHLIST, respectively. For both utility programs,

FIGURE 5.25

Renaming a member of a PDS, scratching a PDS, and scratching a PDS member using IEHPROGM

```
//JCLQB540 JOB ,'J.C.LEWIS',
//          REGION=36K
//LIBPROGM EXEC PGM=IEHPROGM
//SYSPRINT DD SYSOUT=A
//ANYNAME  DD UNIT=SYSDA,
//              VOL=SER=WYL004,
//              DISP=OLD
//SYSIN    DD *
 RENAME MEMBER=MEMB1,DSNAME=WYL.QB.JCL.OLDLIB1,               *
                VOL=SYSDA=WYL004,                             *
                NEWNAME=MEMBA
  SCRATCH DSNAME=WYL.QB.JCL.OLDLIB2,                          *
                VOL=SYSDA=WYL004,                             *
                PURGE
  SCRATCH MEMBER=MEMB2,DSNAME=WYL.QB.JCL.OLDLIB1,             *
                VOL=SYSDA=WYL004
/*
//
```

access to the volume is required and not access to a particular data set. In general you will find that utility programs whose names begin with IEB require access to particular data sets, while those whose names begin with IEH require access to a DASD volume as a whole. For utility programs whose names start with IEH, the user may employ any legal ddname that is desired.

Let us examine the control statements for IEHPROGM. IEHPROGM can perform many functions. However, we will only discuss those that are most commonly used. In this chapter we will discuss only the SCRATCH control statement, which is used to delete a data set or a member of a PDS, and the RENAME control statement, which is used to give a new name to either a data set or a member of a PDS. Additional functions of IEHPROGM will be discussed in Chapter 14.

The RENAME Control Statement

Refer back to Figure 5.23. In the second step of that job, we give a data set that happens to be a library a new name. The first thing we need to know is the name of the data set whose name is to be changed. This is supplied with the DSNAME parameter. Unlike a JCL DD statement, the parameter may not be abbreviated to DSN, but must be coded as shown in the example. The next information provided tells the unit type and volume serial number where the data set may be found. If the data set were not a library and resided on several volumes, we might code the VOL parameter as

```
VOL=SYSDA=(WYL003,WYL004,WYL005)
```

As you remember, a library may not exist on more than one volume. Thus the DSNAME parameter tells which data set is to be operated on and the VOL parameter tells where it is. The parameter NEWNAME supplies the new name.

To summarize, the RENAME control statement show in Figure 5.23 will result in the data set named NEWLIB that resides on volume WYL003 having its name changed to COPYLIB.

Now let us look at the RENAME control statement in Figure 5.25. Comparing that RENAME with the one in Figure 5.23, you can see that the only difference is in the MEMBER parameter in Figure 5.25. Once IEHPROGM finds this parameter, it knows that it is dealing with a library and that a member is to be renamed. The RENAME control statement in Figure 5.25 will result in the changing of the name of member MEMB1, which resides in library OLDLIB1 on volume WYL004, to MEMBA.

You now can rename a data set or member of a library using the utility IEHPROGM. You can also rename a member as you copy it from one library to another using IEBCOPY.

The SCRATCH Control Statement

Now that you understand the RENAME control statement, you will find the SCRATCH statements in Figure 5.25 quite simple. Let's look at the first one. The DSNAME parameter names the data set you want scratched, and the VOL tells where to find it. The PURGE parameter says that you want the data set scratched even if its expiration date has not arrived. As you will learn, you set the expiration date with the LABEL parameter in the DD statement. The result of the first SCRATCH statement is that data set OLDLIB2 will be deleted from volume WYL004. If OLDLIB2 is a cataloged data set, it should be uncataloged when it is deleted. (The CATLG and UNCATLG statements will be discussed in Chapter 14.)

The next SCRATCH statement removes a member from the library. The difference between this SCRATCH statement and the preceding one is in the MEMBER parameter. The MEMBER parameter names the member to be deleted from the library named in the DSNAME parameter.

The parameters MEMBER, DSNAME, VOL, and NEWNAME are keyword parameters and may be coded in any order. In Figure 5.25, you will notice that in the SCRATCH and RENAME control statements the MEMBER parameter was coded

FIGURE 5.26

Scratching a PDS using IEFBR14

```
//JCLQB541 JOB ,'J.C.LEWIS',
//          REGION=32K
//SCRATCH  EXEC PGM=IEFBR14
//DD1      DD DSN=WYL.QB.JCL.SOURCE.LIBRARY,
//            DISP=(OLD,DELETE)
//
```

first when the control statement referenced a library member. If you code the MEMBER parameter first, you probably will not accidentally scratch or rename the entire library.

THE IEFBR14 UTILITY
AND DISPOSITION PROCESSING

If you want to scratch a member of a library, you must use IEHPROGM. However, if you want to scratch, catalog, or uncatalog a data set, you can use either IEHPROGM or IEFBR14. Using IEFBR14 is easier. Earlier in this chapter you saw how IEFBR14 could be used to create and catalog SOURCE.LIBRARY. Figure 5.26 shows how IEFBR14 could be used to scratch SOURCE.LIBRARY. When SOURCE.LIBRARY is scratched, it is automatically uncataloged.

EXERCISES

1. What is a library?

2. What is another name for a library?

3. What type of device may be used for a library?

4. How many volumes may be used for a library?

5. What are the rules governing member names?

6. In what order are members listed in the directory?

7. In what order are members stored in the library?

8. What happens to the space released when a member is deleted?

9. How large is a directory block?

10. What information is stored in a directory block?

11. Name two reasons to use a library instead of separate physical sequential data sets.

12. When you look at JCL, what tells you that a library is being created?

13. Why would you use IEBGENER instead of IEBUPDTE to add a member to a library?

14. How do you assign a name to a member when IEBGENER is used to add a member to a library? How do you assign a name when IEBUPDTE is used?

15. Why would you use IEBPTPCH instead of IEBGENER to print a library member?

16. Why would you use IEBCOPY instead of the REPRO function of IEBUPDTE to copy a member from one library to another?

PROGRAMMING ASSIGNMENTS

1. Use IEFBR14 to create a library named FIRSTLIB. You should request one track and one directory block. The logical record length should be 80 and the blocksize 800.

2. Prepare the following data cards

```
CEREAL
TOAST
COFFEE
AAAAAAAA
BOLOGNA SANDWICH
MILK
ICE CREAM
BBBBBBBB
HAMBURGER
FRENCH FRIES
PIE
COFFEE
```

'With these data cards as input, use IEBGENER to store three members, named BKFAST, LUNCH, and DINNER, in FIRSTLIB.

3. Execute a job that will list members BKFAST and DINNER.

4. Use IEBUPDTE to copy members LUNCH and DINNER from FIRSTLIB to a new library named SCONDLIB. Be sure to number the data records so they can be modified.

5. Use IEBUPDTE to modify member DINNER. Change FRENCH FRIES to MASHED POTATOES, and add STRING BEANS.

6. Use IEBCOPY to copy member BKFAST from FIRSTLIB to SCONDLIB.

7. Execute a job that will list the names of the members in FIRSTLIB.

8. Execute a job that will rename member DINNER to SUPPER.

9. Execute a job that will rename SCONDLIB to SECOND.LIB.

10. Execute a job that will scratch member LUNCH.

11. Execute a job that will scratch SECOND.LIB.

SUMMARY

In this chapter you have learned

- how a library is organized

- how to create a library

- how to use IEBGENER to add members to a library

- how to use IEBPTPCH to list members in a library

- how to use IEBUPDTE to add members to a library, change and replace members in a library, and copy members from one library to another

- how to use IEBCOPY to copy members from one library to another and to compress a library

- how to use IEHLIST to list the names of the members in a library

- how to use IEHPROGM to scratch or rename a physical data set, a library, or a member of a library

- how to use IEFBR14 to create, catalog, uncatalog, and delete, a data set

CHAPTER 6

GENERATION DATA GROUPS

CHAPTER 6 / GENERATION DATA GROUPS

LEARNING OBJECTIVES

IN THIS CHAPTER YOU WILL LEARN

- what a generation data group is
- how to create a generation data group
- how to use a generation data group

YOU WILL ALSO LEARN THE MEANINGS OF THE FOLLOWING TERMS:

- generation
- generation data group
- generation data set
- generation group index
- generation number
- model data set control block (DSCB)

WHAT IS A GENERATION DATA GROUP?

A **generation data group** is a collection or group of cataloged data sets having the same name and related to one another chronologically. Each of these data sets is called **generation data set** or, simply, a **generation**. Each generation contains successive versions of the same data. An example would be a cumulative year-to-date payroll, where a new generation is created every pay day.

Each generation may be a physical sequential data set, a partitioned data set, a direct data set, or, under special conditions, an index sequential data set. (Chapter 12 provides a full discussion of index sequential data sets and some discussion of direct data sets.) Each generation data set may reside on tape or DASD. Usually, all of the generation data sets of a generation data group will be on the same kind of device. However, this is not required. It is possible to have a generation data group in which one generation is a physical sequential data set residing on tape and another is a partitioned data set residing on DASD.

Unlike other data sets for which the data set name may be up to forty-four characters, for a generation data set the data set name is limited to thirty-five characters. Each generation or generation data set is distinguished from the others by the **generation number**. The generation number may be relative or absolute. The system uses the absolute numbers, but application programmers usually employ the relative numbers because the relative numbers are easier to use. If the data set name of the group is GEN.DATA.GROUP, then to access the current generation, you code DSN=GEN.DATA.GROUP(0). To access the previous generation, you code DSN=GEN.DATA.GROUP(-1); the generation before would be DSN=GEN.DATA.GROUP(-2). When you want to create a new generation, you code DSN=GEN.DATA.GROUP (+1). If you want to create a second version, you specify a relative number of +2.

The absolute number used by the system is in the form GxxxxVyy where xxxx is the generation number running from 0000 to 9999 and yy is the version number running from 00 to 99. Thus the generation specified as DSN=GEN.DATA.GROUP(0) might appear to the system, for example, as GEN.DATA.GROUP.G0006V00. Then the data set with a relative number of (-1) would be GEN.DATA.GROUP.G0005V00, and the newly created one whose relative number is (+1) would be GEN.DATA.GROUP.G0007V00. If instead of specifying a relative number of +1, you specify +2, then a data set whose name is GEN.DATA.GROUP.G0008V00 is created. The data set with an absolute generation number of 7 would not exist because one generation would be skipped.

Before a generation data set may be created, the programmer must create a generation group index and a model data set control block. How this is done will be discussed next.

GENERATION GROUP INDEX

The **generation group index** contains information on how many generations are to be retained and what to do when the index gets full. If four generations are specified in the index, then four data sets will be retained. When the fifth is created, the index will indicate what should be done. One possibility is to delete all four previous data sets when the fifth is created. Another possibility is to retain the four data sets but to remove their entries from the index. The usual approach is either to remove the index entry for the oldest data set and delete the oldest data set or to remove the index entry for the oldest data set but retain the data set itself.

Using IEHPROGM

The index may be created in either of two ways. The first applies the BLDG control statement used with the utility program IEHPROGM. The job shown in Figure 6.1 illustrates the BLDG control statement. The result of the execution of this control statement will be the creation of the index in the system catalog.

The BLDG control statement builds an index named WYL.QB.JCL.POLYGEN. ENTRIES=4 requests space for four entries. When a fifth entry is created, the oldest existing data set (whose relative number would be -3) is removed from the index, but the data set itself is kept. However, if you wish to access it, you must use the absolute number; e.g., WYL.QB.JCL.POLYGEN.G0051V00.

The BLDG statement in Figure 6.1 contains only the required parameters, INDEX and ENTRIES. Either one or both of two optional parameters, DELETE and EMPTY, may also be coded.

If we had coded DELETE,

```
BLDG INDEX=WYL.QB.JCL.POLYGEN,ENTRIES=4,DELETE
```

then when the fifth entry was created, not only would the index entry for the oldest generation have been removed, but the oldest generation itself would also have been scratched.

FIGURE 6.1

Building a generation group index using IEHPROGM

```
//JCLQB542 JOB ,'COL. MUSTARD',
//              REGION=36K
//STEPBLD   EXEC PGM=IEHPROGM
//SYSPRINT DD SYSOUT=A
//SYSIN    DD *
 BLDG INDEX=WYL.QB.JCL.POLYGEN,ENTRIES=4
/*
//
```

GENERATION GROUP INDEX

If we had coded EMPTY,

```
BLDG INDEX=WYL.QB.JCL.POLYGEN,ENTRIES=4,EMPTY
```

then when the fifth entry was created, all four entries would have been removed from the index, but the data sets themselves would have been kept.

Finally if we had coded both DELETE and EMPTY,

```
BLDG INDEX=WYL.QB.JCL.POLYGEN,ENTRIES=4,DELETE,EMPTY
```

then when the fifth entry was created, all four entries would have been removed from the index and the data sets would have been scratched.

Using IDCAMS

The index may also be created in a VSAM catalog using the VSAM utility program IDCAMS, which will be discussed in detail in Chapter 13. Figure 6.2 shows the sample JCL using IDCAMS to accomplish the same function as performed in Figure 6.1.* The command format is

```
DEFINE GENERATIONDATAGROUP (parameters)
```

or, to abbreviate both terms,

```
DEF GDG (parameters)
```

FIGURE 6.2

Defining a generation group index using IDCAMS

```
//JCLQB544 JOB ,'MISS SCARLET',
//              REGION=300K
//STEPGDG EXEC PGM=IDCAMS
//SYSPRINT  DD SYSOUT=A
//SYSIN     DD *
 DEFINE    GDG (NAME(VSAM.QB.JCL.POLYGEN) LIMIT(4))
/*
//
```

* I changed the first part of the data set name from WYL to VSAM to conform with the CUNY computer center rules for naming VSAM data sets.

where parameters are defined in Table 6.1. Note that EMPTY has the same meaning as in the BLDG statement of IEHPROGM. LIMIT is equivalent to ENTRIES, and SCRATCH is equivalent to DELETE.

MODEL DATA SET CONTROL BLOCK

Every generation data group must have a **model data set control block (DSCB)** from which the system obtains DCB information. Figure 6.3 illustrates a job that could be run to create the model DSCB. Since we just want the DD statement to be processed, we execute the program IEFBR14, discussed in Chapter 5. This job will create a model DSCB named WYL.QB.JCL.POLYGEN. Notice that the model DSCB is not cataloged. Since the model DSCB has the same name as the generations, either the model DSCB or the generations can be cataloged, but not both.

The model DSCB must reside on the same volume as the system catalog. At the CUNY computer center, the serial number of the appropriate

TABLE 6.1

DEFINE GENERATIONDATAGROUP parameters

Parameter	Abbr	Meaning
NAME (entryname)		Generation data group name.
LIMIT (limit)	LIM	The number of generations permitted for this GDG. The maximum is 255.
EMPTY	EMP	If EMPTY is specified, all data sets are to be removed from
NOEMPTY	NEMP	the index when the limit is reached. NOEMPTY is the default.
OWNER (ownerid)		If specified, names the user identification.
SCRATCH	SCR	If SCRATCH is specified, when a data set is removed from
NOSCRATCH	NSCR	the index, the data set is scratched. NOSCRATCH is the default.
TO (date)		This specifies the data set retention period.
FOR (days)		

FIGURE 6.3

Creating a model data set control block for a generation data group

```
//JCLQB546 JOB ,'PROF. PLUM',
//           REGION=32K
//MODLDSCB EXEC PGM=IEFBR14
//DD1      DD DSN=WYL.QB.JCL.POLYGEN,
//            DISP=(,KEEP),
//            UNIT=SYSDA,
//            VOL=SER=WYL001,
//            SPACE=(TRK,0),
//            DCB=(RECFM=FB,LRECL=80,BLKSIZE=1600)
//
```

volume is WYL001. Your advisor will tell you the serial number to use at your computer center; you should write it in the place provided on the inside front cover. If no one can tell you the serial number of the volume that contains the system catalog, you can get it yourself by reading the allocation messages from a job that uses the catalog. In Figure 4.7, for example, you will see the messages

```
IEF285I    SYSCTLG.VWY001              KEPT
IEF285I    VOL SER NOS=WYL001.
```

These messages tell you that system catalog is on DASD volume WYL001.

Since we are only placing information in the data set label, no space is required and the SPACE parameter requests zero tracks.

Instead of running the job shown in Figure 6.3, we could have created the model DSCB by including the DD1 DD statement in either the job shown in Figure 6.1 or the one in Figure 6.2.

It is not necessary to code DCB information in the model DSCB. You can provide some or all of the information when the generation is created.

CREATING AND ACCESSING A GENERATION

Figure 6.4 illustrates a simple two-step job. In the first step, IEBGENER is used to create a generation data set named POLYGEN using as input the first thirty records listed in Appendix C. (These data were used in Chapter 3 to create

FIGURE 6.4

Two-step job using generation data sets

```
//JCLQB548 JOB ,'MR. GREEN',
//          REGION=40K
//STEP1    EXEC PGM=IEBGENER
//SYSPRINT DD SYSOUT=A
//SYSUT1   DD *
13009REED,TINA              A0842000426072100      74
15174HANDJANY,HAIDEH        H0229000220022900      71
17337BUTERO,MAURICE         H0501000434050100      63
19499LAFER,BRUCE            A0706000819050000      52
21661LEE,SUI               A0390170303030017      76
23821COOPER,LUCY            L0745000730070000      64
25980NELSON,LAWRENCE        L0513000217051300      78
28138KRUKIS,SONIA           A0346000510034600      59
30295CHEN,YIN               H0295000514010000      81
32451SIMPKINS,KEVIN         L0388000321038806      76
34605PORTER,MICHELE         A0627500128042700      65
36759DECICCO,RICHARD        A0255000619010000      71
38912ABREU,JUANITA          H0732001030070000      80
41063HIGH,CAROL             L0311000521031100      82
43214ENGLISH,REYNOLDS       A0443000228043300      82
45363LEE,BOHYON             A0515000214050000      79
47512THOMPSON,STANLEY       H0640750307064075      66
49659VALDEZ,FABIO           L0706000430070600      71
51805AMATO,ROBERT           A0466000417015000      63
53950RIZZUTO,JAMES          A0693000822000000      81
56094SCHWARTZ,MICHAEL       H1037000605050000      67
58238RUFINO,CARLOS          L0673000520047300      64
60380MORLEY,JOHN            A0786000514078600      71
62521BREVIL,JAMES           H0812000314081200      55
64660FALCONER,EDWARD        L1080000227008000      74
66799MARTIN,KATHLEEN        L0895000129089500      65
68937YEUNG,SUK              A0517000816050000      49
71074PAUL,MARINA            A0441000414034100      80
73210FRADIN,SHIRLEY         L0668000728066800      56
75344BURNS,JEFFREY          L0706000226070000      57
/*
//SYSUT2   DD DSN=WYL.QB.JCL.POLYGEN(+1),
//            DISP=(,PASS),
//            UNIT=SYSDA,
//            VOL=SER=WYL005,
//            SPACE=(TRK,(2,1))
//SYSIN    DD DUMMY
//STEP2    EXEC PGM=IEBPTPCH
//SYSPRINT DD SYSOUT=A
//SYSUT1   DD DSN=WYL.QB.JCL.POLYGEN(+1),
//            DISP=(OLD,CATLG)
//SYSUT2   DD SYSOUT=A
//SYSIN    DD *
 PRINT MAXFLDS=1
 RECORD FIELD=(80)
/*
//
```

FIGURE 6.5

Two jobs using generation data sets

```
//JCLQB550 JOB ,'MRS. WHITE',
//          REGION=40K
//STEP1     EXEC PGM=IEBGENER
//SYSPRINT DD SYSOUT=A
//SYSUT1    DD *
13009REED,TINA                A0842000426072100      74
15174HANDJANY,HAIDEH          H0229000220022900      71
17337BUTERO,MAURICE           H0501000434050100      63
19499LAFER,BRUCE              A0706000819050000      52
21661LEE,SUI                  A0390170303030017      76
23821COOPER,LUCY              L0745000730070000      64
25980NELSON,LAWRENCE          L0513000217051300      78
28138KRUKIS,SONIA             A0346000510034600      59
30295CHEN,YIN                 H0295000514010000      81
32451SIMPKINS,KEVIN           L0388000321038806      76
34605PORTER,MICHELE           A0627500128042700      65
36759DECICCO,RICHARD          A0255000619010000      71
38912ABREU,JUANITA            H0732001030070000      80
41063HIGH,CAROL               L0311000521031100      82
43214ENGLISH,REYNOLDS         A0443000228043300      82
45363LEE,BOHYON               A0515000214050000      79
47512THOMPSON,STANLEY         H0640750307064075      66
49659VALDEZ,FABIO             L0706000430070600      71
51805AMATO,ROBERT             A0466000417015000      63
53950RIZZUTO,JAMES            A0693000822000000      81
56094SCHWARTZ,MICHAEL         H1037000605050000      67
58238RUFINO,CARLOS            L0673000520047300      64
60380MORLEY,JOHN              A0786000514078600      71
62521BREVIL,JAMES             H0812000314081200      55
64660FALCONER,EDWARD          L1080000227008000      74
66799MARTIN,KATHLEEN          L0895000129089500      65
68937YEUNG,SUK                A0517000816050000      49
71074PAUL,MARINA              A0441000414034100      80
73210FRADIN,SHIRLEY           L0668000728066800      56
75344BURNS,JEFFREY            L0706000226070000      57
/*
//SYSUT2    DD DSN=WYL.QB.JCL.POLYGEN(+1),
//             DISP=(,CATLG),
//             UNIT=SYSDA,
//             VOL=SER=WYL005,
//             SPACE=(TRK,(2,1))
//SYSIN     DD DUMMY
//
//JCLQB552 JOB ,'J.C.LEWIS',
//          REGION=32K
//STEP1     EXEC PGM=IEBPTPCH
//SYSPRINT DD SYSOUT=A
//SYSUT1    DD DSN=WYL.QB.JCL.POLYGEN(0),
//             DISP=SHR
//SYSUT2    DD SYSOUT=A
//SYSIN     DD *
 PRINT MAXFLDS=1
 RECORD FIELD=(80)
/*
//
```

the original version of POLYFILE.) In the second step, IEBPTPCH is used to print the newly created generation. You will note that in both steps the relative number is (+1).

Figure 6.5 does exactly the same thing using two jobs instead of one job with two steps. The difference to be noted is that the relative number in the second step is (0). This is because there is an index in which the generation number is maintained by the system, and the generation number is updated after the job ends. Thus in Figure 6.4 the generation number is not updated until after both steps are executed. In Figure 6.5, the generation number is updated after the first job ends. In the second job, we want to print the current generation; thus we use a relative number of (0).

Figure 6.6 shows how one generation of POLYGEN may be modified to create a new generation. The input to IEBGENER consists of two data sets. The first data set is the current generation of POLYGEN, which is accessed using the relative number (0); the second data set consists of the last ten records in Appendix C. These two data sets are concatenated to form the input to IEBGENER. Concatenation allows more than one data set to be read with one

FIGURE 6.6

Creating a new generation

```
//JCLQB554 JOB ,'MRS. PEACOCK',
//          REGION=40K
//STEP1     EXEC PGM=IEBGENER
//SYSPRINT DD SYSOUT=A
//SYSUT1    DD DSN=WYL.QB.JCL.POLYGEN(0),
//             DISP=SHR
//          DD *
77478KATZ,HAL              A0485000406038500      64
79610WRIGHT,DONNA          H0926000901092000      75
81742CUOMO,DONNA           L0900000313090000      69
83872LOPEZ,ANNA            A0679000716010000      80
86002ALEXANDER,LISA        A0402000623030200      73
88130GOLDBERG,LORI         H0987000524095000      67
92057HOFMANN,PATRICA       H0737000315040000      77
92384PUGH,CLIFFORD         A0750000423075000      80
94509FERRIS,LAURA          A0135000815013500      73
96633BERGIN,MICHAEL        L1608000116100000      74
/*
//SYSUT2    DD DSN=WYL.QB.JCL.POLYGEN(+1),
//             DISP=(,CATLG),
//             UNIT=SYSDA,
//             VOL=SER=WYL002,
//             SPACE=(TRK,(2,1))
//SYSIN     DD DUMMY
//
```

FIGURE 6.7

Listing an entire generation data group

```
//JCLQB556 JOB ,'J.C.LEWIS',
//             REGION=32K
//STEP1    EXEC PGM=IEBPTPCH
//SYSPRINT  DD SYSOUT=A
//SYSUT1    DD DSN=WYL.QB.JCL.POLYGEN,
//             DISP=SHR
//SYSUT2    DD SYSOUT=A
//SYSIN     DD *
 PRINT MAXFLDS=1
 RECORD FIELD=(80)
/*
//
```

DD statement. Concatenation is throughly discussed in Chapter 8. At this point all you need to know is that the current generation of POLYGEN and the ten input-stream records are read as one data set.

The output of Figure 6.6 consists of a new generation of POLYGEN, which is specified using the relative number (+1). Figure 6.5 may seem similar to Figure 4.13, in which the last ten records in Appendix C were added to the end of the original version of POLYFILE, but in fact the two job streams are very different. In Figure 4.13 there was only one version of POLYFILE. At the end of the job, POLYFILE contained all forty records in Appendix C. In contrast, after the job in Figure 6.6 is run, there exist two generations of POLYGEN. The older generation contains the first thirty records from Appendix C, while the current generation contains all forty records.

If all the generations in a generation data group have the same data control block information, then the entire generation data group may be processed using one DD statement. Figure 6.7 illustrates this with the utility program IEBPTPCH. This job will print all the generations in the generation data group. Notice that when you wish to process the entire generation data group, you code the DSN without a relative number.

USING THE MODEL DSCB

When the data sets were created in Figures 6.4, 6.5, and 6.6, no DCB information was provided; the information was obtained from the model DSCB. However, you don't have to use the information in the model DSCB exactly

FIGURE 6.8

(a) Modifying DCB information from model DSCB

```
//DD1       DD DSN=WYL.QB.JCL.POLYGEN(+1),
//             DISP=(,CATLG),
//             UNIT=SYSDA,
//             VOL=SER=WYL002,
//             SPACE=(TRK,(2,1)),
//             DCB=BLKSIZE=880
```

(b) Using model DSCB from another generation data group

```
//DD2       DD DSN=GEN.DATA.COLLECT(+1),
//             DISP=(,CATLG),
//             UNIT=SYSDA,
//             VOL=SER=WYL001,
//             SPACE=(TRK,(3,1)),
//             DCB=(GEN.DATA.GROUP)
```

(c) Using modified model DSCB from another generation data group

```
//DD3       DD DSN=GEN.DATA.COLECT(+1),
//             DISP=(,CATLG),
//             UNIT=SYSDA,
//             VOL=SER=WYL005,
//             SPACE=(TRK,(3,1),RLSE),
//             DCB=(GEN.DATA.GROUP,LRECL=40)
```

as provided. Figure 6.8a illustrates taking all the DCB information from the model DSCB except the block size.

Figure 6.8b illustrates the creation of a generation using the model DSCB of another generation data group. In this case, a generation of GEN.DATA.COLLECT is created using the model DSCB of GEN.DATA.GROUP.

Figure 6.8c illustrates the use of a modified model DSCB of another generation data group. In this example, the DCB information is taken from the model DSCB of GEN.DATA.GROUP, but the logical record length is set equal to 40.

DELETING A GENERATION GROUP INDEX

The IEHPROGM control statement DLTX is used to delete a generation group index. Before a generation group index may be deleted, all the generations

FIGURE 6.9

Deleting a generation group index using IEHPROGM

```
//JCLQB542 JOB ,'J.C.LEWIS',
//              REGION=36K
//STEPDLTX EXEC PGM=IEHPROGM
//SYSPRINT DD SYSOUT=A
//SYSIN    DD *
 DLTX INDEX=WYL.QB.JCL.POLYGEN
/*
//
```

must be scratched. The generations may be scratched using either IEHPROGM
or IEFBR14. Figure 6.9 shows how to use DLTX to delete the generation group
index created in Figure 6.1.

Generation group indexes that were created using the IDCAMS command
DEFINE GDG are deleted using the IDCAMS command DELETE. The DELETE command is discussed in Chapter 13.

PROS AND CONS

The main advantage of using a generation data group is that it permits the
same JCL to be reused without change. For example, each time the job illustrated in Figure 6.4 is run, a new data set is created. If the output of
IEBGENER were not a generation, the data set would have to be scratched
before the job could be rerun. Similarly, the second job in Figure 6.5 prints
the current generation. No matter how many generations are created, this
job may be used to print the current generation.

The main disadvantage of using a generation data group is that machine
procedures must be strictly enforced. If, for example, a machine operator
starts a job, cancels it, and then starts it again, the results may be disastrous
because the generation numbers may be updated twice.

The system programmer must keep an eye on the generation number
because the results are unpredictable when the maximum value of 9999 is
reached.

EXERCISES

1. What is a generation data group?

2. What kind of data sets may be included in a generation data group?

3. What types of devices may be used with a generation data group?

4. How long may a generation data group DSN be?

5. How is one generation distinguished from another?

6. How would an application programmer usually specify a generation?

7. How might a system programmer specify a generation?

8. When is a generation group index updated?

9. From where may the DCB information be obtained if it is not specified in the DD statement when the generation is created?

10. What two items must be created before a generation data group may be used?

11. What information is included in the index?

12. How would the index be created?

PROGRAMMING ASSIGNMENTS

1. Use IEHPROGM to create a generation group index. In the same job, create a model DSCB.

2. With the first thirty records in Appendix D as input, use IEBGENER to create a generation.

3. With the first generation and the last ten records in Appendix D as input, use IEBGENER to create a new generation.

4. Use IEBPTPCH to print both generations. In how many ways may this be done?

5. Use IEFBR14 to scratch the two generations and the model DSCB you created. Use IEHPROGM to delete the generation group index.

SUMMARY

In this chapter you have learned

- how a generation data group is organized
- how to use IEHPROGM to create a generation group index
- how to create a model data set control block
- how to create and access a generation
- how to use IEBPTPCH to list all the generations in a generation data group

CHAPTER 7

MASS STORAGE

LEARNING OBJECTIVES

IN THIS CHAPTER YOU WILL LEARN

- why a mass storage system is needed

- what a mass storage system is

- how to create a data set on a mass storage volume

- how to access a data set on a mass storage volume

- how to use the parameter MSVGP

YOU WILL ALSO LEARN THE MEANINGS OF THE FOLLOWING TERMS:

- data cartridge, or cartridge

- destaging

- Mass Storage System (MSS)

- mass storage volume (MSV)

- staging

DATA STORAGE—MSS AND MSV

As the volume of data retained in data processing installations has grown, data processing management has been confronted with the problem of where to store the data. The choice in the past has been between tape and DASD.

Tape is relatively inexpensive, quickly and relatively easily mounted, easy to transport from one installation to another, and easy to store. Tape does have its disadvantages, however. Only physical sequential data sets may be stored on tape volumes. Libraries, for example, may be stored on tape only in unloaded form, which is not directly usable. In most installations, an entire volume is used for each data set, even if the data set only requires, say, 300 feet out of the 2400 feet of tape. This results in each installation's storing a large number of tape volumes in its library. When a particular tape volume is needed for a job, the operator must first obtain the tape from the library before he or she can mount it and run the job. Although the mounting of the tape reel on the tape unit may go quickly, the entire process (including retrieving the tape from the library and returning it after the job ends) can require a significant amount of time, depending on the library procedures. In addition, the wrong volume is sometimes mounted. The operator then generally has to go to the library again for the correct tape volume. In some such cases, the job must be canceled and rerun.

Although DASD avoids these problems, magnetic disk tends to be more expensive than tape. While a reel of tape costs about $20, a DASD volume costs about $500. In addition, to mount and dismount a DASD volume takes a considerable amount of time. And DASD volumes tend to be more delicate than tape reels. If you drop a tape reel, it probably will not be damaged. DASD volumes, on the other hand, are more likely to be damaged, and because of their awkward size and weight they are more likely to be dropped. DASD is, however, more desirable than tape in that all types of data sets may reside on it.

What data processing management wants is a device that provides the usability of DASD at the cost of tape. The 3850 **Mass Storage System (MSS)** approaches this ideal. An MSS provides the equivalent of up to 4720 3336 Disk Packs. The MSS is described in *OS/VS MSS Services Reference Information* (GC35-0017).

In an MSS, data are stored on a **data cartridge**, often simply called a **cartridge**. Two of these cartridges can hold the same amount of information as a 3336-disk volume, and the two cartridges together are referred to as a **mass storage volume (MSV)**. Each cartridge in the MSV is stored in a hexagonal (six-sided) cell. When data from a particular cartridge are wanted, an accessor removes the cartridge from its cell. The data are then transferred to a 3336 Disk Pack where they may be accessed by the application program. This process of taking data from the MSV and writing them on a 3336 Disk Pack is called **staging**. A data set that is to reside on an MSS is actually created on a 3330-disk drive using a 3336-disk volume. After the data set is closed, it is copied from the 3336-disk volume to an MSV. This process is called **destaging**.

The important thing to remember is that from the application programmer's point of view a 3336 Disk Pack is being used. There is no difference in the way the programmer writes a program, and there are only some very minor differences in the JCL, which we will discuss later.

An MSS does create more work for the system programmer, however. Since the MSS can have the equivalent of up to 4720 3336 Disk Packs, it is desirable to form groups of cartridges that are related in some way. For example, you would probably want one group for payroll and another for, say, inventory. You would initially establish a certain number of groups, and later, as the system was fine-tuned, create more. Groups are created using the CREATEG command of the utility program IDCAMS. Once a group is established, volumes are created using the CREATEV command of IDCAMS. This creation process gives two cartridges a volume serial number so that they become an MSV. At the same time, the MSV may be assigned to a group. When the group is created, it has a default space allocation. This means that if you create a data set and name a group instead of a volume, the SPACE parameter is not needed; the system can obtain the default space from the group.

MSS JCL PARAMETERS

Setting the UNIT parameter to 3330V indicates that the unit referenced is an MSS. In every other way, the UNIT parameter is coded as it is for any DASD.

The one new parameter is MSVGP, which is coded on the DD statement. This parameter is used only when a data set is being created. When this parameter is used, the serial subparameter in the VOL parameter is not coded. The system assigns an MSV from the group named by the MSVGP parameter.

CREATING A DATA SET ON AN MSS

Figure 7.1 illustrates examples of the DD statements required to create data sets on the MSS. You can tell that all of these examples apply to an MSS because UNIT=3330V is coded.

Let us start with a sequential data set created on any MSV belonging to a particular group; Figure 7.1a illustrates this case. It is particularly interesting to look at what is not coded. There is no VOL parameter. The system will go to group PAYROL and use any available MSV in the group. In addition, the SPACE parameter is not coded. Because an MSV group is named, the system

CREATING A DATA SET ON AN MSS

FIGURE 7.1

(a) Creating a sequential data set on MSS using MSV group

```
//SEQDATA   DD DSN=SEQDAT,
//             DISP=(,CATLG),
//             UNIT=3330V,
//             MSVGP=PAYROL,
//             DCB=(LRECL=30,BLKSIZE=1680,RECFM=FB)
```

(b) Creating a library or MSS using MV group

```
//PDSDATA   DD DSN=PDSLIB,
//             DISP=(,CATLG),
//             UNIT=3330V,   .
//             MSVGP=PAYROL,
//             SPACE=(CYL,(10,2,5)),
//             DCB=(LRECL=80,BLKSIZE=1680,RECFM=FB)
```

(c) Creating a sequential data set on specified volume

```
//SEQDATA   DD DSN=SEQDATA,
//             DISP=(,CATLG),
//             UNIT=3330V,
//             VOL=SER=MSS010,
//             SPACE=(CYL,(100,10),RLSE),
//             DCB=(LRECL=80,BLKSIZE=1680,RECFM=FB)
```

will use the default space allocation that is part of the MSV group. The disposition is coded so that at job end the data set will be cataloged. Since the specific MSV is not named, the MSV would need to be learned from the deallocation messages if the data set were not cataloged. By cataloging the data set, we eliminate the need to know which MSV is selected for use by the system. All other parameters are those that you are familiar with.

Figure 7.1b shows a DD statement that may be used to create a PDS on an MSS. In this example, unlike the previous one, the SPACE parameter is coded. When the group indicated by the MSVGP parameter was created, directory blocks were not specified. As a result, the space default of the group can never be used when a PDS is being created, since the only way the system knows that a PDS is being created is by the specification of the directory blocks in the SPACE parameter. Again, a disposition of CATLG is specified for the PDS, so that we do not need to check the deallocation messages to learn which MSV was used.

The last example specifies in the VOL parameter the MSV that is to be used for the data set. Figure 7.1c illustrates the creation of a sequential data

CHAPTER 7 / MASS STORAGE

set on the MSV named MSS010. Since the MSVGP parameter is not specified, the SPACE parameter must be coded. A disposition of CATLG was chosen, although in this case KEEP could have been coded.

ACCESSING A DATA SET ON AN MSS

Accessing a data set on an MSS is virtually the same as accessing a data set on a DASD. Figure 7.2a illustrates accessing a cataloged data set. Whether the data set is a physical sequential or partitioned data set does not matter in coding this DD statement. The fact that this data set resided on an MSS likewise makes no difference to the DD statement coding.

Figure 7.2b illustrates a DD statement that accesses an uncataloged data set. Since UNIT=3330V is coded, we can see that the data set resides on an MSS. However, there is no way of knowing if this data set is physical sequential or partitioned.

If you use the DD statement in either Figure 7.2a or Figure 7.2b to access a physical sequential data set, the data set will be staged when the open instruction is issued by the program. This means that the first time the program tries to access the data set, it is moved from the MSV to a 3336-disk pack where it is actually processed.

If, on the other hand, the DD statement in either Figure 7.2a or Figure

FIGURE 7.2

(a) Accessing a cataloged data set on MSS

```
//ANYDSN     DD DSN=SEQDAT,
//              DISP=OLD
```

(b) Accessing a data set on MSS

```
//ANYDSN     DD DSN=SEQDAT,
//              DISP=OLD,
//              UNIT=3330V,
//              VOL=SER=MSS010
```

(c) Accessing a library on MSS

```
//PDSLIB     DD DSN=PDSLIB,
//              DISP=OLD,
//              DCB=OPTCD=H
```

7.2b is used to access a PDS, then when the PDS is opened only the directory is staged. Each member is staged as it is needed. If for some reason you want the entire PDS staged when the PDS is opened, then set the OPTCD subparameter in the DCB parameter equal to H. This is illustrated in Figure 7.2c.

MSS usage, in general, puts no additional burden on the application programmer. The system programmer using the utility IDCAMS must create the groups and MSV's and give the group name or the volume serial number to the application programmer.

EXERCISES

1. How many cartridges are in an MSV?

2. Where are the data when your program accesses them?

3. Define staging.

4. Define destaging.

5. What is the unique parameter that applies only to an MSS? On which JCL statement is this parameter coded?

6. When creating a data set, how do you tell the system that it is to reside on an MSV?

7. What utility program is used to create an MSV? Which command is used?

8. When creating a physical sequential data set, why don't you need to specify the SPACE parameter? What must be specified?

9. Why must the SPACE parameter always be specified for a library?

10. What does it mean when the subparameter OPTCD=H is coded for a PDS?

PROGRAMMING ASSIGNMENTS

The following programming assignments can be done only if your computer center has an MSS.

1. Repeat the first programming assignment in Chapter 3, storing the data set on an MSS.

2. Execute a job to have IEBGENER list the data set you created in Programming Assignment 1, above.

3. Execute a job to add the additional records in Appendix D to the data set you created in Programming Assignment 1, above. In the same job, use IEBPTPCH to produce a listing of the complete data set.

SUMMARY

In this chapter you have learned

*   why a mass storage system is needed
*   what a mass storage system is
*   how to create a data set on a mass storage volume
*   how to access a data set on a mass storage volume

CHAPTER 8

USING SYSTEM PROCEDURES

LEARNING OBJECTIVES

IN THIS CHAPTER YOU WILL LEARN

- what a compiler is

- what a procedure is

- how to use cataloged procedures to compile a program

- what the loader is

- how to use cataloged procedures to compile and execute programs

- what the linkage editor is

- how to use cataloged procedures to compile and link edit programs

- how to use cataloged procedures to compile, link edit, and execute programs

- how to add a program to a load library

- how to execute a program from a load library

YOU WILL ALSO LEARN THE MEANINGS OF THE FOLLOWING TERMS:

- assembler

- automatic-call library

- cataloged procedures

- compiler

- concatenation

- external references

- forward reference

LEARNING OBJECTIVES

- linkage editor
- loader
- load module
- map
- module
- object module
- overlay
- override statement
- procedure
- procstep
- procstepname
- segment
- source code
- source module
- symbolic parameters
- temporary data set

The examples in the previous chapters have all involved executing programs. In your EXEC statement you coded PGM=. If you examine JCL used by professionals, you will not usually find PGM= on their EXEC statements, because they usually use procedures. A **procedure** is precoded JCL. You probably have encountered procedures in your language-coding classes, where they are commonly used to compile programs. We will start our study with these commonly used procedures. However, we will first discuss compilers so that you will have a better understanding of what these procedures do. In your professional career, you may never need many of the compiler functions you will be shown; the compiler is being used here as a vehicle to illustrate some aspects of JCL.

FUNCTION OF A COMPILER

Computers can only follow instructions entered in machine language, but people usually have a great deal of difficulty working with machine language. To make computers more accessible, computer specialists developed easier methods of telling the computer what to do.

All instructions consist of an operation (what to do) and one or more operands (what to do it to). In machine language, these instructions are written in binary notation (ones and zeros). The first programming simplification consisted of replacing the binary operation with a symbolic one. The programmer could then write, for example, A instead of 00011010 to mean add. Now, however, the program was no longer directly executable. It became the input to another program that replaced the symbolics with their binary values. The next step in the simplification process was to replace the binary values of the operands with symbolic names, now known as variables. This line of development led to the modern **assembler** language and the assembler program that usually generates one machine-language instruction for each assembly-language instruction.

Assembler languages have many advantages over machine language, but they are difficult to learn and programs written in them usually require a relatively long time for coding and testing. As a result, assembler language does not provide sufficient simplification for most people.

Computer specialists and scientists turned the problem around and developed the requirements for a language that would meet users' needs. The languages that meet these requirements are called high-level languages. FORTRAN, whose name comes from FORmula TRANslation, was developed to meet the needs of the scientific community, and COBOL, whose name comes from COmmon Business Oriented Language, was developed for the business community. Programs were written which would translate a program written in a particular high-level language into machine language. A program that does this translation is called a **compiler**. Each high-level language has its own compiler.

At one time, there was a distinct difference between a compiler and an assembler. A compiler generated several machine-language instructions for each high-level language instruction, while an assembler always generated one machine-language instruction for each assembler instruction. Now the distinction has become blurred because many assembler languages have macro instructions which generate several machine-language instructions for each instruction. For simplicity here references to a high-level language mean assembler language as well as FORTRAN, COBOL, and PL/I.

COMPILING A PROGRAM

Figure 8.1 shows a system flowchart for a standard compilation. With some minor differences, this flowchart applies to FORTRAN, COBOL, and PL/I compilations as well as assembler. The high-level language program, called the **source code**, is input to the compiler using the ddname SYSIN. Figure 8.1 shows cards, but there is no restriction regarding medium. Work data sets used by the compiler for intermediate storage are shown by the ddnames SYSUT1, SYSUT2, SYSUT3, and SYSUT4; however, only the COBOL compiler uses all four. The PL/I compiler uses only one; FORTRAN, two; and assembler, three. The DD statement SYSLIB applies only to the assembler; it is used by the assembler for macro definitions and precoded assembler code accessible with the COPY command. The SYSPRINT data set holds the program listing and compiler messages in all four cases.

There are three more ddnames in Figure 8.1, SYSPUNCH, SYSGO, and SYSLIN. They are used to hold the compiler output, which is usually called an **object module**. The forked output path to these data sets indicates that at any given time you might want one or the other, but usually not both. SYSPUNCH is shown as a deck of cards, and SYSLIN and SYSGO as a disk data set; these are the system defaults. SYSGO is the ddname used by the assembler, and SYSLIN is used by the three other high-level languages we are discussing.

The compilers set return codes which may be tested with the COND parameter in subsequent steps. In general, if the return code is 0, there are no errors in the compilation and the object module, if produced, is good. If the return code is 4, there are warning messages, but the object module is probably good. If the return code is 8, there are errors, but the object module may be good; the programmer should examine the error list before trying to use the object module. If the return code is 12, then the errors are sufficiently serious that the object module is useless. If the return code is 16, then you have a disaster. In this case, it is not unusual for the compiler itself to have failed.

FIGURE 8.1

System flowchart for compilation

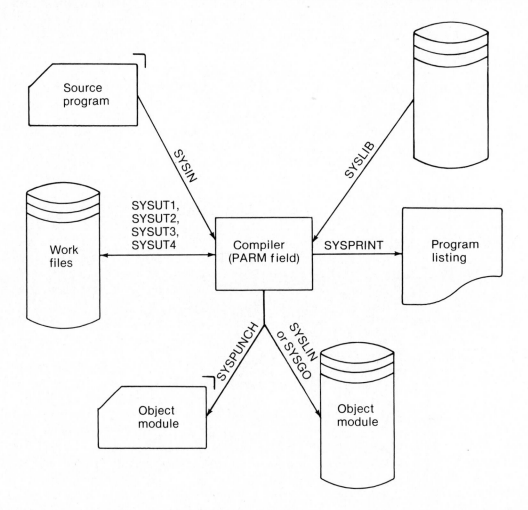

Even though the object module consists of machine-language instructions, it is not executable. To be executable the object module must be processed by the linkage editor or loader. We will discuss these two programs later.

PROCEDURES TO COMPILE A PROGRAM

Whenever a program is written in a high-level language, it must be compiled before it can be used. Obviously, it is necessary to code JCL to compile a program. How will this JCL differ for the various PL/I programs you are working on? How will this JCL differ for your PL/I program and your colleague's? Very little — with minor modification, you can use the same JCL for all your PL/I program compilations and so can anyone else. Why then should you have to code the same JCL for each program you write? You don't; you use procedures, which are precoded JCL. Procedures are stored in a system library usually named SYS1.PROCLIB. If you wished to write a procedure and add it to SYS1.PROCLIB, you would use the utility program IEBUPDTE, which was discussed in Chapter 5. Procedures stored in this library are called **cataloged procedures**. A different kind of procedure, called an in-stream procedure, will be discussed in Chapter 9.

We will discuss how to write a procedure in Chapter 9. In this chapter we will discuss how to use procedures in general and how to use the procedures to compile and execute your programs in particular. Figure 8.2 contains listings of IBM procedures to compile PL/I, COBOL, FORTRAN, and assembler programs. In this section we will study the contents of these procedures and how to use them.

Names of Procedures

The name of a cataloged procedure is its member name in the system library SYS1.PROCLIB. For example, the JCL used to compile a COBOL program is stored in SYS1.PROCLIB as member COBUC.

Names are assigned to cataloged procedures that are used to compile and execute programs in a way that makes it easy to remember which procedure you want to use. The first three or four letters of the name indicate the language the procedure is used with. The COBOL procedures begin with the letters COB, the PL/I procedures with PLI, the FORTRAN procedures with FORT, and the assembler procedures with ASM.

The next letter indicates which version of the compiler is being used. In the procedures discussed here, the COBOL procedures use the letter U, the PL/I and FORTRAN procedures use the letter X, and the assembler procedures use the letter F. This is the most variable part of the name. At your computer center, the FORTRAN procedures might use the letter G and the assembler procedures the letter H, or entirely different letters might be used.

FIGURE 8.2

(a) The COBUC procedure

```
//COB       EXEC PGM=IKFCBL00,PARM='DECK,NOLOAD,SUPMAP',REGION=86K
//SYSPRINT  DD SYSOUT=A
//SYSPUNCH  DD SYSOUT=B
//SYSUT1    DD DSNAME=&&SYSUT1,UNIT=SYSDA,SPACE=(460,(700,100))
//SYSUT2    DD DSNAME=&&SYSUT2,UNIT=SYSDA,SPACE=(460,(700,100))
//SYSUT3    DD DSNAME=&&SYSUT3,UNIT=SYSDA,SPACE=(460,(700,100))
//SYSUT4    DD DSNAME=&&SYSUT4,UNIT=SYSDA,SPACE=(460,(700,100))
```

(b) The PLIXC procedure

```
//PLIXC     PROC
//PLI       EXEC PGM=IEL0AA,PARM='OBJECT,NODECK',REGION=100K
//SYSPRINT  DD SYSOUT=A,
//SYSLIN    DD DSN=&&LOADSET,DISP=(MOD,PASS),UNIT=SYSSQ,
//            SPACE=(80,(250,100))
//SYSUT1    DD DSN=&&SYSUT1,UNIT=SYSDA,SPACE=(1024,(200,50),,CONTIG,ROUND),
//            DCB=BLKSIZE=1024
```

(c) The FORTXC procedure

```
//FORTXC PROC FXPGM=IFEAAB,FXREGN=256K,FXPDECK=DECK,              +39450000
//             FXPOLST=NOLIST,FXPOPT=0,FXLNSPC='3200,(25,6)'       39500000
//*                                                                39550000
//*                                                                39600000
//*      PARAMETER   DEFAULT-VALUE   USAGE                         39650000
//*                                                                39700000
//*      FXPGM       IFEAAB          COMPILER NAME                 39750000
//*      FXREGN      256K            FORT-STEP REGION              39800000
//*      FXPDECK     DECK            COMPILER DECK OPTION          39850000
//*      FXPOLST     NOLIST          COMPILER LIST OPTION          39900000
//*      FXPOPT      0               COMPILER OPTIMIZATION         39950000
//*      FXLNSPC     3200,(25,6)     FORT.SYSLIN SPACE             40000000
//*                                                               +40050000
//FORT   EXEC PGM=&FXPGM,REGION=&FXREGN,COND=(4,LT),               40100000
//           PARM='&FXPDECK,&FXPOLST,OPT(&FXPOPT)'                 40150000
//SYSPRINT DD SYSOUT=A,DCB=BLKSIZE=3429                            40200000
//SYSTFRM  DD SYSOUT=A                                             40250000
//SYSUT1   DD UNIT=SYSSQ,SPACE=(3465,(3,3)),DCB=BLKSIZE=3465       40300000
//SYSUT2   DD UNIT=SYSSQ,SPACE=(2048,(10,10))                     +40350000
//SYSPUNCH DD SYSOUT=B,DCB=BLKSIZE=3440                            40400000
//SYSLIN   DD DSN=&&LOADSET,DISP=(MOD,PASS),UNIT=SYSSQ,
//            SPACE=(&FXLNSPC),DCB=BLKSIZE=3200
```

(d) The ASMFC procedure

```
//ASMFC    PROC MAC='SYS1.MACLIB',MAC1='SYS1.MACLIB'
//ASM      EXEC PGM=IFOX00,REGION=128K
//SYSLIB   DD DSN=&MAC,DISP=SHR
//         DD DSN=&MAC1,DISP=SHR
//SYSUT1   DD DSN=&&SYSUT1,UNIT=SYSSQ,SPACE=(1700,(600,100)),
//         SEP=(SYSLIB)
//SYSUT2   DD DSN=&&SYSUT2,UNIT=SYSSQ,SPACE=(1700,(300,50)),
//         SEP=(SYSLIB,SYSUT1)
//SYSUT3   DD DSN=&&SYSUT3,UNIT=SYSSQ,SPACE=(1700,(300,50))
//SYSPRINT DD SYSOUT=A,DCB=BLKSIZE=1089
//SYSPUNCH DD SYSOUT=B
```

CHAPTER 8 / USING SYSTEM PROCEDURES

In fact, there may be several procedures for different versions of the same language.

The last part of the name indicates what the procedure does. Names of procedures that only compile end with the letter C. Names of procedures that compile a program and invoke the loader to execute it end with the letters CG (the G stands for GO, which is what executing is called). Names of procedures that compile and link edit end with the letters CL, where the L stands for link edit. Finally, names of procedures that compile, link edit, and execute end with the letters CLG.

The COBUC Procedure

Let us examine the procedure COBUC in Figure 8.2a, which is used to compile a COBOL program. There is an EXEC statement with a stepname of COB. We must know the stepname for reasons that will be clear when we use the procedure. The program that is executed is named IKFCBLOO. That is the name of the COBOL compiler.

The EXEC statement in the COBUC procedure uses the PARM keyword parameter. In Chapter 5 the PARM parameter was used to pass the word MOD or NEW to IEBUPDTE. Here it is used to pass three values, DECK, NOLOAD, and SUPMAP, to the compiler. Information is passed to the compiler to request special processing. The values that may be passed, their meanings, and the default values are described in the programmer's guide for each language. (See bibliography.)

The DECK and NOLOAD values cause the compiler to write the object module to the SYSPUNCH data set and not to the SYSLIN data set. You will notice that the SYSLIN DD statement is not included. Since it is not used, it is not necessary.

The SYSIN DD statement is not included in the procedure. The SYSIN data set points to your source code. The source code is frequently in card form, but it can also be on tape or DASD as either a sequential data set or a member of a PDS. Since the DD statement for the source code cannot be defined in advance, it is not included in the procedure. You must code the SYSIN DD statement when you use the procedure.

Temporary Data Sets

The data set names on the SYSUT1, SYSUT2, SYSUT3, and SYSUT4 DD statements do not fit the description of a valid data set name that you learned in Chapter 3; they start with a double ampersand. Something must be wrong!

PROCEDURES TO COMPILE A PROGRAM

This is obviously incorrect, and you would have a JCL error.

The only time a symbolic parameter does not have to have a value assigned to it is when the symbolic parameter stands for a data set name. For example:

```
//TEMP     DD DSN=&NAME,
```

If a value is assigned to NAME, it acts just like a symbolic parameter. But if a value is not assigned, &NAME is assumed to be a temporary data set name, equivalent to &&NAME.

Please note the symbolic parameter FXLNSPC in Figure 8.2c. Unlike the values assigned to other parameters, the value assigned to it includes special characters (in this case, commas and parentheses). To set a symbolic parameter equal to a value that includes special characters, you must include the entire expression within apostrophes. The proper way to do this is illustrated by the value assigned to symbolic parameter FXLNSPC in Figure 8.2c. If, in Figure 8.3c, FXPOLST='LIST', had been coded, there would have been no problem. If, on the other hand, FXLNSPC = 3200,(50,6) had been coded on the EXEC statement, a JCL error would have resulted.

The ASMFC Procedure

CONCATENATION. If you examine the procedure ASMFC in Figure 8.2d, you will observe that following the SYSLIB DD statement is a DD statement without a ddname. This is called **concatenation** and is not restricted to procedures.* If you wrote a program to do some statistical analysis on payroll, for example, and decided that you wanted to use as input both the January and February data instead of just the January data, you would not need to either change the program or run it twice. You could concatenate the two data sets. The following is an example:

```
//INPUT    DD DSN=JAN,
//            DISP=SHR
//         DD DSN=FEB,
//            DISP=SHR
```

In this case, when end of file is reached on the data set JAN, processing con-

---

* Concatenation was used in Figure 6.6.

tinues with the data set FEB. When end of file on FEB is encountered, then the end-of-file processing in the program takes place. Although the above example shows only 2 data sets being concatenated, it would be just as correct to show up to 255 for sequential data sets or 16 for partitioned data sets.

For data sets to be concatenated, they must be the same type. You cannot concatenate a physical sequential data set with a library, although you can concatenate a physical sequential data set with a member of a library provided that they have the same record length.

Concatenated data sets must have the same record length, but they may have different blocksizes. Just remember to code the data set whose blocksize is largest first. If you wish to concatenate two data sets, ALEF and BET, where ALEF's blocksize is 1600 and BET's is 3200, then you code

```
//INCATDD   DD DSN=BET,
//             DISP=SHR
//          DD DSN=ALEF,
//             DISP=SHR
```

The DD statement for data set BET is coded first because BET's blocksize is larger than ALEF's.

JCL TO EXECUTE THE ASMFC PROCEDURE.   Figure 8.3d illustrates use of the procedure ASMC. In the EXEC statement, the symbolic parameter MAC1 is set equal to 'MT.SOURCE'. In the PROC statement in procedure ASMFC in Figure 8.2d are two symbolic parameters, MAC and MAC1. Both are set equal to 'SYS1.MACLIB', which is the system macro library. These symbolic parameters are used in the concatenated SYSLIB statements to supply the data set names. Obviously, we do not need or really want to concatenate 'SYS1.MACLIB' to itself. The second DD statement is a place holder, which makes it easy for a user to supply his or her own library. In Figure 8.3d, this was done by setting MAC1 equal to 'MT.SOURCE'. You will notice that MT.SOURCE is enclosed in apostrophes because it includes a special character, a period. If the assembler program does not find what it is looking for in SYS1.MACLIB, it will search MT.SOURCE.

The three DD statements that follow the EXEC statement in Figure 8.3d are used to change the SYSLIB-concatenated DD statements. The first one contains the ddname ASM.SYSLIB but no parameters because the first SYSLIB DD statement in the procedure is satisfactory and doesn't need to be changed. The disposition of the second procedure DD statement is to be changed from SHR to OLD; thus the second DD statement in Figure 8.3d has no ddname and only the disposition is coded. A third library named SCF.SOURCE is to be made available to the assembler, and this is accomplished with the third DD statement in Figure 8.3d. Please note that to add an additional data set to a concatenation in a procedure, you must code DD statements for all the existing DD statements in the procedure and then the additional DD statement. Thus, two DD statement precede the added DD statement. Coding

```
//ASM.SYSLIB DD DSN=SCF.SOURCE,
//              DISP=SHR
```

would have overridden the first SYSLIB DD statement in the procedure and the assembler would not have had access to the system library SYS1.MACLIB. It would only have had access to SCF.SOURCE and MT.SOURCE.

The SYSPUNCH DD statement is also overridden. A lot of errors are to be expected in the initial testing, so it would be a waste of cards to produce an object module.* The important thing to note is that the override for SYSLIB is coded before the override for SYSPUNCH. The reason, as mentioned earlier, is that override statements must be coded in the same order as the DD statements in the procedure.

The last statement in Figure 8.3d is the SYSIN for the assembler source code. This statement must be last, since you must code all the override statements before you code the statements that are added.

Executing a Compile Procedure

Figure 8.4 is an actual COBOL compilation as run on the CUNY system. Local changes have been purposely left in because you will find that the IBM-supplied procedures are modified to meet local needs in most installations.

Line numbers have been added on the left of the listing to make the discussion easier to follow. Lines 1 through 5 represent the JCL entered to run the compilation.

Let us look at lines 6 through 19. Lines 6, 7, 18, and 19 were actually coded. Lines 8 through 17 are from the cataloged procedure. Since COBUC is a relatively simple procedure, it is easy to distinguish the code written by the programmer from the statements supplied by the procedure. However, in

---

* Coding PARM=NODECK would have suppressed punching the object module, but this method shows you how to code the override statement.

FIGURE 8.4

Actual COBOL compilation

```
 1  //JCLOB682 JOB ,'J.C.LEWIS'
 2  //COBCEX  EXEC COBUC
 3  //COB.SYSIN DD *
 4  /*
 5  //
 6   1    //JCLOB682 JOB ,'J.C.LEWIS'                                          00000100
 7   2    //COBCEX  EXEC COBUC                                                 00000200
 8   3    XXCOBUC  PROC SUT1=15,SOBJ=15                                        00000300
 9   4    XXCOB    EXEC PGM=IKFCBL00                                           00000400
10   5    XXSYSLIN DD   DSNAME=&LOADSET,DCB=BLKSIZE=3120,DISP=(MOD,PASS),      00000500
11        XX           UNIT=3330,SPACE=(6400,(&SOBJ,10))                      00000600
12   6    XXSYSPRINT DD SYSOUT=A,DCB=BLKSIZE=1936                             00000700
13   7    XXSYSPUNCH DD SYSOUT=B,DCB=BLKSIZE=2000                             00000800
14   8    XXSYSUT1  DD  UNIT=3330,SPACE=(TRK,(&SUT1,5))                        00000900
15   9    XXSYSUT2  DD  UNIT=3330,SPACE=(TRK,(&SUT1,5))                        00001000
16  10    XXSYSUT3  DD  UNIT=3330,SPACE=(TRK,(&SUT1,5))
17  11    XXSYSUT4  DD  UNIT=3330,SPACE=(TRK,(&SUT1,5))
18  12    //COB.SYSIN DD *,DCB=BLKSIZE=80
19        //
20  STMT NO. MESSAGE
21   5    IEF653I SUBSTITUTION JCL - UNIT=3330,SPACE=(6400,(15,10))
22   8    IEF653I SUBSTITUTION JCL - UNIT=3330,SPACE=(TRK,(15,5))
23   9    IEF653I SUBSTITUTION JCL - UNIT=3330,SPACE=(TRK,(15,5))
24  10    IEF653I SUBSTITUTION JCL - UNIT=3330,SPACE=(TRK,(15,5))
25  11    IEF653I SUBSTITUTION JCL - UNIT=3330,SPACE=(TRK,(15,5))
26
```

```
27 PP 5734-CB2  V4 RELEASE 1.5 10NOV77      IBM OS AMERICAN NATIONAL STANDARD COBOL                    DATE FEB  5,1982
28     1
29 00001             IDENTIFICATION DIVISION.
30 00002             PROGRAM-ID. LISTER.
31 00003             ENVIRONMENT DIVISION.
32 00004             INPUT-OUTPUT SECTION.
33 00005             FILE-CONTROL.
34 00006                 SELECT INPUT-FILE
35 00007                     ASSIGN TO UR-S-INPUT.
36 00008                 SELECT OUTPUT-FILE
37 00009                     ASSIGN TO UR-S-OUTPUT.
38 00010             DATA DIVISION.
39 00011             FILE SECTION.
40 00012             FD  INPUT-FILE
41 00013                 LABEL RECORDS ARE OMITTED.
42 00014             01  INPUT-REC                       PIC X(80).
43 00015             FD  OUTPUT-FILE
44 00016                 LABEL RECORDS ARE OMITTED.
45 00017             01  OUTPUT-REC                      PIC X(80).
46 00018             PROCEDURE DIVISION.
47 00019             PAR-1.
48 00020                 OPEN INPUT INPUT-FILE
49 00021                      OUTPUT OUTPUT-FILE.
50 00022                 READ INPUT-FILE
51 00023                     AT END
52 00024                         STOP RUN.
53 00025                 MOVE INPUT-REC TO OUTPUT-REC.
54 00026                 WRITE OUTPUT-REC
55 00027                     AFTER ADVANCING 1 LINES.
56 00028                 STOP RUN.
57
58 *STATISTICS*  SOURCE RECORDS =  28    DATA DIVISION STATEMENTS =   4    PROCEDURE DIVISION STATEMENTS =    6
59 *OPTIONS IN EFFECT*  SIZE = 124000 BUF = 30000 LINECNT = 52 SPACE1, FLAGW, SEQ, SOURCE
60 *OPTIONS IN EFFECT*  NODMAP, NOPMAP, NOCLIST,  SUPMAP, NOXREF, NOSXREF,  LOAD, NODECK,  APOST,  NOTRUNC, NOFLOW
61 *OPTIONS IN EFFECT*  NOTERM, NONUM, NOBATCH, NONAME, COMPILE=01, STATE, NORESIDENT, NODYNAM, NOLIB, NOSYNTAX
62 *OPTIONS IN EFFECT*  NOOPTIMIZE, NOSYMDMP, NOTEST, VERB, ZWB, SYST, NOENDJOB, NOADV
```

231

most cases this would not be true, so you need a mechanism to separate your JCL from that supplied by the procedure. Looking at the listing, you will note that the first two positions of the statements supplied by the programmer contain slashes, while those from the procedure COBUC have X's in columns 1 and 2.

Let us digress for a moment. In Chapter 2 we discussed the MSGLEVEL parameter on the JOB statement, for which coding a value of 1 for the first subparameter (the statements subparameter) causes both the input JCL and the JCL from cataloged procedures to be printed. You recall also that at the CUNY computer center the default value for the statements subparameter, which was used in Figure 8.4, is 1. It was this default value of 1 which caused lines 8 through 17 to be printed. If a value of 0 had been coded, only the JOB statement, line 6, would have been printed. If a value of 2 had been coded, only the input JCL, lines 6, 7, 18, and 19, would have been printed.

Unlike the IBM-supplied procedure, the COBUC procedure used here has a PROC statement with default values for symbolic parameters used in the procedure. Lines 21 through 25 show the values of the symbolic parameters being substituted into the procedure's JCL. These lines show the JCL as it looks after the substitution is made.

Lines 29 through 56 contain the program listing. Those of you who are familiar with COBOL will recognize this as a program named LISTER that reads a card and then prints it. If there had been errors in the program, then error messages would have followed the program listing.

The compiler options that are in effect during this compilation are shown on lines 59 through 62. Line 9 shows the EXEC statement for the compiler. Since there is no PARM field to set compiler options, all of the compiler options here are the installation defaults.

Similar output is produced when the other procedures illustrated in Figure 8.2 are executed.

FUNCTION OF THE LOADER

As mentioned earlier, before the object module produced by a compiler can be executed, it must have additional processing. One way of doing the additional processing is to use the loader. The same loader is used irrespective of which programming language is used. The **loader** resolves external references, includes modules from the SYSLIB library, relocates address constants, and then causes the program to begin executing. **External references** are module or program names that are used in a module or program but are

FUNCTION OF THE LOADER

not in that module or program. If, for example, you write a program named TESTMAIN that calls a program named TESTSUB that you have written, the name TESTSUB is an external reference to TESTMAIN. The loader resolves these external references, which means that these modules or programs are loaded in with the main program. Thus the object module of TESTSUB is loaded in with TESTMAIN so that TESTSUB may be referenced by TESTMAIN. If the loader cannot resolve external references, it marks the program not executable. The loader is described in detail in *OS/VS Linkage Editor and Loader* (GC 26-3813).

Figure 8.5 is a system flowchart that illustrates how the loader works. There are two inputs to the loader itself: the object module produced by the

FIGURE 8.5

System flowchart for the loader

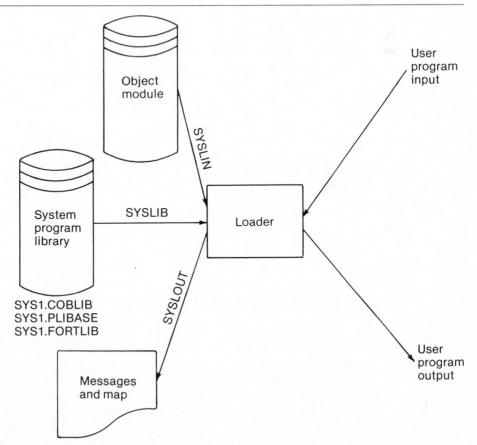

compiler under the ddname SYSLIN and a library under the ddname SYSLIB. The library used depends on the programming language and is not used for assembler. The loader searches these libraries to resolve external references. SYSLOUT is used by the loader for error and warning messages as well as the list of called modules if requested. This list of called modules is referred to as a **map**.

The loader executes the user's program, so Figure 8.5 also shows input to the user's program and output produced by the user's program.

The functions performed by the loader are also performed by the linkage editor, which will be discussed later. The loader is used for testing purposes. When testing is complete, the linkage editor is used. There are situations in which the loader cannot be used because the system under development is too complex. This will become clear when we discuss the linkage editor.

PROCEDURES TO COMPILE AND EXECUTE A PROGRAM

Figure 8.6 contains listings of the IBM-supplied procedures that compile a program and invoke the loader to execute the program. These are called compile and go procedures, and their names end with the letters CG. The procedures listed here are for COBOL, PL/I, FORTRAN, and assembler language. In all four procedures the loader is invoked in the GO step.

In all the procedures, the PARM parameter is coded on the EXEC statement to modify the loader processing and the listing produced. The values that may be coded, their meanings, and the default values are listed in Table 8.1. Usually, the default values are satisfactory. However, as in the case of the compilers, you may change the PARM values by coding an overriding PARM parameter on your EXEC statement. For example:

```
//CGPARM    EXEC COBUCG,
//              PARM.GO='NOMAP,LET'
```

If you wanted to change the PARM values for both the compiler and the loader, you would code

```
//CGPARM    EXEC COBUCG,
//              PARM.COB='FLAGE',
//              PARM.GO='NOMAP,LET'
```

FIGURE 8.6

(a) The COBUCG procedure

```
//COB       EXEC PGM=IKFCBL00,PARM='LOAD',REGION=86K
//SYSPRINT  DD  SYSOUT=A
//SYSUT1    DD  DSNAME=&&SYSUT1,UNIT=SYSDA,SPACE=(460,(700,100))
//SYSUT2    DD  DSNAME=&&SYSUT2,UNIT=SYSDA,SPACE=(460,(700,100))
//SYSUT3    DD  DSNAME=&&SYSUT3,UNIT=SYSDA,SPACE=(460,(700,100))
//SYSUT4    DD  DSNAME=&&SYSUT4,UNIT=SYSDA,SPACE=(460,(700,100))
//SYSLIN    DD  DSNAME=&&LOADSET,DISP=(MOD,PASS),                    X
//          UNIT=SYSDA,SPACE=(80,(500,100))
//GO        EXEC PGM=LOADER,PARM='MAP,LET',COND=(5,LT,COB),REGION=106K
//SYSLIN    DD  DSNAME=*.COB.SYSLIN,DISP=(OLD,DELETE)
//SYSLOUT   DD  SYSOUT=A
//SYSLIB    DD  DSNAME=SYS1.COBLIB,DISP=SHR
```

(b) The PLIXCG procedure

```
//PLIXCG    PROC LKLBDSN='SYS1.PLIBASE'
//PLI       EXEC PGM=IEL0AA,PARM='OBJECT,NODECK',REGION=100K
//SYSPRINT  DD  SYSOUT=A
//SYSLIN    DD  DSN=&&LOADSET,DISP=(MOD,PASS),UNIT=SYSSQ,
//          SPACE=(80,(250,100))
//SYSUT1    DD  DSN=&&SYSUT1,UNIT=SYSDA,SPACE=(1024,(200,50),,CONTIG,ROUND),
//          DCB=BLKSIZE=1024
//GO        EXEC PGM=LOADER,PARM='MAP,PRINT',REGION=100K,
//          COND=(9,LT,PLI)
//SYSLIB    DD  DSN=&LKLBDSN,DISP=SHR
//          DD  DSN=SYS1.PLIBASE,DISP=SHR
//SYSLIN    DD  DSN=&&LOADSET,DISP=(OLD,DELETE)
//SYSLOUT   DD  SYSOUT=A
//SYSPRINT  DD  SYSOUT=A
```

(c) The FORTXCG procedure

```
//FORTXCG PROC FXPGM=IFEAAB,FXREGN=256K,FXPDECK=NODECK,        +46150000
//             FXPOLST=NOLIST,FXPOPT=0,GOF5DD='DDNAME=SYSIN',  +46200000
//             GOF6DD='SYSOUT=A',GOF7DD='SYSOUT=B',GOREGN=100K  46250000
//*                                                             46300000
//*     PARAMETER   DEFAULT-VALUE   USAGE                       46350000
//*                                                             46400000
//*     GOREGN      100K            GO-STEP REGION              46450000
//*     FXPGM       IFEAAB          COMPILER NAME               46500000
```

(cont.)

```
//*                  FXREGN    256K                 FORT-STEP REGION          46550000
//*                  FXPDECK   NODECK               COMPILER DECK OPTION      46600000
//*                  FXPOLST   NOLIST               COMPILER LIST OPTION      46650000
//*                  FXPOPT    0                    COMPILER OPTIMIZATION     46700000
//*                  GOF5DD    DDNAME=SYSIN         GO.FT05F001 OPERAND       46750000
//*                  GOF6DD    SYSOUT=A             GO.FT06F001 OPERAND       46800000
//*                  GOF7DD    SYSOUT=B             GO.FT07F001 OPERAND       46850000
//                                                                           46900000
//FORT     EXEC  PGM=&FXPGM,REGION=&FXREGN,COND=(4,LT),                     +46950000
//               PARM='&FXPDECK,&FXPOLST,OPT(&FXPOPT)'                        47000000
//SYSPRINT DD  SYSOUT=A,DCB=BLKSIZE=3429                                      47050000
//SYSTERM
//SYSUT1   DD  UNIT=SYSSQ,SPACE=(3465,(3,3)),DCB=BLKSIZE=3465                 47100000
//SYSUT2   DD  UNIT=SYSSQ,SPACE=(2048,(10,10))                               47150000
//SYSPUNCH DD  SYSOUT=B,DCB=BLKSIZE=3440                                      47200000
//SYSLIN   DD  DSN=&&LOADSET,DISP=(MOD,PASS),UNIT=SYSSQ,                     +47250000
//               SPACE=(3200,(25,6)),DCB=BLKSIZE=3200                         47300000
//GO       EXEC  PGM=LOADER,COND=(4,LT),REGION=&GOREGN,                      +47350000
//               PARM='LET,NORES,EP=MAIN'                                     47400000
//SYSLOUT  DD  SYSOUT=A                                                       47450000
//SYSLIB   DD  DSN=SYS1.FORTLIB,DISP=SHR                                      47500000
//SYSLIN   DD  DSN=&&LOADSET,DISP=(OLD,DELETE)                                47550000
//FT05F001 DD  &GOF5DD                                                        47600000
//FT06F001 DD  &GOF6DD                                                        47650000
//FT07F001 DD  &GOF7DD                                                        47700000
```

(d) The ASMFCG procedure

```
//ASMFCG   PROC MAC='SYS1.MACLIB',MAC1='SYS1.MACLIB'
//ASM      EXEC PGM=IFOX00,PARM=OBJ,REGION=128K
//SYSLIB   DD  DSN=&MAC,DISP=SHR
//         DD  DSN=&MAC1,DISP=SHR
//SYSUT1   DD  DSN=&&SYSUT1,UNIT=SYSSQ,SPACE= (1700, (600,100)) ,
//         SEP= (SYSLIB)
//SYSUT2   DD  DSN=&&SYSUT2,UNIT=SYSSQ,SPACE= (1700, (300,50)) ,
//         SEP= (SYSLIB,SYSUT1)
//SYSUT3   DD  DSN=&&SYSUT3,UNIT=SYSSQ,SPACE= (1700, (300,50))
//SYSPRINT DD  SYSOUT=A,DCB=BLKSIZE=1089
//SYSPUNCH DD  SYSOUT=B
//SYSGO    DD  DSN=&&OBJSET,UNIT=SYSSQ,SPACE= (80, (200,50)) ,
//             DISP= (MOD,PASS)
//GO       EXEC PGM=LOADER,PARM='MAP,PRINT,NOCALL,LET',
//             COND= (8,LT,ASM)
//SYSLIN   DD  DSN=&&OBJSET,DISP= (OLD,DELETE)
//SYSLOUT  DD  SYSOUT=A
```

PROCEDURES TO COMPILE AND EXECUTE A PROGRAM

TABLE 8.1

Loader options specified in the PARM field

Option	Definition
MAP NOMAP	Instructs loader to produce a list of the module names and where they will be loaded in storage. NOMAP is the default.
RES NORES	Causes the link-pack area to be searched after the SYSLIN data set but before the SYSLIB library. RES is the default.
CALL NCALL	Specifies automatic search of SYSLIB library. CALL is the default.
LET NOLET	Permits execution even if certain types of errors occur. NOLET is the default.
SIZE=n	Specifies the amount of main storage for the loader. 100K is the default.
EP=name	Supplies the name of the entry point.
NAME=name	Supplies a name other than GO to the loaded program. The default name is **GO.
PRINT NOPRINT	Causes informational and diagnostic messages to appear in the SYSLOUT data set. PRINT is the default.
TERM NOTERM	Sends certain messages to the SYSTERM data set. NOTERM is the default.

An interesting point in the listing of these procedures is the use of the COND parameter on the EXEC statement for the loader. All of the procedures except FORTXCG use the format COND=(x,LT,stepname) (the FORTRAN procedure does not include a stepname). Stepname is the compilation step name, and x is 5 for COBOL, 4 for FORTRAN, 8 for assembler, and 9 for PL/I. The result of this COND parameter is that the loader will execute if the compile has a return code of 0 or 4 in all cases. If the return code is 8, the loader will execute only for PL/I and assembler.

Another interesting point is the use of the referback or backwards reference for the data set in the SYSLIN DD statement in the GO step of the COBUCG procedure. In this situation it appears to be more trouble to use the referback than to code the actual data set name. However, you might wish to override the SYSLIN DD statement in the compile step to retain the data set. If you did so, then you would also have to replace the entire SYSLIN DD statement in the GO step. With the referback, only the disposition need be changed, from (OLD,DELETE) to (OLD,KEEP).

Executing a Compile and Go Procedure

We will examine how the loader works by using it to execute the COBOL program named LISTER that was compiled in Figure 8.4. This program reads card input under the ddname INPUT and produces printer output under the ddname OUTPUT. (The methods used in COBOL, FORTRAN, PL/I, and assembler to specify the ddnames used for input and output data sets were discussed in Chapter 2.) Sample JCL to execute the compile and go procedure COBUCG is shown in Figure 8.7. The JCL for the other three languages is very similar.

Notice how GO has been added to the ddnames on the INPUT and OUTPUT DD statements. These DD statements are required during the GO step when the program is executed. Using GO. as the first part of their ddnames allows them to be added to the GO step. This is similar to the way COB. was added to the SYSIN ddname in Figure 8.3a to cause that DD statement to be added to the COB step.

Figure 8.8 shows the output produced when the job in Figure 8.7 is executed using the program LISTER as the COBOL source code. In Figure 8.8, the

FIGURE 8.7

COBOL compile and go

```
//JCLQB630 JOB ,'J.C.LEWIS'
//COBOLCG  EXEC COBUCG
//COB.SYSIN DD *

          COBOL Source Code

/*
//GO.INPUT DD *

          Input Data

/*
//GO.OUTPUT DD SYSOUT=A
//
```

FIGURE 8.8

Actual COBOL compile and go run

```
 1  //JCLQB667 JOB ,'J.C.LEWIS'
 2  //COBEXMPL EXEC COBUCG
 3  //COB.SYSIN DD *
 4  /*
 5  //GO.INPUT DD *
 6  /*
 7  //GO.OUTPUT DD SYSOUT=A
 8  //
 9  //JCLQB687 JOB ,'J.C.LEWIS'                                          00000100
10  //COBEXMPL EXEC COBUCG                                               00000200
11  XXCOBUCG PROC SUT1=15,SOBJ=15,ADDLIB='SYS1.ADDLIB',                  00000300
12  XX            STEPLIB='SYS1.ADDLIB'                                  00000400
13  XXCOB    EXEC PGM=IKFCBL00                                           00000500
14  XXSYSPRINT DD SYSOUT=A,DCB=BLKSIZE=1936                              00000600
15  XXSYSUT1  DD UNIT=3330,SPACE=(TRK,(&SUT1,5))                         00000700
16  XXSYSUT2  DD UNIT=3330,SPACE=(TRK,(&SUT1,5))                         00000800
17  XXSYSUT3  DD UNIT=3330,SPACE=(TRK,(&SUT1,5))                         00000900
18  XXSYSUT4  DD UNIT=3330,SPACE=(TRK,(&SUT1,5))
19  XXSYSUT5  DD UNIT=3330,SPACE=(TRK,(&SUT1,5)),DISP=(,PASS)            00001000
20  XXSYSLIN  DD DSNAME=&LOADSET,DCB=BLKSIZE=3120,DISP=(MOD,PASS),       00001100
21  XX           UNIT=3330,SPACE=(6400,(&SOBJ,10))
22  //COB.SYSIN DD *,DCB=BLKSIZE=80                                      00001200
23  XXGO     EXEC PGM=LOADER,PARM='MAP,LET',COND=(5,LT,COB)              00001300
24  XXSYSLIB  DD DSN=&ADDLIB,DISP=SHR                                    00001400
25  XX           DSN=SYS1.COBLIB,DISP=SHR                               00001500
26  XXSYSLIN  DD DSNAME=*.COB.SYSLIN,DISP=(OLD,DELETE)                   00001600
27  XXSYSLOUT DD SYSOUT=A,DCB=BLKSIZE=1936                               00001700
28  XXSTEPLIB DD DSNAME=SYS1.COBLIB,DISP=SHR                             00001800
29  XX           DSNAME=&STEPLIB,DISP=SHR                               00001900
30  XXSYSUT5  DD DSN=*.COB.SYSUT5,DISP=(OLD,DELETE)                      00002000
31  XXSYSDBOUT DD SYSOUT=A,DCB=BLKSIZE=1936                              00002100
32  XXDISPLAY DD SYSOUT=A,DCB=(RECFM=FA,LRECL=121,BLKSIZE=121,BUFNO=1)   00002200
33  XXSYSOUT  DD SYSOUT=A
34  //GO.INPUT DD *,DCB=BLKSIZE=80
35  //GO.OUTPUT DD SYSOUT=A
36  //
```

(cont.)

```
      STMT NO.  MESSAGE

  -
   6    IEF653I  SUBSTITUTION JCL  - UNIT=3330,SPACE=(TRK,(15,5))
   7    IEF653I  SUBSTITUTION JCL  - UNIT=3330,SPACE=(TRK,(15,5))
   8    IEF653I  SUBSTITUTION JCL  - UNIT=3330,SPACE=(TRK,(15,5))
   9    IEF653I  SUBSTITUTION JCL  - UNIT=3330,SPACE=(TRK,(15,5)),DISP=(,PASS)
  10    IEF653I  SUBSTITUTION JCL  - UNIT=3330,SPACE=(TRK,(15,5))
  11    IEF653I  SUBSTITUTION JCL  - UNIT=3330,SPACE=(6400,(15,10))
  14    IEF653I  SUBSTITUTION JCL  - DSN=SYS1.ADDLIB,DISP=SHR
  19    IEF653I  SUBSTITUTION JCL  - DSNAME=SYS1.ADDLIB,DISP=SHR


                                    VS LOADER

  OPTIONS USED - PRINT,MAP,LFT,CALL,RES,NOTERM,SIZE=163840,NAME=**GO
```

NAME	TYPE	ADDR	NAME	TYPE	ADDR	NAME	TYPE	ADDR	NAME	TYPE	ADDR	NAME	TYPE	ADDR
LISTER	SD	AC010	ILBOSRV *	SD	AC688	ILBOSRV0*	LR	AC6C2	ILBOSR *	LR	AC6C2	ILBOSR3 *	LR	AC6C2
ILBOSRV1*	LR	AC6C6	ILBOSTP1*	LR	AC6C6	ILBOST *	LR	AC6CA	ILBOSTP0*	LR	AC6CA	ILBODBG *	SD	ACA08
ILBODBG0*	LR	ACA3A	ILBODBG1*	LR	ACA3E	ILBODBG2*	LR	ACA42	ILBODBG3*	LR	ACA46	ILBODBG4*	LR	ACA4A
ILBODBG5*	LR	ACA4E	ILBODBG6*	LR	ACA52	ILBODBG7*	LR	ACA56	ILBOEXT *	SD	AD780	ILBOEXT0*	LR	AD782
ILBOCOM0*	SD	AD7F8	ILBOCOM *	LR	AD7F8	ILBOCMM *	LR	AD900	ILBOCMM0*	LR	AD932	ILBOCMM1*	LR	AD936
ILBOBEG *	SD	ADCD0	ILBOBEG0*	LR	ADD02	ILBOMSG *	SD	ADDA0	ILBOMSG0*	LR	ADDD2			

```
  TOTAL LENGTH      1E58
  ENTRY ADDRESS     AC010

  E. T. PHONE HOME
```

output produced by the compiler has been eliminated since it is identical to the output in Figure 8.4.

Again remember that the COBUCG procedure executed was modified to meet the needs of CUNY and consequently is different from the IBM procedures listed in Figure 8.6. You will probably find that these procedures have been changed in your installation as well.

In Figure 8.8, look at lines 9 through 36. As you will recall, those statements starting with // were coded by the programmer and those starting with XX came from the procedure. Please note line 22, the source code input DD statement. Notice how it is inserted immediately prior to the GO step EXEC statement, because it is being added to the compile step COB. Lines 34 and 35 show how our two GO DD statements are inserted at the end of the GO step.

Lines 48 through 58 are output from the loader. Line 49 shows the options used by the loader. Back in line 23, the PARM field contains the options MAP and LET; the remaining options indicated in line 49 are the defaults. Lines 51 through 56 list the names of the modules used. This list is a result of the MAP option. The first name, LISTER, is the program name as indicated in line 30 of Figure 8.4. The remainder are modules that have been called in from libraries referenced by the SYSLIB statement in the GO step. Line 57 gives the length of the program in hexadecimal form, and line 58 is the entry address which corresponds to the entry address given for LISTER on line 51. The result of executing the program is line 60, which is the card that was just read. (Because there is no carriage control field in the output record in the COBOL program, the first character is not printed. Therefore, the message, E. T. PHONE HOME, is started in column 2 of the data card.)

PASSING VALUES TO YOUR PROGRAMS

You have seen how to use the PARM parameter to pass values to compilers and the loader. The PARM parameter may also be used to pass values to your programs. If you are using a compile and go procedure, the PARM values for your program are included in the PARM.GO field after the loader parameters. For example, suppose you have a program that can produce either a full report or a summary report and that you can control the operation of the program by passing it either an F or an S. Furthermore, suppose you want to print the season, FALL, WINTER, etc., on the report. You might code the PARM parameter as follows:

```
PARM.GO='NOMAP,LET/SWINTER'
```

The rule is that the loader options are coded first, followed by a slash, and the data to be passed to your program are coded after the slash. Even if you do not code any loader options, the slash is required.

There is one peculiar feature when you use a PARM field in PL/I. The PL/I compiler adds code that allows your program to accept data from a PARM field. To distinguish between these data and the data you want placed in the PARM field, code an extra slash, e.g.,

```
PARM.GO='NOMAP,LET//SWINTER'
```

If you want to pass an apostrophe to a program, you must code two apostrophes:

```
PARM='RUBIC''S CUBE'
```

Similarly, when you want to pass an ampersand to a program, you must code two ampersands.

Now that you know how to pass information to a program using the PARM field, let us examine how the program receives it.

Upon entry to your assembler program, register 1 points to the field that contains the address of the PARM field. The first two bytes of this field contain the length of the data passed in the PARM field. If the PARM field contains 'SWINTER', these two bytes will contain 7. Your assembler program could access the PARM field using code similar to the following:

```
L       R2,0(R1)  REGISTER 2 POINTS TO LENGTH OF PARM FIELD
LA      R3,2(R2)  REGISTER 3 POINTS TO DATA IN PARM FIELD
```

As befits a high-level language, to handle a PARM field PL/I needs only the following code:

```
PGM1: PROCEDURE (PARMFLD) OPTIONS (MAIN);
      DCL PARMFLD CHAR (100) VARYING;
```

You may use any valid PL/I variable name for the PARM field. You must declare the receiving field with a length of 100 characters, even if you know the data that you pass will be less than that. The PL/I string-handling functions can be used to separate the fields passed in the PARM field.

Handling a PARM field in COBOL is equally easy. A record to receive the PARM data must be defined in the LINKAGE section as follows:

```
01 PARM-FIELD.
     05 PARM-LENGTH          PIC S9(4) COMP.
     05 REPORT-FLAG          PIC X.
     05 SEASON-DATA          PIC X(6).
     05 FILLER               PIC X(93).
```

You may use any legal COBOL identifier names you like, but the first field in the record must be defined with PIC S9(4) COMP, and the remaining fields must have a combined length of 100 bytes.

The PROCEDURE DIVISION header is coded as

```
PROCEDURE DIVISION USING PARM-FIELD.
```

FUNCTION OF THE LINKAGE EDITOR

The main function of the **linkage editor** is to take as input the object module produced by a compiler and to create a load module. A **load module** is a program module in a form suitable for loading into storage for execution. The same linkage editor is used no matter which compiler produced the object module. Like the loader, the linkage editor creates a load module by resolving external references and relocating address constants. Unlike the loader, the linkage editor does not execute the load module. Instead it writes the load module to a disk as a member of a library. The linkage editor is described in *OS/VS Linkage Editor and Loader* (GC26-3813).

Figure 8.9 is a system flowchart which shows how the linkage editor works. The name of the linkage editor is IEWL. Compare Figure 8.9 with Figure 8.5, which illustrates the loader. Both have a SYSLIB DD statement that points to one or more libraries used to resolve external references. In both cases the library used depends on the programming language and is not used by the assembler.

Since the library defined on the SYSLIB DD statement is automatically used by the linkage editor to resolve external references, this library is known as an **automatic-call library**. Any library concatenated with SYSLIB is also an automatic-call library. Additional automatic-call libraries can be defined by the LIBRARY control statement, which we will discuss later.

FIGURE 8.9

System flowchart for the linkage editor

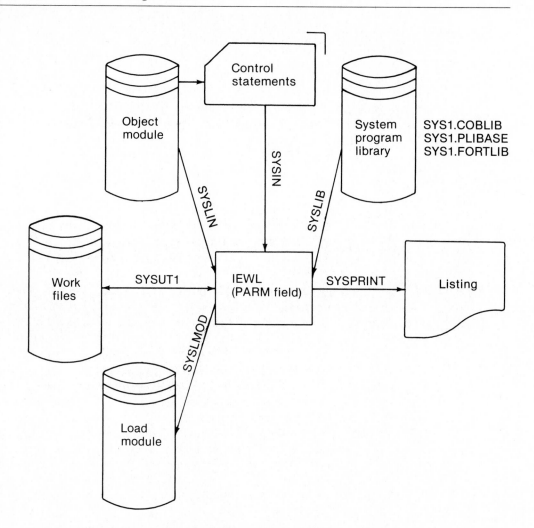

For the loader, the SYSLIN DD statement identifies the input data. For the linkage editor, the SYSLIN DD statement identifies the primary input data, which consist of an object module produced by a compiler. Additional input data in the form of linkage editor control statements may be supplied using the ddname SYSIN. When we study the compile and link edit procedures in the next section, the relationship between SYSLIN and SYSIN DD statements will be explained.

The linkage editor can perform functions that the loader cannot. These additional functions are invoked with the linkage editor control statements. They are illustrated in Table 8.2. The control statements most frequently used by application programmers will be discussed later in this chapter.

TABLE 8.2

Linkage editor control statements

Linkage Editor Control Statement	Function
ALIAS	Supplies additional names for the load module.
CHANGE	Causes an external reference in a module to be replaced with another external reference.
ENTRY	Supplies the name of the first instruction to be executed.
EXPAND	Is used to lengthen one or more control sections.
IDENTIFY	Supplies data to be entered into the identification records for a particular control section.
INCLUDE	Identifies DD statements that supply input to the linkage editor. The input may be sequential or partitioned data sets.
INSERT	Repositions a control section to a segment in an overlay structure.
LIBRARY	Specifies additional automatic-call libraries, restricted no-call function and never-call function.
NAME	Supplies the member name for the load module.
ORDER	Indicates the sequence in which control sections appear in the output load module.
OVERLAY	Indicates the beginning of an overlay segment or region.
PAGE	Aligns a control section on a 4K-page boundary in the load module. (cont.)

CHAPTER 8 / USING SYSTEM PROCEDURES

TABLE 8.2 (cont.)

Linkage editor control statements

Linkage Editor Control Statement	Function
REPLACE	Specifies the replacement of one control section with another or the deletion of a control section or entry name.
SETCODE	Assigns the specified authorization code to the output load module.
SETSSI	Specifies hexadecimal data to be placed in the system status index of the directory entry for the output module.

TABLE 8.3

Linkage editor options specified in the PARM field

Option	Definition
AC=n	Sets an authorization code for the load module. The SETCODE control card may override this value.
ALIGN2	Sets the load module to be loaded on a 2K boundary. 4K is the default.
DCBS	Permits the SYSLMOD blocksize to be specified.
LET	Allows the load module to execute with certain errors.
LIST	Prints the linkage editor control cards.
MAP	Prints a list of the modules in the load module and their relative position.
NCAL	Prevents automatic library calls.
NE	Prevents the load module from being processed by the linkage editor again.

PROCEDURES TO COMPILE AND LINK EDIT A PROGRAM

TABLE 8.3 (cont.)

Linkage editor options specified in the PARM field

Option	Definition
OVLY	Indicates that an overlay program is being processed.
REFR	Permits the load module to be refreshed.
REUS	Permits the load module to be serially reusable.
SCTR	Allows the load module to be loaded into noncontiguous main storage.
SIZE=(v1,v2)	Specifies the amount of main storage for the linkage editor (v1) and for the buffer space (v2).
XCAL	Allows valid exclusive calls.
XREF	Produces a cross reference listing.

The printed linkage editor output goes to the SYSPRINT DD statement. The load module, which is the main linkage editor output, is written as a member of the library specified by the SYSLMOD DD statement.

As with the loader, you can make some modification to the load module produced, invoke special processing, and change the output listings with the PARM field in the EXEC statement. The values that may be specified in the PARM field are listed in Table 8.3. Use the default values unless you have a reason to do otherwise.

PROCEDURES TO COMPILE AND LINK EDIT A PROGRAM

Figure 8.10 shows the listings of the IBM-supplied procedures to compile and link edit a program. The names of these procedures end with the letters CL. Most of these procedures are very similar to one another. The compile step is the same or almost the same as the corresponding compiler procedure in Figure 8.2. In all cases, the object module is written to a temporary data set with the ddname SYSLIN (SYSGO for the assembler).

FIGURE 8.10

(a) The COBUCL procedure

```
//COB      EXEC PGM=IKFCBL00,REGION=86K
//SYSPRINT DD  SYSOUT=A
//SYSUT1   DD  DSNAME=&&SYSUT1,UNIT=SYSDA,SPACE=(460,(700,100))
//SYSUT2   DD  DSNAME=&&SYSUT2,UNIT=SYSDA,SPACE=(460,(700,100))
//SYSUT3   DD  DSNAME=&&SYSUT3,UNIT=SYSDA,SPACE=(460,(700,100))
//SYSUT4   DD  DSNAME=&&SYSUT4,UNIT=SYSDA,SPACE=(460,(700,100))
//SYSLIN   DD  DSNAME=&&LOADSET,DISP=(MOD,PASS),UNIT=SYSDA,          X
//             SPACE=(80,(500,100))
//LKED     EXEC PGM=IEWL,PARM='LIST,XREF,LET',COND=(5,LT,COB),       X
//             REGION=96K
//SYSLIN   DD  DSNAME=&&LOADSET,DISP=(OLD,DELETE)
//         DD  DDNAME=SYSIN
//SYSLMOD  DD  DSNAME=&&GOSET,DISP=(NEW,PASS),UNIT=SYSDA,            X
//             SPACE=(1024,(50,20,1))
//SYSLIB   DD  DSNAME=SYS1.COBLIB,DISP=SHR
//SYSUT1   DD  UNIT=(SYSDA,SEP=(SYSLIN,SYSLMOD)),                    X
//             SPACE=(1024,(50,20))
//SYSPRINT DD  SYSOUT=A
```

(b) The PLIXCL procedure

```
//PLIXCL   PROC LKLBDSN='SYS1.PLIBASE'
//PLI      EXEC PGM=IEL0AA,PARM='OBJECT,NODECK',REGION=100K
//SYSPRINT DD  SYSOUT=A
//SYSLIN   DD  DSN=&&LOADSET,DISP=(MOD,PASS),UNIT=SYSSQ,
//             SPACE=(80,(250,100))
//SYSUT1   DD  DSN=&&SYSUT1,UNIT=SYSDA,SPACE=(1024,(200,50),,CONTIG,ROUND),
//             DCB=BLKSIZE=1024
//LKED     EXEC PGM=IEWL,PARM='XREF,LIST',COND=(9,LT,PLI),REGION=100K
//SYSLIB   DD  DSN=&LKLBDSN,DISP=SHR
//         DD  DSN=SYS1.PLIBASE,DISP=SHR
//SYSLMOD  DD  DSN=&&GOSET(GO),DISP=(MOD,PASS),UNIT=SYSDA,
//             SPACE=(1024,(50,20,1))
//SYSUT1   DD  DSN=&&SYSUT1,UNIT=SYSDA,SPACE=(1024,(200,50),,CONTIG,ROUND),
//             DCB=BLKSIZE=1024
//SYSPRINT DD  SYSOUT=A
//SYSLIN   DD  DSN=&&LOADSET,DISP=(OLD,DELETE)
//         DD  DDNAME=SYSIN
//SYSIN    DD  DUMMY
```

(c) The FORTXCL procedure

```
//FORTXCL PROC FXPGM=IFEAAB,FXREGN=256K,FXPDECK=NODECK,FXPOLST=NOLIST,   +41350000
//             FXPNAME=MAIN,FXPOPT=0,PGMLB='&&GOSET'                       41400000
//*                                                                       41450000
//*     PARAMETER  DEFAULT-VALUE    USAGE                                  41500000
//*                                                                       41550000
//*     FXPGM      IFEAAB           COMPILER NAME                         41600000
//*     FXREGN     256K             FORT-STEP REGION                      41650000
//*     FXPDECK    NODECK           COMPILER DECK OPTION                  41700000
//*     FXPOLST    NOLIST           COMPILER LIST OPTION                  41750000
//*     FXPNAME    MAIN             COMPILER NAME OPTION                  41800000
//*     FXPOPT     0                COMPILER OPTIMIZATION                 41850000
//*     PGMLB      &&GOSET          LKED.SYSLMOD DSNAME                   41900000
//*                                                                       41950000
//FORT   EXEC  PGM=&FXPGM,REGION=&FXREGN,COND=(4,LT),                     +42000000
//      PARM='&FXPDECK,&FXPOLST,NAME(&FXPNAME),OPT(&FXPOPT)'               42050000
//SYSPRINT DD SYSOUT=A,DCB=BLKSIZE=3429                                    42100000
//SYSTERM  DD SYSOUT=A                                                     42150000
//SYSUT1   DD UNIT=SYSSQ,SPACE=(3465,(3,3)),DCB=BLKSIZE=3465               42200000
//SYSUT2   DD UNIT=SYSSQ,SPACE=(2048,(10,10))                             42250000
//SYSPUNCH DD SYSOUT=B,DCB=BLKSIZE=3440                                   +42300000
//SYSLIN   DD DSN=&&LOADSET,DISP=(MOD,PASS),UNIT=SYSSQ,                    42350000
//      SPACE=(3200,(25,6)),DCB=BLKSIZE=3200                              42400000
//LKED   EXEC  PGM=IEWL,REGION=96K,COND=(4,LT),                          +42450000
//      PARM='LET,LIST,MAP,XREF'                                          42500000
//SYSPRINT DD SYSOUT=A                                                     42550000
//SYSLIB   DD DSN=SYS1.FORTLIB,DISP=SHR                                    42600000
//SYSUT1   DD UNIT=SYSDA,SPACE=(1024,(200,20))                           +42650000
//SYSLMOD  DD DSN=&PGMLB.(&FXPNAME),UNIT=SYSDA,                            42700000
//      DISP=(NEW,PASS),SPACE=(TRK,(10,10,1),RLSE)                        42750000
//SYSLIN   DD DSN=&&LOADSET,DISP=(OLD,DELETE)                             42800000
//         DD DDNAME=SYSIN
```

(d) The ASMFCL procedure

```
//ASMFCL    PROC MAC='SYS1.MACLIB',MAC1='SYS1.MACLIB'
//ASM       EXEC PGM=IFOX00,PARM=OBJ,REGION=128K
//SYSLIB    DD   DSN=&MAC,DISP=SHR
//          DD   DSN=&MAC1,DISP=SHR
//SYSUT1    DD   DSN=&&SYSUT1,UNIT=SYSSQ,SPACE= (1700, (600,100)) ,
//          SEP= (SYSLIB)
//SYSUT2    DD   DSN=&&SYSUT2,UNIT=SYSSQ,SPACE= (1700, (300,50)) ,
//          SEP= (SYSLIB,SYSUT1)
//SYSUT3    DD   DSN=&&SYSUT3,UNIT=SYSSQ,SPACE= (1700, (300,50))
//SYSPRINT  DD   SYSOUT=A,DCB=BLKSIZE=1089
//SYSPUNCH  DD   SYSOUT=B
//SYSGO     DD   DSN=&&OBJSET,UNIT=SYSSQ,SPACE= (80, (200,50)) ,
//               DISP= (MOD,PASS)
//LKED      EXEC PGM=IEWL,PARM= (XREF,LET,LIST,NCAL) ,REGION=128K,
//               COND= (8,LT,ASM)
//SYSLIN    DD   DSN=&&OBJSET,DISP= (OLD,DELETE)
//          DD   DDNAME=SYSIN
//SYSLMOD   DD   DSN=&&GOSET (GO) ,UNIT=SYSDA,SPACE= (1024, (50,20,1)) ,
//               DISP= (MOD,PASS)
//SYSUT1    DD   DSN=&&SYSUT1,UNIT= (SYSDA,SEP= (SYSLIN,SYSLMOD)) ,
//               SPACE= (1024, (50,20))
//SYSPRINT  DD   SYSOUT=A
```

250

PROCEDURES TO COMPILE AND LINK EDIT A PROGRAM

The linkage editor steps use the stepname LKED in all four procedures. There are three main differences in these procedures. First, each one specifies slightly different options in the PARM field (they all specify XREF and LIST). You can check Table 8.3 to determine the meaning of the options named.

The second difference is the COND parameter. In each procedure, the COND parameter in the linkage editor EXEC statement specifies a different number. However, the numbers are the same as in the compile and go procedures we saw earlier on the loader EXEC statement.

The third difference lies in the SYSLIB DD statement. While the assembler does not specify an automatic-call library (via the SYSLIB DD statement), each of the high-level languages uses a different automatic-call library.

In all cases, the SYSLMOD data set where the load module is written is a library. Load modules must be written as members of a library because the linkage editor expects to write the load module as a library member. In addition, the operating system only executes programs that are library members. In the four procedures, the SYSLMOD DD statement points to a temporary library named GOSET.

The DDNAME Parameter

If you examine the SYSLIN DD statement in each link edit step of Figure 8.10, you will see another DD statement concatenated to it. The only information coded in the DD statement is DDNAME=SYSIN. DDNAME is a new keyword parameter and is called a **forward reference**.

The DDNAME parameter must be used because the input to the linkage editor, which is supplied under the ddname SYSLIN, actually consists of two concatenated data sets. The first data set is &&LOADSET, which is the object module produced by the compiler, and the second data set is the linkage editor control statements to be used. The DDNAME parameter permits you to concatenate the linkage editor control statements in the job stream with &&LOADSET. In effect, the parameter says that the data set which should be defined in this DD statement so that it will be concatenated with &&LOADSET will in fact be defined later (which is why the coding is called a forward reference) with a DD statement that has the ddname SYSIN. You must therefore code your linkage editor control statements using the ddname SYSIN. Since in our example we want the control statements added to the LKED step, the name we will actually use is LKED.SYSIN.

CHAPTER 8 / USING SYSTEM PROCEDURES

Although you can use up to five forward references in a step, provided all the ddnames are different, use of more than one is rare.

Executing a Compile and Link Edit Procedure

Figure 8.11 illustrates use of the procedure COBUCL. The SYSLMOD DD statement has been overridden so that the load module will be written to the previously created personal load library named LOADLIB.

If LOADLIB did not exist, it could be created in this job by coding the following DD statement:

```
//LKED.SYSLMOD DD DSN=WYL.QB.JCL.LOADLIB,
//             DISP=(NEW,CATLG),
//             VOL=SER=WYL005,
//             SPACE=(CYL,(5,1,10))
```

Notice that the DSN, DISP, VOL, and SPACE parameters are changed, but the UNIT parameter is not. Nor is the DCB parameter coded. The values coded for UNIT and DCB in the SYSLMOD DD statement in the procedure are acceptable.

Linkage Editor Control Statements

As stated earlier, the linkage editor control statements are supplied under the ddname LKED.SYSIN. The linkage editor control statements are described in Table 8.2. In Figure 8.11, the NAME control statement is coded. The NAME

FIGURE 8.11

COBOL compile and link edit

```
//JCLQB635 JOB ,'J.C.LEWIS'
//COMPLKD1 EXEC COBUCL
//COB.SYSIN DD *

            COBOL Source Code

/*
//LKED.SYSLMOD DD DSN=WYL.QB.JCL.LOADLIB,
//             DISP=OLD
//LKED.SYSIN DD *
 NAME LISTER(R)
/*
//
```

PROCEDURES TO COMPILE AND LINK EDIT A PROGRAM

control statement supplies the member name. When you want to execute a program, it is the member name you code on the EXEC statement. In Figure 8.11, (R) is coded following the member name in the NAME control statement. This means that if member LISTER already exists in the library named in the SYSLMOD DD statement then it will be replaced by the version created in this job. If (R) had not been coded in the NAME control statement and the member already existed, the job step would have failed. [It is also possible to specify the member name in the DSN—for example, WYL.QB.JCL.LOADLIB (LISTER). In that case the NAME control statement would not be necessary.]

Let us digress a moment and discuss the general format of the linkage editor control statements. The operations, such as NAME, must start in or after column 2. The first operand must be separated from the operation by at least one blank. If it is necessary or desirable, linkage editor control statements may be continued. The rules for continuing linkage editor control statements are the same as the rules discussed in Chapter 4 for continuing utility control statements: the last operand on a statement ends with a comma and column 72 contains a nonblank character; the continuation statement must start in column 16; there is no limit on the number of continuation statements. Please remember that a symbol cannot be split.

Figure 8.12 shows the output when the job in Figure 8.11 is executed using the program LISTER as the COBOL source code. Once again the output produced by the compiler has been eliminated. Remember that the procedures used in this example and the others in this chapter are not the IBM-supplied procedures, but rather procedures that have been modified to meet the needs of the CUNY system.

In Figure 8.12, statements 1 through 9 represent the coded JCL. Lines 10 through 36 contain the execution JCL, a mixture of the cataloged procedure and the coded JCL. The COBOL source code is input following the COB.SYSIN DD statement, which is line 22 of the execution JCL. It is a DD statement added to the compile step. As mentioned earlier, in the execution JCL you can always spot your JCL because it has // in the first two positions. The JCL from the procedure, on the other hand, has XX in the first two positions. Lines 26 and 27 contain the override information for the SYSLMOD DD statement. Lines 28 and 29 contain the original information from the cataloged procedure.

Line 28 is unusual because it has an X/ in the first two positions, which indicates a statement in the procedure that is being overridden. Whenever you override a DD statement in a procedure, provided the statement subparameter of the MSGLEVEL parameter is 1, your statement will be printed immediately before the statement you are overriding. The overridden statement will be printed with X/ in the first two positions. Notice that the

FIGURE 8.12

Actual COBOL compile and link edit run

```
 1  //JCLQB623 JOB ,'J.C.LEWIS'
 2  //COMPLKD1 EXEC COBUCL
 3  //COB.SYSIN DD *
 4  /*
 5  //LKED.SYSLMOD DD DSN=WYL.QB.JCL.LOADLIB,
 6  //            DISP=OLD
 7  //LKED.SYSIN DD *
 8  /*
 9  //


10   1  //JCLQB623 JOB ,'J.C.LEWIS'                                            00000100
11   2  //COMPLKD1 EXEC COBUCL                                                 00000200
12   3  XXCOBUCL PROC SUT1=15,SOBJ=15,SLUT1=50,SLUT2=20,SLMOD1=50,SLMOD2=20,   00000300
13      XX            ADDLIB='SYS1.ADDLIB'                                     00000400
14   4  XXCOB    EXEC PGM=IKFCBL00                                            00000500
15   5  XXSYSPRINT DD SYSOUT=A,DCB=BLKSIZE=1936                                00000600
16   6  XXSYSUT1  DD DSN=&&SYSUT1,UNIT=3330,SPACE=(TRK,(&SUT1,5))              00000700
17   7  XXSYSUT2  DD DSN=&&SYSUT2,UNIT=3330,SPACE=(TRK,(&SUT1,5))              00000800
18   8  XXSYSUT3  DD DSN=&&SYSUT3,UNIT=3330,SPACE=(TRK,(&SUT1,5))              00000900
19   9  XXSYSUT4  DD DSN=&&SYSUT4,UNIT=3330,SPACE=(TRK,(&SUT1,5))              00001000
20  10  XXSYSLIN  DD DSN=&&LOADSET,DCB=BLKSIZE=3120,DISP=(MOD,PASS),
21      XX            UNIT=3330,SPACE=(6400,(&SOBJ,10))
22  11  //COB.SYSIN DD *,DCB=BLKSIZE=80                                        00001100
23  12  XXLKED    EXEC PGM=IEWL,PARM='LIST,XREF,LET',COND=(5,LT,COB)           00001200
24  13  XXSYSLIN  DD DSN=&&LOADSET,DISP=(OLD,DELETE)                           00001300
25  14  XX        DD DDNAME=SYSIN
26  15  //LKED.SYSLMOD DD DSN=WYL.QB.JCL.LOADLIB,
27      //            DISP=OLD
28      X/SYSLMOD  DD DSN=&&GOSET,DISP=(NEW,PASS),UNIT=3330,                   00001400
29      XX            SPACE=(1024,(&SLMOD1,&SLMOD2,1))                         00001500
30  16  XXSYSLIB   DD DSN=&ADDLIB,DISP=SHR                                     00001600
31  17  XX         DD DSN=SYS1.CCBLIB,DISP=SHR                                 00001700
32  18  XXSYSUT1   DD UNIT=(3330,SEP=(SYSLIN,SYSLMOD)),                        00001800
33      XX            SPACE=(1024,(&SLUT1,&SLUT2))                             00001900
34  19  XXSYSPRINT DD SYSOUT=A,DCB=BLKSIZE=1936                                00002000
35  20  //LKED.SYSIN DD *,DCB=BLKSIZE=80
36      //
```

```
F64-LEVEL LINKAGE EDITOR OPTIONS SPECIFIED LIST,XREF,LET
       DEFAULT OPTION(S) USED  -  SIZE=(196608,65536)
IEW0000        NAME LISTER (R)


                              CROSS REFERENCE TABLE

CONTROL SECTION                ENTRY
 NAME      ORIGIN  LENGTH       NAME     LOCATION    NAME      LOCATION    NAME      LOCATION    NAME      LOCATION
 LISTER      00      676
 ILBOCOM0*   678     102       ILBOCOM     678

 ILBODBG *   780     D78       ILBODBG0    7B2      ILBODBG1    7B6      ILBODBG2    7BA      ILBODBG3    7BE
                               ILBODBG4    7C2      ILBODBG5    7C6      ILBODBG6    7CA      ILBODBG7    7CE
 ILBOEXT *   14F8     72       ILBOEXT0    14FA

 ILBOSRV *   1570    37C       ILBOSRV0    15AA     ILBOSR      15AA     ILBOSR3     15AA     ILBOSRV1    15AE
                               ILBOSTP1    15AE     ILBOST      15B2     ILBOSTP0    15B2
 ILBOBEG *   18F0     CA       ILBOBFG0    1922

 ILBOCMM *   19C0    3C9       ILBOCMM0    19F2     ILBOCMM1    19F6

 ILBOMSG *   1D90     D8       ILBOMSG0    1DC2


 LOCATION   REFERS TO SYMBOL   IN CONTROL SECTION        LOCATION   REFERS TO SYMBOL   IN CONTROL SECTION
   478      ILBOSRV0           ILBOSRV                     47C      ILBODBG0           ILBODBG
   480      ILBOSR             ILBOSRV                     484      ILBODBG4           ILBODBG
   488      ILBOEXT0           ILBOEXT                     48C      ILBOSRV1           ILBOSRV
   400      ILBOCOM0           ILBOCOM0                    13B4     ILBOFLW0           $UNRESOLVED(W)
   13B8     ILBOFLW2           $UNRESOLVED(W)              13BC     ILBOTEF3           $UNRESOLVED(W)
   13C0     ILBOSTN0           $UNRESOLVED(W)              1860     ILBOCOM0           ILBOCOM0
   1864     ILBOCMM0           ILBOCMM                     1868     ILBOBEG0           ILBOBEG
   186C     ILBOMSG0           ILBOMSG

 ENTRY ADDRESS          00
 TOTAL LENGTH         1E68
***LISTER   NOW ADDED TO DATA SET
 AUTHORIZATION CODE IS      0.
```

resulting DD statement, which is a combination of the parameters you coded and the parameters on the original statement, is not printed anywhere. The last DD statement on line 35 is the added statement for the linkage editor control statements.

Linkage Editor Output

The linkage editor output starts on line 37, which shows the options selected for the linkage editor. If you compare them with the PARM field information in line 23, you will see that they are the same. Line 38 shows the default option that specifies the amount of storage reserved for the linkage editor and the amount of storage reserved for the buffer space. Line 39 shows the linkage editor control statement that was entered. This line appears because the LIST option was specified.

Line 41 through 71 appear because the XREF option was specified. The COBOL program is named LISTER. Those of you familiar with COBOL will observe that the code does not explicitly refer to any other modules. The additional modules in the cross reference listing are called in as a result of compiler action. In lines 72 and 73 the entry address is given as 00 and the program length as 1E68. When the program is loaded, it will not actually be loaded into address 00; it will be loaded wherever the system finds space for it. Line 74 indicates that the program LISTER is added to the data set specified in the SYSLMOD DD statement. The authorization code is a security feature which has not been implemented at the CUNY computer center.

In COBOL programs, the PROGRAM-ID entry supplies the internal program name (see line 30 in Figure 8.4). The linkage editor control statement NAME supplies the name of the member under which the load module is stored in the load library. In Figure 8.12, both have the name LISTER. Although using the same name is good practice, it is not necessary.

EXECUTING A PROGRAM FROM A LIBRARY

When we ran Figure 8.11, we added the load module named LISTER to a library; we would now like to execute it. Executing it is relatively simple, as shown in Figure 8.13. The EXEC statement is similar to the EXEC statements we have used to execute IEBGENER and the other utility programs. Looking at

FIGURE 8.13

Execution of a COBOL program

```
//JCLQB627 JOB ,'J.C.LEWIS'
//JOBLIB   DD DSN=WYL.QB.JCL.LOADLIB,
//            DISP=SHR
//LODEXMPL EXEC PGM=LISTER
//INPUT    DD *
/*
//OUTPUT   DD SYSOUT=A
//SYSUDUMP DD SYSOUT=A
//
      1    //JCLQB627 JOB ,'J.C.LEWIS'
      2    //JOBLIB   DD DSN=WYL.QB.JCL.LOADLIB,
           //            DISP=SHR
      3    //LODEXMPL EXEC PGM=LISTER
      4    //INPUT    DD *,DCB=BLKSIZE=80
      5    //OUTPUT   DD SYSOUT=A
      6    //SYSUDUMP DD SYSOUT=A
           //

E. T. PHONE HOME
```

Figure 8.13, we cannot tell that LISTER was originally written in COBOL. Of course, we must provide the INPUT and OUTPUT DD statements, but notice that GO is not included as part of the ddnames. That is because we are executing a program and not a procedure with a GO step. The output is shown in the last line.

JOBLIB DD Statement

The only new feature in Figure 8.13 is the JOBLIB DD statement. Up until now all programs we have executed have been located in a library named SYS1.LINKLIB. You did not know that, and you did not have to know it because the system automatically looks in SYS1.LINKLIB to find programs that are executed. However, LISTER is not in SYS1.LINKLIB, but in WYL.QB.JCL.LOADLIB. In Figure 8.13, the JOBLIB DD statement tells the system to search WYL.QB.JCL.LOADLIB for program LISTER.

The JOBLIB DD statement is coded immediately after the JOB statement and applies to all steps in the job. If you use a JOBLIB DD statement, the system will search the specified library first. The JOBLIB DD statement may point to several libraries if you concatenate them. If the program (actually

FIGURE 8.14

Using a JOBLIB DD statement

```
//JCLQB675 JOB ,'J.C.LEWIS'
//JOBLIB   DD DSN=LOADLIB,
//              DISP=SHR
//STEP1     EXEC PGM=PROG1
//SYSPRINT DD SYSOUT=A
//INPUT     DD DSN=TESTDATA,
//              DISP=OLD
//OUTPUT    DD SYSOUT=A
//STEP2     EXEC PGM=PROG2
//SYSPRINT DD SYSOUT=A
//REPORT    DD SYSOUT=A
//DATA      DD DSN=DATATEST,
//              DISP=OLD
//STEP3     EXEC PGM=IEBGENER
//SYSPRINT DD SYSOUT=A
//SYSUT2    DD SYSOUT=A
//SYSUT1    DD DSN=SOURCE.LIB,
//              DISP=SHR
//SYSIN     DD DUMMY
//
```

load module) is not in the library or libraries pointed to by the JOBLIB DD statement, then the SYS1.LINKLIB library is searched. If the load module is not found in SYS1.LINKLIB, the job abends with a system completion code of 806, which means the load module cannot be found. Perhaps you misspelled the program name, or perhaps the JOBLIB statement points to the wrong library.

Figure 8.14 shows the use of a JOBLIB DD statement in a multistep job. The JOBLIB DD statement points to one library, LOADLIB. The system will search this library first for the programs. PROG1 and PROG2 will be found there, but since IEBGENER is usually in SYS1.LINKLIB, it will not be found in LOADLIB. After the system determines that IEBGENER is not in LOADLIB, it will search SYS1.LINKLIB, where IEBGENER should be found unless the program name is misspelled.

Since we coded only the data set name and disposition on the JOBLIB DD statement in Figure 8.14, the load library named must be cataloged. Load libraries are usually cataloged, but if the one you need is not and you do not want it cataloged, the normal disposition must be coded as PASS. For example, you could code

```
DISP=(NEW,PASS)
```

EXECUTING A PROGRAM FROM A LIBRARY

FIGURE 8.15

Creating and using a load library in the same job

```
//JCLQB680 JOB ,'J.C.LEWIS'
//JOBLIB    DD DSN=WYL.QB.JCL.MODLIB,
//             DISP=(,CATLG),
//             UNIT=DISK,
//             VOL=SER=USR007,
//             SPACE=(1024,(50,10,1))
//STEPCL    EXEC COBUCL
//COB.SYSIN DD *

          COBOL Source Code

/*
//LKED.SYSLMOD DD DSN=*.JOBLIB,
//             VOL=REF=*.JOBLIB,
//             DISP=MOD
//LKED.SYSIN DD *
 NAME LISTER(R)
/*
//STEPEX    EXEC PGM=LISTER
//SYSPRINT DD SYSOUT=A
//OUTPUT    DD SYSOUT=A
//INPUT     DD *

          Input Data

/*
//
```

or you might code

```
DISP=(SHR,PASS)
```

To create the load library in the same job in which it is referenced by a JOBLIB DD statement is very unusual, outside of a manual. Figure 8.15 provides a sample of how this might be done.

The STEPLIB DD Statement

If your job has many steps and the program executed in each step is in a different library, all the libraries would have to be concatenated in the JOBLIB DD statement. This could mean that the search time to find a program to be executed will be quite long. The search time can be reduced by using a STEPLIB statement in each step in place of the JOBLIB statement.

The STEPLIB DD statement is coded like any other DD statement that points to an existing library. Unlike the JOBLIB DD statement, it does not have to be in any particular position within the step, although the STEPLIB DD statement is often coded immediately after the EXEC statement.

If the program named in the EXEC statement is not found in the library or libraries referenced by the STEPLIB DD statement, SYS1.LINKLIB is searched. If the program is not found in SYS1.LINKLIB, the job will abend with a system completion code of 806.

If all but one of the programs to be executed in a job are in the same library, a JOBLIB DD statement would be used to point to that library. A STEPLIB DD statement would be used in the one step that uses a program from another library. When a STEPLIB DD statement is specified and the program is not found in the STEPLIB library, SYS1.LINKLIB will be searched, but not the library indicated by the JOBLIB DD statement. If, for example, in Figure 8.14 we wished to prevent library LOADLIB from being searched in STEP3, then we could have coded a STEPLIB DD statement naming SYS1.LINKLIB as the library to be searched.

You may use the PARM parameter to pass data to your program even when the program is stored in executable form in a load library. You simply code the PARM parameter on the EXEC statement, and of course you do not include a procstepname.

There is one peculiar feature to remember when you use a PARM field with a PL/I program. The PL/I compiler adds code to your program that accepts data from a PARM field. To distinguish between these data and the data you want placed in the PARM field, code a slash before your data. You must code a slash before your values, e.g.,

```
PARM='/SWINTER'
```

Dynamic Linking

In some systems not all modules required by a program are linked to it when it is link edited. Some modules are linked when the program is executing. This is called dynamic linking. If modules are to be linked at execution, the library in which they are stored must be made available to the job. This can be done by concatenating the appropriate library—for example, SYS1.COBLIB—to the JOBLIB or STEPLIB DD statement.

LINKING PROGRAMS

If you are working on a large system in which you are writing one module and your coworker another, the two object modules must be link edited together to form a single load module. Figure 8.16 shows how a main program and a subprogram may be compiled and link edited. The resulting load module is stored in the library named PLILOAD. (It is not necessary to compile a main program and a subprogram separately; they may be compiled together using batch compilation. The rules for batch compilation are explained in the programmer's guide for each language [see the bibliography]. Assembler, however, does not permit batch compilation. Batch compilation is not used in Figure 8.16 because this example leads naturally to the next example, for which batch compilation may not be used.) Figure 8.16 illustrates PL/I, but the other languages are used the same way.

The important point is that in the first step you execute the compile only procedure. This step puts the main program's object module into the temporary data set named &&LOADSET. In the second step, you execute the compile and link edit procedure. This step first puts the subprogram's object module into &&LOADSET, and then link edits the two object modules to form a load module.

You might wonder why the subprogram's object module did not erase

FIGURE 8.16

Compiling and link editing a PL/I program and subroutine

```
//JCLQB640 JOB ,'GROUCHO'
//COMPLKD2 EXEC PLIXC
//PLI.SYSIN DD *

          Main Program

//STEP2    EXEC PLIXCL
//PLI.SYSIN DD *

          Subprogram

//LKED.SYSLMOD DD DSN=WYL.QB.JCL.PLILOAD,
//              DISP=SHR
//LKED.SYSIN DD *
 NAME module-name
/*
//
```

the main program's existing object module when the subprogram was added to &&LOADSET. The answer lies in the clever coding of the DISP parameter for LOADSET. As shown in Figure 8.10, in the procedures for all the languages the status subparameter for the data set that receives the object module is coded as MOD. If a data set does not exist, as LOADSET did not exist at the start of the first step, then MOD has the same effect as NEW. However, if the data set does exist, as LOADSET did at the start of the second step, then, as you learned in Chapter 4, MOD means add to the end of the data set. Because the procedures use MOD this way, you may compile as many programs as you want and have them all added to the same data set.

There is one last point to be made about Figure 8.16. Notice that the main program was compiled first, followed by the subprogram. That is because the computer will start execution with the first program in the linkage editor's input. Since we want to start execution with the main program, we had to make sure the main program was first. Actually, PL/I programs always start execution with the main program, so the order of the programs in Figure 8.16 was not important. However, for other languages the order is important. So it is good practice to make a habit of always compiling the main program first. Sometimes you cannot put the main program first. We will see what to do in those cases a little later.

Linking a Previously Compiled Program

Now let us assume that your coworker has compiled her subprogram and stored the object module in a library. In this case, the linkage editor control statement INCLUDE is used to bring your coworker's object module into the load module. Figure 8.17 illustrates this situation. A PL/I program is compiled and link edited together with an object module found in a private library. This object module was produced from COBOL source code. By the way, it is not usual for a large system to use two high-level languages; usually one language is used. If there is a need to use a second language, it is usually assembler. The example in Figure 8.17 uses two high-level languages because it is a slightly more complex situation. Later you will notice the simplification when both programs are written in the same language.

In Figure 8.17, the first thing to observe is the COBOL library concatenated to the SYSLIB DD statement. This will give the COBOL object module access to the COBOL modules required. How can we know the data set name of the COBOL library—in this case, SYS1.COBLIB? Look at the SYSLIB DD statement in the link edit step of the COBUCL procedure.

FIGURE 8.17

Compiling a PL/I program and link editing it with a COBOL module

```
//JCLQB645 JOB ,'CHICO'
//COMPLKD2 EXEC PLIXCL
//PLI.SYSIN DD *

          PL/I Source Code

/*
//LKED.SYSLIB DD
//        DD DSN=SYS1.COBLIB,
//           DISP=SHR
//LKED.SYSLMOD DD DSN=WYL.QB.JCL.LOADLIB,
//           DISP=OLD
//LKED.PRIVATE DD DSN=WYL.QB.JCL.OBJLIB,
//           DISP=OLD
//LKED.SYSIN DD *
 INCLUDE PRIVATE(COBMOD)
 NAME LOADPLC(R)
/*
//
```

The SYSLMOD override statement in Figure 8.17 points to an existing load library, just as in Figure 8.11. The next DD statement makes a private object module library named OBJLIB available to the linkage editor. The linkage editor control statements following the LKED.SYSIN DD statement will tell the linkage editor how to use this private object module library. After the input is taken from the primary input, which is the SYSLIN data set, the linkage editor control statements are read. The INCLUDE control statement points to the library member named COBMOD that is in a library defined by the DD statement whose name is PRIVATE. The INCLUDE statement must be placed before the NAME statement.

THE INCLUDE STATEMENT.   Let us look at the INCLUDE statement. The object module to be included may reside in a library, or it may reside in a physical sequential data set. If the object module is in a physical sequential data set, then the INCLUDE statement would be coded as

```
INCLUDE dd1
```

where dd1 is the ddname of the DD statement that points to the object module. If you wish to include more than one object module, then, instead of coding several INCLUDE statements, code

```
INCLUDE dd1,dd2,...
```

where dd1,dd2,... are the ddnames of the DD statements that point to the various object modules.

In many computer centers there is a special library for object modules. When the object module is in a library, the INCLUDE statement is coded as illustrated in Figure 8.17. If you want several modules from the same library, then you code the control statement as

```
INCLUDE dd1(mod1,mod2,...)
```

where dd1 is the ddname of the DD statement that points to the object module library and mod1,mod2,... are the particular object modules that you want included. You can use the same INCLUDE statement to point to several libraries. In fact, you can point to sequential data sets and libraries on the same control statement by simply coding the ddnames and, in the case of libraries, the module names and separating the entries by commas.

Returning to Figure 8.17, you see that the load module produced will be named LOADPLC and will replace an existing module in LOADLIB. The order of the modules in the load module is shown in the output listing if MAP is coded in the PARM field of the link edit step. The order of modules in the load module (excluding modules called in by the compiler) is the same as the order in which they are input. The load module produced as a result of executing the job in Figure 8.17 would have the PL/I program first, because it came from the SYSLIN DD statement, followed by the COBOL program.

As mentioned earlier, it is common for the main program and subprogram to be written in the same language. In that case the job stream in Figure 8.17 could be used with the simplification that there would be no need to concatenate a library to the SYSLIB DD statement.

THE ENTRY STATEMENT.   In Figure 8.17, we want to begin execution with the main program. Since the PL/I program is the main program, it is appropriate to code it first. Suppose, however, it were the other way around, and the PL/I program were the subprogram and the COBOL program were the main program. We would need some way to tell the system to begin execution with the COBOL program. We would do this with the ENTRY control statement.

LINKING PROGRAMS

The ENTRY control statement is coded as follows:

ENTRY entryname

where entryname is the name of the program with which execution is to start. The entryname in each language is different. In assembler, it is the name specified in the CSECT instruction of the main program; in COBOL, it is the name specified in the PROGRAM-ID instruction of the main program; in FORTRAN, it is MAIN; and in PL/I, it is PLISTART. The order of the ENTRY and INCLUDE statements does not matter, but they must both be placed before the NAME statement.

Creating Multiple Load Modules

Figure 8.18 illustrates how the linkage editor can create several load modules in one job. The load modules created are stored as members of a library created in this job. SYSLMOD is overridden to create the load library. You will notice that no DCB information is provided; none is required unless you specify DCBS in the linkage editor PARM field. Do not do this unless you must.

FIGURE 8.18

Creating several load modules in one job

```
//JCLQB650 JOB ,'HARPO'
//COMPLKD3 EXEC FORTXCL
//FORT.SYSIN DD *

          FORTRAN Source Code

/*
//LKED.SYSLMOD DD DSN=WYL.QB.JCL.FORTLOAD,
//             DISP=(,KEEP),
//             VOL=SER=SCR002,
//             SPACE=(CYL,(10,1,10))
//LKED.PRIVATE DD DSN=WYL.QB.JCL.FORTOBJ,
//             DISP=SHR
//LKED.SYSIN DD *
 NAME MOD1
 INCLUDE PRIVATE(MOD2)
 NAME MOD2
 INCLUDE PRIVATE(MODA,MODB,MODC)
 NAME MOD3
/*
//
```

The object library named FORTOBJ is made available to the linkage editor with the additional DD statement whose name is PRIVATE. This library contains previously created object modules. The first linkage editor control statement supplies the module name for the object code found in the primary input, the SYSLIN data set. The next two linkage editor control statements belong together. The INCLUDE statement takes the object module named MOD2 from the library pointed to by the DD statement PRIVATE. The linkage editor will process this object module and create a second load module. The NAME statement assigns the name MOD2 to this load module. You will notice that the object and load module members have the same name. If the source code were a member of a source library, the same name would be used for the source code member. The advantage of this approach is that there is only one name to remember for the three states of the program — that is, source, object, and load module.

The last two control statements will result in the creation of a third load module named MOD3. The INCLUDE statement takes three object modules MODA, MODB, and MODC from the library pointed to by the PRIVATE DD statement.

You should understand that there are three separate linkage editor tasks accomplished by Figure 8.18, the creation of load modules MOD1, MOD2, and MOD3, and that these three tasks are independent of one another. The primary function of the job in Figure 8.18 is to compile a FORTRAN program and to link edit the object module produced to create the load module MOD1. It was convenient to create MOD2 and MOD3 at the same time because the job invoked the linkage editor and made available the FORTOBJ library which is required to create MOD2 and MOD3. (Also, it shows you how to create several load modules in one job.)

In this example, assume that all the object modules were originally written in the same language. If different languages were used, additional libraries would have to be made available, as shown in Figure 8.17.

The LIBRARY Statement

The job coded in Figure 8.19 illustrates the use of the LIBRARY linkage editor control statement. In this example, assembler modules are assumed. The extra modules will be found in libraries ASMOBJ1 and ASMOBJ2, which are concatenated together under the ddname PRIVATE. Let us examine the first LIBRARY control statement in Figure 8.19. LIBRARY is the operation, and PRIVATE(MODA,MODB) is the operand. PRIVATE is the ddname of the DD statement pointing to the library in which object modules MODA and MODB will be found.

LINKING PROGRAMS

FIGURE 8.19

Assembling a program and link editing it into a load library

```
//JCLQB655 JOB ,'GUMMO'
//COMPLKD4 EXEC ASMFCL
//ASM.SYSIN DD *

            Assembler Source Code

/*
//LKED.SYSLMOD DD DSN=WYL.QB.JCL.MODLIB,
//             DISP=OLD
//LKED.PRIVATE DD DSN=WYL.QB.JCL.ASMOBJ1,
//             DISP=SHR
//           DD DSN=WYL.QB.JCL.ASMOBJ2,
//             DISP=SHR
//LKED.SYSIN DD *
 LIBRARY PRIVATE(MODA,MODB)
 LIBRARY (CITYTAX)
 NAME PAY(R)
/*
//
```

The general form of the LIBRARY control statement is

```
LIBRARY dd1(mod1,mod2,...)
```

It is possible that these object modules, MODA and MODB, also exist in a standard library and that new versions are being tested. The LIBRARY control statement tells the linkage editor to take the object modules from the library or libraries pointed to by the specified DD statement instead of from the SYSLIB library or libraries.

The LIBRARY and INCLUDE statements are similar, but not the same. Any module specified with an INCLUDE statement is immediately incorporated into the load module. On the other hand, a module named in a LIBRARY statement is not called until the module is required to resolve an external reference. In fact, if no reference is made to a module named in a LIBRARY statement, it will not be incorporated into the load module.

The second LIBRARY control statement in Figure 8.19 is used to exclude a module from a load module. Any reference to CITYTAX in the load module to be named PAY will remain unresolved when the automatic-call library is searched. Why would you want to exclude an object module from a load module? To create a smaller load module. In this example, we do not need a CITYTAX module in a payroll program because no one in the installation

CHAPTER 8 / USING SYSTEM PROCEDURES

lives in the city. The general format of the LIBRARY statement to exclude a module is

```
LIBRARY (mod1,mod2,...)
```

OVERLAY*

In all the cases we have examined so far, the load module created is loaded into storage and remains there until execution ceases. The **overlay** structure creates a load module that will be loaded into storage in pieces. These pieces are called **segments**. When a new piece or segment is needed, it is brought into storage for execution. Figure 8.20 shows a sample hierarchical organization and the related linkage editor control statements. The INSERT statement causes the linkage editor to take a module that it will find in the SYSLIN data set. If the modules were in one or more different libraries, INCLUDE statements would be used in place of the INSERT statement. The OVERLAY statement identifies the point at which the overlay is made. These places are labeled in Figure 8.20 as ONE, TWO, THREE, and FOUR.

When the linkage editor is invoked for overlay structure, OVLY must be specified in the PARM field.

Let us discuss what actually will happen if the modules shown in Figure 8.20 are executed. Initially the segment labeled ROOT will be loaded into storage. This segment will remain in storage for the life of the execution. When called by the ROOT segment, segment A1 will be loaded and executed. After A1 execution ends, control will be returned to the ROOT segment. Notice that the INSERT statements for A1, A2, and A3 are preceded by the statement OVERLAY ONE. This OVERLAY statement means that if segment A2 is called, it will be placed in the same starting location as A1. Similarly, if segment A3 is called, it will be loaded in the same starting storage location as A1 and A2. The INSERT B1 and B2 statements are preceded by a different OVERLAY statement, OVERLAY TWO. Segment A3 can, while remaining in storage, call segments B1 and B2, which would be loaded and executed in storage following segment A3. When control is returned to the ROOT segment, if segment A4 is called, it will be loaded in the same location as A3. If B4 is called, it will be loaded following segment A4. If B4 were to call either C1 or C2, either one would be loaded following segment B4.

---

* This section may be skipped without loss of continuity.

OVERLAY

FIGURE 8.20

Hierarchical organization and linkage editor control statements

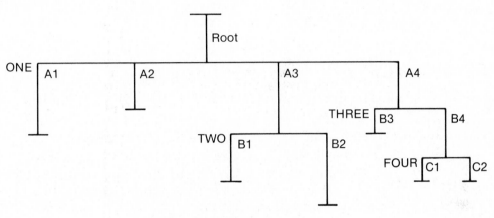

Hierarchical organization

```
ENTRY BEGIN
INSERT ROOT
OVERLAY ONE
INSERT A1
OVERLAY ONE
INSERT A2
OVERLAY ONE
INSERT A3
OVERLAY TWO
INSERT B1
OVERLAY TWO
INSERT B2
OVERLAY ONE
INSERT A4
OVERLAY THREE
INSERT B3
OVERLAY THREE
INSERT B4
OVERLAY FOUR
INSERT C1
OVERLAY FOUR
INSERT C2
```

Overlay structure was an important technique for making the most of limited main storage. It has fallen into disuse because main storage has become relatively inexpensive and because of the development of virtual storage, which gives the illusion of much larger storage than is actually available. However, with the growth of small personal computers, knowledge of this concept may prove helpful.

PROCEDURES TO COMPILE, LINK EDIT, AND EXECUTE A PROGRAM

Figure 8.21 shows listings of IBM-supplied procedures to compile, link edit, and execute. The names of these procedures end with the letters CLG.

The principal difference between the procedures in Figure 8.21 and the compile and link edit procedures in Figure 8.10 is the addition of the third step, which executes the program just compiled and link edited. The third step's name is GO.

If you compare the SYSLMOD statement in the COBUCL procedure with that in COBUCLG, you will see a difference in the data set name. In the COBUCLG procedure, the member name of GO is included in the data set name. In the COBUCL procedure, the user must supply the member name in some fashion, such as with the NAME linkage editor control statement.

The third step in these procedures, which causes the program to execute, uses a new form of the EXEC statement. Instead of naming the program to be executed, it uses a backwards reference. The same rules that apply to a data set backwards reference apply here. The asterisk tells the system that this is a backwards reference. The next element in this field names the step in which the DD statement will be found, and the last one names the DD statement itself. Thus the backwards reference in COBUCLG is pointing to the load library member to be executed. Outside of these procedures, backwards references are rarely used to identify the program to be executed.

Executing a Compile, Link Edit, and Go Procedure

Figures 8.22a and 8.22b illustrate the JCL used to invoke COBUCLG and PLIXCLG. You will notice how similar the JCL is in both jobs. Also, except for the procedure name, the JCL in Figure 8.22a is identical to the JCL in Figure 8.7 used to invoke COBUCG. In both cases, the COBOL source code follows the

FIGURE 8.21 (a) The COBUCLG procedure

```
//COB       EXEC  PGM=IKFCBL00,PARM=SUPMAP,REGION=86K
//SYSPRINT  DD    SYSOUT=A
//SYSUT1    DD    DSNAME=&&SYSUT1,UNIT=SYSDA,SPACE=(460,(700,100))
//SYSUT2    DD    DSNAME=&&SYSUT2,UNIT=SYSDA,SPACE=(460,(700,100))
//SYSUT3    DD    DSNAME=&&SYSUT3,UNIT=SYSDA,SPACE=(460,(700,100))
//SYSUT4    DD    DSNAME=&&SYSUT4,UNIT=SYSDA,SPACE=(460,(700,100))
//SYSLIN    DD    DSNAME=&&LOADSET,DISP=(MOD,PASS),UNIT=SYSDA,         X
//                SPACE=(80,(500,100))
//LKED      EXEC  PGM=IEWL,PARM='LIST,XREF,LET',COND=(5,LT,COB),      X
//                REGION=96K
//SYSLIN    DD    DSNAME=&&LOADSET,DISP=(OLD,DELETE)
//          DD    DDNAME=SYSIN
//SYSLMOD   DD    DSNAME=&&GOSET(GO),DISP=(NEW,PASS),UNIT=SYSDA,       X
//                SPACE=(1024,(50,20,1))
//SYSLIB    DD    DSNAME=SYS1.COBLIB,DISP=SHR
//SYSUT1    DD    UNIT=(SYSDA,SEP=(SYSLIN,SYSLMOD)),                   X
//                SPACE=(1024,(50,20))
//SYSPRINT  DD    SYSOUT=A
//GO        EXEC  PGM=*.LKED.SYSLMOD,COND=((5,LT,COB),(5,LT,LKED))
```

(b) The PLIXCLG procedure

```
//PLIXCLG   PROC  LKLBDSN='SYS1.PLIBASE'
//PLI       EXEC  PGM=IEL0AA,PARM='OBJECT,NODECK',REGION=100K
//SYSPRINT  DD    SYSOUT=A
//SYSLIN    DD    DSN=&&LOADSET,DISP=(MOD,PASS),UNIT=SYSSQ,
//                SPACE=(80,(250,100))
//SYSUT1    DD    DSN=&&SYSUT1,UNIT=SYSDA,SPACE=(1024,(200,50),,CONTIG,ROUND),
//                DCB=BLKSIZE=1024
//LKED      EXEC  PGM=IEWL,PARM='XREF,LIST',COND=(9,LT,PLI),REGION=100K
//SYSLIB    DD    DSN=&LKLBDSN,DISP=SHR
//          DD    DSN=SYS1.PLIBASE,DISP=SHR
//SYSLMOD   DD    DSN=&&GOSET(GO),DISP=(MOD,PASS),UNIT=SYSDA,
//                SPACE=(1024,(50,20,1))
//SYSUT1    DD    DSN=&&SYSUT1,UNIT=SYSDA,SPACE=(1024,(200,20)),
//                DCB=BLKSIZE=1024
//SYSPRINT  DD    SYSOUT=A
//SYSLIN    DD    DSN=&&LOADSET,DISP=(OLD,DELETE)
//          DD    DDNAME=SYSIN
//SYSIN     DD    DUMMY
//GO        EXEC  PGM=*.LKED.SYSLMOD,COND=((9,LT,PLI),(9,LT,LKED)),
//                REGION=100K
//SYSPRINT  DD    SYSOUT=A
```

(cont.)

(c) The FORTXCLG procedure

```
//FORTXCLG PROC FXPGM=IFEAAB,FXREGN=256K,FXPDECK=NODECK,           +42900000
//              FXPQLST=NOLIST,FXPOPT=0,GOREGN=100K,               +42950000
//              GOF5DD='DDNAME=SYSIN',GOF6DD='SYSOUT=A',           +43000000
//              GOF7DD='SYSOUT=B'                                   43050000
//*                                                                43100000
//*        PARAMETER  DEFAULT-VALUE    USAGE                       43150000
//*                                                                43200000
//*        FXPGM      IFEAAB           COMPILER NAME               43250000
//*        FXREGN     256K             FORT-STEP REGION            43300000
//*        FXPDECK    NODECK           COMPILER DECK OPTION        43350000
//*        FXPQLST    NOLIST           COMPILER LIST OPTION        43400000
//*        FXPOPT     C                COMPILER OPTIMIZATION       43450000
//*        GOREGN     100K             GO-STEP REGION              43500000
//*        GOF5DD     DDNAME=SYSIN     GO.FT05F001 OPERAND         43550000
//*        GOF6DD     SYSOUT=A         GO.FT06F001 OPERAND         43600000
//*        GOF7DD     SYSOUT=B         GO.FT07F001 OPERAND         43650000
//*                                                                43700000
//FORT    EXEC PGM=&FXPGM,REGION=&FXREGN,COND=(4,LT),             +43750000
//              PARM='&FXPDECK,&FXPQLST,OPT(&FXPOPT)'             +43800000
//SYSPRINT DD SYSOUT=A,DCB=BLKSIZE=3429                            43850000
//SYSTERM  DD SYSOUT=A
//SYSUT1   DD UNIT=SYSSQ,SPACE=(3465,(3,3)),DCB=BLKSIZE=3465      +3900000
//SYSUT2   DD UNIT=SYSSQ,SPACE=(5048,(10,10))                     43950000
//SYSPUNCH DD SYSOUT=B,DCB=BLKSIZE=3440                           44000000
//SYSLIN   DD DSN=&&LOADSET,DISP=(MOD,PASS),UNIT=SYSSQ,          +44050000
//              SPACE=(3200,(25,6)),DCB=BLKSIZE=3200              44100000
//LKED    EXEC PGM=IEWL,REGION=96K,COND=(4,LT),                 +44150000
//              PARM='LET,LIST,MAP,XREF'                          44200000
//SYSPRINT DD SYSOUT=A                                            44250000
//SYSLIB   DD DSN=SYS1.FORTLIB,DISP=SHR                           44300000
//SYSUT1   DD UNIT=SYSDA,SPACE=(1024,(200,20))                    44350000
//SYSLMOD  DD DSN=&&GOSET(MAIN),DISP=(,PASS),UNIT=SYSDA,         +44400000
//              SPACE=(TRK,(10,10,1),RLSE)                        44450000
//SYSLIN   DD DSN=&&LOADSET,DISP=(OLD,DELETE)                     44500000
//         DD DDNAME=SYSIN                                        44550000
//GO      EXEC PGM=*.LKED.SYSLMOD,REGION=&GOREGN,COND=(4,LT)    +44600000
//FT05F001 DD &GOF5DD                                            44650000
//FT06F001 DD &GOF6DD                                            44700000
//FT07F001 DD &GOF7DD                                            44750000
```

(d) The ASMFCLG procedure

```
//ASMFCLG  PROC  MAC='SYS1.MACLIB',MAC1='SYS1.MACLIB'
//ASM      EXEC  PGM=IFOX00,PARM=OBJ,REGION=128K
//SYSLIB   DD    DSN=&MAC,DISP=SHR
//         DD    DSN=&MAC1,DISP=SHR
//SYSUT1   DD    DSN=&&SYSUT1,UNIT=SYSSQ,SPACE=(1700,(600,100)),
//               SEP=(SYSLIB)
//SYSUT2   DD    DSN=&&SYSUT2,UNIT=SYSSQ,SPACE=(1700,(300,50)),
//               SEP=(SYSLIB,SYSUT1)
//SYSUT3   DD    DSN=&&SYSUT3,UNIT=SYSSQ,SPACE=(1700,(300,50))
//SYSPRINT DD    SYSOUT=A,DCB=BLKSIZE=1089
//SYSPUNCH DD    SYSOUT=B
//SYSGO    DD    DSN=&&OBJSET,UNIT=SYSSQ,SPACE=(80,(200,50)),
//               DISP=(MOD,PASS)
//LKED     EXEC  PGM=IEWL,PARM=(XREF,LET,LIST,NCAL),REGION=128K,
//               COND=(8,LT,ASM)
//SYSLIN   DD    DSN=&&OBJSET,DISP=(OLD,DELETE)
//         DD    DDNAME=SYSIN
//SYSLMOD  DD    DSN=&&GOSET(GO),UNIT=SYSDA,SPACE=(1024,(50,20,1)),
//               DISP=(MOD,PASS)
//SYSUT1   DD    DSN=&&SYSUT1,UNIT=(SYSDA,SEP=(SYSLIN,SYSLMOD)),
//               SPACE=(1024,(50,20))
//SYSPRINT DD    SYSOUT=A
//GO       EXEC  PGM=*.LKED.SYSLMOD,COND=((8,LT,ASM),(4,LT,LKED))
```

CHAPTER 8 / USING SYSTEM PROCEDURES

FIGURE 8.22

(a) Compiling, link editing, and executing a COBOL program

```
//JCLQB660 JOB ,'J.C.LEWIS'
//COMPLG1  EXEC COBUCLG
//COB.SYSIN DD *

          COBOL Source Code

/*
//GO.INPUT DD *

          Input Data

/*
//GO.OUTPUT DD SYSOUT=A
//
```

(b) Compiling, link editing, and executing a PL/I program

```
//JCLQB665 JOB ,'J.C.LEWIS'
//COMPLG2  EXEC PLIXCLG
//PLI.SYSIN DD *

          PL/I Source Code

/*
//GO.CARDIN DD *

          Input Data

/*
//GO.PRINTER DD SYSOUT=A
//
```

COB.SYSIN DD statement, the GO.INPUT DD statement provides the input data, and the GO.OUTPUT DD statement provides the printer output.

You may be wondering why you would bother with the compile, link edit, and execute procedures when you could use the compile and execute procedures. As a general rule, if you can use the loader, use the compile and execute procedure. However, if you want to create a permanent load module, you must use the linkage editor. If you need to use any of the linkage editor control statements discussed earlier in this chapter, you must use the compile, link edit, and execute procedure.

Figure 8.23 is an actual compile, link edit, and execution of the LISTER program. The COBUCLG procedure used in the CUNY system differs in some

FIGURE 8.23

Actual compilation, link editing and execution of a COBOL program

```
1  //JCLQB683 JOB ,'J.C.LEWIS'
2  //COMPLG1  EXEC COBUCLG
3  //COB.SYSIN DD *
4  /*
5  //GO.INPUT DD *
6  /*
7  //GO.OUTPUT DD SYSOUT=A
8  //
```

```
 9   1  //JCLQB683 JOB ,'J.C.LEWIS'                                           00000100
10   2  //COMPLG1 EXEC COBUCLG                                                00000200
11   3  XXCOBUCLG PROC SUT1=15,SOBJ=15,SLUT2=20,SLMOD1=50,SLMOD2=20,          00000300
12      XX        ADDLIB='SYS1.ADDLIB',STEPLIB='SYS1.ADDLIB'
13   4  XXCOB     EXEC PGM=IKFCBL00                                           00000400
14   5  XXSYSPRINT DD SYSOUT=A,DCB=BLKSIZE=1936                               00000500
15   6  XXSYSUT1  DD UNIT=3330,SPACE=(TRK,(&SUT1,5))                          00000600
16   7  XXSYSUT2  DD UNIT=3330,SPACE=(TRK,(&SUT1,5))                          00000700
17   8  XXSYSUT3  DD UNIT=3330,SPACE=(TRK,(&SUT1,5))                          00000800
18   9  XXSYSUT4  DD UNIT=3330,SPACE=(TRK,(&SUT1,5))                          00000900
19  10  XXSYSUT5  DD UNIT=3330,SPACE=(TRK,(&SUT1,5)),DISP=(,PASS)             00001000
20  11  XXSYSLIN  DD DSNAME=&LOADSET,DCB=BLKSIZE=3120,DISP=(MOD,PASS),        00001100
21      XX        UNIT=3330,SPACE=(6400,(&SOBJ,10))
22  12  //COB.SYSIN DD *,DCB=BLKSIZE=80                                       00001200
23  13  XXLKED    EXEC PGM=IEWL,PARM='LIST,XREF,LET',COND=(5,LT,COB)          00001300
24  14  XXSYSLIN  DD DSNAME=&LOADSET,DISP=(OLD,DELETE)                        00001400
25      XX        DDNAME=SYSIN
26  15  XXSYSLMOD DD DSNAME=&&GOSET(GO),DISP=(NEW,PASS),UNIT=3330,            00001500
27      XX        SPACE=(1024,(&SLMOD1,&SLMOD2,1))
28  17  XXSYSLIB  DD DSNAME=&ADDLIB,DISP=SHR                                  00001600
29  18  XX        DSNAME=SYS1.COBLIB,DISP=SHR                                 00001700
30  19  XXSYSUT1  DD UNIT=(3330,SEP=(SYSLIN,SYSLMOD)),                        00001800
31      XX        SPACE=(1024,(&SLUT1,&SLUT2))
32  20  XXSYSPRINT DD SYSOUT=A,DCB=BLKSIZE=1936                               00001900
33  21  XXGO      EXEC PGM=*.LKED.SYSLMOD,COND=((5,LT,COB),(5,LT,LKED))       00002000
34  22  XXSTEPLIB DD DSNAME=SYS1.COBLIB,DISP=SHR                             00002100
35  23  XX        DSNAME=&STEPLIB,DISP=SHR                                   00002200
36  24  XXSYSUT5  DD DSN=*.COB.SYSUT5,DISP=(OLD,DELETE)                      00002300
37  25  XXSYSDROUT DD SYSOUT=A,DCB=BLKSIZE=1936                             00002400
38  26  XXDISPLAY DD SYSOUT=A,DCB=(RECFM=FA,LRECL=121,BLKSIZE=121,BUFNO=1)  00002500
39  27  XXSYSOUT  DD SYSOUT=A                                               00002600
40  28  XXDELETE  DD DSN=&&GOSET,DISP=(OLD,DELETE,DELETE)                   00002700
41  29  //GO.INPUT DD *,DCB=BLKSIZF=80                                      00002800
42  30  //GO.OUTPUT DD SYSOUT=A                                             00002900
43      //
```

(cont.)

275

46
47   CROSS REFERENCE TABLE
48

49 CONTROL SECTION   ENTRY

NAME	ORIGIN	LENGTH	NAME	LOCATION	NAME	LOCATION	NAME	LOCATION	NAME	LOCATION
LISTER	00	676								
ILBOCOM0*	678	102	ILBOCOM	678						
ILBODBG *	780	D78	ILBODBG0	7B2	ILBODBG1	7B6	ILBODBG2	7BA	ILBODBG3	7BE
			ILBODBG4	7C2	ILBODBG5	7C6	ILBODBG6	7CA	ILBODBG7	7CE
ILBOEXT *	14F8	72	ILBOEXT0	14FA						
ILBOSRV *	1570	37C	ILBOSRV0	15AA	ILBOSR	15AA	ILBOSR3	15AA	ILBOSRV1	15AE
			ILBOSTP1	15AE	ILBOST	15B2	ILBOSTP0	15B2		
ILBOBEG *	18F0	CA	ILBOBEG0	1922						
ILBOCMM *	19C0	3C9	ILBOCMM0	19F2	ILBOCMM1	19F6				
ILBOMSG *	1D90	D8	ILBOMSG0	1DC2						

LOCATION	REFERS TO SYMBOL	IN CONTROL SECTION	LOCATION	REFERS TO SYMBOL	IN CONTROL SECTION
478	ILBOSRV0	ILBOSRV	47C	ILBODBG0	ILBODBG
480	ILBOSR	ILBOSRV	484	ILBODBG4	ILBODBG
488	ILBOEXT0	ILBOEXT	48C	ILBOSRV1	ILBOSRV
400	ILBOCOM0	ILBOCOM0	13B4	ILBOFLW0	$UNRESOLVED(W)
13B8	ILBOFLW2	$UNRESOLVED(W)	13BC	ILBOTEF3	$UNRESOLVED(W)
13C0	ILBOSTN0	$UNRESOLVED(W)	1860	ILBOCOM	ILBOCOM0
1864	ILBOCMM0	ILBOCMM	1868	ILBOBEG0	ILBOBEG
186C	ILBOMSG0	ILBOMSG			

78 ENTRY ADDRESS   00
79 TOTAL LENGTH   1E68
80 ****GO   DOES NOT EXIST BUT HAS BEEN ADDED TO DATA SET
81 AUTHORIZATION CODE IS   0.
82
83 E. T. PHONE HOME

FIGURE 8.24

Compiling, link editing, and executing a PL/I program and subroutine

```
//JCLQB670 JOB ,'J.C.LEWIS'
//COMPLKD2 EXEC PLIXC
//PLI.SYSIN DD *

          Main Program

//STEP2    EXEC PLIXCLG
//PLI.SYSIN DD *

          Subprogram

//GO.CARDS DD *

          Input Data

//GO.LINES DD SYSOUT=A
//
```

ways from the IBM-supplied procedure COBUCLG, principally in the step in which the program is executed. From the point of view of our discussion, these changes are not relevant. If you compare Figure 8.23 with the contents of Figure 8.12, which is an actual COBUCL execution, you will see no significant difference. The compiler and linkage editor output are virtually the same. Line 83 of Figure 8.23 contains the COBOL program output.

Executing Subprograms

The compile, link edit, and execute procedures may also be used with subprograms. As an example, the PL/I main program and subprogram which were compiled and link edited in Figure 8.16 are compiled, link edited, and executed in Figure 8.24. The changes are that in Figure 8.24 the PLIXCLG procedure is used in the second step, the SYSLMOD DD statement is not overridden, and the DD statements for the input and output data sets are supplied.

EXERCISES

1. What is the purpose of a compiler or assembler?

2. What is the difference between a compiler and an assembler?

3. What do FORTRAN and COBOL stand for?

4. What is the output of a compiler?

5. What is a procedure?

6. What are the two types of procedures?

7. In what library would you probably find the procedure COBUC?

8. If you wanted to invoke the procedure COBUC, how would you code the EXEC statement?

9. How would you code the DD statement to input the COBOL source code? What is this DD statement called?

10. What is a PROC statement?

11. Where in a procedure must the PROC statement be located?

12. For which type of procedure is the PROC statement required?

13. What information is coded on a PROC statement?

14. If you needed to change information in a DD statement of a procedure for one run, what would you do?

15. What does && appearing at the start of a data set name signify?

16. In Figure 8.2a, if you wished to use the COBUC procedure and change the UNIT of SYSUT2 and SYSUT3 to SYSQ, what would you code?

17. What is a symbolic parameter? How do you assign a value to a symbolic parameter? When must you use apostrophes in assigning a value to a symbolic parameter?

18. What is concatenation? When would you use it?

19. If you wished to add a third library to the SYSLIB DD statement when using ASMFC, what would you code?

20. What does the loader do?

21. When would you use the loader?

22. How do you modify the execution of the loader?

23. What functions are performed by the compile and go procedures?

EXERCISES

24. What function performed by the loader is not performed by the linkage editor?

25. What function do both the linkage editor and the loader perform?

26. What is the output of the linkage editor? Under what ddname is the output produced?

27. How would you invoke the additional functions of the linkage editor?

28. How would you modify the execution of the linkage editor?

29. What is the difference between the linkage editor control statements NAME MOD and NAME MOD(R)?

30. What function does the linkage editor perform that the loader cannot?

31. Which linkage editor control statement is used to obtain an object module from a source other than the primary input?

32. Which linkage editor control statement is used to exclude a module from a load module?

33. Why would overlay structure be used?

34. For a previously compiled and link edited program to be executable, where must it be stored?

35. What parameter is used on a DD statement for a forward reference?

36. How would you change the JCL in Figure 8.17 if the program called for a FORTRAN module?

37. Using the linkage editor, how would you give a name to the load module?

38. In the compile, link edit, and go procedures, how is the program named in the execute or GO step?

39. When executing a previously compiled and link edited program, where does the system look for the program to be executed?

40. Figure 8.25 shows the execution of a job that attempts to add a load module named COBPGM1 to a load library named WYL.QB.JCL.LINKLIB. The output seems to indicate that the job ran perfectly, but when a programmer later tried to execute COBPGM1, using a JOBLIB statement that pointed to WYL.QB.JCL.LINKLIB, the job abended with a completion code of 806. Why?

FIGURE 8.25

Actual execution

```
//JCLQB633 JOB ,'J.C.LEWIS'
//COBLOAD  EXEC COBUCL
//COB.SYSIN DD *
/*
//LKED.SYSIN DD *
/*
//LKED.SYSLMOD DD DSN=WYL.QB.JCL.LINKLIB,
//            DISP=(NEW,CATLG),
//            UNIT=DISK,
//            VOL=SER=WYL004,
//            SPACE=(1024,(50,10,1),RLSE)
```

```
 1    //JCLQB633 JOB ,'J.C.LEWIS'                                                               00000100
 2    //COBLOAD  EXEC COBUCL                                                                     00000200
 3    XXCOBUCL  PROC SUT1=15,SOBJ=15,SLUT1=50,SLUT2=20,SLMOD1=50,SLMOD2=20,                      00000300
      XX             ADDLIB='SYS1.ADDLIB'
 4    XXCOB     EXEC PGM=IKFCBL00                                                                00000400
 5    XXSYSPRINT DD  SYSOUT=A,DCB=BLKSIZE=1936                                                   00000500
 6    XXSYSUT1  DD  DSN=&&SYSUT1,UNIT=3330,SPACE=(TRK,(&SUT1,5))                                 00000600
 7    XXSYSUT2  DD  DSN=&&SYSUT2,UNIT=3330,SPACE=(TRK,(&SUT1,5))                                 00000700
 8    XXSYSUT3  DD  DSN=&&SYSUT3,UNIT=3330,SPACE=(TRK,(&SUT1,5))                                 00000800
 9    XXSYSUT4  DD  DSN=&&SYSUT4,UNIT=3330,SPACE=(TRK,(&SUT1,5))                                 00000900
10    XXSYSLIN  DD  DSN=&&LOADSET,DCB=BLKSIZE=3120,DISP=(MOD,PASS),                              00001000
      XX             UNIT=3330,SPACE=(6400,(&SOBJ,10))
11    //COB.SYSIN DD *,DCB=BLKSIZE=80                                                            00001100
12    XXLKED    EXEC PGM=IEWL,PARM='LIST,XREF,LET',COND=(5,LT,COB)                               00001200
13    XXSYSLIN  DD  DSN=&&LOADSET,DISP=(OLD,DELETE)
```

```
14   XX           DD   DDNAME=SYSIN                                    00001300
15   XXSYSLMOD    DD   DSN=&&GOSET,DISP=(NEW,PASS),UNIT=3330,          00001400
     XX                SPACE=(1024,(&SLMOD1,&SLMOD2,1))                00001500
16   XXSYSLIB     DD   DSN=&ADDLIB,DISP=SHR                            00001600
17   XXSYSUT1     DD   DSN=SYS1.COBLIB,DISP=SHR                        00001700
18   XXSYSUT1     DD   UNIT=(3330,SEP=(SYSLIN,SYSLMOD)),               00001800
     XX                SPACE=(1024,(&SLUT1,&SLUT2))                    00001900
19   XXSYSPRINT   DD   SYSOUT=A,DCB=BLKSIZE=80                         00002000
20   //LKED.SYSIN  DD *,DCB=BLKSIZE=1936
21   //LKED.SYSLMOD DD DSN=WYL.QB.JCL.LINKLIB,
     //                 DISP=(NEW,CATLG),
     //                 UNIT=DISK,
     //                 VOL=SER=WYL004,
     //                 SPACE=(1024,(50,10,1),RLSE)

F64-LEVEL LINKAGE EDITOR OPTIONS SPECIFIED LIST,XREF,LET
         DEFAULT OPTION(S) USED -  SIZE=(196608,65536)
IEW0000
         NAME COBPGM1
LOCATION REFERS TO SYMBOL  IN CONTROL SECTION    LOCATION REFERS TO SYMBOL  IN CONTROL SECTION
  478    ILBOSRV0          ILBOSRV                 47C     ILBODBG0          ILBODBG
  480    ILBOSR            ILBOSRV                 484     ILBODBG4          ILBODBG
  488    ILBOEXT0          ILBOEXT                 48C     ILBOSRV1          ILBOSRV
  400    ILBOCOMO          ILBOCOMO                13B4    ILBOFLW0          $UNRESOLVED(W)
  13B8   ILBOFLW2          $UNRESOLVED(W)          13BC    ILBOTEF 3         $UNRESOLVED(W)
  13C0   ILBOSTNO          $UNRESOLVED(W)          1860    ILBOCOM           ILBOCOMO
  1864   ILBOCMMO          ILBOCMM                 1868    ILBOBEG0          ILBOBEG
  186C   ILBOMSGO          ILBOMSG

ENTRY ADDRESS      00
TOTAL LENGTH       1E68
****COBPGM1   NOW ADDED TO DATA SET
AUTHORIZATION CODE IS    0.
```

PROGRAMMING ASSIGNMENTS

1. Using the COBOL program LISTER or any other simple program in either COBOL, PL/I, FORTRAN, or assembler language, execute each of the four procedures we have discussed. Modify the compile and link edit procedure execution so that the load module is stored in either a new or an existing load library. After the module is stored in a load library, execute the program from the load library once using a JOBLIB DD statement and once using a STEPLIB DD statement.

2. In any language you like, write a main program and a subprogram. Compile the subprogram and store the object module as a sequential data set. Using a compile, link edit, and execute procedure, compile the main program, link edit it with the subprogram, and execute the resulting load module.

SUMMARY

In this chapter you have learned

- the functions of a compiler

- the functions of the loader and when to use it

- the functions of the linkage editor and when to use it

- how to use system procedures to compile, load, link edit, and execute programs

- how to override a DD statement in a procedure

- how to add a DD statement to a procedure

- what a symbolic parameter is and how to code a value for one

- how to use the DDNAME parameter to create a forward reference

- how to store a load module in a private library

- how to execute a load module that is stored in a private library

CHAPTER 9

USER-WRITTEN PROCEDURES

LEARNING OBJECTIVES

IN THIS CHAPTER YOU WILL LEARN

- how to write, test, and use user-written procedures
- how to code in-stream procedures
- how to use symbolic parameters in user-written procedures

YOU WILL ALSO LEARN THE MEANING OF THE FOLLOWING TERM:

- nullify

In Chapter 8 you learned how to use system procedures. In this chapter you will learn how to create, test, and use your own procedures.

CREATING AN IN-STREAM PROCEDURE

As our first example, let us write a procedure that uses the program IEFBR14 to create a library. The coding we need is shown in Figure 9.1. When the coding in Figure 9.1 is executed, it will catalog a library named MYLIB on disk

FIGURE 9.1

JCL to create a PDS using IEFBR14

```
//LIBMAKE    EXEC PGM=IEFBR14,
//                REGION=32K
//LIBDD      DD DSN=WYL.QB.JCL.MYLIB,
//              DISP=(,CATLG),
//              UNIT=DISK,
//              VOL=SER=WYL003,
//              SPACE=(TRK,(5,,7)),
//              DCB=(RECFM=FB,LRECL=80,BLKSIZE=1600)
```

CREATING AN IN-STREAM PROCEDURE

FIGURE 9.2

An in-stream procedure to create a PDS using IEFBR14

```
//CREATE    PROC
//LIBMAKE   EXEC PGM=IEFBR14,
//               REGION=32K
//LIBDD     DD DSN=WYL.QB.JCL.MYLIB,
//             DISP=(,CATLG),
//             UNIT=DISK,
//             VOL=SER=WYL003,
//             SPACE=(TRK,(5,,7)),
//             DCB=(RECFM=FB,LRECL=80,BLKSIZE=1600)
//          PEND
```

pack WYL003. The library will occupy 5 tracks, and contain 7 directory blocks; the record size will be 80 bytes; the blocksize will be 1600 bytes.

To convert the coding in Figure 9.1 into a cataloged procedure, we would have to add it to the procedure library. However, first it would be a good idea to execute it to make sure there are no errors. The way to do that is to convert it into an in-stream procedure.

Figure 9.2 shows how the coding in Figure 9.1 is converted into an in-stream procedure. (Notice the name. A procedure in the input stream is called an in-stream procedure. Data in the input stream are called input stream data.)

As you can see, the conversion is very easy. All we do is add a PROC statement at the start of the procedure and a PEND statement at the end. We studied the PROC statement in Chapter 8. There you learned that in cataloged procedures the PROC statement is optional. For in-stream procedures the PROC statement is required and must have a name coded in the name field. In Figure 9.2, the name is CREATE, which is used when the in-stream procedure is executed.

The PEND statement is used only to mark the end of an in-stream procedure. The rules for coding the PEND statement are the same as for all the other JCL statements: slashes in columns 1 and 2; a name field, which is optional; and at least one space before and after the operation PEND. It is not customary to code a name on the PEND statement, and in Figure 9.2 none is coded.

There are some general rules about procedures—both cataloged and in-stream—that you should know. A procedure may not contain a JOB statement, a delimiter statement (/*), or a null statement (//). It may not contain a JOBLIB DD statement, input stream data, or a DD statement for input stream

FIGURE 9.3

Executing the in-stream procedure in Figure 9.2

```
//JCLQB710 JOB ,'J.C.LEWIS'
//CREATE   PROC
//LIBMAKE  EXEC PGM=IEFBR14,
//             REGION=32K
//LIBDD     DD DSN=WYL.QB.JCL.MYLIB,
//             DISP=(,CATLG),
//             UNIT=DISK,
//             VOL=SER=WYL003,
//             SPACE=(TRK,(5,,7)),
//             DCB=(RECFM=FB,LRECL=80,BLKSIZE=1600)
//         PEND
//CREATLIB EXEC CREATE
//
```

data (such as DD *). Finally, an EXEC statement in a procedure may execute only programs and not procedures.

Now that we have created an in-stream procedure, the next thing we must do is execute it to make sure it is correct. Figure 9.3 shows how the in-stream procedure in Figure 9.2 is executed. The important point in Figure 9.3 is that the EXEC statement that executes the procedure must follow the procedure. The procedure name coded on the EXEC statement is the name on the PROC statement—CREATE.

When an in-stream procedure is executed, the source of the JCL statements in the effective job stream is identified on the output listing (if you code 1 for the statements subparameter in the MSGLEVEL parameter). The identification method used is similar to the method used to identify the source of JCL statements when a cataloged procedure is executed, which was discussed in Chapter 8. In-stream procedure statements that you did not override are identified by a ++ in columns 1 and 2. In-stream procedure statements that you did override are identifed by a +/ in columns 1 and 2. Comment statements are identified by a *** in columns 1, 2, and 3.

ADDING A PROCEDURE
TO THE PROCEDURE LIBRARY

After proper execution has proven that an in-stream procedure does not contain any errors, the procedure may be added to the procedure library. IEBUP-DTE is usually used to do this.

that this DD statement refers to a report which you sometimes want to print and sometimes want to suppress. The way to suppress a report is to DUMMY its DD statement. You might think that the following coding solves the problem:

```
//RUNPROC  PROC DUM=DUMMY
     .
     .
     .
//REPORT    DD &DUM,SYSOUT=A
```

If you execute the procedure by simply calling it,

```
//STEP1    EXEC RUNPROC
```

&DUM will be assigned the default value DUMMY and the REPORT DD statement will become

```
//REPORT    DD DUMMY,SYSOUT=A
```

This will cause the report to be suppressed, which is what you want.

The trouble comes in when you nullify &DUM to print the report. In that case, the EXEC statement will be

```
//STEP1    EXEC RUNPROC,
//              DUM=
```

When &DUM is nullified, the REPORT DD statement will look like

```
//REPORT    DD ,SYSOUT=A
```

The leading comma in this statement is a syntax error, and the job will not run.

The way to solve this problem is to use a period as the separator between &DUM and SYSOUT=A. The correct way to write this procedure is

```
//RUNPROC  PROC DUM='DUMMY,'
     .
     .
     .
//REPORT    DD &DUM.SYSOUT=A
```

Notice that it is necessary to include the comma in the default value for DUM. Since the comma is a special character, the whole value must be enclosed in apostrophes.

If you execute the procedure without nullifying &DUM, the REPORT DD statement will look like

```
//REPORT    DD DUMMY,SYSOUT=A
```

Notice that the period, which is only a separator, is removed when the value of the symbolic parameter is substituted. On the other hand, if you execute the procedure and nullify &DUM, the REPORT statement will look like

```
//REPORT    DD SYSOUT=A
```

The leading comma, which caused a syntax error before, has been eliminated.

The rule is

IF A SYMBOLIC PARAMETER STANDS FOR A POSITIONAL PARAMETER AND IF IT IS FOLLOWED BY A KEYWORD PARAMETER, YOU SHOULD USE A PERIOD AS THE SEPARATOR BETWEEN THEM.

The fact that the period used as a separator is eliminated when a value is substituted for a symbolic parameter means that if you *want* a period to appear you must code two of them. For example, as explained in Chapter 3, at the CUNY computer center, data set names start with WYL. followed by two letters which identify the programmer's school (QB stands for Queensborough Community College), followed by three letters which identify the programmer. Suppose a procedure named ALLOCATE, which can be used by any programmer at Queensborough to create a data set named LIB, is written. In the procedure the DSN could be coded as follows:

```
DSN=WYL.QB.&INIT..LIB
```

If a student whose initials are XYZ used this procedure, he or she would code

```
//STEP1    EXEC ALLOCATE,
//              INIT=XYZ
```

When &INIT is replaced by its value, one of the periods will be eliminated and the resulting DSN will be

```
DSN=WYL.QB.XYZ.LIB
```

which is correct.

You do not have to be concerned about commas that remain when a symbolic parameter that stands for the value of a keyword parameter is nullified. For example, suppose in a procedure you have the following coding:

```
//DD1      DD DSN=&NAME,
//            DISP=&DISP,
//            UNIT=TAPE,
//            VOL=SER=&NO
```

If you nullify &NAME, &DISP, and &NO when you execute the procedure which contains this DD statement, the statement will become

```
//DD1      DD DSN=,
//            DISP=,
//            UNIT=TAPE,
//            VOL=SER=
```

This statement is perfectly legal.

CREATING A MORE COMPLICATED PROCEDURE

The various versions of the CREATE procedure have illustrated a number of points about user-written procedures, but in fact the CREATE procedures are too simple to be very useful. User-written procedures really show their value when they include all the JCL needed to execute a complicated system.

A system flowchart for a more complicated system is shown in Figure 9.12. This system updates a master file. The transactions are edited, sorted, and then used to update a master file. In the last step a report is printed. This system involves a generation data set, which you studied in Chapter 6, and a sort, which you will study in Chapter 10. Even though at this point you may

FIGURE 9.12

System flowchart for an inventory update system

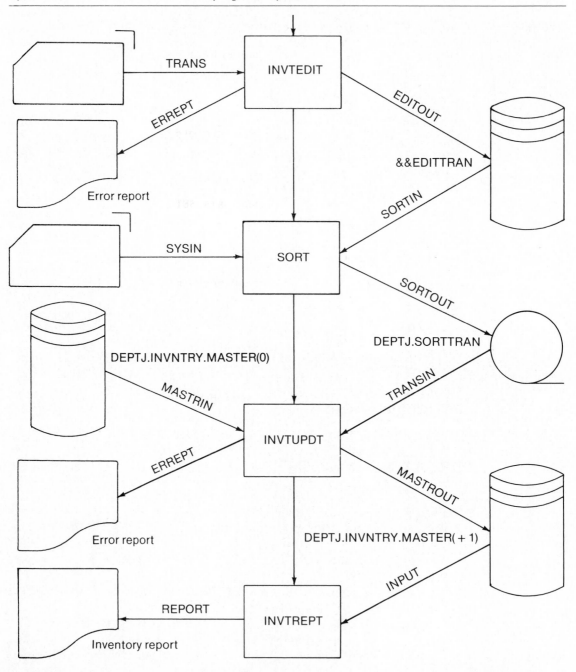

CREATING A MORE COMPLICATED PROCEDURE

FIGURE 9.13

The INVTUPDT procedure for the inventory update system

```
//INVTUPDT PROC PRI=5,
//            SEC=1
//*
//*      THIS PROCEDURE IMPLEMENTS DEPT J'S
//*      INVENTORY UPDATE SYSTEM
//*
//*      SYMBOLIC      MEANING                      DEFAULT
//*      PRI           PRIMARY ALLOCATION              5
//*                    (IN CYLINDERS) OF EDITED
//*                    TRANSACTIONS  DATA SET
//*
//*      SEC           SECONDARY ALLOCATION            1
//*                    AS ABOVE
//*
//*      EDITSTEP READS THE RAW TRANSACTIONS
//*      AND PRODUCES A TEMPORARY DATA SET OF
//*      EDITED TRANSACTIONS AND AN ERROR REPORT
//*
//EDITSTEP EXEC PGM=INVTEDIT,
//            REGION=80K
//STEPLIB  DD DSN=DEPTJ.UPDTLIB,
//            DISP=SHR
//ERREPT   DD SYSOUT=A
//EDITOUT  DD DSN=&&EDITTRAN,
//            DISP=(,PASS),
//            UNIT=DISK,
//            SPACE=(CYL,(&PRI,&SEC))
//*
//*      SORTSTEP SORTS THE EDITED TRANSACTIONS ON
//*      INVENTORY NUMBER AND DATE AND CREATES SORTTRAN
//*
//SORTSTEP EXEC PGM=SORT,
//            PARM='SIZE=MAX',
//            COND=(4,LT,EDITSTEP),
//            REGION=192K
//SORTLIB  DD DSN=SYS1.SORTLIB,
//            DISP=SHR
//SORTWK01 DD UNIT=SYSDA,
//            SPACE=(CYL,5,,CONTIG)
//SORTWK02 DD UNIT=SYSDA,
//            SPACE=(CYL,5,,CONTIG)
//SORTWK03 DD UNIT=SYSDA,
//            SPACE=(CYL,5,,CONTIG)
//SYSOUT   DD SYSOUT=A
//SORTIN   DD DSN=*.EDITSTEP.EDITOUT,
//            DISP=(OLD,DELETE)
//SORTOUT  DD DSN=DEPTJ.SORTTRAN,
//            DISP=(,PASS),
//            UNIT=TAPE
```

(cont.)

FIGURE 9.13 (cont.)

```
//*
//*      UPDTSTEP UPDATES AND CREATES A
//*      NEW GENERATION OF THE INVENTORY
//*      MASTER DATA SET
//*
//UPDTSTEP EXEC PGM=INVTUPDT,
//               COND=((4,LT,EDITSTEP),(0,NE,SORTSTEP)),
//               REGION=132K
//STEPLIB  DD DSN=DEPTJ.UPDTLIB,
//               DISP=SHR
//TRANSIN  DD DSN=*.SORTSTEP.SORTOUT,
//               DISP=(OLD,KEEP)
//MASTRIN  DD DSN=DEPTJ.INVNTRY.MASTER(0),
//               DISP=OLD
//MASTOUT  DD DSN=DEPTJ.INVNTRY.MASTER(+1),
//               DISP=(,PASS),
//               UNIT=DISK,
//               VOL=SER=DISK01,
//               SPACE=(CYL,(10,5))
//ERREPT   DD SYSOUT=A
//*
//*      REPTSTEP PRODUCES A REPORT BASED
//*      ON THE NEW MASTER FILE
//*
//REPTSTEP EXEC PGM=INVTREPT,
//               COND=((4,LT,EDITSTEP),(0,NE,SORTSTEP),(4,LE,UPDTSTEP)),
//               REGION=64K
//STEPLIB  DD DSN=DEPTJ.UPDTLIB,
//               DISP=SHR
//INPUT    DD DSN=*.UPDTSTEP.MASTOUT,
//               DISP=(OLD,CATLG)
//REPORT   DD SYSOUT=A
```

not know anything about sorting, you can still use the procedure, just as you were able to use the compile and link edit procedures in Chapter 8 without being an expert on compilers or the linkage editor.

The procedure to carry out the processing in Figure 9.12 is shown in Figure 9.13. There are a number of important points about Figure 9.13. First, the SORT program obtains SORT program modules and prints messages using data sets that are not shown in Figure 9.12, because Figure 9.12 shows the flow of data through the system and not incidental data sets. (You may recall that in Figure 3.3 we did not show the SYSIN and SYSPRINT data sets used by IEBGENER.)

Second, the fact that programs INVTEDIT, INVTUPDT, and INVTREPT reside in DEPTJ.UPDTLIB might lead you to think that one JOBLIB statement could have been coded instead of three `STEPLIB DD` statements. Remember, however, that a procedure may not contain a `JOBLIB` statement. Third, every `EXEC` statement, except the first, has a `COND` parameter coded on it to control the execution of the step. Finally, all the data sets required by the system are included in the procedure, except the `TRANS` input to the `INVTEDIT` program and the `SYSIN` input to the `SORT` program. `TRANS` supplies the transactions to the `EDIT` program. `SYSIN` supplies the control statements to the `SORT` program in much the same way that `SYSIN` supplies the control statements to the utilities we have studied. Both `TRANS` and `SYSIN` will be coded as input stream data, and you recall that a procedure may not contain input stream data. The `TRANS` and `SYSIN` `DD` statements will be coded as part of the JCL when the procedure is executed.

EXECUTING THE INVTUPDT PROCEDURE

A job that executes the `INVTUPDT` procedure is shown in Figure 9.14. This is the simplest possible job which uses this procedure, since only the required two `DD` statements have been coded. The two `DD` statements must be in the order shown in Figure 9.14, since that is the order of the two steps in Figure 9.13.

Since the same `SORT` control statements will be used every time this procedure is executed, it would be more convenient to obtain the `SORT` control statements from a library, rather than supplying them as input stream data. Exercise 14 explores this idea.

FIGURE 9.14

Executing the INVTUPDT procedure

```
//JCLQB745 JOB ,'J.C.LEWIS'
//UPDATE1  EXEC INVTUPDT
//EDITSTEP.TRANS DD *

        Transaction Records

/*
//SORTSTEP.SYSIN DD *

        Sort Control Statements

/*
//
```

Overriding and Adding Parameters on an EXEC Statement

A more complicated execution of the INVTUPDT procedure is shown in Figure 9.15. In this example we want to execute INVTUPDT with several changes. In the EDITSTEP we want to add a TIME parameter to limit the step to 3.5 minutes and increase the REGION to 120K. In the SORTSTEP we want to decrease the REGION to 164K. We want to set the symbolic parameter PRI to 10 and SEC to 2. We want to use a new version of the INVTEDIT program which is stored in a library named DEPTJ.TESTLIB. We want to add a SORTWK04 DD statement to the SORTSTEP. And finally, in the REPTSTEP we want to direct the REPORT to output class C. All of these changes are made in Figure 9.15.

As Figure 9.15 shows, any parameters you want to add or override on any of the EXEC statements in a procedure are coded on the EXEC statement that invokes the procedure. To add or override a parameter on an EXEC statement in a procedure, you code

```
parameter.procstepname=value
```

FIGURE 9.15

Executing the INVTUPDT procedure with changes

```
//JCLQB750 JOB ,'J.C.LEWIS'
//UPDATE2   EXEC INVTUPDT,
//               TIME.EDITSTEP=(3,30),
//               REGION.EDITSTEP=120K,
//               REGION.SORTSTEP=164K,
//               PRI=10,
//               SEC=2
//EDITSTEP.STEPLIB DD DSN=DEPTJ.TESTLIB
//EDITSTEP.TRANS    DD *

       Transaction Records

/*
//SORTSTEP.SORTWK04 DD UNIT=SYSDA,
//               SPACE=(CYL,5,,CONTIG)
//SORTSTEP.SYSIN DD *

       Sort Control Statements

/*
//REPTSTEP.REPORT DD SYSOUT=C
//
```

EXECUTING THE INVTUPDT PROCEDURE

So in this example, to add a TIME parameter on the EDITSTEP EXEC statement, we coded

```
TIME.EDITSTEP=(3,30)
```

and to override the REGION parameter on the EDITSTEP EXEC statement we coded

```
REGION.EDITSTEP=120K
```

This is what was done in Chapter 8 for the PARM parameter, and you can now see that the same rule applies to all the EXEC statement parameters. Parameters to be added or overridden are coded in the same way. If you code a parameter that does not exist on the EXEC statement, the parameter will be added. That is what will happen to the TIME parameter shown in Figure 9.15. If, on the other hand, you code a parameter that does exist on the EXEC statement, the value you code will replace the value coded on the EXEC statement. That is what will happen to the two REGION parameters shown in Figure 9.15. You will recall that this is exactly the same way parameters coded on overriding DD statements are processed

You must code all the parameters for one step before you code the parameters for a later step. In Figure 9.15, both EDITSTEP parameters are coded before the SORTSTEP parameter. The order in which you code the parameters for a particular step is not significant. In Figure 9.15, for the EDITSTEP, the TIME parameter is coded first, followed by REGION, but REGION could just as well have been coded first. In Figure 9.15, the symbolic parameters are coded last, but they could be coded in any position.

OMITTING THE STEPNAME. You do not have to code the procedure stepname when coding a parameter. What happens when you omit the procedure stepname depends on which parameter you are coding. If you omit the procedure stepname on the TIME parameter, the value you code applies to the whole procedure. If Figure 9.15 had been coded

```
TIME=(3,30)
```

the 3.5 minute limitation would apply to the whole procedure, not to any particular step.

If you omit the procedure stepname on the PARM parameter, the value you code applies only to the first procedure step. If a PARM parameter is coded on any other EXEC statement in the procedure, it is nullified. It is hard to imagine under what circumstances you would want to do that, so in most cases the PARM parameter would be coded with a procedure stepname.

If you omit the procedure stepname on any parameter other than TIME or PARM, the parameter you code applies to all the steps in the procedure. So, for example, coding

```
REGION=212K
```

has the effect of making the REGION 212K on every step in the procedure.

If you omit the procedure stepname on any parameter, that parameter must be coded before any parameters that do have a procedure stepname.

Overriding and Adding DD Statements

The DD statements in Figure 9.15 require careful study. Recall that the DD statements must be coded in the order in which the steps they refer to are coded in the procedure. So in Figure 9.15, the DD statements for the EDITSTEP are coded before the DD statements for the SORTSTEP, which in turn are coded before the DD statement for the REPTSTEP. Within a step, the overriding DD statements must be coded in the order in which they occur and before the additional DD statements. In the EDITSTEP, the STEPLIB DD statement, which is an overriding DD statement, must be coded before the TRANS DD statement, which is an additional DD statement. In the SORTSTEP, both DD statements are additional statements, so their order does not matter.

The STEPLIB DD statement applies only to the EDITSTEP. The programs INVTUPDT and INVTREPT in Figure 9.13 will still be taken from DEPTJ.UPDTLIB. Taking INVTREPT, for example, from DEPTJ.TESTLIB would require a REPTSTEP.STEPLIB DD statement pointing to DEPTJ.TESTLIB.

EXERCISES

1. What is the function of the PEND statement?

2. Which JCL statements may not be used in a procedure?

3. Under what circumstances do in-stream procedures require a PROC statement?

EXERCISES

4. Under what circumstances do cataloged procedures require a PROC statement?

5. On the output listing, how can you recognize JCL statements that were added to your job stream as a result of calling an in-stream procedure?

6. In Figure 9.6, is the order in which the DD parameters are coded important or could a different order be used?

7. What are the rules for naming symbolic parameters?

8. Why are symbolic parameters assigned default values?

9. How are symbolic parameters assigned default values?

10. How are symbolic parameters assigned values when a procedure is executed?

11. How is a symbolic parameter nullified?

12. When should you use a period instead of a comma as a separator between a symbolic parameter and the coding that follows it?

13. How do you override parameters on EXEC statements in a procedure?

14. The same sort control statements will be used every time the INVTUPDT procedure in Figure 9.13 is executed. Therefore, it would be more convenient to obtain the control statements from a control statement library rather than coding them as input stream data. Modify the INVTUPDT procedure to obtain the sort control statement from member UPDATE from a library named SORT.CNTLLIB.

15. Modify the CREATE3 procedure in Figure 9.9 to make the values of RECFM, LRECL, and BLKSIZE symbolic parameters. Assign default values of FB to RECFM, 150 to LRECL, and 1500 to BLKSIZE. Show how you would use this procedure to create a library named BKUPLIB, which resides on disk pack DISK43 and has 10 tracks, 5 directory blocks, a logical record length of 100, and a blocksize of 500.

16. Below is a cataloged procedure named SUMMARY.

```
//SUMMARY   PROC
//EDIT      EXEC PGM=EDIT
//OUTPUT    DD DSN=&&OUTPUT,
//             DISP=(NEW,PASS),
//             UNIT=SYSDA,
//             SPACE=(TRK,10)                    (cont.)
```

```
//RUN      EXEC PGM=SALES
//INPUT    DD DNS=&&OUTPUT,
//              DISP=(OLD,DELETE)
//REPORT       DD SYSOUT=A
```

Code the JCL required to execute this procedure with the following modifications:

a. Program EDIT should have a REGION of 80K.

b. Program SALES should not be executed if program EDIT returns a condition code equal to 100.

c. Program EDIT requires input stream data supplied under the ddname CARDFILE.

d. Data set &&OUTPUT requires 20 tracks.

17. Below is a cataloged procedure named ABCXYZ.

```
//ABCXYZ    PROC TRACKS=10,
//               DISP=DELETE
//ABC       EXEC PGM=ABC,
//               REGION=80K
//ABCOUT    DD DSN=&NAME,
//               UNIT=3330,
//               DISP=(NEW,PASS),
//               SPACE=(TRK,(&TRACKS)),
//               VOL=SER=PACK07
//XYZ       EXEC PGM=XYZ
//XYZIN     DD DSN=*.ABC.ABCOUT,
//               DISP=(OLD,&DISP)
//XYZOUT    DD SYSOUT=A
```

Code the JCL required to execute this procedure with the following modifications:

a. Program ABC should have a REGION of 100K.

b. Program XYZ should not be run if program ABC returns a condition code of 12 or higher.

c. The disk data set's name should be ABC.DATAFILE, and its final disposition should be KEEP.

d. Program ABC requires input stream data supplied under the ddname ABCCARDS.

18. A system flowchart for a payroll system is shown in Figure 9.16. Write a

FIGURE 9.16

System flowchart for a payroll system

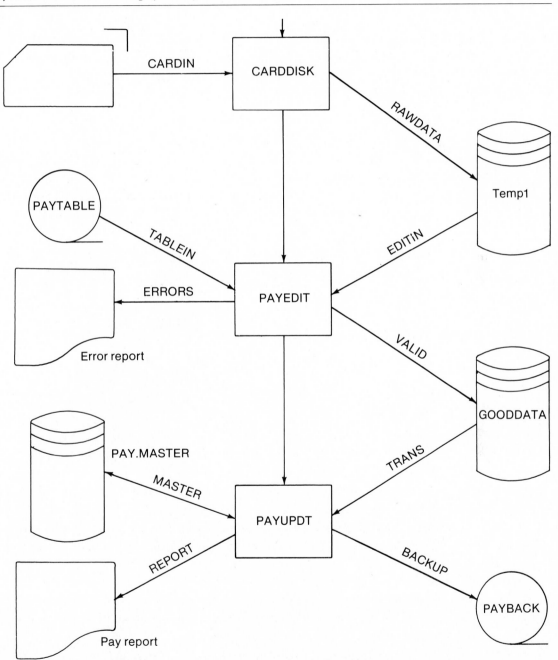

procedure to implement this system. Additional information is given below.

General information: All tape units are TAPE and all disk units are DISK. Any names required but not given may be invented.

Program information:

Step	Program Name	Library	Region	Time	Conditions
1	CARDDISK	LIB1	50K	20 sec	—
2	PAYEDIT	PAYLIB	130K	4 min	Do not run unless the condition code from step 1 is 0.
3	PAYUPDT	PAYLIB	100K	10 min	Do not run unless the condition code from step 1 is 0 and from step 2 is less than 8.

Data set information: All data sets that existed before a job is run should be retained at the end of the job.

Data Set	Volume	Space	Comments
Temp1	nonspecific	In 800-byte blocks. Primary 5000, secondary 500. Release unused space.	Invent a legal temporary DSN. Use a backward reference to this data set in step 2.
GOODDATA	PACK46	In cylinders. Primary 20, secondary 5.	Delete if job runs, keep if job abends.
PAYTABLE	cataloged	—	—
PAY.MASTER	cataloged	—	Do not allow any other programs to access this data set while it is being updated.
PAYBACK	nonspecific	—	—

After you have written the procedure, write the JCL to execute it, supplying the required input stream data DD statement.

PROGRAMMING ASSIGNMENTS

1. Write a procedure named LISTER which uses IEBGENER to list any cataloged data set. Make the name of the data set to be listed a symbolic parameter. Execute the procedure as an in-stream procedure, listing the data set you created in Chapter 3.

2. Write a procedure named COMPRESS which uses IEBCOPY to compress a library. Make the name of the library to be compressed a symbolic parameter. Execute the procedure as an in-stream procedure, compressing FIRSTLIB, which you created in Chapter 5.

3. Write a two-step procedure named COPYMEMB. In the first step use IEBCOPY to copy a member from one library into another. In the second step use IEBPTPCH to list the member just copied. The second step should not be executed if the condition code from the first step is greater than 4. The names of the two libraries should be symbolic parameters. Execute the procedure as an in-stream procedure to copy a member either from a fellow student's library or from a library your advisor suggests to FIRSTLIB, which you created in Chapter 5.

SUMMARY

In this chapter you have learned

*   how to write, test, and use user-written procedures
*   how to code in-stream procedures
*   when and how to use the PROC and PEND statements
*   when and how to use the DATA parameter
*   how to code symbolic parameters in procedures
*   how to assign default values to symbolic parameters
*   how to override and add parameters to EXEC statements when a procedure is executed

CHAPTER 10

SORTING
AND MERGING

LEARNING OBJECTIVES

IN THIS CHAPTER YOU WILL LEARN

- how to use the sort/merge program

YOU WILL ALSO LEARN THE MEANINGS OF THE FOLLOWING TERMS:

- collating sequence

- control field, major and minor

- key field, major and minor

Sorting, which means putting records in a data set into a specified order, is an important computer task. Merging, which is closely related to sorting, means combining records from two or more sorted data sets into one data set that is in the same order. IBM provides a sort/merge program which is described in *OS/VS Sort/Merge Programmer's Guide* (SC33-4035). In addition, many software companies sell their own sort/merge programs.

Sort/merge programs may be invoked from user-written programs in assembler, COBOL, or PL/I. In this chapter you will learn how to perform a sort or merge directly by coding JCL statements and sort/merge control statements.

SORTING

When you perform a sort, you have to give the sort program* three pieces of information: where the input data can be found, which fields in the records you want the sorting done on, and where to put the sorted output data set.

---

* In this text, the discussions about sorting will refer to the sort program, and the discussions about merging will refer to the merge program. You should keep in mind, however, that sorting and merging are done by the same program.

SORTING

The sort program expects its input to be supplied under the ddname SORTIN. The input data might be input stream data or a tape or disk data set, but no matter where the data are coming from, with all your experience coding DD statements you should have no trouble coding the SORTIN DD statement. Similarly, the sort program writes its output under the ddname SORTOUT. You might want to make the output a tape or disk data set or direct it to a printer or card punch, but again, no matter where the output is going you should have no trouble writing the SORTOUT DD statement.

So you see that the only new thing you have to learn in order to use the sort program is how to specify which fields you want the sort done on. This information is provided by the sort control statements, so a large part of this chapter will be devoted to learning how to code sort control statements.

Major and Minor Control Fields

Before we begin discussing the details of how to code sort control statements, let us look a little more carefully at what is meant by specifying the fields in the records you want the sorting done on. As an example, we will sort the seven records shown in Figure 10.1. These records contain three fields. The first field contains the person's name, the second the person's marital status (Y = married and N = not married), and the third the person's sex (F = female, M = male).

Initially we will sort on only one field. The selected field is called the **control field** or the **key field**. We must also specify whether we want the sort to be done in ascending order from A to Z or descending order from Z to A. If we sort this data set in ascending order using the name as the control field, we get the results shown in Figure 10.2. If we had sorted in descending order, the results would have been reversed, with West being the first record and

FIGURE 10.1

Data used for sorting illustrations

```
WEST       NF
NUTLEY     YF
KOREN      NM
STANLEY    NF
BRYCE      YF
EVANS      YM
ROONEY     YM
```

FIGURE 10.2

Data in 10.1 sorted in ascending order by name

```
BRYCE      YF
EVANS      YM
KOREN      ⇥NM
NUTLEY     YF
ROONEY     YM
STANLEY    NF
WEST       NF
```

Bryce being the last. Notice that when you sort records, the complete records are rearranged, not just the control field you specify.

More interesting situations result when more than one control field is specified. The first field specified is called the **major control field**, or **major key**, and the other fields are called the **minor control fields**, or **minor keys**. If we sort the records in Figure 10.1 in ascending order using marital status as the major control field and name as the minor control field, we get the results shown in Figure 10.3. The sort program first sorts on the major control field. Then those records that have the same value in the major control field are sorted on the minor control field. In this case, the records are first sorted by marital status. Then the records that have a marital status of N are sorted by name, and the records that have a marital status of Y are sorted by name separately.

If we wanted the married people listed first, we would specify we wanted the sort done in descending order by marital status and ascending order by name. In that case we would get the results shown in Figure 10.4. Notice that these results are *not* simply the results in Figure 10.3 in reverse order.

FIGURE 10.3

Data in 10.1 sorted in ascending order by marital status and name

```
KOREN      NM
STANLEY    NF
WEST       NF
BRYCE      YF
EVANS      YM
NUTLEY     YF
ROONEY     YM
```

FIGURE 10.4

Data in 10.1 sorted in descending order by marital status and ascending order by name

```
BRYCE      YF
EVANS      YM
NUTLEY     YF
ROONEY     YM
KOREN      NM
STANLEY    NF
WEST       NF
```

It is important to understand that the sort on the minor control field is done only for records that have the same value in the major control field. If we sort in ascending order using name as the major control field and marital status as the minor control field, we get the same result we got when we sorted by name only. This is because no two records have the same value for the name field.

You can specify more than one minor control field. Suppose we want to sort the records in Figure 10.1 in ascending order using marital status as the major control field and sex and name, in that order, as the minor control fields. When several control fields are specified, they are frequently simply listed; it is understood that the major control field is listed first and the minor control fields follow in order of importance. So the problem can be restated as sorting the records in Figure 10.1 in ascending order by marital status, sex, and name. The results are shown in Figure 10.5.

Sometimes programmers refer to the major control field as the primary sort field, the first minor as the secondary, and the second minor as the tertiary. In this example marital status is the primary field, sex is the secondary, and name the tertiary.

FIGURE 10.5

Data in 10.1 sorted in ascending order by marital status, sex, and name

```
STANLEY    NF
WEST       NF
KOREN      NM
BRYCE      YF
NUTLEY     YF
EVANS      YM
ROONEY     YM
```

The sort program first sorts on the major or primary control field, and then on the minor control fields in the order named. In this case the records are first sorted by marital status. Then the records that have a marital status of N and those that have a marital status of Y are separately sorted by sex. Finally, records that have the same value of marital status and sex, such as Stanley and West, and Evans and Rooney, are sorted by name.

Equal Control Fields

What happens if two or more records have the same value in the control fields? Suppose in the previous example the name was omitted as a control field and the sorting was done only by marital status and sex. When the sorting was finished there would be three pairs of records, Stanley and West, Bryce and Nutley, and Evans and Rooney, with the same value of marital status and sex. What would their order be in the output?

Sometimes the final order is not important; Stanley followed by West and West followed by Stanley might be equally acceptable. But sometimes you would like records with the same value in the control fields to have the same order in the output as they have in the input. In that case the pairs would be West followed by Stanley, Bryce followed by Nutley, and Evans followed by Rooney (see the original order in Figure 10.1). You will learn later how to tell the sort program to keep the original order for records that have the same value in the control fields.

Collating Sequence

In the previous examples of sorting on alphabetic fields, the meanings of ascending order (A to Z) and descending order (Z to A) were easily understood. When sorting is done on numeric fields, it is equally obvious what is meant by ascending and descending order. (Remember negative numbers are considered less than positive numbers.) But in sorting on alphanumeric fields, things get a little more complicated. Suppose you were sorting on an address field, and the address on one record was 123 Elm Street and on another was 123 59th Avenue. The control fields on these two records are equal until you get the E on the first record and the 5 on the second record. To put these two records in order you have to know whether E is greater or less than 5, which means that you must know the collating sequence used by the computer. The **collating sequence** is simply the sequence used by the computer to sort data stored in character form. IBM computers use the

EBCDIC collating sequence, which is shown in Table 1.2. In the EBCDIC collating sequence, E is less than 5, so 123 Elm Street would be less than 123 59th Avenue.

Although IBM computers usually use the EBCDIC collating sequence, you can specify that you want a sort performed using a modified collating sequence. How to specify the modifications will be discussed later.

JCL TO INVOKE THE SORT PROGRAM

Every computer center has a cataloged procedure to invoke the sort program. This procedure is usually named SORTD and is tailored to meet local requirements. The SORTD procedure at the CUNY computer center is shown in Figure 10.6.

The PROC statement assigns default values to the symbolic parameters, and the EXEC statement executes the sort program and assigns a default value to the PARM field. The values that may be coded in the PARM field will be explained a little later. The SORTLIB DD statement points to the library that contains the sort/merge program modules. The DD statements SORTWK01 through SORTWK06 provide work areas for the sort program. Depending on which version of the sort you are using, you must have a minimum of one, two, or three work areas. The more work areas you provide, the faster the sort is done. The six work areas provided in this procedure will be enough for even the largest sorts. The SYSOUT DD statement is used by the sort program for messages.

FIGURE 10.6

The SORTD cataloged procedure

```
//SORT     PROC SIZE=MAX,SPACE=3
//SORT     EXEC PGM=SORT,PARM='SIZE=&SIZE'
//SORTLIB  DD   DSN=SYS1.SORTLIB,DISP=SHR
//SORTWK01 DD   UNIT=3330,SPACE=(CYL,&SPACE)
//SORTWK02 DD   UNIT=(3330,SEP=SORTWK01),SPACE=(CYL,&SPACE)
//SORTWK03 DD   UNIT=3330,SPACE=(CYL,&SPACE)
//SORTWK04 DD   UNIT=3330,SPACE=(CYL,&SPACE)
//SORTWK05 DD   UNIT=3330,SPACE=(CYL,&SPACE)
//SORTWK06 DD   UNIT=3330,SPACE=(CYL,&SPACE)
//SYSOUT   DD   SYSOUT=A
```

FIGURE 10.7

Job stream to sort the data in 10.1

```
//JCLQB755 JOB ,'J.C.LEWIS'
//SORT     EXEC SORTD
//SORT.SORTIN DD *
WEST      NF
NUTLEY    YF
KOREN     NM
STANLEY   NF
BRYCE     YF
EVANS     YM
ROONEY    YM
/*
//SORT.SORTOUT DD SYSOUT=A
//SORT.SYSIN DD *

         Sort Control Statements

/*
//
```

When you use the SORTD procedure, you have to provide three additional DD statements. The SORTIN DD statement defines the input data set, the SORTOUT DD statement defines the output data set, and the SYSIN DD statement defines the control statement data set. If the records in Figure 10.1 were punched on cards and if we wanted to direct the output to the printer, the job stream we would use is shown in Figure 10.7.

Ddnames in One-Step Procedures

When the ddnames on the three DD statements in Figure 10.7 were coded, the rules you learned in Chapters 8 and 9 for creating ddnames were followed: the procedure stepname (SORT) was combined with the required ddname (SORTIN, SORTOUT, or SYSIN). This coding is correct, but unnecessarily complicated. When you have a one-step procedure such as SORTD, the DD statements can only be added to that one step, so it is not necessary to include a procedure stepname as part of the ddname. In future examples in this chapter SORT will be omitted from the ddnames.

You may even omit the procedure stepname from the ddname when you have a multistep procedure. In that case the system assumes the DD statements apply to the first step. This means that in Figure 9.15, EDITSTEP could have been omitted from the ddnames. But since omitting the procedure stepname in a multistep procedure makes your coding less clear, it is not recommended. You may, however, see such coding sometimes, and you should understand it.

SORT CONTROL STATEMENTS

All that needs to be done to execute the job stream in Figure 10.7 is to code the sort control statements. The most commonly used sort control statements are the SORT and MERGE statements. The parameters used with these two statements are identical, so they are described together in Table 10.1.

The FIELDS Parameter*

Let us assume that in the records in Figure 10.7, the name field is in the first ten positions of the record, the marital status is in the eleventh position, and the sex is in the twelfth position. Then to sort these records in ascending order on the name field, we would code the following SORT statement:

```
SORT FIELDS=(1,10,CH,A)
```

We can use the description of the FIELDS parameter in Table 10.1 to interpret this. The 1 means the control field begins at the first byte in the record. The 10 means the control field is 10 bytes long. (Notice that the order of the position and length subparameters in the SORT FIELDS parameter is the opposite of their order in the IEBGENER and IEBPTPCH FIELD parameters. That is to make it easy—to get mixed up.) The CH means the data in the control field are in EBCDIC character form. The name field starts at the first byte, is 10 bytes long, and is in EBCDIC character form, so these three values specify the name as the control field. The A means the sort should be in ascending order. If this control statement were used in Figure 10.7, the records would be sorted as shown in Figure 10.2. (Table 10.1 shows two formats for the FIELDS parameter. When to use each one will be explained a little later.)

The coding rules for the sort control statements are similar to the coding rules for the other utility control statements you have studied. Unless the statement contains a label, which is usually omitted, column 1 must be

---

* Notice that the SORT parameter is FIELDS, while for IEBGENER and IEBPTPCH it is FIELD.

TABLE 10.1

Parameters for SORT and MERGE statements

Parameter	Meaning

`FIELDS=(position, length, format, sequence...)`
 	
or
 	
`FIELDS=(position,length, sequence...), FORMAT=format`
	`position` is starting byte of the control field in the record.
	
	`length` is the length in bytes of the control field.
	
	`format` is the format of the data in the control field. Commonly used values are
	`ZD` for zoned decimal,
	`PD` for packed decimal,
	`BI` for binary,
	`AC` for ASCII character,
	`CH` for EBCDIC character,
	`AQ` for EBCDIC character using alternative collating sequence.
	
	`sequence` is either `A` for ascending or `D` for descending.

`FILSZ=x`	`x` is the number of records to be sorted. If `x` is an estimate, precede it with `E`; e.g., `FILSZ=E1000`. Optional.
`SKIPREC=z`	Skip `z` records before sorting. Optional. Not permitted for a merge.
`EQUALS` `NOEQUALS`	`EQUALS` means that records with the same value of the control fields should retain the order they have in the input. `NOEQUALS` means the order need not be retained. Optional. Default set when sort program was installed. Not permitted for a merge.
`CKPT`	Checkpoints should be taken.

SORT CONTROL STATEMENTS

blank. The operand SORT may start anywhere, usually in column 2. SORT must be separated from the parameters by one or more blanks; one blank is common. There must not be any embedded blanks within the parameters. The parameters may be coded in any order, although the order shown in Table 10.1 is used most often. Control statements may not extend beyond column 71. If a control statement must be continued, it should be interrupted at a comma and continued in the following line between columns 2 and 16. It is not necessary to have a nonblank character in column 72.

The control statement that could be used to sort the records in ascending order by marital status and name is

```
SORT FIELDS=(11,1,CH,A,1,10,CH,A)
```

In this statement two control fields are defined. The first four values (11,1,CH,A) define the major control field, and the last four values (1,10, CH,A) define the minor control field. The major control field starts at the eleventh byte in the record, is 1 byte long, and is in EBCDIC character form. These values correspond to the marital status field, which is therefore the major control field. As before, the A means the sort should be done in ascending order. The coding for the minor control field is identical to the coding in the previous example, as it should be, since both cases describe the name field. If this control statement were used in Figure 10.7, the records would be sorted as shown in Figure 10.3.

This sort control statement can be simplified slightly. When all the control fields have the same format, as they do in this case, the second form of the FIELDS parameter shown in Table 10.1 may be used. Using the second form, the control statement would be

```
SORT FIELDS=(11,1,A,1,10,A),FORMAT=CH
```

The point of this form of the FIELDS parameter is that since all the control fields have the same format, it needs to be specified only once.

If we want to sort in descending order by marital status and ascending order by name, we have only to change the first A to a D:

```
SORT FIELDS=(11,1,D,1,10,A),FORMAT=CH
```

Used in Figure 10.7, this control statement would produce the output in Figure 10.4.

The control statement that could be used to sort the records in ascending order by marital status, sex, and name is

```
SORT FIELDS=(11,1,A,12,1,A,1,10,A),FORMAT=CH
```

Used in Figure 10.7, this control statement would produce the output in Figure 10.5.

Other SORT Statement Parameters

Four additional SORT statement parameters are described in Table 10.1. All four are optional.

The purpose of the FILSZ parameter is to improve the efficiency of the sort by giving the sort program either the exact number or an estimate of the number of records to be sorted. If the SORTIN data set contains exactly 15,357 records, you can code

```
FILSZ=15357
```

If the actual number of records is not 15,357, the sort will terminate.

Frequently you do not know the exact number of SORTIN records. In that case you can specify an estimate of the number of records. The estimate should be at least as great as the number of records. So, for example, if you have approximately 15,357 records, you can code

```
FILSZ=E16000
```

The E indicates that 16,000 is an estimate.

Although it is optional, FILSZ should be coded because it improves the efficiency of the sort.

SKIPREC causes records in SORTIN to be skipped before the sort begins. To skip the first 250 records, you would code

```
SKIPREC=250
```

EQUALS means you want records that have equal values in the control fields to retain the same order they had in the input. NOEQUALS means that the order does not have to be retained. When the sort program is installed, the computer center can decide whether to make EQUALS or NOEQUALS the default. EQUALS may slow down the sort, so most computer centers make NOEQUALS the default.

CKPT causes checkpoints to be taken. Checkpoints are fully discussed in the next chapter.

As an example of how all the parameters could be used, assume you want to sort a data set that contains approximately 20,000 records. The major control field begins at byte 5, is 4 bytes long, and contains packed decimal data. The minor control field begins at byte 96, is 20 bytes long, and contains character data. The sort should be in ascending order on both fields. Records that have the same value in the control fields should retain the same order in the output as they have in the input. The first 500 records should be skipped. Checkpoints should be taken. The control statement that could be used for this problem is

```
SORT FIELDS=(5,4,PD,A,96,20,CH,A),
     FILSZ=E20000,SKIPREC=500,EQUALS,CKPT
```

As is usual with control statements, there may not be embedded blanks in the parameter list.

Specifying a Modified Collating Sequence

As mentioned earlier, it is possible to specify that you want the sort done using a modified collating sequence. Suppose, for example, you are sorting by account number. The first byte of the account number contains a code. This code can be a blank, an asterisk, or an A. For this particular sort, you want the records that contain an asterisk to be listed first. If you sort in ascending order, the records that contain a blank will be first. If you sort in descending order, the records that contain an A will be first. To force the records that contain an asterisk to be first, you have to change the position of the asterisk in the collating sequence.

You must do two things. First you must specify that you want the field sorted using a modified collating sequence. You do this by coding AQ for the format of that field. If the account number begins at byte 1 and is 8 bytes long and you want the sort to be in ascending order, the SORT statement would be

```
SORT FIELDS=(1,8,AQ,A)
```

The AQ coded for the format tells the sort that this field should be sorted using a modified collating sequence.

THE ALTSEQ STATEMENT. The second thing you have to do is specify the modified collating sequence. This is done using the `ALTSEQ` statement. Since you are sorting in ascending order, to force the records that have an asterisk to be listed before those that have a blank, you must move the asterisk from its normal position in the collating sequence to a position before the blank. The following statement does this:

```
ALTSEQ CODE=(5C00)
```

To use the `ALTSEQ` statement, you must use the hexadecimal representation in the EBCDIC code, as given in Table 1.2, of the characters whose positions you are changing. The hexadecimal representation of an asterisk is `5C`. This `ALTSEQ` statement moves the asterisk from its normal position to the position whose hexadecimal representation is `00`. Since `00` is the lowest hexadecimal value, this change puts the asterisk before the blank.

The format of the `ALTSEQ` statement is

```
ALTSEQ CODE=(fftt,fftt,...,fftt)
```

where `ff` is the hexadecimal representation of the character whose position is to be changed and `tt` is the hexadecimal representation of the position to which it is to be moved. The ellipses (...) indicate that you may code as many sets of `fftt` as you want. Suppose you want to move the digits 0 through 9 from their normal position following the upper-case letters to a position between the lower-case letters and the upper-case letters. The following statement could be used:

```
ALTSEQ CODE=(F0B0,F1B1,F2B2,F3B3,F4B4,F5B5,F6B6,F7B7,F8B8,F9B9)
```

Table 1.2 shows that `F0` through `F9` represent the digits 0 through 9 and that the hexadecimal values `B0` through `B9` fall between the lower-case and upper-case letters. Notice that the sets of four hexadecimal digits are separated by commas.

Coding Parameters for the Sort Program

You may code a `PARM` field on the `EXEC` statement to pass parameter values to the sort program. These parameters specify the sorting technique that should be used and whether diagnostic messages and sort control statements should be printed. In most cases accepting default values for these parameters is satisfactory.

You may also specify how much main storage the sort program is allowed to use. The amount of main storage is specified using the SIZE parameter, as in

    SIZE=130000

or

    SIZE=MAX

In the first example you are allocating 130,000 bytes of storage to the sort program. In the second example you are instructing the sort to use all the available main storage. MAX is recommended because it makes the sort more efficient. The procedure in Figure 10.6 uses a symbolic parameter named &SIZE to assign a value to the SIZE parameter. The default value of &SIZE is MAX. In most computer centers the default value assigned to the SIZE parameter is MAX, and since MAX is the recommended value, most of the time users do not have to code any PARM values.

MERGING

Merging is closely related to sorting. When you merge, you start with two or more sorted data sets and create a new data set that is in the same sorted order. The JCL and control statements used for merging are very similar to those used for sorting.

The only difference in the JCL used for merging is that you must specify more than one input data set. These data sets have the ddnames SORTINnn, where nn may range from 01 to 16. This means that up to 16 data sets may be merged in one operation. The DD statements must be coded in order: SORTIN01, followed by SORTIN02, and so on. The input data sets may have different blocksizes, but the data set with the largest blocksize must be defined by the SORTIN01 DD statement. The input data sets may not be concatenated.

The major difference in the control statements is that the operation specified is MERGE instead of SORT. An example will clarify how a merge is coded. Suppose we have four data sets named FRESHMEN, SOPHS, JUNIORS, and SENIORS. The record formats in all the data sets are identical. Among other data, each record contains the student's major as character data in bytes 56 and 57, and his or her grade point average as zoned decimal data in bytes 43 through 45. The data sets have previously been sorted by each student's major as the major control field and by grade point average as the minor control field. We now want to merge all four data sets to produce a new data set named STUDENTS. STUDENTS will also be in order, with student's major as the major control field and grade point average as the minor control field. A job stream that does this processing is shown in Figure 10.8.

Notice that even though we are merging, we execute the SORTD procedure. The fact that we want to perform a merge is indicated by the word MERGE coded in the control statement. The rest of the control statement is identical to the statement we would code if we were sorting these data sets by major and grade point average rather than merging them. As required, each input data set is named by its own DD statement, SORTIN01 through SORTIN04. Also as required, the SORTINnn statements are coded in numerical order. As mentioned earlier, it is not necessary to include the procedure stepname SORT as part of the ddname, so in Figure 10.8 it is omitted.

There are several minor differences between the MERGE and SORT statements. SKIPREC and EQUALS/NOEQUALS options are not used on the MERGE statement. For merging, the value specified for FILSZ should be the total number of records in all the input data sets.

FIGURE 10.8

Job stream to merge four data sets

```
//JCLQB760 JOB ,'J.C.LEWIS'
//MERGE     EXEC SORTD
//SORTIN01 DD DSN=FRESHMEN,
//             DISP=OLD
//SORTIN02 DD DSN=SOPHS,
//             DISP=OLD
//SORTIN03 DD DSN=JUNIORS,
//             DISP=OLD
//SORTIN04 DD DSN=SENIORS,
//             DISP=OLD
//SORTOUT  DD DSN=STUDENTS,
//             DISP=(,CATLG),
//             UNIT=DISK,
//             VOL=SER=DISK89,
//             SPACE=(TRK,(3,1),RLSE)
//SYSIN    DD *
 MERGE FIELDS=(56,2,ZD,A,43,3,CH,A)
/*
//
```

EXERCISES

1. What ddnames are used to supply the sort program with its input, its output, and its control statements?

2. What is a major control field? What is a minor control field?

3. Show the result if the records in Figure 10.1 are sorted in ascending order by sex, marital status, and name.

4. In the following records, the brand is in positions 1 through 10, the type in positions 11 through 19, and the price in positions 20 through 22.

Brand	Type	Price
Taylor	Burgundy	279
Taylor	Burgundy	500
Taylor	Chablis	419
Gallo	Rhine	288
Gallo	Chablis	300
Gallo	Burgundy	295
Gallo	Rhine	165
Masson	Chablis	345
Masson	Rhine	318

Show the results if these records are sorted in ascending order by

a. price
b. brand and price
c. price and brand
d. type, brand, and price
e. brand, type, and price

5. Which collating sequence is used by IBM computers?

6. In the collating sequence used by IBM computers, which is highest—a, A, or 1? Which is lowest?

7. What is the name of the cataloged procedure that is used to execute the sort/merge program?

8. In the SORT statement

   SORT FIELDS=(a,b,c,d)

   what are the meanings of a, b, c, and d?

9. Code the sort control statements required to perform the sorting indicated in Exercise 4, parts a through e.

10. True or false: If a sort is performed in ascending order on the major control field, it must also be in ascending order on the minor control fields.

11. How do you indicate that records that have equal values in the control fields should keep in the output the same order they have in the input?

12. What is the purpose of the FILSZ parameter?

13. How do you indicate that you want a field sorted using a modified collating sequence?

14. Code the ALTSEQ statement that will cause a blank to collate higher than a 9.

15. What does coding the parameter SIZE=MAX do?

16. What ddname is used for the input data sets in a MERGE operation? How many input data sets may be merged in one operation?

17. Instead of merging the four sorted data sets FRESHMEN, SOPHS, JUNIORS, and SENIORS to produce the STUDENTS data set, you could concatenate them and use the concatenation as the input to a sort. Can you think of any advantage of merging over sorting in this case?

18. The data in the following three sets start in column 1.

Set 1	Set 2	Set 3
627A	318B	136C
714A	712B	419C
863A	713B	984C

You will notice that the data in each set have been sorted using the first three columns as the key. Show what the results would be if these three data sets were merged, using the first three columns as the key. Could these three data sets be merged using the first four columns as the key? If they could be, show what the results would be.

PROGRAMMING ASSIGNMENTS

1. Enter the data listed in Exercise 4, and then sort them as requested in Exercise 4, parts a through e. Direct the output to the printer.

2. Enter the data listed in Exercise 18, and then merge them as requested in Exercise 18.

3. As mentioned before, when the sort/merge program is installed, the computer center chooses to make either EQUALS or NOEQUALS the default. Design and execute an experiment that will indicate whether EQUALS or NOEQUALS is the default at your computer center.

SUMMARY

In this chapter you have learned

*   how to sort using major and minor control fields

*   how to use the SORTD procedure to perform a sort

*   how to code the SORT and MERGE statements

*   how to modify the collating sequence used in a sort or merge

*   how to use the parameters FILSZ, SKIPREC, and EQUALS/NOEQUALS

CHAPTER 11

ADVANCED JCL FEATURES

CHAPTER 11 / ADVANCED JCL FEATURES

LEARNING OBJECTIVES

IN THIS CHAPTER YOU WILL LEARN

- additional parameters that may be coded on the JOB, EXEC, and DD statements

- how to use the checkpoint/restart feature

YOU WILL ALSO LEARN THE MEANINGS OF THE FOLLOWING TERMS:

- affinity

- buffer

- channel

- checkpoint

- Julian date

- performance group

JOB STATEMENT PARAMETERS

The MSGCLASS Parameter

The MSGCLASS parameter may be used to direct system messages and JCL statements to a particular output class. MSGCLASS is coded as

```
MSGCLASS=output-class
```

MSGCLASS is very similar to SYSOUT, which also directs output to a particular output-class, but SYSOUT applies to the DD statement it is coded on, while

JOB STATEMENT PARAMETERS

MSGCLASS applies to all system messages and JCL statements. If MSGCLASS is not coded, a default value applies, which usually directs the output to the same device as SYSOUT=A.

The MPROFILE Parameter

The MPROFILE parameter may be used only in VS1 systems to assign an output class to a job's messages. It may be used in place of the MSGCLASS parameter.

The format of the MPROFILE parameter is

```
MPROFILE='message-profile-string'
```

The message-profile-string describes the job's requirements. The format is established at each computer center. For example, you might code

```
MPROFILE='FORM=CARBON'
```

This message-profile-string specifies that the job's messages should be printed on carbon paper. The system will use this specification to assign an output class to the job's messages. This message-profile-string is valid only if the values FORM and CARBON have been given meanings at your computer center.

The NOTIFY Parameter

The NOTIFY parameter is used only in MVS systems to request that a message be sent to a time-sharing terminal when a job submitted from that terminal has completed processing.

The format of the NOTIFY parameter is

```
NOTIFY=user-id
```

The PROFILE Parameter

The PROFILE parameter may be used only in VS1 systems to assign a job class and a priority to each job. (PROFILE may also be coded on a DD statement, as explained later in this chapter.) You describe the job's requirements, and the system translates these requirements into a job class and a priority.

The format of the PROFILE parameter is

```
PROFILE='profile-string'
```

The profile-string describes the job's requirements. The format of the profile-string is established at each computer center. For example, you might code

```
PROFILE=('RUN=PROD','LANG=COBOL','TIME=5')
```

This profile-string describes this job as a production job, written in COBOL, requiring 5 minutes. The system uses these specifications to assign a job class and priority to the job. This profile-string is valid only if the values RUN, PROD, LANG, etc., have been assigned meanings at your computer center.

The PRTY Parameter

The PRTY parameter specifies a job's priority for execution within its job class. PRTY is coded as

```
PRTY=n
```

where n is a number representing the job's priority. The lowest priority is 0. The highest priority is 13 (JES3) or 15 (JES2). If two jobs with the same job class are waiting in the input work queue, the job with the higher priority will be selected first. If PRTY is not coded, an installation-defined default applies. Usually the accounting system will increase charges for a job run at a high priority.

The TYPRUN Parameter

The two main functions of the TYPRUN parameter are to hold a job for later processing and to have a job's JCL checked for syntax errors. To have your job held, code

```
TYPRUN=HOLD
```

If a job uses a data set that is created by a different job, you might want to hold the job until the data set has been created. You must tell the operator when the held job should be released.

In VS1 and MVS you can have your job's JCL checked by coding

```
TYPRUN=SCAN
```

This causes the job's JCL to be checked for syntax errors and prevents the job from executing. Suppose a job uses a data set that has not yet been created. The job obviously cannot be executed, but you might like to check the JCL syntax. This is the kind of situation for which TYPRUN=SCAN is useful. *

JOB AND EXEC STATEMENT PARAMETERS

The two parameters discussed here, ADDRSPC and PERFORM, may be coded on either the JOB statement or an EXEC statement.

The ADDRSPC Parameter

In VS1 and MVS systems the ADDRSPC parameter is used to permit or prevent paging of a job or a step between real and virtual storage. When ADDRSPC is coded on the JOB statement it applies to the whole job, and when it is coded on an EXEC statement it applies to that step.

```
ADRSPC=REAL
```

means that the job or step must occupy real storage, and therefore paging is prevented.

```
ADDRSPC=VIRT
```

means that the job or step may occupy virtual storage, and therefore paging is permitted. If ADDRSPC is not coded, paging is permitted. Most programs may be paged, and preventing paging degrades the system's performance, so

---

* TYPRUN=SCAN is also useful if you are writing a JCL textbook and want to be sure that the examples do not contain syntax errors.

most often you will either code VIRT or omit the ADDRSPC parameter altogether. In fact, at some computer centers you may not be allowed to code ADDRSPC=REAL unless you get special permission.

The PERFORM Parameter

The PERFORM parameter is used only in MVS systems to associate a job with a **performance group**. Performance groups, which are defined by the computer center, specify the workload-dependent processing rate under which a job or jobstep should execute. When the workload is light all performance groups are given good processing rates, but when the workload becomes heavier some performance groups will be given lower processing rates than others.

The PERFORM parameter is coded as

```
PERFORM=n
```

where n, which is the number of the performance group, must be between 1 and 255.

When PERFORM is coded on the JOB statement it applies to the whole job, and when it is coded on the EXEC statement it applies to that step.

EXEC STATEMENT PARAMETER— THE DPRTY PARAMETER

The DPRTY parameter is used only in MVS systems to assign a dispatching priority to a jobstep. The dispatching priority determines the order in which jobsteps that are executing but are in a wait state are given control of the CPU. This is different from the JOB statement PRTY parameter, which sets the priority controlling the order in which jobs in the input work queue are selected for execution.

The format of DPRTY parameter is

```
DPRTY=(value1,value2)
```

where value1 and value2 are numbers from 0 through 15. These values are used in an equation to calculate the dispatching priority.

If the DPRTY parameter is not coded, the system assigns a default priority.

DD STATEMENT PARAMETERS

This section will discuss additional features of the UNIT, VOL, SPACE, SYSOUT, and DCB parameters, additional parameters which are coded with SYSOUT, and some new parameters.

The UNIT Parameter

In Chapter 3 you learned how to use the UNIT parameter to specify the kind of unit required. The complete format for the UNIT parameter is

$$
\text{UNIT} = \left(\begin{bmatrix} \text{address} \\ \text{device-type} \\ \text{group-name} \end{bmatrix} \begin{bmatrix} ,\text{unit-count} \\ ,\text{P} \end{bmatrix} [,\text{DEFER}][,\text{SEP}=\text{ddname}] \right)
$$

You know how to code address, device-type, and group-name. The unit-count subparameter is used with data sets that extend over more than one volume. Suppose you have a data set that occupies three tape volumes. You can request that all three tape volumes be mounted at the start of the job by coding a 3 for the unit-count. For example,

    UNIT=(TAPE,3)

requests that three tape drives be allocated to this data set. Notice the required parentheses.

Instead of coding a number for the unit-count, you can code the letter P, which stands for parallel mounting. Coding a P means that the number of units to be allocated to this data set is to be obtained from information given in the VOL parameter. (How the VOL parameter is coded for multivolume data sets is the next topic.) If you do not code a unit-count value or the letter P, one unit is allocated to the data set, in which case, as each volume is finished the job stops executing and the system informs the operator that the current volume must be demounted and the next volume be mounted.

Requesting multiple units for a multivolume data set improves operating efficiency, since the jobstep does not have to be interrupted to allow the operator to demount and mount volumes. On the other hand, if you request many units, your job may have to wait a long time for all the units to be available before it can begin execution. Furthermore, while your job is using the units, they are not available to other jobs.

Code DEFER when you want to defer mounting a volume—for example, if there is a data set that might not be used during an execution of your program. When you code DEFER, the system does not request the operator to mount the volume until your program opens the data set. If your program never opens the data set, the volume will not be mounted. If DEFER is coded for a new data set on a direct access device, it is ignored.

Except for SEP, the UNIT subparameters are positional, so if you omit one and want to code a later one, you must code a comma to indicate the missing parameter. Suppose you have a cataloged data set. You do not want to code the device type, but you do want to request 5 units. You code

```
UNIT=(,5)
```

As another example, suppose you have a cataloged data set that requires only one unit, but for which you want to specify deferred mounting. You code

```
UNIT=(,,DEFER)
```

Sometimes getting the right number of commas can be confusing. One way of making sure you have the right number of commas is to code all the parameters, with their commas, and then to erase the parameters you want to omit, leaving the commas.

The SEP subparameter is available only for MFT, MVT, and VS1 systems and applies only to DASD. The ddname must be the name of an earlier DD statement in the same jobstep. SEP means that you want this data set and the earlier data set to be on separate units. If two data sets are heavily used, you might want them on separate units to reduce access arm movement. However, most computer centers that use VS1 have installed a program that does I/O load balancing, so that unit separation is done automatically. Therefore for VS1 systems you generally do not have to code the SEP subparameter. The SORTWK02 DD statement in Figure 10.6 requests separation from SORTWK01.

THE AFF SUBPARAMETER. The UNIT parameter has a second format which is sometimes used. It is

```
UNIT=AFF=ddname
```

AFF stands for **affinity**, and ddname is the name of an earlier DD statement in the same jobstep. AFF is the opposite of SEP. You code this form of the UNIT

DD STATEMENT PARAMETERS

parameter when you want two data sets to use the same unit. The two data sets are said to have unit affinity.

Consider the following coding:

```
//STEP1     EXEC PGM=STATS
//DD1       DD DSN=SALETBLE,
//             DISP=SHR,
//             UNIT=TAPE,
//             VOL-SER=111111
//DD2       DD DSN=SALESTAT,
//             DISP=(NEW,KEEP),
//             UNIT=AFF=DD1,
//             VOL-SER=222222
```

When this step begins execution, volume 111111 will be mounted. When SALESTAT is opened by the program, the system will tell the operator to mount volume 222222 on the same tape drive.

Coding AFF reduces the number of units used by a jobstep, but it can only be used if the circumstances are right. In the example, for AFF to work properly the program must be finished with SALETBLE before it starts writing SALESTAT.

AFF and SEP Parameters

In MFT, MVT, and VS1 systems, the AFF and SEP parameters may be used to request channel separation. A **channel** is a device over which data are transmitted between main storage and I/O devices. Processing time may be shortened if data sets that are used in a jobstep are transmitted over separate channels.

The format of the SEP parameter is

```
SEP=(ddname,...)
```

As an illustration of how the SEP parameter is used, consider the following example:

```
//DDA       DD DSN=ALPHA,
//             DISP=OLD
//DDB       DD DSN=BETA,
//             DISP=(NEW,KEEP),                              (cont.)
```

```
//              UNIT=TAPE
//DDC       DD DSN=GAMMA,
//              DISP=OLD,
//              SEP=(DDA,DDB)
//DDD       DD DSN=DELTA,
//              DISP=(NEW,PASS),
//              UNIT=2400,
//              SEP=(DDA,DDB)
```

The system will attempt to assign the data sets named GAMMA and DELTA to a channel other than those assigned to ALPHA and BETA. ALPHA and BETA may or may not be assigned to the same channel.

The AFF parameter offers an alternative way of requesting channel separation. The format of the AFF parameter is

```
AFF=ddname
```

where ddname is the name of an earlier DD statement which contains the SEP parameter. The AFF parameter copies the separation specified on the earlier DD statement. This means that in the previous example, the last DD statement could have been coded as

```
//DDD       DD DSN=DELTA,
//              DISP=(NEW,PASS),
//              UNIT=2400,
//              AFF=DDC
```

This coding means that DELTA is to have the same channel separation that is specified in the DD statement whose name is DDC. This is exactly the same channel separation requested previously when SEP=(DDA,DDB) was coded.

The VOL Parameter

In Chapter 3 you learned how to use the VOL parameter to specify a serial number, and in Chapter 4 you learned how to code a backwards reference. The complete format of the VOL parameter is

$$VOL=\left([PRIVATE]\ [,RETAIN]\ [,vol\text{-}seq\text{-}no]\ [,vol\text{-}count] \begin{bmatrix} SER=(ser\text{-}no,...) \\ REF=reference \end{bmatrix} \right)$$

SER and REF are keyword parameters; the other parameters are positional.

DD STATEMENT PARAMETERS

THE PRIVATE SUBPARAMETER. PRIVATE means that no other output data set is to be allocated to this volume unless a specific volume request is made. Suppose you are using a disk volume that has been assigned to your use. There should not be any other jobs that specifically request that volume. But the system might assign that volume to satisfy a nonspecific volume request. You can prevent that, and ensure that your job has exclusive use of the volume, by coding PRIVATE. Tape volumes for which you make a specific volume request are automatically made private. Also, tape volumes used for permanent data sets are automatically made private. In these cases you do not have to code PRIVATE.

If you specify or imply PRIVATE, the system will request that the operator demount the volume after its last use in the jobstep, unless the data set is passed or you code RETAIN.

THE RETAIN SUBPARAMETER. RETAIN has meaning only for tape volumes. For private tape volumes RETAIN means the volume should not be demounted at the end of a jobstep. If a volume will be used in more than one step, coding RETAIN saves the operator the trouble of demounting and mounting the volume.

THE VOLUME SEQUENCE NUMBER SUBPARAMETER. If you do not want to start processing multivolume data sets with the first volume, vol-seq-no, which is an abbreviation for volume sequence number, is used. For example, suppose a data set is in sequence by name and occupies four volumes. Names beginning with A to E are on the first volume, F to L are on the second volume, M to R are on the third volume, and S to Z are on the fourth volume. If you wanted to begin processing with names starting with M, you code

```
//INPUT    DD DSN=NAMEFILE,
//             DISP=OLD,
//             VOL=(,,3)
```

NAMEFILE is a cataloged data set. The UNIT information and volume serial numbers are recorded in the catalog, and therefore you do not have to code them. Notice that you may specify that processing should begin with the third volume, even though you do not explicitly code the volume serial numbers. The two commas in the coding for the VOL parameter indicate that the positional subparameters PRIVATE and RETAIN are omitted.

THE SER SUBPARAMETER.   The elipses (...) in the description of the SER subparameter mean that more than one serial number may be coded. Suppose you are creating on tape a data set that requires three reels of tape. You could code

```
//DD1       DD DSN=BIGFILE,
//             DISP=(NEW,KEEP),
//             UNIT=(2400,2),
//             VOL=SER=(TAPE06,TAPE18,TAPE42)
```

Notice the parentheses that are required when more than one serial number is coded. This coding means that BIGFILE will be written to TAPE06, TAPE18, and TAPE42, in that order. As mentioned earlier in the discussion of the UNIT parameter, the 2 specified for the unit-count indicates that two tape drives should be allocated to this data set. When the step begins, the system will request the operator to mount TAPE06 and TAPE18. When TAPE06 is full, the operator will demount it and mount TAPE42 on the same tape drive.

THE VOLUME COUNT SUBPARAMETER.   vol-count, which is an abbreviation for volume count, is used only for output data sets, either a new data set or an existing data set which is being extended. For example,

```
//OUTPUT    DD DSN=NEWFILE,
//             DISP=(NEW,CATLG),
//             UNIT=(TAPE,P),
//             VOL=(,,,5,SER=(TAPE46,TAPE47))
```

defines a data set that is being created. You expect that two tape volumes, TAPE46 and TAPE47, will be enough to hold the data set, but by coding a volume count of 5 you are telling the system that, if they are required, up to three more volumes may be allocated. The need for additional volumes will be treated as a nonspecific volume request. Notice that a P is coded in the UNIT parameter. This P means that the number of units which should be allocated to this data set is either the number specified for the volume count subparameter or the number of serial numbers coded, whichever is higher. In this case, five tape units will be allocated. Tying up five tape drives when only two are needed is wasteful. Many computer centers limit the number of drives that may be requested.

DD STATEMENT PARAMETERS

Notice that in this example SER is preceded by a comma, while in the previous example SER was not preceded by a comma. The rule is that when SER is coded with one or more other subparameters it must be preceded by a comma, but when it is the only subparameter it is not preceded by a comma.

The SPACE Parameter

In Chapter 3 you learned how to request and release primary and secondary space allocations, and in Chapter 5 you learned how to request directory blocks when creating a library. The complete format of the SPACE parameter is

$$\text{SPACE} = \left(\left\{ \begin{matrix} \text{TRK} \\ \text{CYL} \\ \text{blocksize} \end{matrix} \right\}, \left(\text{primary[,secondary]} \begin{bmatrix} \text{,directory} \\ \text{,index} \end{bmatrix} \right) \text{[,RLSE]} \begin{bmatrix} \text{,CONTIG} \\ \text{,MXIG} \\ \text{,ALX} \end{bmatrix} \text{[,ROUND]} \right)$$

(index will be discussed in Chapter 8). All the SPACE subparameters are positional.

THE CONTIG, MXIG, AND ALX SUBPARAMETERS. You may recall that an extent is a group of contiguous tracks. Chapter 3 explained that the system always tries to satisfy the primary request using one extent. If the specified volume does not contain an extent large enough to satisfy the primary request, up to five extents will be used. The subparameters CONTIG, MXIG, and ALX offer three different ways to ensure that the whole primary allocation is made in contiguous space.

When you code CONTIG, you specify that the primary allocation must be contiguous. If the specified volume does not contain enough contiguous space to satisfy the primary allocation, the job will fail. MXIG specifies that the space allocated to the data set must be the largest area of contiguous space on the volume. Furthermore, this space must be equal to or greater than the primary request or the job will fail. ALX specifies that up to five extents should be allocated to the data set. Each extent must be at least as large as the primary request. The system will allocate as many extents as it can find on the volume that are as least as large as the primary request, up to a maximum of five extents. If it cannot find at least one extent as large as the primary request, the job will fail.

THE ROUND SUBPARAMETER. Coding ROUND offers a way of getting cylinders when space is requested by blocksize. When you request space by blocksize, the request is normally converted into the equivalent whole number of tracks, and the allocation is made in tracks. When you code ROUND, however, the system calculates the smallest number of cylinders needed to satisfy the request, and the allocation is made in cylinders. For example, you might code

```
//BLKS      DD DSN=BLOCKS,
//             DISP=(NEW,CATLG),
//             UNIT=3330,
//             VOL=SER=WYL002,
//             SPACE=(600,(1000,200),,,ROUND)
```

The SPACE parameter requests a primary allocation of 1000 600-byte records. If ROUND had not been coded, Table E.1 in Appendix E shows that 56 tracks would have been allocated. ROUND means that this request should be allocated in cylinders. The 56 tracks will be rounded up to 3 cylinders. The secondary allocation for 200 600-byte records will also be made in cylinders. The three commas indicate that two positional parameters have been omitted.

MULTIVOLUME DATA SETS. When space is requested for a multivolume data set, the primary request must be satisfied on the first volume specified or the job will fail. Secondary requests may be satisfied on either the first volume or subsequent volumes. Take the following example:

```
//CREATE    DD DSN=LARGESET,
//             DISP=(NEW,KEEP),
//             UNIT=DISK,
//             VOL=SER=(WYL004,WYL006),
//             SPACE=(TRK,(100,20))
```

Disk pack WYL004 must contain at least 100 tracks in 5 or fewer extents or the job will fail. If secondary space is required, the system will allocate 20 tracks at a time, taking them from WYL004. This will continue either until there is not enough space on WYL004 to allocate 20 tracks or until a total of 16 extents have been allocated on WYL004 to the data set. At that point the system will begin allocating 20 tracks at a time from WYL006. Each disk pack may contain a total of 16 extents.

DD STATEMENT PARAMETERS

REQUESTING SPECIFIC TRACKS.   There is another form of the SPACE parameter in which you specify the tracks you want to be used for the data set:

$$\mathrm{SPACE}{=}\left(\mathrm{ABSTR},\left(\mathrm{primary},\mathrm{address}\begin{bmatrix}\mathrm{,directory}\\\mathrm{,index}\end{bmatrix}\right)\right)$$

In this form, primary specifies the number of tracks, address specifies the relative track number, and directory specifies the number of directory blocks.

For example,

```
SPACE=(ABSTR,(100,500))
```

requests 100 tracks, starting at relative track number 500. If any of the requested tracks are being used, the job will fail.

This form of the SPACE parameter is used only when there is a special reason for wanting a data set to be on particular tracks. For example, some direct access devices have both fixed and moveable heads. The data on tracks serviced by the fixed heads can be read and written much faster than the data on tracks serviced by the moveable heads. It might therefore be desirable for a critical data set to be located on the track serviced by the fixed heads. You can specify that by using this form of the SPACE parameter.

The SPLIT Parameter

In MFT, MVT, and VS1 systems, the SPLIT parameter is used to allocate space to two or more data sets in such a way that the data sets share tracks in a cylinder. This is useful when data sets have corresponding records. For example, one data set may contain customers' names and addresses, and a second data set may contain their financial data. If these data sets share tracks in a cylinder, access arm motion will be reduced.

The SPLIT parameter allows space to be requested in cylinders or blocks. When cylinders are used, the format is

```
SPLIT=(n,CYL,(primary[,secondary]))
```

and

```
SPLIT=n
```

346

Here n is the number of tracks per cylinder you want allocated, and the other subparameters have their usual meaning. As an example, suppose you want to allocate 13 cylinders on a 3330 for three data sets named RED, ORANGE, and YELLOW. On a 3330 each cylinder contains 19 tracks, and you want RED to occupy 11 tracks per cylinder, ORANGE 5 tracks per cylinder and YELLOW the remaining 3 tracks per cylinder. You code

```
//DD1       DD DSN=RED,
//             DISP=(,KEEP),
//             UNIT=3330,
//             VOL-SER=123456
//             SPLIT=(11,CYL,13)
//DD2       DD DSN=ORANGE,
//             DISP=(,KEEP),
//             SPLIT=5
//DD3       DD DSN=YELLOW,
//             DISP=(,KEEP),
//             SPLIT=3
```

Notice that volume and unit information are coded for RED, but not for ORANGE or YELLOW. Since ORANGE and YELLOW are using space allocated to RED, they must have the same volume and unit. Notice also that when you code SPLIT you do not also code SPACE; SPLIT allocates the space.

The format to use when you want to allocate space in blocks is

```
SPLIT=(percent,blocksize,(primary[,secondary]))
```

and

```
SPLIT=percent
```

Here percent is the percent of each cylinder you want to allocate. As an example, suppose the average blocksize is 2000 bytes, and you need space for 1500 blocks for two data sets named GREEN and BLUE. You want GREEN to occupy 70% of the tracks per cylinder and BLUE 30% of the tracks per cylinder. You code

```
//DDA       DD DSN=GREEN,
//             DISP=(,KEEP),
//             UNIT=DISK,
```

DD STATEMENT PARAMETERS

```
//                 VOL=SER=ABC123,
//                 SPLIT=(70,2000,1500)
//DDB    DD DSN=BLUE,
//                 DISP=(,KEEP),
//                 SPLIT=30
```

The percentage you request is converted into tracks and is rounded down. Therefore, the percent you request must equal at least one track.

The SUBALLOC Parameter

In MFT, MVT, and VS1 systems, the SUBALLOC parameter offers another way to allocate space to a data set. You first create a master data set which contains a lot of space, and then suballocate that space to other data sets.

The format of the SUBALLOC parameter is

$$\text{SUBALLOC} = \left(\begin{Bmatrix} \text{TRK} \\ \text{CYL} \\ \text{blocksize} \end{Bmatrix} , (\text{primary}[,\text{secondary}][,\text{directory}]), \text{ddname} \right)$$

As you can see, the format is similar to the format of the SPACE parameter, except for the ddname subparameter. The ddname is the name of the DD statement defining the master data set which has the space that is being suballocated.

Let us clarify these ideas by examining the following coding:

```
//ONE      DD DSN=APPLES,
//                DISP=(NEW,CATLG),
//                UNIT=DISK,
//                VOL=SER=DISK07,
//                SPACE=(CYL,20,,CONTIG)
//TWO      DD DSN=PEACHES,
//                DISP=(NEW,CATLG),
//                SUBALLOC=(CYL,5,ONE)
//THREE    DD DSN=CHERRIES,
//                DISP=(NEW,KEEP),
//                SUBALLOC=(TRK,(20,5),ONE)
```

The master data set is named APPLES and is defined on the DD statement named ONE. APPLES is allocated 20 contiguous cylinders. (When space is to be suballocated, it must be contiguous.) The data set named PEACHES requests 5 cylinders of the space allocated to APPLES. Notice that unit or volume information is not coded for PEACHES. Since PEACHES is suballocating space allocated to APPLES, it must have the same volume and unit as APPLES. The data set named CHERRIES requests 20 tracks of the space allocated to APPLES and also requests a secondary allocation of 5 tracks.

You may suballocate space from an existing data set, but your job must include a DD statement defining the master data set. This DD statement need not be in the same jobstep as the DD statement for the data set that is suballocating space. If the DD statement defining the master data set is in an earlier jobstep, you replace the ddname subparameter by stepname.ddname. Similarly, if the DD statement defining the master data set is in a procedure step that is called by an earlier jobstep, you replace ddname by stepname.procstepname.ddname. This is the usual technique for backwards references to earlier steps.

The SYSOUT Parameter

So far you have used only the simple form of the SYSOUT parameter,

```
SYSOUT=class
```

where class has usually been A for the printer and B for the punch. The complete format for the SYSOUT parameter is

```
SYSOUT=(class[,program-name][,form-name])
```

If you code an asterisk for the class, the output is directed to the same output class you specified in the MSGCLASS parameter on the JOB statement.

If you want to have the output data set written by a program in the system library rather than by the job entry system, you use program-name to specify the name of the program. This subparameter is rarely used.

form-name is the name of the form you want the output printed on. The form-name is assigned by the computer center. A form-name of A1 might mean unlined paper, A2 might mean two-part paper, and so on.

```
SYSOUT=(C,,A2)
```

directs the output to output class C and indicates that you want this output printed on the form identified by A2.

DD STATEMENT PARAMETERS

THE PROFILE SUBPARAMETER. The following form of the SYSOUT parameter may be used only in VS1 systems:

```
SYSOUT=PROFILE='sysout-profile-string'
```

The PROFILE subparameter is used to assign an output class. You use the sysout-profile-string to describe the data set's printing requirements, and the system assigns an output class. The format of the sysout-profile-string is established at each computer enter. For example, you could code

```
//PAYOUT   DD SYSOUT=PROFILE='FORM=CHECKS'
```

This sysout-profile-string specifies that this data set should be printed on check forms. The system uses this specification to assign an output class to this data set. This sysout-profile-string is valid only if FORM and CHECKS have been assigned meanings at your computer center.

Parameters Used with SYSOUT

Several parameters are used with SYSOUT to give more control over printing or punching.

THE COPIES PARAMETER. The COPIES parameter specifies the number of copies of the data set to be printed. The statement

```
//REPORT   DD SYSOUT=A,
//            COPIES=24
```

will cause 24 copies of the data set to be printed. A maximum of 255 copies may be requested, except for JES3, for which the limit is 254 copies. COPIES has an additional feature used only with the IBM 3800 printer; it will be discussed later.

THE DEST PARAMETER. Normally output is routed to the workstation from which the job was submitted. You can use the DEST parameter to route the output to a different location. Suppose a job stream contains the following two DD statements:

```
//ABC      DD SYSOUT=A
//XYZ      DD SYSOUT=A,
//            DEST=RMT1
```

CHAPTER 11 / ADVANCED JCL FEATURES

The workstation from which the job was submitted receives the output defined by the ABC DD statement, and the workstation named RMT1 receives the output defined by the XYZ DD statement. The names of the workstations are assigned by the computer center, except for LOCAL or ANYLOCAL, which mean an output device attached to the central CPU.

THE HOLD PARAMETER.   The HOLD parameter is used to prevent a data set from being printed or punched until it is released. For example, you might code

```
//BIGONE    DD SYSOUT=A,
//             COPIES=200,
//             HOLD=YES
```

Since 200 copies of this data set are requested, printing can take a long time. Therefore, the coding specifies that the data set should be held, and a message is left with the operator to release it for printing on a late shift, when the printer is not very busy.

THE OUTLIM PARAMETER.   The OUTLIM parameter is used to limit the number of lines printed or cards punched. It is particularly useful during debugging, when a program may go into a loop and print thousands of lines of garbage. It is coded as follows:

```
//OUTPUT    DD SYSOUT=A,
//             OUTLIM=2000
```

If the program tries to write more than 2000 lines to this data set, the job abends. If OUTLIM is omitted, under JES2 there is no default for the number of output records. Under JES3 there is a default limit defined by the computer center.

THE UCS PARAMETER.   The UCS parameter is used to request that a particular character set be used to print the data set. This parameter has meaning only if output is directed to a printer with the universal character feature, i.e., the 1403, 3203-5, and 3211 printers. The parameter is used as follows:

```
//TEXT      DD SYSOUT=A,
//             UCS=TN
```

DD STATEMENT PARAMETERS

This requests that the data set be printed using the TN print chain. The character sets that may be requested are defined by IBM. You can only use those IBM character sets for which the corresponding print chain is available at your computer center. User-defined character sets are also permitted.

PARAMETERS USED WITH 3800 PRINTING SUBSYSTEM. IBM's laser printer is called the 3800 Printing Subsystem. Special features offered by this printer are invoked by coding keyword parameters on the DD statement that defines a data set routed to a 3800 printer. The printer is described in *IBM 3800 Printing Subsystem, Programmer's Guide* (GC26-3846).

The COPIES Parameter. When the COPIES parameter is used with a 3800 printer, you can specify how you want multiple copies to be printed by coding group values. For example, in

```
//REPORT   DD SYSOUT=A,
//            COPIES=(0,(1,4,2))
```

the 1, 4, and 2 are the group values. This coding causes 7 copies of the data to be printed in three groups. The first group contains 1 copy of each page in the data set, the second group contains 4 copies of each page, and the third group contains 2 copies of each page. Notice that when group values are coded, the value specified for the number of copies, which in this example is 0, is ignored. Up to 8 group values may be coded.

The BURST Parameter. Before we discuss the other features of this printer, it is useful to examine in general how the 3800 Printing Subsystem works. Figure 11.1 shows the path of the paper through the system. The paper starts at the input station and is brought into contact with the photoconductor drum at the transfer station, where the data are transferred to the paper. The data are fused on the paper at the fuser. From there the paper goes either to the continuous forms stacker or to an optional burster and trimmer which bursts it into separate sheets. The burster and trimmer is very useful for producing letters for a mass mailing. To use the 3800 burster and trimmer, you code the DD statement as follows:

```
//REPORT   DD SYSOUT=A,
//            BURST=Y
```

FIGURE 11.1

Overview of the IBM 3800 Printing Subsystem

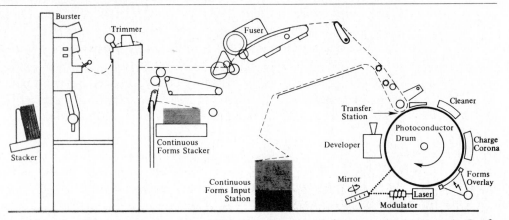

Reprinted by permission from *IBM 3800 Printing Subsystem Programmer's Guide* (GC26-3846-3). © 1975 by International Business Machines Corporation.

If you do not want it used, you code

```
//REPORT   DD SYSOUT=A,
//            BURST=N
```

The FLASH Parameter.   Let us look at what happens around the photo-conductor drum in Figure 11.1. First the cleaner removes whatever is currently on the drum. Then the charge corona prepares the surface to receive the image. The next station is one of the special features of the 3800, the forms overlay. With standard printers special forms are required for certain jobs. The 3800 Printing Subsystem, however, eliminates the need for supplies of different types of forms. Plain paper is used with the forms overlay, a device that is inserted in the 3800 and causes the desired form to be printed on plain paper. Once a particular form is no longer required, the forms overlay is disposed of, without the loss of a large supply of now unneeded forms. When you want a particular forms overlay inserted in the system, you code the FLASH parameter on the DD statement, as in

```
//REPORT   DD SYSOUT=A,
//            FLASH=SCRN
```

FIGURE 11.2

Sample of Germanic script

Thif if a fample of the old germanic fcript created at one inftallation.
It maf created for fun and not for ufe fince even in Germany it if not
commonly ufed. The fentence, "The quicf brown for jumped over the lazn
dogf", illuftratef the ufe of the entire alfabet. The fentence when
written in capital letterf appearf af "THE QUICK BROWN FOX JUMPED OVER
THE LAZY DOGG".

On the operator's terminal a message will appear informing the operator
that the forms overlay named SCRN is to be inserted in the system. The name
of the forms overlay is from one to four characters. There may be occasions
when you want one copy of a report printed on a form and a second copy
printed on plain paper. In this case, the DD statement is coded as

```
//REPORT    DD SYSOUT=A,
//              COPIES=2,
//              FLASH=(SCRN,1)
```

Specifying 1 with the FLASH parameter prevents the forms overlay from being
used to produce the form on both copies of the output.

The CHARS Parameter.   The 3800 Printing Subsystem also offers the
user a variety of type styles. Certain styles such as Gothic come with the
system, but users can create additional type styles using the utility program
IEBIMAGE, which will be discussed in Chapter 14. In one installation the old
Germanic script was implemented for use. Figure 11.2 contains a sample of
this type style. It is invoked with the DD statement

```
//REPORT    DD SYSOUT=A,
//              CHARS=GRMN
```

The CHARS parameter specifies that the type style named GRMN is to be used
when this data set is printed. The name used to invoke the type style with
the CHARS parameter may be from one to four characters in length.

The MODIFY Parameter.   Frequently printed documents must include
a legal disclaimer of some sort. This legal disclaimer may have to appear on

several documents and may change based on current legal activity. In the past the program for each document had to include this disclaimer, and the programs had to be changed every time the disclaimer changed. With the 3800 Printing Subsystem, this is no longer the situation. Through the utility program IEBIMAGE, a copy modification module is stored in a system library named SYS1.IMAGELIB. This facility is invoked with the DD statement

```
//REPORT   DD SYSOUT=A,
//              MODIFY=MODI
```

The MODIFY parameter specifies that the copy modification module named MODI is to be used when this data set is printed. The name of the module used with the MODIFY parameter may be from one to four characters in length.

The copy modification module also offers the user the ability to print information on one copy but not on another. For example, in a manufacturing environment it might be desirable to include the unit cost on the manufacturer's copy of the invoice but not on the customer's copy.

The FCB Parameter.   Vertical spacing on the old impact printers was handled with a carriage control tape that was made of paper. The carriage control tape had 12 columns on it. These columns were referred to as channels. By tradition, channel 1 had a hole punched in it to indicate the start of a new page. When forms or specially sized paper was used, the operator had to physically change the carriage control tape. Being made of paper, carriage control tapes were fragile and had to be replaced frequently. Modern impact printers, such as the 3211, use a forms control buffer (FCB) to supply the information previously provided by the carriage control tape. For the 3800 Printing Subsystem the FCB is a module stored in library SYS1.IMAGELIB by the utility program IEBIMAGE. To invoke a particular FCB module, you code the DD statement as

```
//REPORT   DD SYSOUT=A,
//              FCB=CCT1
```

The FCB parameter specifies that the module named CCT1 is to be used when the data set is printed. The FCB module name may be one to four characters in length.

DD STATEMENT PARAMETERS

The LABEL Parameter

The format of the LABEL parameter is

$$\text{LABEL=} \left(\text{[seq-no][,label-type]} \begin{bmatrix} \text{,PASSWORD} \\ \text{,NOPWREAD} \end{bmatrix} \begin{bmatrix} \text{,IN} \\ \text{,OUT} \end{bmatrix} \begin{bmatrix} \text{RETPD=nnnn} \\ \text{EXPDT=yyddd} \end{bmatrix} \right)$$

All the subparameters are positional except RETPD and EXPDT.

THE DATA SET SEQUENCE NUMBER SUBPARAMETER. seq-no, which is an abbreviation for data set sequence number, applies only to tape. A tape volume may contain more than one data set. The data set sequence number specifies the number of the data set where processing is to begin. If you wanted to read or write the third data set on a tape volume, you would code

    LABEL=3

If the data set sequence number is not specified, the system assumes that the data set is the first one on the volume, unless the data set is passed or cataloged. If the data set is passed, the system obtains the data set sequence number from the passing step. If the data set is cataloged, the system obtains the data set sequence number from the catalog.

Although a tape volume may contain more than one data set, if you write over a particular data set, the following data sets are no longer accessible. For example, if a tape volume contains five data sets and you write over the second data set, the third, fourth, and fifth are no longer usable.

THE LABEL-TYPE SUBPARAMETER. label-type specifies the kind of labels the data set has. The values that may be coded and their meanings are shown in Table 11.1. Data sets on direct access devices must have either IBM standard labels (SL) or IBM standard and user labels (SUL). If label-type is not coded, IBM standard labels are assumed. label-type is not stored in the catalog or passed with passed data sets, so if a data set has other than IBM standard labels you must code the LABEL parameter whenever you access the data set.

In the previous chapters, discussions concerning data sets on tape always assumed that the data set accessed was the first one on the tape volume and that it had standard labels. Since these are the default values, it was not necessary to code the LABEL parameter.

CHAPTER 11 / ADVANCED JCL FEATURES

TABLE 11.1

Label-types and their meanings

Label-type	Meaning
SL	IBM standard labels.
SUL	IBM standard and user labels.
AL	American National standard labels.
AUL	American National standard and user labels.
NSL	Nonstandard labels.
NL	No labels.
BLP	System should bypass label processing.
LTM	A leading tapemark may be present.

DATA SET PROTECTION.   PASSWORD and NOPWREAD are used to protect a data set against unauthorized access. If PASSWORD is coded, a protection byte in the label is turned on. When the protection byte is on, the system requests the operator to enter the data set's password whenever a job attempts to read, write to, or delete the data set. NOPWREAD works the same way except that jobs may read the data set without supplying a password. However, if a job attempts to write to or delete the data set, the operator must enter the data set's password. If the operator enters the incorrect password twice, the job is terminated. (To err is human, but to err twice causes an abend.) Passwords are assigned using the system utility IEHPROGM to enter a data set's name and password into a data set named PASSWORD. Since PASSWORD itself is password-protected, this may be done only by authorized personnel. If neither PASSWORD nor NOPWREAD is coded, the data set is not password-protected.

RESTRICTING DATA SET USAGE.   The next subparameter, which may be coded as either IN or OUT, is used to restrict the way a data set is used. IN means the data set can be used only for input, and OUT means the data set can be used only for output. If the program attempts to violate these restrictions, the job will abend.

DD STATEMENT PARAMETERS

SPECIFYING A RETENTION PERIOD. The final subparameter offers two ways to specify a time period during which a data set may not be deleted or written over. One way is to specify a retention period; the number of days specified must be a one- to four-digit number. To specify a retention period of 60 days, for example, code

```
RETPD=60
```

The other method is to specify a date before which the data set may not be deleted or written over. The date is specified by giving a two-digit year number and a three-digit day number in the form yyddd. This form of the date is frequently called the Julian date.* For example, January 1, 1984 is 84001, and February 1, 1984 is 84032. The coding

```
EXPDT=84366
```

sets the expiration date as the 366th day of 1984 (December 31, 1984).

To delete a data set before its retention period or expiration date has passed, you can use the system utility IEHPROGM, described in Chapter 14.

LABEL PARAMETER EXAMPLES. As mentioned earlier, the default value for seq-no is 1 and for label-type is IBM standard labels. Frequently these are the values you want, so you may accept the default values and not code the LABEL parameter. If the other subparameters are not coded, they do not apply. Therefore, if you want password protection, or if you want to specify that the data set should be used only for input or only for output, or if you want to assign a retention period, you must code the LABEL parameter.

The parameter

```
LABEL=(5,,PASSWORD,RETPD=90)
```

indicates that the data set is the fifth on the tape volume, that it has standard labels, that it is to be password-protected, and that it is to be protected against accidental erasure for 90 days.

The LABEL parameter

```
LABEL=EXPDT=90365
```

* In some cases the Julian date is specified in the form dddyy. You must be careful to use the form that is required.

sets the expiration date as December 31, 1990.

Notice that in this example EXPDT is not preceded by a comma, while in the previous example RETPD was preceded by a comma. The rule is that when EXPDT or RETPD is the only subparameter coded it is not preceded by a comma, but if any other subparameter is coded EXPDT and RETPD must be preceded by a comma.

The following uses all the appropriate subparameters:

```
LABEL=(2,AL,NOPWREAD,OUT,RETPD=10)
```

This parameter specifies that the data set is the second on the volume, that it has American National standard labels, and that it is to be password-protected, used only for output, and protected against accidental erasure for 10 days.

Additional DCB Subparameters

In Chapter 3 you learned the most frequently used DCB subparameters, RECFM, LRECL, BLKSIZE, and DEN. In Chapter 12 you will learn some additional subparameters that are used with ISAM data sets. Here we will discuss several other subparameters that you may have occasion to use. However, be aware that there are more than 30 DCB subparameters. Many of them are used only under very special circumstances and will not be discussed.

BUFNO is used to specify the number of buffers to be used with the data set. When data are read or written, they are temporarily held in an area of main storage called a **buffer**. Usually two buffers are used, so that the data in one can be processed while the other is being filled. To request 6 buffers you would code

```
BUFNO=6
```

The DISPLAY DD statement in Figure 8.8 is requesting one buffer. If BUFNO is not coded, a default number of buffers, which depends on the operating system and access method being used, is assigned.

PRTSP is used to control the line spacing used with an on-line printer. For example,

```
PRTSP=2
```

specifies double spacing. You may code values from 0 (no spacing) to 3 (triple spacing). If PRTSP is not coded, single spacing is used. This parameter is not

THE CHECKPOINT/RESTART FEATURE

resources used, a device or a volume, are made available to other users sooner. The format of the FREE parameter is

$$FREE = \begin{Bmatrix} END \\ CLOSE \end{Bmatrix}$$

Coding END causes the data set to be deallocated at the end of the jobstep, and coding CLOSE causes the data set to be deallocated when the data set is closed. If FREE is not coded, the data set is deallocated at the end of the jobstep.

The TERM Parameter

The TERM parameter is used with time-sharing systems to indicate that the data set is coming from or going to a time-sharing system. (In VS1 systems the TERM parameter is used differently.) The format of the TERM parameter is

    TERM=TS

The only parameters that may be coded with the TERM parameter are SYSOUT and DCB. The following DD statement illustrates the use of the TERM parameter:

    //RESULTS   DD TERM=TS

THE CHECKPOINT/RESTART FEATURE

If a job is interrupted because of a system error or because of a program error, it may be desirable to save computer time by restarting the job from where the interruption occurred, rather than from the beginning of the job. This ability is provided by the checkpoint/restart feature. The job may be restarted either from the beginning of the step in which the interrupt occurred, which is called step restart, or from within the step in which the interrupt occurred, which is called checkpoint restart. The restart may be either automatic, which means the job will be rerun immediately, or deferred, which means the job will be rerun when the programmer resubmits it. Checkpoint/restart is described in *OS/VS1 Checkpoint/Restart* (GC26-3876) for VS1 systems and *OS/VS2 MVS Checkpoint/Restart* (GC26-3877) for MVS systems.

Deferred restarts from the beginning of a step are the easiest to understand and code, so we will begin with these.

Deferred Step Restart

Suppose you run a job that has eight steps named STEP1 through STEP8, and the job fails during STEP6. If a system error caused the failure, you may be able simply to resubmit the job starting at STEP6. If a program error caused the failure, you may be able to examine the output, correct the error, and resubmit the job starting at STEP6.

You can resubmit the job and start at STEP6 by coding the RESTART parameter on the JOB statement as follows:

```
RESTART=STEP6
```

Rerunning a job may sound simple, and indeed coding the RESTART parameter is simple, but many other factors must be considered. For example, STEP4 may create a temporary data set and pass it to STEP6. In that case it will be necessary to restart the job from STEP4. Or suppose STEP6 creates a disk data set. Depending on how the DISP parameter is coded, that data set may not have been deleted when the job failed. When you rerun the job and STEP6 tries again to create the data set, you will get the message DUPLICATE NAME ON DIRECT ACCESS VOLUME. In this case you have to delete the data set or change the disposition from NEW to OLD.

If STEP6 updates a data set, those records which were updated before the failure occurred will be updated a second time if STEP6 is rerun. To prevent records from being updated twice it may be necessary to include, for example, a last-date-updated field in each record. When the step is rerun, that field may be tested to determine if the record was updated on the run that failed. Even that strategy does not work if records may legally be updated more than once during a run.

You should also be aware that COND parameters that refer to a step preceding the restarted step will be ignored.

You can restart a job from a step within a procedure by coding the stepname and procstepname. For example,

```
RESTART=(STEP6.GO)
```

means that the job should restart at the GO step within the procedure invoked on the STEP6 EXEC statement.

Checkpoint Restart

Instead of restarting a job from the beginning of a step, it is possible to request checkpoint restart, in which case execution starts within a step. To use checkpoint restart you must establish checkpoints in your program. At a **checkpoint** the status of your job and of the system is written to a checkpoint data set. Writing this status information is called taking a checkpoint. This status information may be used to restart the job at the checkpoint within a step.

To establish checkpoints you must code the appropriate instruction in your program. Assembler programs use the CHKPT macro; COBOL programs use the RERUN clause; and PL/I programs use the CALL PLICKPT instruction. FORTRAN does not permit checkpointing. You specify that you want checkpoints taken during a sort or merge by coding the CKPT parameter on the SORT or MERGE control statement.

For multivolume data sets you can request that a checkpoint be taken when the end of a volume is encountered by coding the CHKPT parameter on the DD statement for that data set. For example, coding

```
//DD1        DD DSN=LARGE,
//              DISP=OLD,
//              UNIT=TAPE,
//              VOL=SER=(TAPE01,TAPE02,TAPE03),
//              CHKPT=EOV
```

means checkpoints will be taken at the end of TAPE01 and TAPE02. CHKPT may be coded only for sequential data sets.

You must also provide either a sequential or partitioned data set to which the checkpoint records are written. Assembler, COBOL, and PL/I programmers specify the ddname of the checkpoint data set in their programs. The ddname of the data set used for sort checkpoints is SORTCKPT. The ddname of the data set used for checkpoints generated by the CHKPT parameter is SYSCKEOV.

Saving all the checkpoints written requires that the disposition of this data set be MOD. If the disposition is NEW, each checkpoint overwrites the previous one. A DD statement that could be used is

```
//CHEK      DD DSN=CHECKPNT,
//             DISP=(MOD,CATLG),
//             UNIT=TAPE
```

Each time a checkpoint is taken, the system prints a message which includes the checkpoint identification, a seven-digit number preceded by the letter C. The first checkpoint is C0000001, the second is C0000002, etc. As you will see later, these identifications may be used to perform a delayed checkpoint restart.

If your program takes checkpoints, it is assumed that you want automatic checkpoint restart. Therefore, if a program that has taken one or more checkpoints is interrupted because of failure or because of an abend that returned one of the eligible completion codes, the system sends a message to the operator asking if the job should be restarted. If the operator gives permission, the job will be automatically restarted from the latest checkpoint. The eligible completion codes are established by IBM, but may be changed by the computer center. If you want automatic checkpoint restart, you do not have to do anything. If you do not want automatic checkpoint restart, you can tell the operator not to give permission. It is, however, more convenient to control automatic restart using the RD parameter.

The RD Parameter

The RD parameter is used to request automatic step restart or suppress automatic checkpoint restart. It is also used to prevent checkpoints from being taken. The RD parameter may be coded on either the JOB or EXEC statements. If it is coded on the JOB statement, it overrides any RD parameters coded on EXEC statements.

The RD parameter is coded as follows:

```
RD=request
```

The values that may be coded for request and their meanings are shown in Table 11.2.

If you code R you will get automatic step restart, provided that the interrupt was due to a system failure or an abend that returned one of the eligible completion codes. However, if the program contains instructions to take

THE CHECKPOINT/RESTART FEATURE

TABLE 11.2

Values that may be coded for the RD parameter

Value	Meaning
R	Requests automatic step restart. Has no effect on checkpoint instructions.
NR	Does not request automatic step restart. Allows checkpoints to be taken, but suppresses automatic checkpoint restart.
RNC	Requests automatic step restart. Suppresses all checkpoint instructions.
NC	Does not request automatic step restart. Suppresses all checkpoint instructions.

checkpoints and one or more checkpoints were taken before failure, you will get automatic checkpoint restart instead of automatic step restart. In this case you can still get automatic step restart by coding RNC. Coding RNC prevents checkpoints from being taken, even if the program contains instructions to take checkpoints. Coding R or RNC is the only way you can get automatic step restart.

You would code NC if your program contained instructions to take checkpoints and you wanted to suppress those instructions. Coding NC allows a program containing checkpoint instructions to be used when the checkpoint function is not wanted.

You would code NR if your program contained instructions to take checkpoints and you wanted the checkpoints taken, but you did not want automatic checkpoint restart. The checkpoints could be used to perform a delayed checkpoint restart. To perform a delayed checkpoint restart, you must code the RESTART parameter, and you must include the checkpoint data sets in the job stream.

In coding the RESTART parameter you must identify the checkpoint at which you want to restart, as well as the stepname. For example,

```
RESTART=(STEP6,C0000004)
```

specifies that the job is to be restarted within STEP6 at the checkpoint named C0000004.

The checkpoint data set must have the ddname SYSCHK. The SYSCHK DD statement must be placed immediately before the first EXEC statement in the job. If you wrote the checkpoints using the DD statement given earlier, then the SYSCHK statement could be

```
//SYSCHK    DD DSN=CHECKPNT,
//              DISP=OLD
```

EXERCISES

1. What is the function of the PRTY parameter?

2. What are the functions of the TYPRUN parameter?

3. What is the function of the ADDRSPC parameter?

4. What is the function of the PERFORM parameter?

5. Code a UNIT parameter that requests five model 2400 tape drives. Specify deferred mounting.

6. What is parallel mounting and how do you get it?

7. What is unit affinity and how do you get it?

8. What is a private volume and how do you get one?

9. Code a VOL parameter that will cause processing to start at the second volume of a cataloged data set.

10. Code a VOL parameter that could be used to create a four-volume data set on tape. The serial numbers of the four volumes are A, B, C, and D. Code the associated UNIT parameter, requesting two model 3420 tape drives.

11. What are the functions of the CONTIG, MXIG, and ALX subparameters?

12. What is wrong with the following coding?

```
SPACE=(TRK,10,RLSE,,ROUND)
```

13. Code a SPACE parameter that requests a primary allocation of 100 cylinders and a secondary allocation of 20 cylinders. The space should be contiguous. Release unused space.

EXERCISES

14. Code a SYSOUT parameter that directs output to class G and uses a form with labels. The name of the form is LBLS.

15. Code a SYSOUT parameter that directs the output to class F, requests 15 copies, directs the output to WKS7, and limits the output to 5000 lines.

16. Which print chains are available at your computer center? How do you request them?

17. If the output were directed to a 3800 printer, how many copies would the parameter

    ```
    COPIES=(5,(1,2,3,4))
    ```

    cause to be printed?

18. What is the function of the BURST parameter?

19. What is the function of the FLASH parameter?

20. What is the function of the CHARS parameter?

21. What is the function of the MODIFY parameter?

22. What is the function of the FCB parameter?

23. GRADES is the fifth data set on a tape. It is accessed using the following statement:

    ```
    //INPUT     DD DSN=GRADES,
    //                DISP=SHR
    ```

    Why isn't the LABEL parameter coded to specify the data set sequence number? What kind of labels does this data set have?

24. What is the difference between PASSWORD and NOPWREAD?

25. What does coding the LABEL subparameters IN and OUT do?

26. What is the difference between RETPD and EXPDT?

27. Code a LABEL parameter to protect a data set. Allow the data set to be read without a password.

28. Code a LABEL parameter that will set a retention period of 100 days.

29. Code a LABEL parameter for a data set that is the third on a tape volume, that has IBM standard and user labels, that may be used only for output, and that has an expiration date of December 31, 1999.

30. What is the function of the DLM parameter?

31. Code a DLM parameter on a DD DATA statement to change the delimiter to !!. What record must you put at the end of the input stream data?

32. What is the purpose of the checkpoint/restart feature?

33. What is the difference between an automatic restart and a deferred restart? How is each requested?

34. What is the difference between step restart and checkpoint restart? How is each requested?

35. What is the function of the CHKPT parameter?

36. Code the RESTART parameter to restart a job at the seventh checkpoint taken in STEP3.

37. When is the ddname SYSCHK used?

SUMMARY

In this chapter you have learned

- how to code the JOB statement parameters MPROFILE, NOTIFY, PROFILE, PRTY, and TYPRUN

- how to code the JOB and EXEC statement parameters ADDRSPC and PERFORM

- how to code the EXEC statement parameter DPRTY

- how to code the full form of the UNIT, VOLUME, SPACE, and LABEL parameters

- how to code the DD statement parameters AFF, SEP, SPLIT, SUBALLOC, FREE, and TERM

- how to code the following parameters used with SYSOUT: COPIES, DEST, HOLD, OUTLIM, PROFILE, and UCS

- how to request special features of the 3800 printer by using the parameters COPIES, BURST, FLASH, CHARS, MODIFY, and FCB

- how to code the DCB subparameters BUFNO, PRTSP, STACK, and TRTCH

- how to use the checkpoint/restart feature

CHAPTER 12

ISAM DATA SETS

LEARNING OBJECTIVES

IN THIS CHAPTER YOU WILL LEARN

- what ISAM is
- how to code JCL to create an ISAM data set
- how to code JCL to access an ISAM data set
- how to use the utility programs IEBISAM and IEBDG

YOU WILL ALSO LEARN THE MEANINGS OF THE FOLLOWING TERMS:

- basic direct access method (BDAM)
- batch processing
- cylinder index
- cylinder overflow
- delete character
- index area
- indexed sequential access method (ISAM)
- key
- master index
- overflow area
- prime area
- random access
- relative key position (RKP)
- reorganization

PROCESSING DATA SETS

Up to this point, we have discussed data sets that are processed sequentially. In sequential processing records can be directly added only to the end of the data set—provided, of course, that a disposition of MOD has been specified. If you want to add a record in the middle of the data set, you must completely re-create the data set. Figure 12.1 illustrates one sequence of operations to accomplish this. As you can see, this involves three separate steps which have to be executed every time a record is to be added to the data set, unless the decision is made to group the undated records together and run the job,

FIGURE 12.1

System flowchart to add a record to a sequential data set

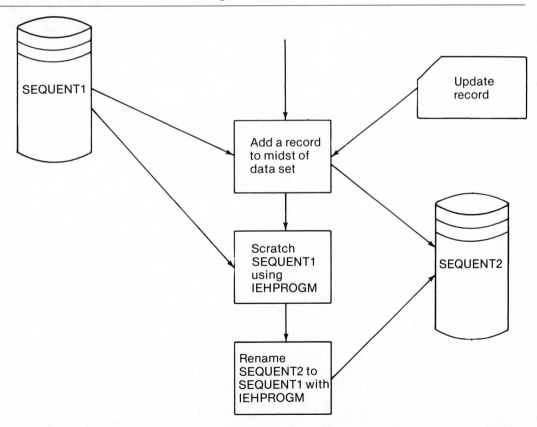

say, once a day. Such grouping is called **batch processing**. One disadvantage of batch processing is that the data set is accurate only once a day, immediately after the batch run.

Similarly, if you wish to read a particular record that is somewhere in the middle of a sequential data set, you must start with the first record and read each record until you find the one you want. If you are in a situation where you are responding to inquiries that do not come in any special order, you have to start reading at the beginning of the data set for each inquiry. This means you cannot answer the questions very quickly because of the massive I/O required.

What is needed is the ability to read the desired record directly and change a particular record or add a new record in the middle of the data set without re-creating the entire data set. This is called **random access**. Random access requires that the records be identified by keys. A **key** is a field within the record used to uniquely identify the record. All keyed data sets must reside on DASD.

THE BASIC DIRECT ACCESS METHOD

The first access method to accomplish this goal is called the **basic direct access method** or **BDAM**. The key of the record is used in some fashion to point to the record's location on DASD. The data set may be created by specifying each record's location on DASD either as a relative address or as an absolute address. If you use the absolute address, the data usually cannot be moved. The absolute address is given as MBBCCHHR, where M is a one-byte value that gives the relative location of an entry in a data extent block, BB is a two-byte number for bin or cell, CC is the two-byte number that identifies the cylinder, HH is the two-byte number that names the reading head or track address, and R is a one-byte number that identifies which block contains the data sought.

A relative address may be a relative block address or a relative track address. The relative block address is a three-byte number that tells the location of the block in the data set. The relative block address of the first block is 0. If relative block address is used, the records must be fixed length and unblocked, because the system uses the relative block address to calculate the absolute address of the record. The relative track address which may be used with blocked or unblocked records of fixed or variable length is three bytes in length. The first two bytes are the relative track address, and the third byte is the record number on the track. The relative track address of the first block is 0.

If you want to create a data set that contains information about nuts, you cannot use the name of the nut as the key since the name is alphabetic and each of the methods described requires that the key be a number. Many ways were developed to resolve this problem. For example, algorithms were developed to convert the actual key, such as 'ACORN', to a relative or absolute address. These algorithms were frequently very difficult to develop and did not always work well for long. If, for example, an algorithm is developed for a tool manufacturer's inventory, when a new line of tools is made with very different names it is necessary to develop a new algorithm and re-create the inventory file. This is obviously time consuming and expensive. There had to be a better way, and it is called the **indexed sequential access method** or **ISAM**.

Before we go on to discuss ISAM, please be aware that there are times when BDAM is the best choice. If the keys can be used as the addresses without any complex manipulation, your access time with BDAM will be much better than ISAM can provide. BDAM data sets do not usually need reorganization, which will be discussed in detail later. For the present, it is enough to know that reorganization is a time-consuming operation that generally must be performed at regular intervals for ISAM data sets.

WHAT IS ISAM?

What made ISAM unique when it was developed was its index. The index keeps track of the DASD addresses of the records in the data sets. The index is created by the system, so with ISAM, unlike BDAM, the programmer need not be concerned with developing DASD addresses. With BDAM, for example, the system can normally read a particular record in one read operation, with the programmer supplying the DASD address. With ISAM the index is read first, and from it the system learns the DASD address, which is then used to read the desired record. Therefore the system must perform at least two read operations in order to retrieve the record.

ISAM ORGANIZATION

An ISAM data set may consist of up to three parts: the prime area, the index area, and the independent overflow area. Space for an ISAM data set is allocated in cylinders. If you specify tracks, the system will round up to the nearest cylinder.

Prime Area

Unlike the index and independent overflow areas, the **prime area** is always required. In addition to data, each cylinder of the prime area must contain a track index and may contain an overflow area. Figure 12.2 illustrates a prime area cylinder with the required track index and the optional overflow area called the **cylinder overflow**. For convenience, the cylinder shown in Figure 12.2 only contains six tracks, numbered from 0 to 5. The prime area shows only the keys of the records, since for this discussion the rest of the record is unimportant.

FIGURE 12.2

A cylinder in the prime area

Track

0	147	Trk 1 Rec 1	147	Trk 1 Rec 1	175	Trk 2 Rec 1	175	Trk 2 Rec 1	230	Trk 3 Rec 1	230	Trk 3 Rec 1	274	Trk 4 Rec 1	274	Trk 4 Rec 1	Track index
1	106			124			131			139			147				Prime area
2	152			159			168			171			175				
3	186			195			208			222			230				
4	238			246			253			261			274				
5																	Cylinder overflow

FIGURE 12.3

Entry in a track index

Normal entry		Overflow entry	
Key of highest record on prime data track	Address of prime data track	Key of highest overflow record associated with track	Address of lowest overflow record associated with track

You will notice that all the records are in sort sequence. The records in the prime area are always in sort sequence. In Figure 12.2, the overflow area is shown as empty. When an ISAM data set is created, the overflow area is always empty.

There is an entry in the track index for each prime data track in the cylinder. This entry contains the highest key on the track and the address of the first record on that track. The apparent doubling of the data in the track index in Figure 12.2 is explained by Figure 12.3, which shows that each entry in the track index actually consists of two parts: a normal entry and an overflow entry. We will see how this works when we discuss adding records to an ISAM data set.

Index Area

If the ISAM data set occupies more than one cylinder, the system will automatically create a **cylinder index**. In addition, you can request that the system create a **master index**. These indexes may be stored on the first cylinder of the prime area, but if the data set is even moderately large, it is recommended that a separate **index area** be created. (How a separate index area is created will be discussed later in this chapter.)

There is one entry in the cylinder index for each cylinder in the prime area. This entry contains the highest key on the cylinder and the address of the track index of that cylinder.

FIGURE 12.4

Three cylinders of an ISAM data set with their cylinder index

Cylinder index

| Cylinder 178 | 274 | Cyl 42 Trk 0 | 362 | Cyl 43 Trk 0 | 451 | Cyl 44 Trk 0 |

Separate index area

Track index

Prime area

| Cylinder 42 | 147 | T1 R1 | 147 | T1 R1 | 175 | T2 R2 | 175 | T2 R2 | 230 | T3 R1 | 230 | T3 R1 | 274 | T4 R1 | 274 | T4 R1 |

106	124	131	139	147
152	159	168	171	175
186	195	208	222	230
238	246	253	261	274

Cylinder 43

269	T1 R1	269	T1 R1	311	T2 R1	311	T2 R1	337	T3 R1	337	T3 R1	362	T4 R1	362	T4 R1

278	281	287	294	296
299	301	305	307	311
314	318	326	334	337
341	342	356	359	362

Track indexes

Cylinder 44

384	T1 R1	384	T1 R1	399	T2 R1	399	T2 R1	413	T3 R1	413	T3 R1	451	T4 R1	451	T4 R1

368	372	373	379	384
387	388	392	397	399
400	406	409	411	413
426	432	437	446	451

Figure 12.4 shows the ISAM data set we started in Figure 12.2 expanded to three cylinders and the cylinder index that would be created. In Figure 12.4, assume that the prime area occupies cylinders 42, 43, and 44 and that the cylinder index is on cylinder 178.

The purpose of a cylinder index is to speed up access when a particular record is being sought. Without a cylinder index, the track index of each cylinder would have to be read to locate the desired record. In Figure 12.4, at most three track indexes would have to be read, but if there were, say, twenty cylinders in the data set, an average of ten track indexes would have to be read to locate a specific record, with the disk read/write head moving each time.

With the cylinder index, locating a record requires reading only two tracks: the track in the cylinder index, which sends us to the correct cylinder, and the track index of that cylinder. The disk read/write head only moves twice, since it is in position to read the data once it is positioned to read the track index.

However, if the data set is very large, the cylinder index can expand to

FIGURE 12.5

Index area showing master and cylinder indexes

Master index

451	Cyl 178 Trk 1	695	Cyl 178 Trk 2	919	Cyl 178 Trk 3

Cylinder index

Cylinder 178

Track						
1	274	Cyl 42 Trk 0	362	Cyl 43 Trk 0	451	Cyl 44 Trk 0
2	537	Cyl 45 Trk 0	603	Cyl 46 Trk 0	695	Cyl 47 Trk 0
3	737	Cyl 48 Trk 0	808	Cyl 49 Trk 0	919	Cyl 50 Trk 0

several tracks and slow down record retrieval. Creating a master index eliminates this problem. As shown in Figure 12.5, one entry is made in the master index for each track in the cylinder index.

Overflow Area

There are two kinds of **overflow areas**. One is the cylinder overflow, which is part of the prime area and is shown in Figures 12.2 and 12.4. If there is no room for a record in the track where it belongs and there is space in a cylinder overflow, the record may be written in the cylinder overflow and the access arm of the DASD need not be moved. If either there is no more space available in the cylinder overflow or there is no cylinder overflow, the record is written in the independent overflow area, if one exists. The independent overflow area is not required, but it is recommended, particularly if there are many additions to the data set.

Adding Records to an ISAM Data Set

Figures 12.6, 12.8, and 12.9 illustrate what happens in the prime area when records are added to an ISAM data set. Refer back to Figure 12.3, which defines the fields in the track index entry, and compare that information with the information in the original track index entry at the top of Figure 12.2. You will notice that those fields that are supposed to contain overflow information actually contain the same information as the normal entry. Notice also that before any additions are made to the data set, the cylinder overflow in Figure 12.2 is empty.

We now wish to add a record whose key is 137 to the data set. The first thing the system does is locate in which track the record belongs. The system compares the key of the record to be added with the highest key on each track. The first key that is higher than the key to be added indicates the track on which the record belongs. In our example, we are adding a record whose key is 137. The highest key on the first track is 147; therefore the record belongs on the first track. (If the highest key on track 1 had been 50, for example, the highest key of the second track would have been examined.)

However, since there is no room on the first track for another record, we must use an overflow area. Since the cylinder overflow is not full (in fact, at this point it is empty), the system will use it instead of the independent

FIGURE 12.6

Cylinder after the record with key 137 is added

Track

0	139	Trk 1 Rec 1	147	Trk 5 Rec 1	175	Trk 2 Rec 1	175	Trk 2 Rec 1	230	Trk 3 Rec 1	230	Trk 3 Rec 1	274	Trk 4 Rec 1	274	Trk 4 Rec 1
1		106			124			131			137			139		
2		152			159			168			171			175		
3		186			195			208			222			230		
4		238			246			253			261			274		
5	147		Trk 1													

overflow area. The new record is inserted in its proper place in the prime area. This means that there is no room left for the record whose key is 147, which is then placed in the cylinder overflow area with a pointer back to track 1. The track index entry must be changed. The highest record on the prime data track is now 139, but the prime data track address remains the same (track 1). The field that contains the highest overflow record associated with track 1 remains 147, but the field that has the address of the lowest overflow record associated with the track is changed to track 5, record 1.

ISAM ORGANIZATION

FIGURE 12.7

Cylinder after the record with key 112 is added

Track

0	137	Trk 1 Rec 1	147	Trk 5 Rec 2	175	Trk 2 Rec 1	175	Trk 2 Rec 1	230	Trk 3 Rec 1	230	Trk 3 Rec 1	274	Trk 4 Rec 1	274	Trk 4 Rec 1

Track					
1	106	112	124	131	137
2	152	159	168	171	175
3	186	195	208	222	230
4	238	246	253	261	274
5	147	Trk 1	139	Trk 5 Rec 1	

Now let us add a second record to this data set, as shown in Figure 12.7. Since the record we are adding has a key of 112, it also belongs on track 1, which means that the record whose key is 139 falls off and must be added to the cylinder overflow. A pointer is added to that record to point to the next record in the data set that belongs to track 1. This record, whose key is 147, is the first record in the track of the cylinder overflow. Two fields in the track index entry must be changed: the key of the highest record on the prime data track goes from 139 to 137, and the field that contains the address of the lowest overflow record changes from track 5, record 1 to track 5, record 2.

CHAPTER 12 / ISAM DATA SETS

Figure 12.8 shows the addition of two more records. The first record added has a key of 165. It is inserted in its proper position on track 2, and record 175 is placed in the overflow area. The track index entry for track 2 is modified to reflect these changes.

The next record added has a key of 143. It belongs on track 1, whose highest key is 147. However, at the present time the highest key on track 1 is 137. This means that the new record should be added directly to the cylinder overflow. This addition does not require any changes in the track index. The record whose key is 143 is added to the overflow, with a pointer to the record whose key is 147. The pointer of the record whose key is 139 is

FIGURE 12.8

Cylinder after records with keys 165 and 143 are added

changed so that it no longer points to the record whose key is 147, but instead points to the new record.

Let us see what happens when we try to read the record whose key is 147. The overflow entry in the track index for track 1 sends us to record 2 on track 5. We read the key of that record and discover it is not the record we want. The pointer of that record directs us to record 4 on track 5. We read the key of that record and again find that it is not the record we want. This time the pointer directs us to record 1 on track 5, and when we read the key of that record we finally find that it is the record we are looking for. Reading

FIGURE 12.9

Cylinder after the record with key 230 is deleted and the record with key 214 is added

Track

0	137	Trk 1 Rec 1	147	Trk 5 Rec 2	171	Trk 2 Rec 1	175	Trk 5 Rec 3	222	Trk 3 Rec 1	222	Trk 3 Rec 1	274	Trk 4 Rec 1	274	Trk 4 Rec 1

1	106	112	124	131	137

2	152	159	168	171	175

3	186	195	208	214	222

4	238	246	253	261	274

5	147	Trk 1	139	Trk 5 Rec 4	175	Trk 2	143	Trk 5 Rec 1	

all these records takes time, which is why after a number of records have been added to an ISAM data set it is desirable to reorganize the data set. When an ISAM data set is reorganized, all the records in the overflow area are inserted in their proper sequential position in the prime area. How an ISAM data set is reorganized will be explained latter.

Notice the logical similarity between the normal and overflow index entries. In Figure 12.8, the normal entry for track 1 indicates that a sequence of records starts at the beginning of track 1, the last record having a key of 137. The overflow entry indicates that a sequence of records starts with the second record of track 5, the last record having a key of 147.

Deleting Records

Figure 12.9 illustrates deleting the record whose key is 230. What actually happens is that the delete byte, which is the first byte in a fixed-length record or the fifth byte in a variable-length record, is set to hexadecimal FF. Under certain conditions, this record can still be read. However, if a record whose key is 214 is added, the record whose key is 230 is now actually deleted. The system would normally place the record whose key is 230 in the cylinder overflow, but before it does so the delete byte is checked. Since there is a hexadecimal FF in the delete byte, the record is discarded.

JCL TO CREATE AN ISAM DATA SET

When an ISAM data set is created, there are four possible forms it may assume. The ISAM data set may consist of three different parts: index, prime, and overflow. It may consist of two parts: index and prime or prime and overflow. It also may consist only of the prime. Creating the data set may require one, two, or three DD statements, depending on which form you want.

Using One DD Statement

Figure 12.10 illustrates a DD statement that could be used to create an ISAM data set using one DD statement. Most of the information in the DD statement is familiar to you. The principal differences are in the SPACE parameter and the DCB parameter. Let us examine the SPACE parameter first. The space allocation is in cylinders as opposed to tracks, because cylinders are required

JCL TO CREATE AN ISAM DATA SET

FIGURE 12.10

Creating an ISAM data set using one DD statement

```
//ISAMDD1  DD DSN=WYL.QB.JCL.ISAM1,
//            DISP=(,KEEP),
//            UNIT=SYSDA,
//            VOL=SER=WYL004,
//            SPACE=(CYL,(5,,1)),
//            DCB=(DSORG=IS,RECFM=FB,LRECL=80,BLKSIZE=1680,
//            KEYLEN=5,RKP=1,CYLOFL=2,NTM=4,OPTCD=LMRUWY)
```

for ISAM. If you code tracks, the system will round up to the nearest cylinder.

If you specify ABSTR instead of CYL in the SPACE parameter, the primary quantity, which must be tracks when ABSTR is specified, must be equal to a whole number of cylinders. The second parameter, which gives the secondary allocation when CYL or TRK is specified, for ABSTR gives the address of a particular track and in this case must be the first track in a cylinder. The use of ABSTR is definitely not recommended.

In the SPACE parameter in Figure 12.10, a primary allocation of 5 cylinders is requested. There is no secondary space allocation because for ISAM it is forbidden. The 1 represents the space to be reserved for the index. How does the system know the request is for one cylinder for an index and not for one 256-byte directory block for a library, as discussed in Chapter 5? In the DCB parameter, the subparameter DSORG is set equal to IS, which identifies this data set as an ISAM data set. DSORG=IS *must* always be present when an ISAM data set is created or accessed. We will not discuss the DCB subparameters LRECL, BLKSIZE, and RECFM, since there is no difference between their use here and in earlier discussions.

The DCB subparameter KEYLEN tells how long the record key is. In the example in Figure 12.10, it is 5 bytes. RKP stands for **relative key position**. If the record is variable in length, RKP must be greater than or equal to 4 since the first four bytes are reserved for system use, as discussed in Appendix E. If you specify RKP=0 for fixed-length or RKP=4 for variable-length records, the key will start in the first data byte of the record and the records in the data set cannot be deleted because the delete byte is part of the key. In Figure 12.10, RKP is equal to 1, meaning that the key starts in the second byte of the record and the first byte is available for use as a delete byte.

The subparameter OPTCD may be set equal to I, L, M, R, U, W, and/or Y. I means that an independent overflow area is desired. To actually create the independent overflow area requires a special DD statement which we will discuss later. Y means that cylinder overflow is desired. If you code Y, you must also code CYLOFL to specify the number of tracks in each prime area cylinder which should be reserved for cylinder overflow. In Figures 12.2, 12.6, 12.7, 12.8, and 12.9, one track in the prime area is labeled as cylinder overflow. In Figure 12.10, CYLOFL=2 reserves two tracks of each cylinder for overflow.

If L is specified, the first byte of the record is to be used as the delete byte; RKP must be set equal to a value that leaves the first byte available for use as the delete byte. The M requests that the system create and maintain a master index after the cylinder index in the index area (see Figures 12.4 and 12.5) occupies a certain number of tracks. The number is specified in the DCB subparameter NTM. In this example NTM is set equal to 4, which means that after there are four tracks in the cylinder index, a master index will be created. The R causes reorganization data to be placed in the data control block. U, which can be used only with fixed-length records, causes the system to accumulate the data for the track index and write them as a group. W requests a validity check for each write operation. This means that after the record is written, it is immediately read and compared with what was written. This obviously decreases the speed of the operation, but increases its accuracy.

In COBOL programs, the key length and position are specified in the RECORD KEY clause, so COBOL programmers usually do not code KEYLEN or RKP subparameters on the DD statement. The other ISAM DCB subparameters, CYLOFL, NTM, and OPTCD, must be coded on the DD statement. In PL/I programs, the key length and position may be specified either in the ENV entry for the file or on the DD statement. As in the case of COBOL, the other ISAM subparameters must be coded on the DD statement. In assembler programs, all the subparameters may be coded either within the program in the DCB macro or on the DD statement. Generally, when a parameter may be coded either in the program or on the DD statement, it is better to code it on the DD statement, because that makes the program more flexible.

You will notice that the disposition specifies that the data set is to be kept at job end. CATLG could have been specified in this case, because only one DD statement is used. If two or three DD statements are used, CATLG may not be specified in the DISP parameter.

If you choose not to code the index value in the SPACE parameter, the system will create an index at the end of the prime area anyway. Therefore, in Figure 12.10, the SPACE parameter could have been coded as

```
SPACE=(CYL,(6))
```

JCL TO CREATE AN ISAM DATA SET

If you want to specify the size of the index area, code the index value in the SPACE parameter, but if you are willing to let the system determine the size, you can omit the index value. Omitting the index value is a good idea when you are creating a small ISAM data set of one or two cylinders, because if you specify an index value in the SPACE parameter, the index alone must be at least one cylinder.

Using Two DD Statements

Figure 12.11 illustrates the JCL used to create an ISAM data set with an index and prime DD statement, and Figure 12.12 shows the JCL needed to create an ISAM data set with a prime and independent overflow DD statement. When more than one DD statement is used to define an ISAM data set, you indicate which part of the data set the DD statement is defining by including INDEX, PRIME, or OVFLOW in parentheses following the data set name. The DD statements must be concatenated and must be coded in the following order: INDEX, PRIME, OVFLOW. You will notice that the SPACE parameter for the prime DD statement in Figure 12.11 does not have an index value, while that in Figure 12.12 does. The reason is that the index is explicitly defined in Figure 12.11. None of the additional subparameters of the SPACE parameter have been coded; all but CONTIG are forbidden for ISAM.

The DCB information in the DD statements must be the same in all of the statements; the backward reference in the second DD statement in both Figure 12.11 and Figure 12.12 ensures agreement.

FIGURE 12.11

Creating an ISAM data set with index and prime areas

```
//DD2ISAMA DD DSN=WYL.QB.JCL.ISAM2(INDEX),
//             DISP=(,KEEP),
//             UNIT=SYSDA,
//             VOL=SER=WYL004,
//             SPACE=(CYL,(1)),
//             DCB=(DSORG=IS,RECFM=FB,LRECL=80,BLKSIZE=1680,
//             KEYLEN=5,RKP=1,CYLOFL=2,NTM=4,OPTCD=LMRUWY)
//          DD DSN=WYL.QB.JCL.ISAM2(PRIME),
//             DISP=(,KEEP),
//             UNIT=SYSDA,
//             VOL=SER=WYL004,
//             SPACE=(CYL,(5)),
//             DCB=*.DD2ISAMA
```

FIGURE 12.12

Creating an ISAM data set with prime and overflow areas

```
//DD2ISAMB DD DSN=WYL.QB.JCL.ISAM3(PRIME),
//            DISP=(,KEEP),
//            UNIT=SYSDA,
//            VOL=SER=WYL004,
//            SPACE=(CYL,(10,,1)),
//            DCB=(DSORG=IS,RECFM=FB,LRECL=80,BLKSIZE=1680,
//            KEYLEN=5,RKP=1,CYLOFL=2,NTM=4,OPTCD=ILMRUWY)
//         DD DSN=WYL.QB.JCL.ISAM3(OVFLOW),
//            DISP=(,KEEP),
//            UNIT=SYSDA,
//            VOL=SER=WYL005,
//            SPACE=(CYL,(5)),
//            DCB=*.DD2ISAMB
```

The disposition for the data sets is KEEP. In these two cases, CATALG cannot be specified. If you wish to catalog an ISAM data set defined with two or three DD statements, the utility IEHPROGM may be used. IEHPROGM may be used to catalog an ISAM data set as long as all the parts of the data set reside on the same type of device. For example, in Figure 12.12, the prime and index areas of ISAM3 are on disk pack WYL004, while the overflow area is on WYL005. Both these disk packs are 3350s, so IEHPROGM may be used to catalog ISAM3. If the volumes were different types (for example, if WYL004 were a 3350, but WYL005 were a 2314), the data set could not be cataloged.

FIGURE 12.13

Cataloging an ISAM data set

```
//JCLQB810 JOB ,'J.C.LEWIS',
//             REGION=48K
//CATALOG  EXEC PGM=IEHPROGM
//SYSPRINT DD SYSOUT=A
//DD2      DD UNIT=SYSDA,
//            VOL=SER=(WYL004,WYL005),
//            DISP=OLD
//SYSIN    DD *
 CATLG DSNAME=WYL.QB.JCL.ISAM3,
            VOL=SYSDA=(WYL004,WYL005)
/*
//
```

FIGURE 12.14

Creating an ISAM data set using three DD statements

```
//ISAMDD3   DD DSN=WYL.QB.JCL.ISAM4(INDEX),
//             DISP=(,KEEP),
//             UNIT=SYSDA,
//             VOL=SER=WYL004,
//             SPACE=(CYL,(1)),
//             DCB=(DSORG=IS,RECFM=FB,LRECL=80,BLKSIZE=1680,
//             KEYLEN=5,RKP=1,CYLOFL=2,NTM=4,OPTCD=ILMRUWY)
//          DD DSN=WYL.QB.JCL.ISAM4(PRIME),
//             DISP=(,KEEP),
//             UNIT=SYSDA,
//             VOL=REF=*.ISAMDD3,
//             SPACE=(CYL,(10)),
//             DCB=*.ISAMDD3
//          DD DSN=WYL.QB.JCL.ISAM4(OVFLOW),
//             DISP=(,KEEP),
//             UNIT=SYSDA,
//             VOL=REF=*.ISAMDD3,
//             SPACE=(CYL,(5)),
//             DCB=*.ISAMDD3
```

Figure 12.13 shows how IEHPROGM may be used to catalog ISAM3. Notice that all the volumes the data set resides on must be named in both the DD statement and the control statement. The use of IEHPROGM is discussed more fully in Chapter 14.

Using Three DD Statements

Figure 12.14 illustrates the JCL used to create an ISAM data set with all three DD statements. All three parts of the ISAM data set are on the same volume. However, if speed of operation were important, it would be wise to place the index area and the prime on different volumes, thus eliminating the need for the access arm to move with each read.

Multivolume Data Sets

If you are dealing with a very large ISAM data set, you want to use more than one volume. Figure 12.15 illustrates this case. You will notice that INDEX consists of 10 cylinders on volume WYL001, OVFLOW consists of 50 cylinders on volume WYL005, and PRIME consists of 300 cylinders (100 cylinders each on volumes WYL002, WYL003, and WYL004).

FIGURE 12.15

Creating an ISAM data set on multiple volumes

```
//ISAMDD4   DD DSN=WYL.QB.JCL.ISAM5(INDEX),
//             DISP=(,KEEP),
//             UNIT=SYSDA,
//             VOL=SER=WYL001,
//             SPACE=(CYL,(10)),
//             DCB=(DSORG=IS,RECFM=FB,LRECL=80,BLKSIZE=1680,
//             KEYLEN=5,RKP=1,CYLOFL=2,NTM=4,OPTCD=ILMRUWY)
//          DD DSN=WYL.QB.JCL.ISAM5(PRIME),
//             DISP=(,KEEP),
//             UNIT=(SYSDA,3),
//             VOL=SER=(WYL002,WYL003,WYL004),
//             SPACE=(CYL,(100)),
//             DCB=*.ISAMDD4
//          DD DSN=WYL.QB.JCL.ISAM5(OVFLOW),
//             DISP=(,KEEP),
//             UNIT=SYSDA,
//             VOL=SER=WYL005,
//             SPACE=(CYL,(50)),
//             DCB=*.ISAMDD4
```

You might not have expected that 100 cylinders would be taken from each of the three volumes, since, as you learned in Chapter 11, for sequential data sets the primary request is taken from the first-named volume and the other volumes are used only to satisfy the secondary requests. But the space allocation works differently for ISAM data sets. When the DD statement that defines the prime area names more than one volume, the number of cylinders requested is taken from each of the volumes.

JCL TO ACCESS AN ISAM DATA SET

When an ISAM data set is created, from one to three DD statements are used, as illustrated in Figures 12.10, 12.11, 12.12, 12.14, and 12.15. Accessing any of these data sets requires only one DD statement. Figure 12.16 shows how ISAM4, which was created in Figure 12.14 using three DD statements, may be accessed using only one DD statement. Notice that to access an ISAM data set you do not have to include the qualifiers INDEX, PRIME, or OVFLOW, even though they may have been used when the data set was created. To update a data set, code a disposition of OLD, as shown in Figure 12.16. This prevents another program from reading the data set while this program is in the pro-

JCL TO ACCESS AN ISAM DATA SET

FIGURE 12.16

Accessing an ISAM data set

```
//ISAMREAD DD DSN=WYL.QB.JCL.ISAM4,
//              DISP=OLD,
//              UNIT=SYSDA,
//              VOL=SER=WYL004,
//              DCB=DSORG=IS
```

cess of changing it. If you wish to read a data set, you do not need exclusive control; you do not care if other programs are reading the data set at the same time. Consequently you code a disposition of SHR, which permits multiple use of the data set.

In Figure 12.16, the one required DCB subparameter, DSORG=IS, is coded. The other DCB information is not necessary, since it can be found in the data set control block. DSORG=IS tells the system that this data set is an ISAM data set, something the system must know before it reads the data set control block (DSCB). There are a few conditions under which it is not necessary to code DCB=DSORG=IS, but they are rather complex, so why bother remembering them when it is always correct to code DCB=DSORG=IS?

Figure 12.17 shows JCL to access ISAM data sets on multiple volumes. The first example shows how to access ISAM5, which was created in Figure

FIGURE 12.17

Accessing multivolume ISAM data sets

```
//ISAMUPD1 DD DSN=WYL.QB.JCL.ISAM5,
//              DISP=SHR,
//              UNIT=(SYSDA,5),
//              VOL=SER=(WYL001,WYL002,WYL003,WYL004,WYL005),
//              DCB=DSORG=IS


//ISAMUDD2 DD DSN=WYL.QB.JCL.ISAM6,
//              DISP=SHR,
//              UNIT=3330,
//              VOL=SER=WYL003,
//              DCB=DSORG=IS
//          DD DSN=WYL.QB.JCL.ISAM6,
//              DISP=SHR,
//              UNIT=(2314,2),
//              VOL=SER=(DISK01,DISK02),
//              DCB=DSORG=IS
```

CHAPTER 12 / ISAM DATA SETS

12.15 using three DD statements and which resides on five volumes. The unit parameter indicates five devices, and five serial numbers are specified in the volume parameter. Even though the data set may have been created with multiple DD statements, since all the volumes are the same type only one DD statement is required to access it. The second example illustrates the situation when multiple DD statements are required. In this situation, the unit on the first DD statement indicates a 3330 disk drive, while the second shows a 2314. It is the difference in device type that creates the need for multiple DD statements. When multiple DD statements are used to access an ISAM data set, they must be concatenated and coded in the order in which they were coded when the data set was created.

If the ISAM data set is cataloged, as ISAM3 was cataloged in Figure 12.13, then, like any other cataloged data set, it can be accessed through coding of only DSN and DISP; UNIT and VOL can be omitted. However, for ISAM data sets you must always code DCB=DSORG=IS to be safe.

ISAM AND GENERATION DATA GROUPS

ISAM data sets do not naturally form generation data groups; they have to be forced into the mold. After the ISAM data set is created, perhaps using JCL similar to that shown in Figure 12.14, a job similar to that shown in Figure 12.18 is run. The first command for the utility program IEHPROGM renames the ISAM data set to give it the next generation number and any version

FIGURE 12.18

Creating a generation data group from an ISAM data set

```
//JCLQB820 JOB ,'RICK',
//              REGION=48K
//ISAMGDG  EXEC PGM=IEHPROGM
//SYSPRINT DD SYSOUT=A
//DD1      DD UNIT=SYSDA,
//              VOL=SER=WYL004,
//              DISP=OLD
//SYSIN    DD *
 RENAME DSNAME=WYL.QB.JCL.ISAM4,VOL=SYSDA=WYL004,
             NEWNAME=WYL.QB.JCL.ISAM4.G0036V00
 CATLG DSNAME=WYL.QB.JCL.ISAM4.G0036V00,VOL=SYSDA=WYL004
/*
//
```

number you wish. In the example in Figure 12.18, the generation number is 36 and the version is 00. After the data set is renamed, it is cataloged and becomes part of the generation data group.

LOADING AN ISAM DATA SET

Loading an ISAM data set usually requires a program written in assembler, COBOL, or PL/I. The creation program is used once and then discarded. This is wasteful of programming effort. (Remember that you, the programmer, are the most expensive part of a data processing installation.) There must be a better way, and its name is IEBDG.

IEBDG

IEBDG is a utility program designed to produce test data, but it may also be used to create an ISAM data set. Let us first consider a simple case in which we will use POLYFILE as input and create an ISAM file named POLYISAM. The job stream is shown in Figure 12.19.

FIGURE 12.19

Creating an ISAM data set using IEBDG

```
//JCLQB830 JOB ,'ILSA LUND',
//              REGION=32K
//CREATE EXEC PGM=IEBDG
//SYSPRINT DD SYSOUT=A
//SEQIN    DD DSN=WYL.QB.JCL.POLYFILE,
//              DISP=SHR
//ISAM     DD DSN=WYL.QB.JCL.POLYISAM,
//              DISP=(NEW,CATLG),
//              UNIT=DISK,
//              VOL=SER=SCR001,
//              SPACE=(CYL,1),
//              DCB=(DSORG=IS,RKP=1,KEYLEN=5,OPTCD=YL,CYLOFL=2,
//              RECFM=FB,LRECL=81,BLKSIZE=810)
//SYSIN DD *
 DSD OUTPUT=(ISAM),INPUT=(SEQIN)
 FD NAME=BYTE0,LENGTH=1,STARTLOC=1,FILL=X'00'
 FD NAME=FLD1,LENGTH=80,STARTLOC=2,FROMLOC=1,INPUT=SEQIN
 CREATE NAME=(BYTE0,FLD1),INPUT=SEQIN
 END
/*
//
```

CHAPTER 12 / ISAM DATA SETS

When an ISAM data set is created, the data must be presented in sort sequence. Each time a record is written, the system checks the key to make sure that it is greater than the key of the previously written record. For that reason it is usual for the input data set to be sorted before it is used to create the ISAM data set. By inspecting the listing of POLYFILE in Chapter 4, we can see that it is already in sort sequence. Consequently, we do not have to sort it. You should keep in mind, however, the general requirement that data sets used to create ISAM data sets must be in sort sequence.

Look at the control statements in Figure 12.19. The first control statement is the DSD statement, which must be first and which is used to supply the ddnames of the data sets to be used. Notice that the ddnames must be in parentheses.

The next two statements are FD (field definition) statements. These statements define the fields that are used to create the output record. The first FD statement creates data. It names and describes a field that starts in the first byte of the output record and is 1 byte long. The name supplied is BYTE0. You know that it is the first byte because STARTLOC=1 is coded, and you know its length is 1 byte because LENGTH=1 is coded. The FILL parameter specifies that this field will contain hexadecimal zeros, which is exactly what is desired for the delete byte.

The second FD statement copies data from the input data set. FLD1 is 80 bytes long and starts in the second byte of the output record. The data for this field will be copied from the input data set identified by the ddname SEQIN. Eighty bytes will be copied, starting in the first byte (FROMLOC=1) of each input record.

The next control statement is the CREATE statement, which is used to specify the data to be included in the output record. In this case the output record will consist of the two fields named BYTE0 and FLD1. INPUT=SEQIN is also coded to specify the ddname of the data set that will provide the input data. Notice that the ddname of the input data set is specified on both the FD and the CREATE statements.

The last control statement in the job is the END statement. It marks the end of the group of control statements that apply to the creation of the data set named in the previous DSD control statement. Another group of control statements starting with a DSD statement could follow this END statement. Since in this case no other control statements are coded, the END statement could have been omitted.

Notice that because POLYISAM was created using only one DD statement, a disposition of CATLG could be legally coded.

The result of executing this job will be the creation of a cataloged ISAM data set named POLYISAM, containing the same data as in POLYFILE.

LOADING AN ISAM DATA SET

The control statements in Figure 12.19 are complicated because the delete byte had to be added to the data record in POLYFILE. The control statements could be simplified if the records in POLYISAM were made exactly the same as the records in POLYFILE. In that case the DSD statement would remain the same, but the two FD statements would be eliminated and the CREATE statement would be simplified to

```
CREATE INPUT=SEQIN
```

There are situations where the information used for an ISAM record is computed from multiple sources. In such cases you cannot create the data set by copying information from a sequential data set. However, you do not want to invest time developing another program whose purpose would be to create the ISAM data set with dummy records. Figure 12.20 illustrates a job that copies the input information without requiring a separate create program.

In the DSD control statement, you will note that there is no input parameter. Since there is no input data set in this example, the input parameter is not required. The data to be written in the output records are generated in the two FD control statements. The first sets the delete byte in the output record to hexadecimal FF. The only difference between this FD

FIGURE 12.20

Creating an ISAM data set with dummy records using IEBDG

```
//JCLQB840 JOB ,'VICTOR LASZLO',
//            REGION=32K
//ISAMDUM EXEC PGM=IEBDG
//SYSPRINT DD SYSOUT=A
//ISAMOUT  DD DSN=WYL.QB.JCL.ISAM8,
//            DISP=(,CATLG),
//            UNIT=SYSDA,
//            VOL=SER=SCR001,
//            SPACE=(CYL,1),
//            DCB=(DSORG=IS,RECFM=FB,LRECL=75,BLKSIZE=1500,
//            KEYLEN=10,RKP=1,CYLOFL=2,OPTCD=LY)
//SYSIN    DD *
 DSD OUTPUT=(ISAMOUT)
 FD NAME=BYTE0,LENGTH=1,STARTLOC=1,FILL=X'FF'
 FD NAME=KEYFD,LENGTH=10,STARTLOC=2,FORMAT=PD,INDEX=10
 CREATE NAME=(BYTE0,KEYFD),QUANTITY=100,FILL=X'40'
/*
//
```

control statement and the first one in Figure 12.19 is the value coded for the FILL parameter. In this example the FILL parameter is used to set the field equal to hexadecimal FF.

The next FD control statement sets the value of the key field. Note that the LENGTH agrees with the KEYLEN subparameter of the DCB parameter, and the STARTLOC agrees with the RKP subparameter. The FORMAT=PD parameter indicates that the field should contain packed decimal data. Zoned decimal (ZD), binary (BI), alphameric (AN), or alphabetic (AL) could have been specified instead of PD. For numeric fields the first value generated is plus 1. For packed and binary numbers, SIGN=- can be coded to generate minus 1.

INDEX=10 means that 10 will be added to this packed decimal field each time it is used. Consequently, the first record will have a packed decimal field containing a 1, the second an 11, and so on. The value coded for INDEX must be positive.

The CREATE statement defines the output record as consisting of the two fields defined with the FD statements. The record length in the DCB parameter of the DD statement is 75. The combined length of the two defined fields is 11, leaving 64 bytes to be defined. The FILL parameter in the CREATE statement supplies the data for these 64 bytes. The record created as a result of this operation will have a hexadecimal FF in the first or delete byte, a packed decimal number in the second through eleventh bytes and blanks (hexadecimal 40) in the rest of the record. The QUANTITY parameter indicates that 100 records are to be created.

The example in Figure 12.20 should be studied carefully, because you are likely to need this coding. You do not often have the data prepared as a sequential data set, as illustrated in Figure 12.19. Usually you must write a program that creates the data from multiple sources. If you understand the example in Figure 12.20, you can avoid writing the create program. Use IEBDG to create the data set with dummy records, and then use your update program to actually store information in the ISAM data set.

You will find more information about IEBDG in Chapter 14.

USING IEBISAM

IEBISAM is the utility program used to process ISAM data sets. It offers four functions: load, unload, copy, and print. IEBISAM is different from most utility programs in that there are no control cards. The PARM field is used to tell IEBISAM what should be done.

FIGURE 12.21

Printing an ISAM data set using IEBISAM

```
//JCLQB850 JOB ,'LOUIS RENAULT',
//             REGION=32K
//LIST   EXEC  PGM=IEBISAM,PARM='PRINTL,N'
//SYSPRINT DD  SYSOUT=A
//SYSUT1    DD  DSN=WYL.QB.JCL.POLYISAM,
//             DISP=SHR,
//             DCB=DSORG=IS
//SYSUT2    DD  SYSOUT=A
//
```

IEBISAM Print

The basic print function is the easiest to understand. Figure 12.21 illustrates the JCL required to print a data set in character format. The job consists of a JOB statement, an EXEC statement, and three DD statements whose ddnames are SYSPRINT, SYSUT1, and SYSUT2.

The three DD statements have the same functions for IEBISAM as they do for IEBGENER and IEBPTPCH. SYSPRINT is for messages, SYSUT1 is for the input data set, and SYSUT2 is for the output data set. Since IEBISAM does not use control statements, a SYSIN DD statement is not required.

For the print operation, SYSUT1 is the ISAM data set to be printed, and SYSUT2 directs the output to the printer. In the EXEC statement, coding PARM='PRINTL,N' causes the ISAM data set to be printed in character form. The apostrophes are necessary because of the comma in the PARM field. If PARM=PRINTL is coded, the ISAM data set is printed in hexadecimal form.

IEBISAM Copy

Figure 12.22 illustrates the copy operation. IEBISAM knows that a copy operation is to be performed because PARM=COPY is coded in the EXEC statement. SYSUT1 points to the ISAM data set to be copied. SYSUT2 defines the new ISAM data set named COPYISAM. For the DCB parameter only the required DSORG=IS is coded. The other DCB parameters will be copied from POLYISAM. Since L was specified for the DCB subparameter OPTCD when POLYISAM was created, records marked for deletion will not be copied to COPYISAM. Any records that are in the cylinder overflow area will be inserted in their proper place in the prime area of COPYISAM. If POLYISAM had an independent overflow area, records from it would also be inserted in their proper place in the prime area.

FIGURE 12.22

Copying an ISAM data set using IEBISAM

```
//JCLQB860 JOB ,'STRASSER',
//          REGION=32K
//COPYISM  EXEC PGM=IEBISAM,PARM=COPY
//SYSPRINT DD SYSOUT=A
//SYSUT1   DD DSN=WYL.QB.JCL.POLYISAM,
//            DISP=SHR,
//            DCB=DSORG=IS
//SYSUT2   DD DSN=WYL.QB.JCL.COPYISAM,
//            DISP=(,CATLG),
//            UNIT=SYSDA,
//            VOL=SER=SCR001,
//            SPACE=(CYL,(1),),
//            DCB=DSORG=IS
//
```

IEBISAM Unload

The unload operation creates a physical sequential data set from the ISAM data set. The physical sequential data set produced by IEBISAM consists of 80-byte records regardless of the record length of the ISAM data set. In Figure 12.23, which illustrates the JCL for the unload operation, the output is blocked, but you may choose not to block the output or to block at a different value. The ISAM data set is unloaded to a volume of tape. Depending on your needs you might choose to unload to a disk pack. Why bother to unload at all? One reason, indicated by the data set name selected, is to create a

FIGURE 12.23

Unloading an ISAM data set using IEBISAM

```
//JCLQB870 JOB ,'FERRARI',
//          REGION=32K
//UNLOAD   EXEC PGM=IEBISAM,PARM=UNLOAD
//SYSPRINT DD SYSOUT=A
//SYSUT1   DD DSN=WYL.QB.JCL.POLYISAM,
//            DISP=SHR,
//            DCB=DSORG=IS
//SYSUT2   DD DSN=WYL.QB.JCL.BACKUP,
//            DISP=(,CATLG),
//            UNIT=TAPE,
//            DCB=(RECFM=FB,LRECL=80,BLKSIZE=1600)
//
```

REORGANIZATION

FIGURE 12.27

(a) System flowchart to reorganize an ISAM data set using IEBISAM

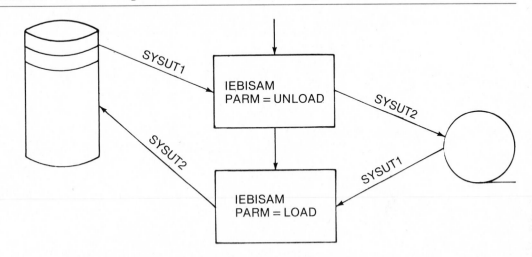

(b) System flowchart to reorganize an ISAM data set using IEBISAM and IEHPROGM

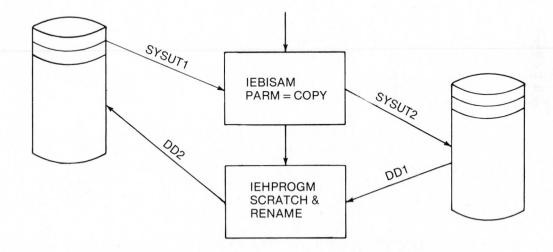

overflow area are integrated into the prime area. Consequently, when you reorganize your ISAM data set, you recover lost space from the deleted records and you get faster access time because all the records are in the prime area and only one data access is required.

There are two principal ways to reorganize an ISAM data set. Both methods involve two steps and are illustrated in Figure 12.27. In the first case IEBISAM is executed twice. The first time the ISAM data set is being unloaded to tape, and the second time the data set on tape is being loaded back to disk. The unloaded data set is shown as residing on tape; you could specify disk instead. The advantage of tape is that the tape may be retained for use as your back-up. Using this approach you accomplish two maintenance tasks with one job. It reorganizes your ISAM data set and provides you with a back-up.

The advantage to the second approach shown in Figure 12.27 is that it is faster. The system only processes the ISAM data set once. In the first step, IEBISAM is used to copy the ISAM data set to another DASD location, which may be on the same disk pack if there is enough space. In the second step the utility program IEHPROGM is used first to scratch the original ISAM data set and second to change the name of (rename) the new ISAM data set from the current value to the original name.

ISAM AND HIGHER-LEVEL LANGUAGES

The purpose of this section is not to teach you how to access ISAM data sets from your COBOL and PL/I programs, but rather to give you sufficient background so that you can tie together your newly acquired JCL knowledge with your COBOL and PL/I knowledge.

ISAM and COBOL*

CREATING AN ISAM DATA SET. Your COBOL program must have a SELECT statement for the ISAM data set. For example, you could code

```
SELECT ISAM-DATA-FILE
    ASSIGN TO DA-I-ISAMDD
    RECORD KEY IS KEY-VAL
    ACCESS IS SEQUENTIAL.
```

Since ACCESS IS SEQUENTIAL is the default, that clause is optional. The

* Those who are not familiar with COBOL should skip this section.

ddname on the DD statement referencing the ISAM data set is ISAMDD. The record key KEY-VAL must be part of the ISAM data set's record. You might have coded

```
FD   ISAM-DATA-FILE
     RECORD CONTAINS...
     BLOCK CONTAINS...
     LABEL RECORDS ARE STANDARD.
01   ISAM-RECORD.
     05 DELETE-BYTE          PIC X.
     05 KEY-VAL              PIC ...
     05 ...
```

To create an ISAM data set, you must access it sequentially and open it as OUTPUT. For example, you could code

```
OPEN OUTPUT ISAM-DATA-FILE.
```

The data set is created using a WRITE statement with an INVALID KEY clause, such as

```
WRITE ISAM-RECORD
     INVALID KEY PERFORM BAD-WRITE-RTN.
```

The INVALID KEY clause is executed if the record key of the current record is less than or equal to the record key of the previously written record.

RANDOMLY UPDATING AN ISAM DATA SET.   The SELECT sentence to randomly access an ISAM data set could be

```
SELECT ISAM-DATA-FILE
     ASSIGN TO DA-I-ISAMDD
     RECORD KEY IS KEY-VAL
     NOMINAL KEY IS KEY-VAL-WS
     ACCESS IS RANDOM.
```

The NOMINAL KEY field must be defined in WORKING-STORAGE and must have the same PICTURE and USAGE as the RECORD KEY field.

CHAPTER 12 / ISAM DATA SETS

To update an ISAM data set, you must open it as I-O. For example; you could code

```
OPEN I-O ISAM-DATA-FILE.
```

To randomly update an ISAM data set, you must move the key of the record that is to be updated into the NOMINAL KEY field, as for example, by coding

```
MOVE KEY-IN TO KEY-VALUE-WS.
```

A READ statement retrieves the record:

```
READ ISAM-DATA-FILE
    INVALID KEY PERFORM BAD-READ-RTN.
```

The INVALID KEY clause is executed if the file does not contain a record whose key is equal to the value in the NOMINAL KEY field.

After the record has been updated, it is placed back in the data set using the REWRITE statement

```
REWRITE ISAM-RECORD
    INVALID KEY PERFORM BAD-REWRITE-RTN.
```

The INVALID KEY clause will be executed if the NOMINAL KEY and RECORD KEY fields do not contain the same value. It is hard to see how that could happen, but imaginative students have been known to find a way.

Deleting records is a variation on updating. The first byte must be changed to hexadecimal FF, as, for example, by the statement

```
MOVE HIGH-VALUES TO DELETE-BYTE.
```

Then the record is rewritten. Records may be deleted only if L was specified as a value for the DCB subparameter OPTCD.

To add a record, use the WRITE statement. First the key value is moved to the NOMINAL KEY field, and then a WRITE statement is executed:

```
WRITE ISAM-RECORD
    INVALID KEY PERFORM BAD-ADD-RTN.
```

The INVALID KEY clause is executed if the data set already contains a record with a key equal to the value in the NOMINAL KEY field.

ISAM AND HIGHER-LEVEL LANGUAGES

ISAM and PL/I*

Your PL/I program must have a DECLARE statement for the ISAM data set. If the data set is to be accessed sequentially,

```
DCL ISAMFLE FILE RECORD INPUT ENV (INDEXED);
```

is valid. If the data set is to be accessed randomly, the DECLARE statement must include the parameter KEYED, as in

```
DCL ISAMFLE FILE RECORD INPUT KEYED ENV (INDEXED);
```

In any case, ISAMFLE would be the ddname in the DD statement referencing the ISAM data set.

If you are reading the records sequentially, either

```
READ FILE (ISAMFLE) INTO (SPACE);
```

or

```
READ FILE (ISAMFLE) SET (PTR);
```

will work. If you wish to read a particular record, the READ statement becomes

```
READ FILE (ISAMFLE) INTO (SPACE) KEY (KEY_VAL);
```

or

```
READ FILE (ISAMFLE) SET (PTR) KEY (KEY_VAL);
```

The variable KEY_VAL would be the length of the key and would be set equal to the key of the record you are seeking.

If you wish to add a record to an ISAM data set, the file declaration must specify OUTPUT instead of INPUT and the WRITE statement should be in the form

```
WRITE FILE (ISAMFLE) FROM (REC) KEYFROM (KEY_VAL);
```

---

* Those who are not familiar with PL/I should skip this section.

The KEYFROM parameter indicates where the record key may be found. The key field is usually indicated in the record to be written.

If you wish to change a record, the file declaration must specify UPDATE. For example, you could code

```
DCL ISAMFLE FILE RECORD KEYED UPDATE ENV (INDEXED);
```

The rewrite may be coded as

```
REWRITE FILE (ISAMFLE);
```

in which case the record is written as it appears in the input buffer, or

```
REWRITE FILE (ISAMFLE) FROM (REC);
```

in which case the record to be written is found in the variable REC.

Records may be deleted either by using the DELETE statement, as in

```
DELETE FILE (ISAMFLE) KEY (KEY_VAL);
```

or by rewriting the record after setting the delete byte (byte 0) equal to hexadecimal FF.

Your program should include the ONKEY condition in which the ONCODE value is tested. Within the ONKEY condition, an ONCODE value of 51 indicates the record is not in the file, 52 indicates an attempt to add a duplicate record, 53 indicates an attempt to load a record out of sequence, and 57 means there is no more space left for the record.

EXERCISES

1. Can an ISAM or BDAM file be written on tape?

2. What is a key?

3. How does the system locate a record in a BDAM data set?

4. How many parts may an ISAM data set contain? What are they?

5. How many different types of indexes are there in an ISAM data set? What are they? Where are they found?

6. What has to be done to data before they are loaded into an ISAM data set?

7. Would an allocation of seven tracks for the prime area be enough?

8. When you examine a DD statement, what tells you that it represents an ISAM data set?

9. What are the functions that may be performed by the utility program IEBISAM?

10. Why would you reorganize an ISAM data set?

PROGRAMMING ASSIGNMENTS

1. Execute a job using IEBDG to create an ISAM data set. As input use the sequential data set you created in Chapter 3.

2. Execute a job to have IEBISAM print the data set you created in Programming Assignment 1.

3. Execute a job to reorganize the data set you created in Programming Assignment 1.

SUMMARY

In this chapter you have learned

- how ISAM data sets are organized

- how to write DD statements to create and access ISAM data sets

- how to use IEBDG to create an ISAM data set

- how to use IEBISAM to print, copy, load, and unload an ISAM data set

- how to reorganize an ISAM data set and why ISAM data sets must be reorganized

- how to use ISAM data sets in your programs (if you are a COBOL or PL/I programmer)

- how to code an exit from IEBISAM (if you are an assembler programmer)

CHAPTER 13

PROCESSING VSAM DATA SETS

LEARNING OBJECTIVES

IN THIS CHAPTER YOU WILL LEARN

- types and organization of VSAM data sets

- the JCL used to access VSAM data sets

- how to use access method services to
  delete a VSAM data set
  print a VSAM data set
  load a VSAM data set
  create a VSAM data set
  create a VSAM user catalog
  correct a cluster

YOU WILL ALSO LEARN THE MEANINGS OF THE FOLLOWING TERMS:

- Access Method Services (AMS)

- alternate index

- alternate key

- base cluster

- cluster

- control area (CA)

- control area split

- control interval (CI)

- control interval definition field (CIDF)

- control interval split

- dynamic allocation

TYPES OF VSAM DATA SETS

- entry sequence data set (ESDS)

- freespace

- index set

- key sequence data set (KSDS)

- prime key

- record definition field

- relative byte address (RBA)

- relative record data set (RRDS)

- sequence set

TYPES OF VSAM DATA SETS

VSAM data sets come in three flavors. There are key sequence data sets, entry sequence data sets, and relative record data sets.

Key sequence data sets (KSDS) have keys in the records which may be used to read a particular record. As in ISAM, KSDS have an index portion and a data portion. In VSAM these two pieces form a **cluster**, and usually it is the cluster name that is given as the data set name in the DD statement. Unlike ISAM, VSAM has no overflow area. When the KSDS is created, unused space may be scattered throughout the data set, and later when records are added they are inserted in this unused space, or **freespace**.

The VSAM KSDS may have more than one key field. In this situation, there would be an index portion for each key field. The original key is called the **prime key**. The original index and data portions together are called the **base cluster**. The second key is called an **alternate key**. There may be more than one alternate key and consequently more than one **alternate index**.

Entry sequence data sets (ESDS) have their records stored in the order in which they are entered, as you might guess from the entry sequence name. New records may be added only to the end of an ESDS. Unlike KSDS, ESDS consist of only one piece, the data portion. As a result, the ESDS cluster has only one piece unless an alternate index is set up for the data set. Here is the apparently crazy case of a data set in its base form being equivalent to a physical sequential data set, but capable of being accessed by a key. As with a KSDS, there may be more than one alternate index. Each record in the ESDS is located by its **relative byte address** or **RBA**, which is the number of bytes from the beginning of the data set.

A **relative record data set (RRDS)** is halfway between a KSDS and an ESDS. Like an ESDS, the cluster has only the data portion. On the other hand, records can be inserted randomly in a manner reminiscent of a KSDS. In RRDS each record is uniquely identified by its position in the data set—that is, its record number. All RRDS must consist of fixed-length records. Unlike KSDS and ESDS, RRDS may not have a secondary key.

CONTROL INTERVALS AND CONTROL AREAS

All VSAM data sets store their records in control intervals which are fixed-size units. When information is transferred from a DASD (all VSAM data sets must reside on a DASD) to virtual storage, a **control interval (CI)** is the unit of information moved. A control interval is between .5K and 32K in size. Several control intervals are grouped together to form a **control area (CA)**, and one or more control areas form the VSAM data set.

Let us look at the format of the control interval in a little more detail. Figure 13.1 illustrates a KSDS control interval. The control interval is fixed in size, but the records may be variable in length. Data records are stored starting on the left. Control information is stored starting on the right. The first piece of information on the right is the **control interval definition field (CIDF)**, in which the amount and location of the freespace are defined. If you want to add a record to a KSDS, the system determines to which control interval it belongs and checks the CIDF to see if there is sufficient space in

FIGURE 13.1

A KSDS control interval

FIGURE 13.2

An RRDS control interval

Record 1	Record 2	Record 3			Record N	RDF 2	RDF 1

that control interval. If there is sufficient space, the record is added to that control interval. Later we will discuss what happens if there is not enough space for the record.

The next field shown on the right is the **record definition field (RDF)**. If each record in the control interval is a different length, there will be one RDF for each record. If all the records are the same length, there will be two RDFs in the CI: one defining the record length and one indicating how many contiguous records are of this length.

Figure 13.2 shows an RRDS CI. There is no CIDF, since there is no free-space in an RRDS. There are only two RDFs, one for length and one for record count, since the records in an RRDS must be fixed length.

An ESDS CI may have some freespace between the data records and the RDFs. As in a KSDS, the records in an ESDS may be of variable length, although the CI is fixed in size.

ADDING AND DELETING RECORDS

Table 13.1 shows which operations may be performed on each of the three types of VSAM data sets. Let us look more closely at the operations as they apply to RRDS. As mentioned earlier, the RRDS consists of numbered record positions. Deleting a record means emptying the record position, but the record position still exists. Inserting a record means placing information in an empty record position. Replacing a record means exchanging the information in the record position for new information. Please remember that for an RRDS, deleting a record does not recover space and inserting a record does not expand the size of the data set.

With KSDS, adding a record may expand the data set and deleting a record will recover the space. When a KSDS record is deleted, the CI is rewritten without the new record, and the size of the freespace is increased. When a KSDS record is added, the CI is rewritten with the new record added,

TABLE 13.1

VSAM operations

	ESDS	*RRDS*	*KSDS*
Records added to end of data set	Yes	N/A	Yes
Records deleted	No	Yes	Yes
Records replaced	Yes*	Yes	Yes
Records inserted	No	Yes	Yes

*If same length.

and the freespace is decreased. This is illustrated in Figure 13.3. The record whose key is 23 is inserted. Notice the decrease in the size of the freespace and the addition of an RDF. If the three records were fixed length, or variable length and all the same size, the additional RDF would not be required.

Another record whose key is 18 and whose length is greater than the available freespace in the CI obviously will not fit into this CI. Adding it to

FIGURE 13.3

Adding a record to a KSDS

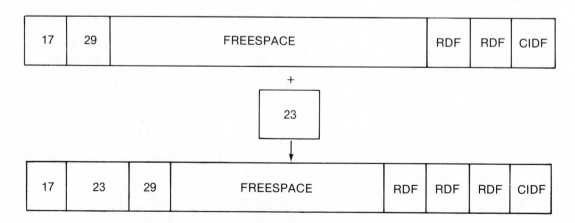

ADDING AND DELETING RECORDS

the KSDS causes a **control interval split**, which is illustrated in Figure 13.4. The new record plus the CI becomes two CIs.

Just as the CI may have freespace for additional records, the CA may have one or more unused CIs. One of these unused CIs is used as the second CI in the split. If there is no unused CI in the CA, a **control area split** occurs. This requires more DASD space for the data set. If none is available or if all the secondary extents have already been used, the record cannot be added to the data set. The program attempting this insertion will either abend or perform an error routine, if one was provided in the program.

Both Figure 13.3 and Figure 13.4 show how records are added to the data portion of a KSDS. What these figures do not show is how the system knows that the record should be inserted in this particular CI. This information is obtained from the index portion of the KSDS. Figure 13.5 illustrates the index CI as it applies to the data CI as shown in Figures 13.3 and 13.4 before the split. Each entry in the index CI contains the highest key in that data CI as well as location information for that data CI. Figure 13.6 shows the index CI after the split. The first entry points to the first CI and the second to the

FIGURE 13.4

A control interval split

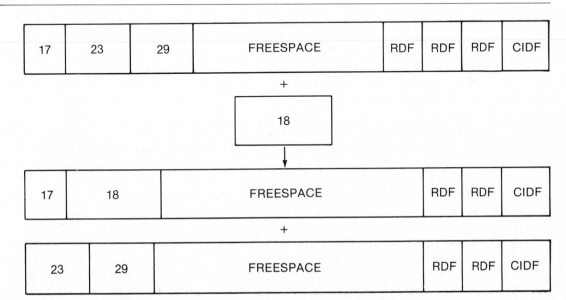

FIGURE 13.5

An index control interval (Reference 13.3)

29		Freespace pointer

FIGURE 13.6

An index control interval (Reference 13.4)

18	29	Freespace pointer

second, but what is in the entry labeled freespace pointer? If you think back to the CI split discussion, you will remember that the system had to find an empty CI in the CA, but no mention was made of how this was done. The freespace pointer points to the available CIs.

Let us now look at what happens when we wish to read the record whose key is 23 (refer to Figures 13.4 and 13.6). First the index CI is read and the key of the desired record is compared with those in the index. Since 23 is greater than 18, the record cannot be in the first data CI; 23 is then compared with 29. Since 23 is less than 29, the record is in the CI pointed to by the second index entry.

What happens with a large data set where more than one CI is needed to hold the index? If there are, for example, 100 CIs in the index, on the average 50 index CIs would have to be read to find a particular data record. To avoid this, the system creates an index to the index, as illustrated in Figure 13.7. The low-level index that points to each data CI is called the **sequence set**, and the index that points to the sequence set CI is called the **index set**. When the system searches for a particular data record, it reads the index set, which directs it to the proper CI in the sequence set, so that 2 CIs are now read instead of 50.

In very large data sets the index set could have several layers. However, we as application programmers need not be concerned, since the system handles the building of the indexes.

FIGURE 13.7

Index structure

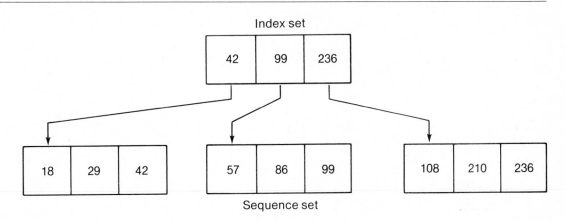

CATALOGS

Unlike other types of data sets, all VSAM data sets must be cataloged in special VSAM catalogs. There is one master VSAM catalog that is usually created by the system programmer. In an OS/MVS system this is done at system generation time. In OS/VS1 systems it may be done later. In addition to the master catalog, there may be VSAM user catalogs. VSAM user catalogs are not required, but if your computer center has many VSAM data sets, grouping them by area (such as payroll) in user catalogs will reduce search time and accelerate the execution of jobs.

VSAM ELEMENTS

VSAM itself consists of three pieces: (1) Access Method Services, (2) the ISAM interface program, and (3) VSAM access method routines. Obviously we cannot cover VSAM completely in one chapter. Our objective here is to supply you, the application programmer, with the information you will need to do your job.

CHAPTER 13 / PROCESSING VSAM DATA SETS

JCL to Access VSAM Data Sets

Since all VSAM data sets must be cataloged in a VSAM catalog, the DD statement is quite simple. All you need specify is the data set name (actually the cluster name) and the disposition, which should be SHR if you are only reading and OLD if you are writing and/or changing the data set.

```
//VSAMFLE DD DSN=VSAMCLST,
//            DISP=SHR
```

and

```
//FLEVSAM  DD DSN=CLSTVSAM,
//            DISP=OLD
```

are valid DD statements for VSAM data sets. The same DD statement form is used for KSDS, ESDS, and RRDS.

How does the system know which type of VSAM data set is to be used? The information is in the VSAM catalog. In the JCL in Figure 13.8, a VSAM cluster named VSAMFLE is accessed using the ddname VSAMIN. Since no other information is supplied, the system will search the VSAM master catalog for the information about this data set. Suppose a VSAM user catalog had been used instead of the VSAM master catalog; how do you tell the system to look in the user catalog? You can supply either a JOBCAT or STEPCAT DD statement. The JOBCAT DD statement is coded after the JOB statement and after the

FIGURE 13.8

JCL to access a VSAM data set

```
//JCLQB100 JOB ,'J. C. LEWIS'
//STEP1    EXEC PGM=MYPROG
//STEPLIB  DD DSN=MYLIB,
//            DISP=SHR
//SYSPRINT DD SYSOUT=A
//SYSUDUMP DD SYSOUT=A
//VSAMIN   DD DSN=VSAMFLE,
//            DISP=SHR
//REPORT   DD SYSOUT=A
//
```

VSAM ELEMENTS

JOBLIB statement, if one is coded, but before the first EXEC statement; for example,

```
//JOBNAME1 JOB ,MSGCLASS=A
//JOBLIB    DD DSN=MYLIB,
//              DISP=SHR
//JOBCAT    DD DSN=UCAT01,
//              DISP=SHR
//STEP1     EXEC PGM=MYPROG
```

The VSAM user catalog (or catalogs, if you concatenate) applies to the entire job when you code the JOBCAT DD statement. The STEPCAT DD statement is coded after the EXEC statement and applies only to that step; for example,

```
//JOBNAME2 JOB ,MSGCLASS=A
//STEP1     EXEC PGM=MYPROG
//STEPCAT   DD DSN=UCAT02,
//              DISP=SHR
```

If both JOBCAT and STEPCAT are coded, the STEPCAT applies to that step and the JOBCAT applies to the rest of the job. For example, look at the following coding:

```
//JOBNAME3 JOB ,MSGLEVEL=1
//JOBCAT    DD DSN=UCAT,
//              DISP=SHR
//STEP1     EXEC PGM=MYPROG1
               .
               .
               .
//STEP2     EXEC PGM=MYPROG2
//STEPCAT   DD DSN=UCAT01,
//              DISP=SHR
               .
               .
               .
//STEP3     EXEC PGM=MYPROG3
               .
               .
               .
```

The VSAM user catalog, UCAT01, named in the STEPCAT statement, is used in STEP2; UCAT, named in the JOBCAT statement is used in STEP1 and STEP3. You will notice that the disposition of SHR is used for all STEPCAT and JOBCAT statements. This ensures that the catalogs may be shared among jobs.

Access Method Services

Access Method Services (AMS) is the VSAM utility program. The facilities of AMS are invoked by executing the utility program IDCAMS. This single utility program provides for VSAM data sets services for which many different utility programs are required for non-VSAM data sets. For example, to print a physical sequential data set you would use IEBPTPCH, and to delete it you would use IEHPROGM. On the other hand, there is only one VSAM utility program, named IDCAMS. It is described in *OS/VS1 Access Method Services* (GC26-3840) for VS1 systems and *OS/VS2 Access Method Services* (GC28-3841) for MVS systems.

AMS BASIC JCL.   Figure 13.9 shows the basic JCL required for any invocation of AMS. Additional DD statements will be needed to perform most commands. However, let us examine this basic JCL. The JOB statement is required for all jobs. IDCAMS requires about 300K bytes of storage and since at the CUNY computer center the default is 192K, the REGION parameter is used to request 300K. The EXEC statement names the AMS utility program IDCAMS. The SYSPRINT DD statement provides a location for the messages that IDCAMS will write. The SYSIN DD statement provides a location for the AMS commands which tell the program IDCAMS what you want done.

FIGURE 13.9

Access Method Services basic JCL

```
//JCLQB110 JOB ,'J. C. LEWIS',
//              REGION=300K
//STEP     EXEC PGM=IDCAMS
//SYSPRINT DD SYSOUT=A
//SYSIN    DD *

    AMS Commands

/*
//
```

VSAM ELEMENTS

AMS COMMAND FORMAT. The AMS command statement usually consists of the command, the parameters, and the terminator. Here we will deal with a limited subset of the commands available—namely, DELETE, PRINT, REPRO, VERIFY, and part of DEFINE.

A command statement may begin in column 2 or later, and may extend to column 72. The commands and parameters are separated by one or more blanks. To make the command statements easy to read, code only one parameter on a line; if the command has more than one parameter, continue the statement onto the next line. A statement is continued by coding a hyphen as the last character. A blank or parenthesis must separate the parameter from the hyphen. The continuation statement may begin anywhere between columns 2 and 72. Again, to make the statements easy to read, line up the parameters. For example, instead of coding

```
DELETE VSAMCLS CLUSTER
```

you should write

```
DELETE VSAMCLS -
       CLUSTER
```

Another way to show continuation is with a plus sign, which does not work exactly the same way as the hyphen; for example,

```
DELETE VSAMCLS CLUSTER ERA+
       SE
```

is the same as

```
DELETE VSAMCLS CLUSTER ERASE
```

When you use the plus sign for continuation, the system looks for the first nonblank character on the next line and concatenates it to that which preceded the plus sign.

You will notice that in the above examples, the parameters are separated with blanks. Commas could have been used instead; the choice is yours. Each statement is ended by not continuing it. A semicolon may instead be used to terminate a statement, as in

```
DELETE VSAMCLS -
       CLUSTER,ER+
       ASE;
```

A parameter may have a subparameter; for example, in

```
DELETE VSAMCLS CLUSTER FILE (DD1)
```

the parameter `FILE` has a subparameter, `DD1`, which is coded within parentheses. The blank between the `E` of `FILE` and the opening parenthesis is optional. It does make reading easier.

CREATING VSAM DATA SETS

Let us now look at how a VSAM data set is created. First, however, let us recall how you create a non-VSAM data set. Normally you just run a program which has been either specially written or bought, and the data set is created on the fly. The `SPACE` parameter tells the system how much DASD to reserve, the `DISP` parameter indicates that the data set is new and what you want done with it when the jobstep ends, and the `DCB` parameter supplies descriptive information. Of course the `DCB` information may be given in the program instead of with the `DCB` parameter on the `DD` statement. Any of several utility programs could also be used to accomplish many of these functions. Running `IEFBR14` would reserve the space on a DASD and supply the `DCB` information, as in

```
//JOBC1     JOB
//STEP      EXEC PGM=IEFBR14
//DD1       DD DSN=NONVSAM,
//             DISP=(NEW,KEEP),
//             UNIT=DISK,
//             VOL=SER=DISK01,
//             DCB=(RECFM=FB,LRECL=80,BLKSIZE=800)
```

Executing `IEHPROGM` would catalog the data set, as in

```
//JOBC2     JOB
//STEP      EXEC PGM=IEHPROGM
//SYSPRINT DD SYSOUT=A
//DD1       DD UNIT=DISK,
```

CREATING VSAM DATA SETS

```
//              VOL=SER=DISK01,
//              DISP=OLD
//SYSIN    DD *
 CATLG DSNAME=NONVSAM,                                    *
              VOL=DISK=DISK01
 /*
```

You could use IEBGENER to load a deck of cards for the data set, for example,

```
//JOBC3    JOB
//STEP     EXEC PGM=IEBGENER
//SYSPRINT DD SYSOUT=A
//SYSIN    DD DUMMY
//SYSUT1   DD *
  (Card deck to be loaded)
/*
//SYSUT2   DD DSN=NONVSAM,
//              DISP=(MOD,KEEP)
//
```

After loading, you would want to see what you have, so you could use IEB-PTPCH to print the data set, as in the following:

```
//JOBC4    JOB
//STEP     EXEC PGM=IEBPTPCH
//SYSPRINT DD SYSOUT=A
//SYSIN    DD *
  PRINT MAXFLDS=1
  RECORD FIELD=(80)
/*
//SYSUT1   DD DSN=NONVSAM,
//              DISP=SHR
//SYSUT2   DD SYSOUT=A
```

To summarize, let us review the steps that are taken to create a non-VSAM data set:

1. Allocate space on a DASD.

2. Supply a description of the data set (DCB information).

3. Set the data set's disposition (CATLG or KEEP).

4. Load the data set.

5. Make sure that the correct data are in the data set.

Obviously these same or similar functions will have to be performed for a VSAM data set, but they are not done in the same way. Unlike the case for non-VSAM data sets, for VSAM data sets a utility program must be used to perform these functions (with the exception of loading the data set, where either a user-written COBOL, PL/I, or assembler program or a utility program could be used). The utility program that performs all of these functions is IDCAMS.

The first thing to do is to decide where to catalog the VSAM data set. Do you want to use the VSAM master catalog or a VSAM user catalog? If you choose to use the master catalog, you can go on to the next step. If you choose to use a user catalog, you must define it if it does not already exist. Defining a user VSAM catalog may be done by the system programmer or by the lead programmer on a team. How to define a user catalog is explained later in this chapter.

The next step is to decide which DASD space to use for the data set. If the decision is that this data set is to occupy space by itself, you can go to the next step. However, if the decision is to group several VSAM data sets in the same space, the space must be obtained for use with VSAM by executing IDCAMS using a DEFINE SPACE command. Again, this is not usually performed by the application programmer, but by a system programmer or lead programmer. In some computer centers, there is a group responsible for controlling the use of DASDs. If your computer center has such a group, this group would execute the DEFINE SPACE function.

The next step is to use the DEFINE CLUSTER command, with which all the descriptive information about the VSAM data set is supplied. This command is the most complex that we will discuss and also the most important.

The REPRO command may be used to load data into a VSAM data set. The input may come from a physical sequential, ISAM, or even VSAM data set. REPRO is also used to back up and to reorganize a VSAM data set. REPRO does not have to be used to load the data set initially. As mentioned earlier, the loading may be done with a user-written program.

Finally, the PRINT command is used to obtain a listing of a VSAM data set. Printing your data set immediately after loading is best, so that you are sure that what you have is what you want.

CREATING VSAM DATA SETS

PRINT Command

We will discuss five commands involved in creating a VSAM data set. Because it is the easiest of the five, we will begin with the PRINT command. The parameters used with the PRINT command are shown in Table 13.2. The job stream in Figure 13.10a prints all of the VSAM data set VSAM.QB.JCL.PLYKSDS1. On the CUNY system, all VSAM data set names must start with VSAM, just as non-VSAM data set names start with WYL. Your computer center may or may not have rules for the data set names of VSAM data sets. If rules have been established, you should write them in the place provided on the inside front cover. Frequently, for convenience, instead of the fully qualified name, such as VSAM.QB.JCL.DATASET, only the last part of the name, such as DATASET, will be used.

Notice that the INFILE parameter names the DD statement DD1, which describes the VSAM data set to be printed. Since the OUTFILE parameter is

TABLE 13.2

PRINT command parameters

Parameter	Abbreviation	Definition
INFILE (ddname/password) INDATASET (entryname/ password)*	IFILE IDS	INFILE names the DD statement of the VSAM data set to be printed. INDATASET actually names the VSAM data set.
OUTFILE (ddname)	OFILE	The output data set is pointed to by the named DD statement. If this parameter is not supplied, SYSPRINT is used.
CHARACTER HEX DUMP	CHAR	CHARACTER means that each byte will be printed in character format. HEX means that each byte will be printed in hexadecimal format. DUMP, which is the default, means that both character and hexadecimal will be printed.
FROMKEY (key) FROMADDRESS (address)	FKEY FADDR	FROMKEY names the key of the first record to be printed and is used with KSDS. (cont.)

TABLE 13.2 (cont.)

PRINT command parameters

Parameter	Abbreviation	Definition
FROMNUMBER (number) SKIP (count)	FNUM	FROMNUMBER gives the relative record number of the first record to be printed and is used with RRDS. FROMADDRESS names the relative byte address (RBA) of the first record and may be used with all three types. SKIP indicates the number of records to be bypassed.
TOKEY (key) TOADDRESS (address) TONUMBER (number) COUNT (count)	TADDR TNUM	TOKEY, TOADDRESS, or TONUMBER indicates the last record to be printed. COUNT tells the number of records to be printed.

*For MVS systems only.

not coded, the output is automatically directed to the output class specified in the SYSPRINT DD statement, which is the printer.

Since the desired format for the listing is not specified, we get DUMP, which is the default. DUMP means the data set will be printed in both character and hexadecimal representations. The output produced by this job stream is shown in Figure 13.10b.

In MVS systems only, the same output is produced by using the IN-DATASET parameter instead of the INFILE parameter. To use INDATASET, we would replace the control statement in Figure 13.10a with

```
PRINT INDATASET (VSAM.QB.JCL.PLYKSDS1)
```

and eliminate the DD1 DD statement. Without the DD1 DD statement, the system will not be able to determine the name of the data set being processed when it scans the JCL. It will find out the name of the data set only when the job goes into execution and the control statements are interpreted. At that time the data set will be allocated. Allocating a data set after a job

FIGURE 13.10

(a) Printing a VSAM data set

```
//JCLQB140 JOB  ,'ARIES',
//              REGION=300K
//PRNT1    EXEC PGM=IDCAMS
//STEPCAT  DD DSN=USERCAT,
//              DISP=SHR
//SYSPRINT DD SYSOUT=A
//DD1      DD DSN=VSAM.QB.JCL.PLYKSDS1,
//              DISP=SHR
//SYSIN    DD *
 PRINT INFILE (DD1)
/*
//
```

(b) Sample output of the print operation

```
LISTING OF DATA SET -VSAM.QB.JCL.PLYKSDS1
KEY OF RECORD - F1F3F0F0F9
000000  F1F3F0F0 F9D9C5C5 C46BE3C9 D5C14040  40404040 40404040 C1F0F8F4     *13009REED,TINA
000020  F2F0F0F0 F4F2F6F0 F7F2F1F0 F0404040  40F7F440 40404040 40404040     *200042607210 0       74
000040  40404040 40404040 40404040                                         *

KEY OF RECORD - F1F5F1F7F4
000000  F1F5F1F7 F4C8C1D5 C4D1C1D5 E86BC8C1  C9C4C5C8 40404040 C8F0F2F2     *15174HANDJANY,HAIDEH
000020  F9F0F0F0 F2F2F0F0 F2F2F9F0 F0404040  40F7F140 40404040 40404040     *90002200022900       71
000040  40404040 40404040 40404040                                         *

KEY OF RECORD - F1F7F3F3F7
000000  F1F7F3F3 F7C2E4E3 C5D9D66B D4C1E4D9  C9C3C540 40404040 C8F0F5F0     *17337BUTERO,MAURICE
000020  F1F0F0F0 F4F3F4F0 F5F0F1F0 F0404040  40F6F340 40404040 40404040     *10004340501 00       63
000040  40404040 40404040 40404040                                         *

KEY OF RECORD - F1F9F4F9F9
000000  F1F9F4F9 F9D3C1C6 C5D96BC2 D9E4C3C5  40404040 40404040 C1F0F7F0     *19499LAFER,BRUCE
000020  F6F0F0F0 F8F1F9F0 F5F0F0F0 F0404040  40F5F240 40404040 40404040     *60008190500 00       52
000040  40404040 40404040 40404040                                         *

KEY OF RECORD - F2F1F6F6F1
000000  F2F1F6F6 F1D3C5C5 6BE2E4C9 40404040  40404040 40404040 C1F0F3F9     *21661LEE,SUI
000020  F0F1F7F0 F3F0F3F0 F3F0F0F1 F7404040  40F7F640 40404040 4040404C     *01703030017          76
000040  40404040 40404040 40404040                                         *
```

has begun execution is called **dynamic allocation**. For dynamic allocation of a data set to be successful, it is necessary that the volume on which the data set resides be mounted before the job begins execution.

Since INFILE and OUTFILE are correct for both VS1 and MVS systems, while INDATASET and OUTDATASET are correct only for MVS systems, all examples here will use INFILE and OUTFILE.

If the PRINT command were

```
PRINT INFILE (DD1) -
      CHARACTER -
      SKIP (20) -
      COUNT (20)
```

the twenty-first through the fortieth records would be printed in character format.

```
PRINT INFILE (DD1) -
      HEX -
      FROMKEY (19499) -
      TOKEY (43214)
```

implies that the VSAM data set is a KSDS. In fact if VSAM.QB.JCL.PLYKSDS1 is not a KSDS, this command will fail. Printing will start with the record

FIGURE 13.11

Printing selected records of an RRDS

```
//JCLQB150 JOB ,'TAURUS',
//            REGION=300K
//JOBCAT   DD DSN=USERCAT,
//            DISP=SHR
//PRNT2    EXEC PGM=IDCAMS
//SYSPRINT DD SYSOUT=A
//DD1      DD DSN=VSAM.QB.JCL.POLYRRDS,
//            DISP=SHR
//DD2      DD SYSOUT=C
//SYSIN    DD *
 PRINT INFILE (DD1) -
       OUTFILE (DD2) -
       FROMNUMBER (6) -
       TONUMBER (20)
/*
//
```

CREATING VSAM DATA SETS

whose key is 19499 and proceed to the record whose key is 43214. The listing will be in hexadecimal format. If the key specified in either FROMKEY or TOKEY contains any special characters, it must be enclosed in quotes—for example, TOKEY('A=B'). The key may be given in hexadecimal format as well—for example, FROMKEY(X'3CFF').

The job illustrated in Figure 13.11 shows the use of the OUTFILE parameter to name the DD2 DD statement that directs the output to output class C. POLYRRDS is an RRDS, and the command will print from record number 6 to record number 20.

REPRO Command

The REPRO command is quite useful. It can be used to load a VSAM data set, to convert an ISAM data set to VSAM, to reorganize a VSAM KSDS, to merge two VSAM data sets, or to create a back-up copy.

Table 13.3 shows the parameters of the REPRO command. The examples will not use FROMKEY, FROMADDRESS, FROMNUMBER, SKIP, TOKEY, TOADDRESS,

TABLE 13.3

REPRO command parameters

Parameter	Abbreviation	Definition

INFILE (ddname/password)
  ENVIRONMENT (DUMMY)
INDATASET (entryname/password)*
  ENVIRONMENT (DUMMY)
	IFILE
	ENV (DUM)
	IDS
		The ddname of INFILE points to the DD statement that names the input data set.
		The entryname of INDATASET is the entry to be copied.
		ENVIRONMENT (DUMMY) means that dummy ISAM records are to be copied.

OUTFILE (ddname/password) OUTDATASET (entryname/password)*	OFILE ODS	The ddname of OUTFILE points to the DD statement that names the output data set. The entryname of OUTDATASET is the output data set. (cont.)

TABLE 13.3 (cont.)

REPRO command parameters

Parameter	Abbreviation	Definition
REPLACE NOREPLACE	REP NREP	In copying a KSDS into an existing KSDS, REPLACE means to take the input record for equal keys. NOREPLACE is the default.
REUSE NOREUSE	RUS NRUS	REUSE means that the data set is to be rebuilt every time it is opened. NOREUSE is the default.
FROMKEY (key) FROMADDRESS (address) FROMNUMBER (number) SKIP (count)	FKEY FADDR FNUM	FROMKEY gives the key of the first record in a KSDS to be copied. FROMADDRESS gives the RBA of the first record to be copied. FROMNUMBER gives the relative record number of the first record to be copied. SKIP tells how many records to bypass before copying.
TOKEY (key) TOADDRESS (address) TONUMBER (number) COUNT (count)	 TADDR TNUM	TOKEY gives the key of the last record to be copied. TOADDRESS gives the RBA of the last record to be copied. TONUMBER gives the relative record number of the last record to be copied. COUNT tells how many records are to be copied.

*For MVS systems only.

TONUMBER, and COUNT, since these parameters are used in the same way here as in the PRINT command.

The job shown in Figure 13.12 uses the REPRO command to load data from the sequential data set POLYFILE into the previously created VSAM

CREATING VSAM DATA SETS

FIGURE 13.12

Loading a VSAM KSDS with data from an SDS

```
//JCLQB160 JOB ,'GEMINI',
//             REGION=300K
//REPRO1    EXEC PGM=IDCAMS
//STEPCAT   DD DSN=USERCAT,
//             DISP=SHR
//SYSPRINT  DD SYSOUT=A
//DD1       DD DSN=WYL.QB.JCL.POLYFILE,
//             DISP=SHR
//DD2       DD DSN=VSAM.QB.JCL.PLYKSDS1,
//             DISP=OLD
//SYSIN     DD *
 REPRO INFILE (DD1) -
       OUTFILE (DD2)
/*
//
```

cluster PLYKSDS1. (In Figure 13.18, PLYKSDS1 is defined as a KSDS.) This job, therefore, uses as input a sequential data set and creates a KSDS. The job shown in Figure 13.13 uses the REPRO command to load data from the ISAM data set POLYISAM into the previously created cluster PLYKSDS2. PLYKSDS2 was previously defined as a KSDS, so this job uses as input an ISAM data set and creates a KSDS. Because ENVIRONMENT (DUMMY) was specified, dummy records

FIGURE 13.13

Loading a VSAM KSDS with data from an ISAM data set

```
//JCLQB170 JOB ,'CANCER',
//             REGION=300K
//JOBCAT    DD DSN=USERCAT,
//             DISP=SHR
//REPRO2    EXEC PGM=IDCAMS
//SYSPRINT  DD SYSOUT=A
//DD1       DD DSN=WYL.QB.JCL.POLYISAM,
//             DISP=SHR,
//             DCB=DSORG=IS
//DD2       DD DSN=VSAM.QB.JCL.PLYKSDS2,
//             DISP=OLD
//SYSIN     DD *
 REPRO INFILE (DD1 ENVIRONMENT (DUMMY)) -
       OUTFILE (DD2) -
       REPLACE
/*
//
```

and records marked for deletion (those records which contain a hexadecimal value of FF in the first byte) will be copied to PLYKSDS2.

The REPRO command can accomplish several functions depending on what type of data set the input and output data sets are and on whether the output data set contains data or is empty. Let us assume that you have a job like those shown in Figure 13.12 and Figure 13.13, but that the DSN of the input data set is INPUT and of the output data set is OUTPUT.

If OUTPUT is empty, the REPRO command will load it with data from INPUT, no matter what kind of data set INPUT or OUTPUT is.

If OUTPUT contains data, what happens depends on what kind of VSAM data set OUTPUT is, as well as what INPUT is. If OUTPUT is an ESDS, all the records in INPUT will be added to the end of OUTPUT, no matter what kind of data set INPUT is. If OUTPUT is a KSDS, the records in INPUT will be merged into OUTPUT based on the value of the key, no matter what kind of data set INPUT is. In the case of duplicate keys, the record in OUTPUT will be kept and the record in INPUT not used. If the command were

```
REPRO INFILE (DD1) -
      OUTFILE (DD2) -
      REPLACE
```

the record in INPUT would replace the record in OUTPUT with the same key.

The job will fail if OUTPUT is an RRDS with data, unless INPUT is also an RRDS. If both are RRDSs, the records are merged by relative record number.

FIGURE 13.14

Creating a tape back-up of a VSAM data set

```
//JCLQB180 JOB ,'LEO',
//             REGION=300K
//JOBCAT   DD DSN=USERCAT,
//             DISP=SHR
//REPRO3   EXEC PGM=IDCAMS
//SYSPRINT DD SYSOUT=A
//DD1      DD DSN=VSAM.QB.JCL.PLYKSDS1,
//             DISP=SHR
//DD2      DD DSN=WYL.QB.JCL.BACKUP,
//             DISP=(,KEEP),
//             UNIT=TAPE,
//             DCB=(RECFM=FB,LRECL=80,BLKSIZE=1600)
//SYSIN    DD *
 REPRO INFILE (DD1) -
       OUTFILE (DD2)
/*
//
```

CREATING VSAM DATA SETS

In case of duplicate relative record numbers, the record in OUTPUT is retained unless REPLACE is specified.

Figure 13.14 shows a job stream to create a back-up copy of a VSAM file on tape. The job stream assumes that the records are 80 bytes in length. The records will be blocked on tape. You will note that REPLACE is not coded because it would be meaningless. Part of the VSAM file could be backed up by using a FROM value together with a TO value.

Reorganizing a KSDS

After a number of CI and CA splits have occurred, the physical sequence of the KSDS will be different from the logical sequence. This condition is illustrated in Figure 13.15. The index shows the logical sequence and the data the physical sequence. At this point it would be desirable to reorganize the KSDS to make the physical and logical sequence the same, which would result in faster read time, particularly in sequential access.

Reorganizing a VSAM KSDS cannot be accomplished in one step. The job stream in Figure 13.16 illustrates one sequence of steps that would do the reorganization. A JOBCAT DD statement is used, since both data sets are cataloged in one user catalog. A STEPCAT statement could have been used in each step; if the master VSAM catalog had been used, neither a JOBCAT nor STEPCAT would be needed. The first step defines the temporary cluster TEMP1. The coding of this will be discussed in the next section. The second step

FIGURE 13.15

Physical and logical sequence differ

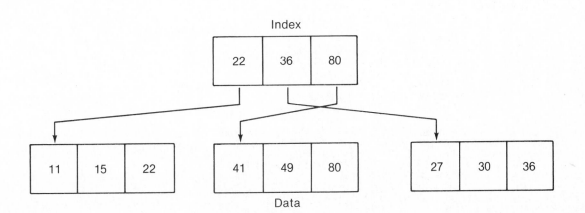

FIGURE 13.16

Reorganizing a VSAM cluster

```
//JCLQB190 JOB ,'VIRGO',
//          REGION=300K
//JOBCAT    DD DSN=USERCAT,
//          DISP=SHR
//REPRO4A   EXEC PGM=IDCAMS
//SYSPRINT DD SYSOUT=A
//SYSIN     DD *
 DEFINE CLUSTER (NAME (VSAM.QB.JCL.TEMP1) -
                 RECORDS (1000 200) -
                 FREESPACE (20 20) -
                 INDEXED -
                 KEYS (5 0) -
                 RECORDSIZE (80 80) -
                 UNIQUE -
                 VOLUMES (SCR001) )
/*
//REPRO4B   EXEC PGM=IDCAMS,
//          COND=(0,NE)
//SYSPRINT DD SYSOUT=A
//DD1       DD DSN=VSAM.QB.JCL.PLYKSDS1,
//          DISP=SHR
//DD2       DD DSN=VSAM.QB.JCL.TEMP1,
//          DISP=OLD,
//          UNIT=SYSDA,
//          VOL=SER=SCR001,
//          AMP=AMORG
//SYSIN     DD *
 REPRO INFILE (DD1) -
       OUTFILE (DD2)
/*
//REPRO4C   EXEC PGM=IDCAMS,
//          COND=(0,NE)
//SYSPRINT DD SYSOUT=A
//DD1       DD UNIT=SYSDA,
//          DISP=OLD,
//          VOL=SER=SCR001
//SYSIN     DD *
 DELETE VSAM.QB.JCL.PLYKSDS1 -
        CLUSTER -
        FILE (DD1)
/*
//REPRO4D   EXEC PGM=IDCAMS,
//          COND=(0,NE)
//SYSPRINT DD SYSOUT=A
//SYSIN     DD *
 ALTER VSAM.QB.JCL.TEMP1 NEWNAME (VSAM.QB.JCL.PLYKSDS1)
/*
//
```

CREATING VSAM DATA SETS

copies the data from the original VSAM KSDS to the temporary one. You will notice that COND=(0,NE) is coded on the EXEC statements of all but the first step. Each step depends on the successful execution of the preceding steps; by checking the return code, we make sure each execution was successful. The third step deletes the original VSAM KSDS. You can see that we would be in serious trouble if we deleted the data set without having a copy of it. The last step uses the ALTER command to rename the temporary VSAM KSDS and make it *the* VSAM KSDS.

This job contains one complication which must be explained. You will notice that in the second step the UNIT and VOL parameters are coded for TEMP1. Since TEMP1 is cataloged, you might wonder why the UNIT and VOL parameters are coded. Recall that before a job starts executing, the reader-interpreter searches the catalog to obtain information about all the cataloged data sets used in the job. But before the job starts executing, TEMP1 does not exist; if the reader-interpreter searched the catalog, it would not find an entry for TEMP1, and the job would fail. TEMP1 will be defined and cataloged in the first step, but it is defined and cataloged using control statements, not JCL statements, and the reader-interpreter does not read control statements.

Briefly then, UNIT and VOL are coded for TEMP1 to prevent the reader-interpreter from searching the catalog to obtain information about TEMP1. But that raises another problem: if the catalog is not read for TEMP1, the system will not learn that TEMP1 is a VSAM data set. To tell the system that TEMP1 is a VSAM data set requires a parameter that is new to us,

```
AMP=AMORG
```

which follows the first VOL parameter in Figure 13.16.

DEFINE CLUSTER Command

The DEFINE CLUSTER command is used to supply the descriptive information about a VSAM data set that is stored in the specified VSAM user catalog or in the VSAM master catalog. If UNIQUE (which means the data set has its own DASD space) is specified, space is also allocated with this command. The general form of the command is

```
DEFINE CLUSTER (parameters) -
       DATA (parameters) -
       INDEX (parameters) -
       CATALOG (catname/password)
```

CHAPTER 13 / PROCESSING VSAM DATA SETS

DEFINE may be abbreviated as DEF, CLUSTER as CL, INDEX as IDX, and CATALOG as CAT. The catname supplies the name of the VSAM user catalog in which the information is to be stored. INDEX information is given only for KSDS.

The parameters are defined in Table 13.4. In the columns labeled *CL*, *DATA*, and *INDEX*, R means the parameter is required, O means it is optional or there is a default value, P means it is optional but its use is recommended, and N/A means not applicable. R/O means that the information is required, but that the user chooses where to supply it. Those parameters which explicitly apply to security have not been included in Table 13.4, but are listed in Table 13.5 without definition.

When coding DEFINE CLUSTER, let the system select the sizes for buffer space and for the CI.

Let us start with defining a KSDS, since more parameters are needed than with any other type of VSAM data set.

The job shown in Figure 13.17 will define a KSDS cluster named VSAM.QB.JCL.KSDS. The parameter INDEXED indicates that this cluster is a KSDS. Space sufficient for 1000 records will be taken from previously defined space as a result of RECORDS (1000 100). The 100 is for the secondary allocation, should it be necessary. The space will be on disk pack SCR001 as a result of the VOLUMES (SCR001) parameter. The RECORDSIZE (100 320) parameter specifies that the logical record length averages 100 bytes with a maximum length of 320 bytes. The KEYS (10 5) parameter tells us that the key is 10 bytes long and starts in the sixth byte of the record. (Remember that the first byte is position 0.) The FREESPACE (20 30) specifies that when data are loaded into this data set, 20% of each of the CIs and 30% of each of the CAs will be left free for expansion.

Since the CATALOG entry was not used as part of the command, the system defaults to the catalog available with the job, which in this case is USERCAT, made available with the STEPCAT DD statement. The catalog could also be supplied via a JOBCAT DD statement. If neither a JOBCAT nor a STEPCAT DD statement were included, the VSAM master catalog would be used.

As explained earlier, a KSDS cluster consists of an index and a data component. In the job in Figure 13.17, the DATA and INDEX parameters supply names for these components.

The job in Figure 13.18 defines a KSDS cluster named PLYKSDS1 in a VSAM user catalog. This job shows how to use the UNIQUE parameter. The UNIQUE entry, which can be abbreviated as UNQ, requests space for this data set that will not be shared by another data set. The VOLUMES (SCR001) parameter supplies the name of the volume on which the data set will reside. Information from this parameter goes into the VSAM user catalog,

TABLE 13.4

DEFINE CLUSTER command parameters

Parameter	Abbreviation	CL	DATA	INDEX	Definition
BUFFERSPACE (size)	BUFSP	O	O	O	Gives minimum space for buffers.
CONTROLINTERVALSIZE (size)	CISZ	O	O	O	Gives size of the control interval.
CYLINDER (prim sec) RECORDS (prim sec) TRACKS (prim sec)	CYL REC TRK	R	O	O	Gives amount of DASD space for data set. If specified in DATA and INDEX, it must equal CLUSTER as a whole.
DESTAGEWAIT NODESTAGEWAIT	DSTGW NDSTGW	O	O	O	Applies to mass storage device data sets.
ERASE NOERASE	ERAS NERAS	O	O	N/A	ERASE specifies that binary zeros are to be written over the data set when it is deleted. The default is NOERASE.
EXCEPTIONEXIT (entry point)	EEXT	O	O	O	Names a user-written routine that takes control when an I/O error occurs.
FILE (ddname)		R/O	O	O	Identifies the device and volume to be used for space allocation. If UNIQUE is specified, this parameter is required for VS1 systems.
FREESPACE (CI% CA%)	FSPC	O	O	N/A	Specifies the percent of the CI and the percent of the CA to be left free when the KSDS is loaded. The default is 0.

(cont.)

TABLE 13.4 (cont.)

DEFINE CLUSTER command parameters

Parameter	Abbreviation	CL	DATA	INDEX	Definition
IMBED NOIMBED	IMBD NOIMBD	O	N/A	O	IMBED specifies that the sequence set is to be placed with the data. It applies to KSDS. NOIMBED is the default.
INDEXED NONINDEXED NUMBERED	IXD NIXD NUMD	O	N/A	N/A	INDEXED is the default and means the data set is KSDS. NONINDEXED means it is ESDS. NUMBERED means it is RRDS.
KEYRANGES ((lowkey highkey) (lowkey highkey)....)	KRNG	O	O	N/A	For a multivolume KSDS, identifies key ranges for each volume.
KEYS (length offset)		O	O	N/A	Specifies key length and position in record. The first byte is position 0. The default is 64 and 0. This applies to KSDS.
MODEL (entryname/password catname/password)		O	O	O	Names an existing entry to be used as a model for this entry.
NAME (entryname)		R	P	P	Supplies the name.
ORDERED UNORDERED	ORD UORD	O	O	O	ORDERED specifies that the volumes are to be used in the order in which they were listed in the VOLUMES parameter. UNORDERED is the default.
OWNER (owner-id)		O	O	O	Names the cluster's owner.

Parameter	Abbrev.	N/A	R/O	R/O	Description
RECORDSIZE (average maximum)	RECSZ	N/A	R/O	R/O	Gives the average and maximum record size. This value must be supplied with either CLUSTER or DATA.
REPLICATE NOREPLICATE	REPL NREPL	O	N/A	O	REPLICATE means each index record is written on a track as many times as it will fit. Rotational delay time is saved this way. NOREPLICATE is the default.
REUSE NOREUSE		O	O	O	REUSE specifies that the cluster can be opened frequently as a temporary data set. NOREUSE is the default.
SHAREOPTIONS (crossregion crosssystem)	SHR	O	O	O	Specifies how a component or cluster can be shared among various users.
SPANNED NOSPANNED	SPND NSPND	N/A	O	O	SPANNED indicates that a record can be bigger than the control interval. NOSPANNED is the default.
SPEED RECOVERY	RCVY	N/A	O	O	RECOVERY, the default, means the data area is preformatted and if the load fails it can be recovered. SPEED does not preformat and is faster.
STAGE BIND CYLINDERFAULT	CYLF	O	O	O	Used with mass storage.

(cont.)

441

TABLE 13.4 (cont.)

DEFINE CLUSTER command parameters

Parameter	Abbreviation	CL	DATA	INDEX	Definition
TO (date) FOR (days)		O	N/A	N/A	Gives the retention period. It may be given as a Julian date. 82264 is 21 September 1982. Alternatively, a number of days may be specified.
UNIQUE	UNQ	O	O	O	UNIQUE means the data set has its own space.
SUBALLOCATION	SUBAL				SUBALLOCATION, which is the default, means the data set shares the space with other data sets.
VOLUMES (volser...)	VOL	R/O	R/O	R/O	Names the volumes on which the entry is located. This parameter must be given either for the cluster as a whole or for the data and index which permits the data to be on one volume and the index on another.
WRITECHECK	WCK	O	O	O	WRITECHECK causes the hardware to check that the data were written correctly.
NOWRITECHECK	NWCK				

TABLE 13.5

Security parameters

Parameter	Abbreviation	CL	DATA	INDEX
ATTEMPTS (number)	ATT	O	O	O
AUTHORIZATION (entrypoint string)	AUTH	O	O	O
CODE (code)		O	O	O
CONTROLPW (password)	CTLPW	O	O	O
MASTERPW (password)	MRPW	O	O	O
READPW (password)	RDPW	O	O	O
UPDATEPW (password)	UPDPW	O	O	O

FIGURE 13.17

Defining a KSDS cluster

```
//JCLQB200 JOB ,'LIBRA',
//           REGION=300K
//DEFCLK1  EXEC PGM=IDCAMS
//STEPCAT  DD DSN=USERCAT,
//           DISP=SHR
//SYSPRINT DD SYSOUT=A
//SYSIN    DD *
 DEFINE CLUSTER (NAME (VSAM.QB.JCL.KSDS) -
                RECORDS (1000 100) -
                FREESPACE (20 30) -
                INDEXED -
                KEYS (10 5) -
                RECORDSIZE (100 320) -
                VOLUMES (SCR001) ) -
        DATA (NAME (VSAM.QB.JCL.KSDSDAT) ) -
        INDEX (NAME (VSAM.QB.JCL.KSDSIND) )
 /*
 //
```

FIGURE 13.18

Defining a unique KSDS cluster

```
//JCLQB210 JOB ,'SCORPIO',
//          REGION=300K
//JOBCAT   DD DSN=USERCAT,
//          DISP=SHR
//DEFCLU2  EXEC PGM=IDCAMS
//SYSPRINT DD SYSOUT=A
//DD1      DD UNIT=SYSDA,
//          DISP=OLD,
//          VOL=SER=SCR001
//SYSIN    DD *
 DEFINE CLUSTER (NAME (VSAM.QB.JCL.PLYKSDS1) -
                RECORDS (1000 200) -
                FILE (DD1) -
                FREESPACE (20 20) -
                INDEXED -
                KEYS (5 0) -
                RECORDSIZE (80 80) -
                UNIQUE -
                VOLUMES (SCR001) ) -
        DATA (NAME (VSAM.QB.JCL.KSDS1DAT) ) -
        INDEX (NAME (VSAM.QB.JCL.KSDS1IND) )
/*
//
```

but does not enable the system to access that disk pack. Access to disk pack
SCR001 is obtained via the FILE (DD1) parameter which points to the DD statement that names the actual disk pack. If the requested space is not available
on SCR001, the job will fail. The FREESPACE allocation is the same as in the
previous example. As mentioned earlier, in MVS systems the FILE
parameter is not required.

The records in this KSDS are fixed in length, since the average and maximum lengths are the same (RECORDSIZE (80 80)). The key is 5 bytes long
and starts in the first position in the record (KEYS (5 0)). The RECORDSIZE
and KEYS parameters are coded to be consistent with POLYFILE. PLYKSDS1 was
loaded with data from POLYFILE in Figure 13.12.

The job to define PLYKSDS2, the cluster that was loaded with data from
POLYISAM in Figure 13.13, is not shown. The job would be similar to Figure
13.18, except that RECORDSIZE (81 81) and KEYS (5 1) would be coded to be
consistent with POLYISAM.

The job in Figure 13.19 defines the KSDS cluster in the VSAM master
catalog because that is the only VSAM catalog available to this job. The

FIGURE 13.19

Defining a KSDS cluster with data and index portions on separate volumes

```
//JCLQB220 JOB ,'SAGITTARIUS',
//           REGION=300K
//DEFCLU3  EXEC PGM=IDCAMS
//SYSPRINT DD SYSOUT=A
//SYSIN    DD *
 DEFINE CLUSTER (NAME (VSAM.QB.JCL.KSDS3) -
               RECORDS (1000 100) -
               FREESPACE (20 10) -
               INDEXED -
               KEYS (10 90) -
               RECORDSIZE (100 100) ) -
        DATA (NAME (VSAM.QB.JCL.KSDS3DAT) -
               VOLUMES (SCR001) ) -
        INDEX (NAME (VSAM.QB.JCL.KSDS3IND) -
               VOLUMES (SCR002) )
/*
//
```

fixed-length records have the key as the last ten bytes. Space for 1000 records will be reserved on volume SCR001, but the index will be on volume SCR002. Since UNIQUE is not coded, we know that space on these two volumes has previously been obtained and will be shared with other data sets.

The jobs shown in Figures 13.17, 13.18, and 13.19 all define KSDS clusters. The system knew KSDS were wanted because the parameter INDEXED was specified. The parameters KEYS and FREESPACE are specified only for KSDS.

The job in Figure 13.20 defines the cluster for an ESDS. The parameter NONINDEXED is what tells the system that an ESDS is being defined. The variable-length records average 320 bytes and have a maximum size of 670. Space for 1000 records is reserved on volume SCR001. The space was previously defined to VSAM user catalog UCAT02. You will notice that the CATALOG entry in the command names the catalog to be used.

The job in Figure 13.21 defines an ESDS cluster to be used as a workfile. Since REUSE is specified, the data set is reloaded every time it is opened. Space for 1000 records will be reserved on volume SCR001. However, if an attempt is made to write more than 1000 records, the job will fail because no secondary allocation is specified.

In Figure 13.20, the data component was given a name. In Figure 13.21, the system supplies all the information for the data component. Since the data component is not named, the system will supply a name in the form

FIGURE 13.20

Defining an ESDS cluster

```
//JCLQB230 JOB ,'CAPRICORN',
//          REGION=300K
//JOBCAT   DD DSN=USERCAT,
//            DISP=SHR
//          DD DSN=UCAT02,
//            DISP=SHR
//DEFCLE1  EXEC PGM=IDCAMS
//SYSPRINT DD SYSOUT=A
//SYSIN    DD *
  DEFINE CLUSTER (NAME (VSAM.QB.JCL.ESDS1) -
                  RECORDS (1000 100) -
                  NONINDEXED -
                  RECORDSIZE (320 670) -
                  VOLUMES (SCR001) ) -
          DATA (NAME (VSAM.QB.JCL.ESDS1DAT) ) -
          CATALOG (UCAT02)
/*
//
```

FIGURE 13.21

Defining a work ESDS cluster

```
//JCLQB240 JOB ,'AQUARIUS',
//          REGION=300K
//JOBCAT    DD DSN=USERCAT,
//            DISP=SHR
//DEFCLE2  EXEC PGM=IDCAMS
//SYSPRINT DD SYSOUT=A
//SYSIN    DD *
  DEFINE CLUSTER (NAME (VSAM.QB.JCL.ESDS2) -
                  RECORDS (1000) -
                  NONINDEXED -
                  RECORDSIZE (80 320) -
                  REUSE -
                  VOLUMES (SCR001) )
/*
//
```

```
VSAMDSET.Tbbbbbbb.DFDyyddd.Taaaaaaa.Tbbbbbbb
```

in which yy is the year, ddd is the Julian date, and aaaaaaabbbbbbb is the time stamp. Allowing the system to supply this information is not recommended. Your VSAM catalog will have entries that you will not recognize, and it will be significantly more difficult to control your DASD.

FIGURE 13.22

Defining an RRDS cluster

```
//JCLQB250 JOB ,'PISCES',
//          REGION=300K
//DEFCLR1  EXEC PGM=IDCAMS
//STEPCAT  DD DSN=USERCAT,
//          DISP=SHR
//SYSPRINT DD SYSOUT=A
//DD1      DD UNIT=SYSDA,
//          DISP=OLD,
//          VOL=SER=SCR001
//SYSIN    DD *
 DEFINE CLUSTER (NAME (VSAM.QB.JCL.POLYRRDS) -
                 RECORDS (1000 100) -
                 FILE (DD1) -
                 NUMBERED -
                 RECORDSIZE (80 80) -
                 UNIQUE -
                 VOLUMES (SCR001) ) -
        DATA (NAME (VSAM.QB.JCL.PLYRRDAT) )
/*
//
```

The job in Figure 13.22 must define an RRDS because the parameter NUMBERED appears in the command. You will also notice that the records are of fixed length (average equals maximum), a requirement for RRDS. The space for this data set will be obtained with this command because UNIQUE is specified.

As with the SPACE parameter for non-VSAM data sets, space can be requested in units of cylinders or tracks as well as of record count. Specifying the space allocation in units of record count is easier. You will probably know about how many records are to go into the data set, and this coding lets the system do the arithmetic to determine how many tracks and/or cylinders are required.

DEFINE SPACE Command

The DEFINE SPACE command reserves space on a DASD volume and records the reservation in a VSAM catalog. Space obtained in this way may hold more than one VSAM data set. As you recall, if you specify UNIQUE with the DEFINE CLUSTER command, space is obtained for only that data set.

Once a data space is defined on a volume, all future data spaces defined on that volume must be defined in the same VSAM catalog. If, as illustrated in Figure 13.23, we define a data space of 10 cylinders on volume SCR001 in

FIGURE 13.23

Defining space

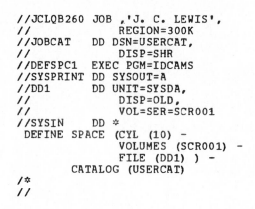

```
//JCLQB260 JOB ,'J. C. LEWIS',
//             REGION=300K
//JOBCAT   DD DSN=USERCAT,
//             DISP=SHR
//DEFSPC1  EXEC PGM=IDCAMS
//SYSPRINT DD SYSOUT=A
//DD1      DD UNIT=SYSDA,
//             DISP=OLD,
//             VOL=SER=SCR001
//SYSIN    DD *
  DEFINE SPACE (CYL (10) -
               VOLUMES (SCR001) -
               FILE (DD1) ) -
        CATALOG (USERCAT)
/*
//
```

TABLE 13.6

DEFINE SPACE command parameters

Parameter	Abbreviation	Definition
CANDIDATE	CAN	Means that the entire volume or volumes named are reserved for VSAM.
CYLINDERS (prim sec) TRACKS (prim sec)	CYL TRK	Reserves the named quantity on the volume named.
RECORDS (prim sec) and RECORDSIZE (aver max)	REC RECSZ	Reserves space for the given number of records of the named size.
VOLUMES (volser...)	VOL	Names the volume or volumes on which the data space is to be defined.
FILE (ddname)		Points to the DD statement for the volume on which the data space is to be defined.
CATALOG (catname/password)	CAT	Names the VSAM catalog in which the data space is to be defined.

CREATING VSAM DATA SETS

FIGURE 13.24

Defining multivolume space

```
//JCLQB270 JOB ,'J. C. LEWIS',
//          REGION=300K
//DEFSPC2  EXEC PGM=IDCAMS
//STEPCAT  DD DSN=USERCAT,
//            DISP=SHR
//SYSPRINT DD SYSOUT=A
//DDX      DD UNIT=SYSDA,
//            DISP=OLD,
//            VOL=SER=(SCR001,SCR002)
//SYSIN    DD *
 DEFINE SPACE (RECORDS (2000 200) -
              RECORDSIZE (100 300) -
              VOLUMES (SCR001 SCR002) -
              FILE (DDX) ) -
         CATALOG (USERCAT)
/*
//
```

VSAM user catalog USERCAT, when we wish to define another data space on volume SCR001, we must again specify VSAM user catalog USERCAT. The largest possible data space would be the entire volume. A data space cannot exist on multiple volumes. However, if you look at the command parameters shown in Table 13.6, you will see that more than one volume can be named, which lets you define data spaces on several volumes with one command. The job in Figure 13.24 illustrates this. You will notice that the two volumes are named in one DD statement; you may not use concatenated DD statements to describe more than one volume. Also, the space requirement is given in record count and record size to let the system compute the number of tracks and/or cylinders. As a result of this job, data space on volumes SCR001 and SCR002 will be defined in VSAM user catalog USERCAT.

We will not discuss the CANDIDATE parameter, which reserves entire volumes for VSAM, because this is something that an application programmer would not normally handle.

DEFINE USERCATALOG Command

Defining of a VSAM user catalog is usually done by a system programmer. It may also be done by the lead programmer on a team and upon occasion by an application programmer, which is why it is included here. The discussion will not go into great depth, but will tell you enough to do the job.

TABLE 13.7

DEFINE USERCATALOG command parameters

Parameter	Abbreviation	UCAT	DATA	INDEX	Definition
BUFFERSPACE (size)	BUFSP	O	O	N/A	Gives minimum space for buffers. 3072 bytes is the default size.
CYLINDERS (prim sec)	CYL	R	O	O	Gives the amount of space to be reserved on the volume.
RECORDS (prim sec)	REC				
TRACKS (prim sec)	TRK				
DESTAGEWAIT	DSTGW	O	O	O	Applies to mass storage.
NODESTAGEWAIT	NDSTGW				
FILE (ddname)		R/O	N/A	N/A	Points to the DD statement that identifies the volume on which the user catalog is being defined.
MODEL (entryname/password catname/password)		O	N/A	N/A	Names an existing VSAM user catalog that is to be used as a sample.
OWNER (owner-id)		O	N/A	N/A	Identifies catalog owner.
RECOVERABLE	RVBL	O	O	O	RECOVERABLE creates a catalog recovery space on each volume owned by catalog. The default is NOTRECOVERABLE.
NOTRECOVERABLE	NRVBL				
NAME (entryname)		R	N/A	N/A	Names the catalog.
TO (date)		O	N/A	N/A	Specifies expiration date.
FOR (days)					
WRITECHECK	WCK	O	O	O	WRITECHECK causes the hardware to check that the data were written correctly.
NOWRITECHECK	NWCK				
VOLUME (volser)	VOL	R	N/A	N/A	Names the volume on which the user catalog is to be defined.

CREATING VSAM DATA SETS

Using separate VSAM user catalogs for each application is a good idea. It makes controlling the data sets easier, and since the catalogs will be smaller, it results in faster execution times.

The general form of the command is

```
DEFINE USERCATALOG (parameters) -
       DATA (parameters) -
       INDEX (parameters) -
       CATALOG (mastercatname/password)
```

With all the abbreviations, it becomes

```
DEF UCAT (parameters) -
    DATA (parameters) -
    INDEX (parameters) -
    CAT (mastercatname/password)
```

The parameters, excluding those that apply to security, are defined in Table 13.7. Those that apply to security are the same as those of the DEFINE CLUSTER command and are shown in Table 13.5.

A user catalog, like a KSDS, consists of a data and an index component. If you examine Table 13.7, you will notice that none of the parameters are required for DATA or INDEX. Unless you have a reason to code them, they should not be coded.

FIGURE 13.25

Defining a user catalog

```
//JCLQB280 JOB ,'J. C. LEWIS',
//           REGION=300K
//DEFUCAT   EXEC PGM=IDCAMS
//SYSPRINT DD SYSOUT=A
//DD1      DD UNIT=SYSDA,
//            DISP=OLD,
//            VOL=SER=SCR001
//SYSIN    DD *
 DEFINE USERCATALOG (NAME (NEWUCAT) -
                     FILE (DD1) -
                     CYL (4 1) -
                     VOLUMES (SCR001) )
/*
//
```

The catalog entry shows that the user catalog is cataloged in the master catalog. You need only specify this parameter if a password is required.

The job shown in Figure 13.25 will result in the creation of a VSAM user catalog on volume SCR001. The catalog will be given a primary allocation of 4 cylinders.

SECONDARY KEYS

Unlike ISAM, VSAM permits more than one field in a record to be treated as a key. Why would you want to do this? As an example, let us examine typical school problems. While it is desirable to maximize the use of classrooms, no more than one class may use a room at any one time. In addition, the administration usually wants to know how many courses a particular instructor is teaching. A typical master course record might contain a unique course number, a course name, the days and time of meeting, the room number, the instructor's name, and the number of students registered.

The course number would be used as the prime key. However, the administration might want to access this data set by room number to determine which courses use that room. To do this, the programmer would make room number an alternate key. The administration might also want to access this data set by the instructor's name to determine which courses each instructor is teaching. To do this, the programmer would make the instructor's name an additional alternate key.

Maintaining secondary keys is expensive in both CPU time and DASD space. Consequently, you must weigh these maintenance costs against the cost of obtaining the data in another way.

DEFINE ALTERNATEINDEX Command

To create a secondary key for either a KSDS or an ESDS, you must first create and load the base cluster. This includes defining the space if the cluster is not unique, defining the cluster, and loading data. Once you have your base cluster, you may issue the command to define the alternate index. This command is in the form

```
DEFINE ALTERNATEINDEX (parameters) -
      DATA (parameters) -
      INDEX (parameters) -
      CATALOG (parameters)
```

SECONDARY KEYS

With all legal abbreviations, this command has the form

```
DEF AIX (parameters) -
    DATA (parameters) -
    INDEX (parameters) -
    CAT (parameters)
```

If you refer back to the DEFINE CLUSTER command, you will notice that the only difference is that ALTERNATEINDEX replaces the word CLUSTER in the command. In fact, the parameters shown in Tables 13.4 and 13.5 also apply to this command with minor exceptions.

Figure 13.26 shows how to create an alternate index using the instructor's name as a secondary key. The NAME, KEYS, and VOLUMES parameters have the same meanings they have in the DEFINE CLUSTER command. In this example coding of the KEYS parameter is based on the assumption that the instructor's name starts at byte 38 and is 15 bytes long. The RECORDSIZE parameter is not required. If it is not coded, the default values of an average size of 4086 bytes and a maximum size of 32,600 bytes are used. The use of these default values is recommended, since the record size depends on the number of records that have the same value for the alternate key, which is difficult to estimate.

FIGURE 13.26

Defining an alternate index

```
//JCLQB290 JOB ,'J. C. LEWIS',
//            REGION=300K
//STEPAIX   EXEC PGM=IDCAMS
//STEPCAT   DD DSN=USERCAT,
//             DISP=SHR
//SYSPRINT DD SYSOUT=A
//SYSIN    DD *
 DEFINE ALTERNATEINDEX (NAME (VSAM.QB.JCL.NAMEINDX) -
                         RELATE (VSAM.QB.JCL.CLASMSTR) -
                         RECORDS (1000 100) -
                         KEYS (15 37) -
                         VOLUMES (SCR001) -
                         FREESPACE (20 10) -
                         NONUNIQUEKEY -
                         UNIQUE -
                         UPGRADE )
/*
//
```

Three new parameters that apply to the alternate index are shown in Figure 13.26. The RELATE parameter is required; the base cluster to which this alternate index applies is named in it. In Figure 13.26, NAMEINDX is related to a previously defined base cluster named CLASMSTR. UNIQUEKEY or NONUNIQUEKEY indicates whether or not more than one record may have the same alternate key. You recall that for a KSDS the prime key must be unique, while for an ESDS there is no prime key. The default value is NON-UNIQUEKEY. In Figure 13.26, NONUNIQUEKEY is coded because each instructor usually teaches several courses. If an alternate index is created based on room number, NONUNIQUEKEY should again be specified because several classes use the same room. On the other hand, if room number were combined with day and time of meeting for use as an alternate key, UNIQUEKEY would be coded because only one class may use a class room at a particular time. The third parameter, UPGRADE or NOUPGRADE, specifies whether or not the alternate index is to be updated when the base cluster is updated. The default value is UPGRADE.

As in the case of defining the user catalog, do not supply parameters separately for the data and index components. Again, supply only required information and allow the system to use default values whenever possible. In Figure 13.26, NONUNIQUEKEY or UPGRADE did not have to be coded, since these are the default values. They are coded to show you how to do it.

BLDINDEX Command

The secondary index cannot be built until there is at least one record in the base cluster. If the alternate index has been defined specifying the UPGRADE parameter, the alternate index will probably be modified every time a record is added, changed, or deleted in the base cluster. The alternate index does not have to be modified, for reasons we will discuss later.

The parameters of the BLDINDEX command are shown in Table 13.8. Just looking at the table may prove a little confusing. Let us stop a minute and talk about the form of the alternate index. Earlier we said that the alternate index, like a KSDS, consists of an index and a data part. The index part is obviously like the index part of a KSDS, as illustrated in Figure 13.7, but what information is in the data part? That depends on whether the base cluster is a KSDS or an ESDS. If it is an ESDS, the data part contains the secondary key and the RBA of the record in the base cluster that contains the secondary key. For a KSDS the data part contains the secondary key and the prime key of the record in the base cluster that contains the secondary key. Thus accessing a record using a secondary key requires accessing the

TABLE 13.8

BLDINDEX command parameters

Parameter	Abbreviation	Definition
INFILE (ddname/password) INDATASET (entryname/password) *	IFILE IDS	INFILE names the DD statement that points to the base cluster. INDATASET may be used instead of INFILE. INDATASET names the base cluster.
OUTFILE (ddname/password) OUTDATASET (entryname/password) *	OFILE ODS	OUTFILE names the DD statement that points to the alternate index or path. OUTDATASET actually names the alternate index or path.
CATALOG (catname/password)	CAT	CATALOG names the VSAM catalog in which the workfiles used in building the index are defined.
EXTERNALSORT INTERNALSORT	ESORT ISORT	Determines if the sort needed in building the index is internal or external. INTERNALSORT is the default. If EXTERNALSORT is specified, workfiles are required.
WORKFILES (ddname ddname)	WFILE	IDCUT1 and IDCUT2 are the default ddnames used by the external sort.

*For MVS systems only.

alternate index first. The record in the alternate index supplies the RBA for an ESDS or the prime key for a KSDS, which is then used to access the base cluster.

If the secondary key is nonunique and the base cluster is an ESDS, the data part of the alternate index contains the secondary key and the RBAs of all the records in the base cluster that contain the secondary key. If the base cluster is a KSDS, the data part of the alternate index contains the secondary key and the prime keys of all the records in the base cluster that contain the secondary key.

Now that we have an understanding of how the alternate index is used, let us consider how it would be built. The base cluster is read and alternate index records containing the secondary key and either the prime key or the RBA are created. In these alternate index records the secondary keys will usually not be in sequence. As a result, the alternate index records must be sorted into the proper order. This sort may be performed internally if there is sufficient virtual storage, or externally if there is not. You may specifically request that an external sort be done, although an internal sort is faster.

Let us now look at Figure 13.27, which illustrates a job used to build the alternate index that was defined in Figure 13.26. The first DD statement refers to the alternate index. For simplicity the ddname of AIX is used, but any valid name may be used. The second DD statement refers to the base cluster. The third and fourth DD statements are the workfiles that IDCAMS will use if there is insufficient virtual storage for an internal sort. Since the WORKFILES parameter is not coded in the BLDINDEX command, the ddnames IDCUT1 and IDCUT2 had to be used. Had the WORKFILES parameter been coded, any valid ddnames could have been used. The parameters for the workfiles DD statements must be coded as shown. Although DISP for these workfiles is

FIGURE 13.27

Building an alternate index

```
//JCLQB300  JOB ,'J. C. LEWIS',
//                REGION=300K
//STEPBLD   EXEC PGM=IDCAMS
//AIX       DD DSN=VSAM.QB.JCL.NAMEINDX,
//                DISP=OLD
//BASE      DD DSN=VSAM.QB.JCL.CLASMSTR,
//                DISP=OLD
//IDCUT1    DD DSN=VSAM.QB.JCL.WORKONE,
//                DISP=OLD,
//                UNIT=SYSDA,
//                VOL=SER=SCR001,
//                AMP=AMORG
//IDCUT2    DD DSN=VSAM.QB.JCL.WORKTWO,
//                DISP=OLD,
//                UNIT=SYSDA,
//                VOL=SER=SCR001,
//                AMP=AMORG
//SYSPRINT  DD SYSOUT=A
//SYSIN     DD *
  BLDINDEX  INFILE (BASE) -
            OUTFILE (AIX) -
            CATALOG (USERCAT)
/*
//
```

specified as OLD, they are defined by BLDINDEX while the job is executing and deleted when the sort is finished. Neither EXTERNALSORT or INTERNALSORT is specified in the command; consequently, the default value of INTERNALSORT is used.

Once the BLDINDEX (abbreviated as BIX) command has been successfully executed, the secondary index exists. However, one more step must be performed before the secondary index can be used.

DEFINE PATH Command

The AIX DD statement in Figure 13.27 does not access the base cluster named CLASMSTR via the alternate index, but rather accesses the alternate index itself as if it were a VSAM KSDS. Accessing the base cluster via an alternate index requires defining a path from the alternate index to the base cluster. The form of this command is

```
DEFINE PATH (parameters) -
       CATALOG (catname/password)
```

The parameters used in the command are defined in Table 13.9; the parameters related to security are defined in Table 13.5.

An example of defining a path is shown in Figure 13.28. The JCL is virtually the same as that shown in Figure 13.26, where the alternate index was defined. In the DEFINE PATH statement the two required parameters are NAME and PATHENTRY. The NAME parameter supplies the name for the path. The PATHENTRY parameter names the alternate index this path refers to. Notice that the name of the base cluster does not have to be supplied.

In the example in Figure 13.28, NOUPDATE is coded, otherwise the default of UPDATE would be used. This parameter overrides the UPGRADE parameter in the definition of any other alternate index. Thus if the base cluster CLASMSTR has other alternate indexes in addition to NAMEINDX, those other alternate indexes will not be updated when a change is made using the path NAMEPATH. A record added via path NAMEPATH will not be known about if the data set is accessed via a different path. Why would anyone let this happen? Usually you do not want your indexes to be out of synchronization, but there are times when it may be acceptable. If UPDATE is specified for a path, all alternate indexes with UPGRADE specified must be opened and available when that path is opened. If your program is only reading the data set, why waste resources by having all the alternate indexes available when they will not be used? A second path for which UPDATE is specified could be defined to be used when the data set will actually be changed.

TABLE 13.9

DEFINE PATH command parameters

Parameter	Abbreviation	Definition
NAME (entryname)		Supplies the path name. This name appears on the DD statement when the alternate index is used.
PATHENTRY (entryname/password)	PENT	Supplies the alternate index name. Under special conditions, a cluster name may be given.
FILE (ddname)		Supplies the ddname of the DD statement that points to the volume used for recovery purposes.
MODEL (entryname/password catname/password)		Supplies the name of an existing path to be used as a model.
OWNER (owner-id)		Identifies the owner of the path.
TO (date) FOR (days)		Specifies expiration date.
UPDATE NOUPDATE	UPD NUPD	UPDATE, the default, indicates that the other alternate indexes will be updated when this path is processed.

FIGURE 13.28

Defining a path

```
//JCLQB310 JOB ,'J. C. LEWIS',
//          REGION=300K
//STEPATH   EXEC PGM=IDCAMS
//STEPCAT   DD DSN=USERCAT,
//             DISP=SHR
//SYSPRINT DD SYSOUT=A
//SYSIN     DD *
 DEFINE PATH (NAME (VSAM.QB.JCL.NAMEPATH) -
             PATHENTRY (VSAM.QB.JCL.NAMEINDX) -
             NOUPDATE )
/*
//
```

FIGURE 13.29

Printing using a path

```
//JCLQB320 JOB ,'J. C. LEWIS',
//           REGION=300K
//PRINT3   EXEC PGM=IDCAMS
//STEPCAT  DD DSN=USERCAT,
//           DISP=SHR
//SYSPRINT DD SYSOUT=A
//PRINT    DD DSN=VSAM.QB.JCL.NAMEPATH,
//           DISP=OLD
//SYSIN    DD *
 PRINT INFILE (PRINT)
/*
//
```

If you want to access a base cluster via an alternate index, it is the path's data set name that is coded on the DD statement. This may surprise you, so let us look at an illustration. Suppose we want to print the base cluster CLASMASTR in alphabetical order by instructor's name. This can be done by accessing CLASMSTR via the alternate index NAMEINDX. In Figure 13.29, the data set name of the path NAMEPATH is coded on the PRINT DD statement.

In Table 13.9, the definition indicates that the PATHENTRY parameter may name a base cluster instead of an alternate index. This is one way to supply an alias for a VSAM data set. In addition, the security specified for the path may differ from that of the base cluster. Thus a path known to an entire group could permit read-only access, while the base cluster known only to a few would permit update access as well.

Secondary Key Summary

Using a secondary key for your VSAM data set requires that an alternate index and path be defined and the index then be built. The index cannot be built until at least one record is loaded into the base cluster.

Secondary keys may be used with KSDS and ESDS, but not with RRDS.

DELETE COMMAND

Once we no longer are using a cluster, user catalog, alternate index, or other VSAM entity, we wish to get rid of it. This is accomplished with the DELETE command.

TABLE 13.10

DELETE command parameters

Parameter	Abbreviation	Definition
(entryname/password...) what is		See Table 13.11.
ERASE	ERAS	ERASE means that binary zeros will be
NOERASE	NERAS	written over deleted data. NOERASE is the default.
FILE (ddname)		Points to the DD statement that names either what is being deleted or the volume that contains what is being deleted.
FORCE	FRC	FORCE enables, for example, the deletion of
NOFORCE	NFRC	a VSAM user catalog that is not empty. NOFORCE is the default.
PURGE	PRG	PURGE allows an entry to be deleted even if
NOPURGE	NPRG	the retention period has not expired. NOPURGE is the default.
CATALOG (catname/password)	CAT	Names the catalog that contains the entries to be deleted.

The parameters used with this command are shown in Table 13.10. Table 13.11 is referenced by the "what is" line in Table 13.10. "What is" tells what may be deleted with the DELETE command. The items in Table 13.11 marked with an asterisk are the elements we will discuss in this chapter. You already know what a cluster and a user catalog are, and we will discuss the others later.

The first parameter, entryname/password, is a positional parameter and must be named first. entryname is the name of what you want deleted. More than one entry may be deleted at a time; for example, you could code

```
DELETE (VSAMCL1 VSAMCL2) ...
```

Notice that when there is more than one entry, the entries must be enclosed

DELETE COMMAND

TABLE 13.11

What may be deleted

"What is"	Abbreviation
ALIAS	
ALTERNATEINDEX*	AIX
CLUSTER*	CL
GENERATIONDATAGROUP	GDG
NONVSAM	NVSAM
PAGESPACE	PGSPC
PATH*	
SPACE*	SPC
USERCATALOG*	UCAT

*Discussed in this chapter.

in parentheses. Although a password was not used here, one may be used for security. We do not have the space to give the subject of security the attention it deserves; however, where passwords may be used is indicated in Table 13.10.

The job stream in Figure 13.30 deletes a VSAM data set; let us look at it in more detail. Two VSAM user catalogs are made available with the JOBCAT DD statement (since this is a one-step job, a STEPCAT DD statement would have produced the same results). The DD1 DD statement points to the entry to be deleted. In the DELETE command, VSAM.QB.JCL.DATASET is again named as the entry to be deleted. CLUSTER indicates that VSAM.QB.JCL.DATASET is a cluster, as are all VSAM data sets. ERASE means that binary zeros are to be written over the data so that if the disk pack were dumped, the data would not be there. FILE (DD1) points to the DD statement DD1. PURGE means that VSAM.QB.JCL.DATASET is to be deleted even if the expiration date has not arrived. CATALOG (UCAT02) says that the entry for DATASET is in the VSAM user catalog UCAT02, and only that catalog will be searched. If this parameter had been left out, both USERCAT and UCAT02 would have been searched. When a cluster is deleted, related alternate indexes and paths are also deleted.

The DD1 DD statement is somewhat special. Because ERASE is coded as part of the DELETE command, this DD statement points to DATASET, which is

FIGURE 13.30

Deleting a VSAM cluster

```
//JCLQB120 JOB ,'J. C. LEWIS',
//             REGION=300K
//JOBCAT    DD DSN=USERCAT,
//             DISP=SHR
//          DD DSN=UCAT02,
//             DISP=SHR
//DELETE1   EXEC PGM=IDCAMS
//SYSPRINT DD SYSOUT=A
//DD1       DD DSN=VSAM.QB.JCL.DATASET,
//             DISP=OLD
//SYSIN     DD *
  DELETE VSAM.QB.JCL.DATASET -
         CLUSTER -
         ERASE -
         FILE (DD1) -
         PURGE -
         CATALOG (UCAT02)
/*
//
```

the entry to be deleted and erased. If ERASE had not been coded, the DD1 DD
statement would point to the volume that DATASET is on, as in

```
//DD1       DD UNIT=SYSDA,
//             VOL=SER=SCR001,
//             DISP=OLD
```

FIGURE 13.31

Deleting a user catalog

```
//JCLQB130 JOB ,'J. C. LEWIS',
//             REGION=300K
//DELETE2   EXEC PGM=IDCAMS
//*
//*           DELETE USER CATALOG
//*
//SYSPRINT DD SYSOUT=A
//SYSIN     DD *
  DELETE UCAT02 -
         USERCATALOG -
         FORCE -
         PURGE
/*
//
```

VERIFY COMMAND

In MVS systems, the FILE parameter and its associated DD statement are not required.

The job in Figure 13.31 deletes a VSAM user catalog named UCAT02 even if the expiration date has not arrived and even if the catalog is not empty.

VERIFY COMMAND

When a job abends or is canceled or the system fails, the VSAM data sets are not properly closed. This means that the end-of-data in the data set does not agree with what the catalog says is the end-of-data. A VSAM data set in this condition cannot be used. The VERIFY command is used to correct this problem.

Table 13.12 illustrates the parameters used with the VERIFY command.

TABLE 13.12

VERIFY command parameters

Parameter	Abbr	Definition
FILE (ddname/password)		Points to the DD statement that names the object to be corrected.
DATASET (entryname/password)	DS	Names the object to be corrected.

FIGURE 13.32

Verifying a data set

```
//JCLQB350 JOB ,'J. C. LEWIS',
//            REGION=300K
//VERIFY   EXEC PGM=IDCAMS
//STEPCAT  DD DSN=USERCAT,
//            DISP=SHR
//SYSPRINT DD SYSOUT=A
//DD1      DD DSN=VSAM.QB.JCL.PLYKSDS1,
//            DISP=OLD
//SYSIN    DD *
 VERIFY FILE (DD1)
/*
//
```

To use the DATASET parameter, your system must have the ability to dynamically allocate the data set. Since not all systems have this ability, the parameter FILE is used in the example shown in Figure 13.32. You will note that OLD is used for the disposition on the DD statement of the data set to be corrected, to ensure that no one else attempts to use it while it is being corrected.

LISTCAT COMMAND

From time to time you might want to know what is in the master or user catalogs. For instance, after you run a job defining some entity, such as a cluster or an alternate index, you might like to see if the entity is listed in the catalog. Or you might define some entity and then forget the name you gave it. You can see what is in a catalog by using the LISTCAT command.

As you will learn in Chapter 14, non-VSAM catalogs may be listed using the LISTCTLG command of the utility program IEHLIST. By changing parameters in the LISTCTLG command, you can modify the listing. Similarly, by changing parameters in the LISTCAT command of IDCAMS, you can make modifications to the listing which are more extensive than those supplied with the IEHLIST utility program. The LISTCAT parameters may be found in Table 13.13. We will discuss those which you as an application programmer will probably need.

Figure 13.33 illustrates a LISTCAT job. You will note that the LISTCAT command is abbreviated LISTC and that no parameters are specified. Since no catalog is named in the job, the master catalog will be listed. The listing will include only the names of the entities in the master catalog. If more information about the entities had been required, any of the following could have been coded:

```
LISTC ALLOC
```

or

```
LISTC HISTORY
```

or

```
LISTC VOLUME
```

TABLE 13.13

LISTCAT command parameters

Parameter	Abbreviation	Description
CATALOG (catname/ password)	CAT	Specifies which catalog is to have its contents listed.
ALIAS		Any or all of these parameters may be specified to limit the scope of the LISTCAT command. If none of these parameters are specified, the listing includes everything in the catalog.
ALTERNATEINDEX	AIX	
CLUSTER	CL	
GENERATIONDATAGROUP	GDG	
DATA		
INDEX	IX	
NONVSAM	NVSAM	
PAGESPACE	PGSPC	
PATH		
SPACE	SPC	
USERCATALOG	UCAT	
ALL		These parameters, which are mutually exclusive, indicate the information to be provided for each entry. The default is NAME.
HISTORY	HIST	
ALLOCATION	ALLOC	
NAME		
VOLUME	VOL	
CREATION (days)	CREAT	Specifies that the listing is to include only those entries created on or before the number of days in this parameter.
ENTRIES (entryname/ password...)	ENT	Names the entries to be included in the listing.
LEVEL (level)	LVL	Is similar to the NODE parameter of the LISTCTLG command of IEHLIST. An asterisk can be used in the middle, e.g., LEVEL (SYS1.*.OUT).
EXPIRATION (days)	EXPIR	Specifies that the listing is only to include those entries due to expire the specified number of days from now or earlier.
NOTUSABLE	NUS	Indicates that the listing is only to include those entries marked not usable.
OUTFILE (ddname)	OFILE	Specifies a data set other than the SYSPRINT data set for output.

FIGURE 13.33

Listing a catalog

```
//JCLQB330 JOB ,'J. C. LEWIS',
//             REGION=300K
//STEPLCAT EXEC PGM=IDCAMS
//SYSPRINT DD SYSOUT=A
//SYSIN    DD *
 LISTC
/*
//
```

If all possible information had been desired,

```
LISTC ALL
```

could have been coded, but be warned, ALL gives you a lot of output.

In Figure 13.33, the LISTCAT job is run as a separate job rather than as a step in a larger job. The reason for this is that in some situations the catalog may not be updated until a job ends. If you define an entity in one step and then execute a LISTCAT in a later step in the same job, you cannot be sure the output you get represents the true state of the catalog.

If we want information about a catalog other than the master catalog, there are three alternatives. A JOBCAT DD statement can be coded naming the desired catalog. Or a STEPCAT DD statement can be coded. Finally, the desired catalog can be named in the LISTCAT command as follows:

```
LISTC CATALOG (UCAT)
```

If we are only interested in the clusters in our user catalog, UCAT, the LISTCAT command is coded as

```
LISTC CATALOG (UCAT) -
      CLUSTER
```

The LEVEL parameter is useful if a group of people share a common user catalog and you are only interested in your clusters. As you recall, the convention at the CUNY computer center requires that all my VSAM data sets start with the qualifiers VSAM.QB.JCL. Consequently, to list my clusters in the common user catalog, I would code

COMMAND EXECUTION CONTROL

```
LISTC CATALOG (UCAT) -
      CLUSTER -
      LEVEL (VSAM.QB.JCL)
```

If all the students in a particular class at Queensborough Community College were given an assignment that involved creating a VSAM data set whose last qualifier was TRANS, the LISTCAT command would be coded as follows to determine which data sets were created:

```
LISTC CATALOG (UCAT) -
      CLUSTER -
      LEVEL (VSAM.QB.*.TRANS)
```

Notice how an asterisk is coded in place of the user's initials required by the convention.

COMMAND EXECUTION CONTROL

Frequently you will want to perform a series of IDCAMS commands. However, you will not want the second command to be executed unless the first has executed successfully, and the third should not be executed unless the second was successful. IDCAMS provides a convenient way to control execution of a series of commands.

Condition Codes

After each IDCAMS command is executed, a condition code is set which is similar to the condition code set by the other utilities we have studied. A condition code of 0 means the command was successfully executed; a 4 means that a problem was encountered, but that it is probably safe to continue; an 8 means that the command was completed, but not with the desired results; a 12 indicates that the command could not be executed at all, but that processing will resume with the next command in the input stream; a 16 shows that an error of such severity occurred that this invocation of IDCAMS must terminate.

These condition codes may be tested with the COND parameter in the JOB or EXEC statement to determine whether or not processing should continue. However, IDCAMS allows you to check the condition code of each command as it is performed within a step. Therefore several IDCAMS commands may be executed in one jobstep, instead of in several jobsteps. This is an advantage because there is a certain amount of overhead involved in initializing each step.

IF-THEN-ELSE Command

Those of you who are familiar with the IF statement of PL/I will find the rest of this section trivial. The rest of you will find it quite simple.

Figure 13.34 contains a simple but realistic example of command execu-

FIGURE 13.34

Testing condition codes

```
//JCLQB340 JOB ,'J. C. LEWIS',
//            REGION=300K
//STEPDEF   EXEC PGM=IDCAMS
//STEPCAT   DD DSN=USERCAT,
//            DISP=SHR
//DD1       DD UNIT=SYSDA,
//            DISP=OLD,
//            VOL=SER=SCR001
//SYSPRINT DD SYSOUT=A
//SYSIN     DD *
        DEFINE SPACE (CYL (10) -
                      VOLUMES (SCR001) -
                      FILE (DD1) ) -
               CATALOG (USERCAT)
    IF LASTCC = 0 -
       THEN -
        DEFINE CLUSTER (NAME (VSAM.QB.JCL.KSDS) -
                        RECORDS (1000 100) -
                        FREESPACE (20 30) -
                        INDEXED -
                        KEYS (10 5) -
                        RECORDSIZE (100 320) -
                        VOLUMES (SCR001) ) -
               DATA (NAME (VSAM.QB.JCL.KSDSDAT) ) -
               INDEX (NAME (VSAM.QB.JCL.KSDSIND) )
    /*
    //
```

COMMAND EXECUTION CONTROL

tion control. First space is defined just as it was in Figure 13.23. Then the command

```
IF LASTCC = 0 -
```

tests the return code resulting from the execution of the DEFINE SPACE command. If the return code is 0, the DEFINE CLUSTER command will be executed just as it was in Figure 13.17. If the return code were any other value, the DEFINE CLUSTER command would not be executed. Notice that the IF and THEN lines contain hyphens to indicate continuation.

Coding could have specified a command to be executed if the DEFINE SPACE had not had a zero return code; for example,

```
DEFINE SPACE ...
IF LASTCC = 0 -
    THEN -
        DEFINE CLUSTER...
    ELSE -
        DELETE SPACE...
```

In this example, if the return code of the DEFINE SPACE is 0, the cluster is defined; if not (ELSE), the space is deleted. (There are conditions under which the space would be defined and a nonzero return code produced.)

If instead of defining a single cluster, you wished to define several, you would code

```
DEFINE SPACE...
IF LASTCC = 0 -
    THEN DO
        DEFINE CLUSTER...
        DEFINE CLUSTER...
            .
            .
            .
        END
    ELSE -
        DELETE SPACE...
```

THEN DO indicates the start of the group of commands to be executed, and END shows the stopping point. Notice that the THEN DO line does not have a hyphen indicating continuation.

If you wished to define a user catalog, space, and several clusters, you might code the commands as

```
DEFINE USERCATALOG...
DEFINE SPACE...
IF MAXCC = 0 -
   THEN DO
        DEFINE CLUSTER...
        DEFINE CLUSTER...
          .
          .
          .
        END
```

In this example, the last return code is not tested as in the previous examples, but the maximum return code MAXCC is tested. MAXCC refers to the maximum return code that has been established by any previous command. If the return code for DEFINE SPACE or DEFINE USERCATALOG had been greater than 0, the DEFINE CLUSTER commands would not have been executed. To undo those commands,

```
DEFINE USERCATALOG...
DEFINE SPACE...
IF MAXCC = 0 -
   THEN DO
        DEFINE CLUSTER...
        DEFINE CLUSTER...
          .
          .
          .
        END
   ELSE DO
        DELETE USERCATALOG...
        DELETE SPACE...
        END
```

might be coded.

Let us summarize the IF-THEN-ELSE command sequence as follows:

VSAM AND HIGHER-LEVEL LANGUAGES

TABLE 13.14

IF-THEN-ELSE comparands

Comparand	Meaning
= or `EQ`	equal to
¬= or `NE`	not equal to
> or `GT`	greater than
< or `LT`	less than
>= or `GE`	greater than or equal to
<= or `LE`	less than or equal to

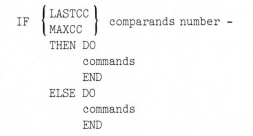

```
IF  { LASTCC }  comparands number -
    { MAXCC  }
       THEN DO
           commands
           END
       ELSE DO
           commands
           END
```

Legal comparands and their meanings are listed in Table 13.14.

These comparands are the same as the operators that may be coded with the `COND` parameter (see Table 4.4), except that for these comparands you may code the symbols as well as the two-letter abbreviation. `number` may be any value between 0 and 16.

While the general form of the command permits complex comparisons, you will find that most of the time you will test for 0 as in the examples earlier in this section.

VSAM AND HIGHER-LEVEL LANGUAGES

The purpose of this section is to give you sufficient background so that you can tie together your newly acquired JCL knowledge with your COBOL and PL/I knowledge.

VSAM and COBOL

We will discuss only KSDS, which is the most common type of VSAM data set processed by COBOL programs. Your COBOL program must have a SELECT statement for the VSAM data set. As an example, you could code

```
SELECT VSAM-DATA-FILE
    ASSIGN TO VSAMDD
    ORGANIZATION IS INDEXED
    ACCESS IS SEQUENTIAL
    RECORD KEY IS KEY-VALUE
    FILE STATUS IS VSAM-STATUS.
```

Since ACCESS IS SEQUENTIAL is the default, that clause is not required. The ddname on the DD statement that references this data set is VSAMDD. The record key, KEY-VALUE, must be defined as part of the VSAM data set's record. You might have

```
FD  VSAM-DATA-FILE
    .
    .
    .
01  VSAM-RECORD.
    05 KEY-VALUE          PIC...
```

The FILE STATUS field must be defined in WORKING-STORAGE, and its PICTURE should be XX. After every I/O operation on the data set, the system places in the FILE STATUS field a value that indicates the results of the operation. A value of 00 means that the operation was successful. A value of 02 can occur only when the data set is accessed via an alternate index, which we will discuss later. Other values indicate that the operation was unsuccessful. The values that may occur and their meanings are described in *IBM/VS COBOL for OS/VS* (GC26-3857).

To create a VSAM data set, use IDCAMS first to create the cluster. Then the records may be loaded into the data set by a COBOL program. The data set must be accessed sequentially and opened as OUTPUT, as, for example,

```
OPEN OUTPUT VSAM-DATA-FILE.
IF VSAM-STATUS NOT = '00'
    PERFORM BAD-OPEN-RTN.
```

VSAM AND HIGHER-LEVEL LANGUAGES

After every I/O operation the FILE STATUS field should be tested to ensure that the operation was successful.

The data set is created using a WRITE statement as in

```
WRITE VSAM-RECORD.
IF VSAM-STATUS NOT = '00'
    PERFORM BAD-WRITE-RTN.
```

Records must be written so that their keys are in sequential order. If you try to write a record whose key is not greater than the key of the previously written record, the record will not be written, and the FILE STATUS field will be set equal to 21.

To sequentially read a VSAM data set, you open it as INPUT and use the standard READ statement, as in the following:

```
READ VSAM-DATA-FILE
    AT END ...
```

Randomly accessing a VSAM data set requires that the ACCESS clause in the SELECT statement on page 472 be changed to ACCESS IS RANDOM. The rest of the SELECT statement may be used without change.

To randomly read a particular record, you must move the key of the desired record into the RECORD KEY field. For example, you might code

```
MOVE KEY-IN TO KEY-VALUE.
```

A READ statement, such as

```
READ VSAM-DATA-FILE.
IF VSAM-STATUS NOT = '00'
    PERFORM BAD-READ-RTN.
```

retrieves the record. If the record is not found, the FILE STATUS field will be set equal to 23.

VSAM data sets may be accessed dynamically by coding ACCESS IS DYNAMIC in the SELECT statement. When a data set is accessed dynamically, both sequential and random access are permitted. A typical sequence would be to randomly read a particular record and then to sequentially read the following records. The random read is done as shown above. The sequential read is done using the NEXT option in the READ statement, as in

```
READ VSAM-DATA-FILE NEXT
    AT END ...
```

VSAM data sets are usually updated randomly. The data set is opened as I-O. For example, you would code

```
OPEN I-O VSAM-DATA-FILE.
```

The records are read as discussed above.

After the record has been updated, it is placed back in the data set using a REWRITE statement, such as

```
REWRITE VSAM-RECORD.
```

Records are deleted using a DELETE statement, such as

```
DELETE VSAM-DATA-FILE.
```

The record deleted is the record whose key matches the value in the RECORD KEY field. If no record exists with that key value, the FILE STATUS field will be set equal to 23.

The WRITE statement is used to add a record. First the key of the record is moved to the RECORD KEY field, and then a WRITE statement is executed, as in

```
WRITE VSAM-DATA-FILE.
IF VSAM-STATUS NOT = '00'
    PERFORM BAD-WRITE-RTN.
```

If the data set already contains a record with a key equal to the value in the RECORD KEY field, the record is not added and the FILE STATUS field is set equal to 22.

ALTERNATE KEYS.   COBOL programs can access a VSAM data set via an alternate index. However, COBOL is not used to create the alternate index. In fact, the COBOL program that loads the base cluster should not refer to the alternate index. After the base cluster is loaded, IDCAMS is used to define the alternate index, build it, and define the path.

VSAM AND HIGHER-LEVEL LANGUAGES

The clause

```
ALTERNATE RECORD KEY IS ALT-KEY
WITH DUPLICATES
```

must be added to the SELECT statement. The WITH DUPLICATES option means that there may be more than one record with the same alternate key value and is used only if that is the case. (The primary key must, as always, be unique.) ALT-KEY must be defined as part of the VSAM data set's record.

The SELECT statement provides only one ddname, yet you must have two DD statements: one for the base cluster and one for the path. The second ddname is constructed by concatenating the digit 1 to the first seven characters of the base cluster's ddname. Using the ddname VSAMDD given in the above SELECT statement, the two DD statements would be

```
//GO.VSAMDD  DD DSN=VSAM.BASE.CLUSTER,
//           DISP=OLD
//GO.VSAMDD1 DD DSN=VSAM.ALTINDX.PATH,
//           DISP=OLD
```

Suppose you want to read a data set sequentially based on the alternate key. Before you execute the READ statement, you must inform COBOL that you want the reading done based on the alternate key. One way to do this is to use the START statement. For example, you could code

```
MOVE ALT-KEY-IN TO ALT-KEY.
START VSAM-DATA-FILE KEY IS = ALT-KEY.
IF VSAM-STATUS NOT = '00'
    PERFORM BAD-START.
```

If the START is successful, the first READ will retrieve the record whose alternate key is equal to ALT-KEY-IN, and subsequent READs will retrieve succeeding records in alternate key order.

The following statements could be used to read the whole data set sequentially in alternate key order:

```
MOVE LOW-VALUES TO ALT-KEY.
START VSAM-DATA-FILE
    KEY IS NOT < ALT-KEY.
```

To randomly read a record based on its alternate key, you move the key of the desired record to the ALTERNATE KEY field. For example, you could code

```
MOVE ALT-KEY-IN TO ALT-KEY.
```

The READ statement must use the KEY option, for example,

```
READ VSAM-DATA-FILE
    KEY IS ALT-KEY.
```

If the record is not found, the FILE STATUS field will be set equal to 23. If the record is found, the FILE STATUS field will be set equal to either 00 or 02. Both values mean the record was found, but 02 means there is at least one more record in the data set whose alternate key is the same as the alternate key of the record just read. These additional records cannot be retrieved by a random read; they must be retrieved using a sequential read, such as

```
READ VSAM-DATA-FILE NEXT.
```

Since both random and sequential access are being used, ACCESS IS DYNAMIC must have been specified for the data set.

VSAM and PL/I

The DECLARE statement for a VSAM data set must include VSAM in the ENVIRONMENT parameter, that is,

```
DCL RECFLE FILE RECORD ENV (VSAM)...
```

There is no point to specifying any other information normally specified with the DCB parameter, since by definition all VSAM data sets are cataloged. If you do specify this information, it will be compared with data found in the VSAM catalog. If the data supplied by you are correct, there is no problem. However, if your information disagrees with the data found in the VSAM catalog, at best it will be ignored and at worst your program will abend. Consequently, no information beyond that required should be specified.

The performance or usage of the VSAM data set is affected by a few options you might wish to specify in the ENVIRONMENT parameter. These are BKWD, REUSE, GENKEY, SKIP, SIS, BUFSP(n), BUFNI(n), and BUFND(n). We cannot discuss these here, so you must refer either to your PL/I textbook or the manufacturer's manual for more detailed information.

In the following discussion, whatever is applied to a KSDS also applies to an alternate index. The difference is where the DD statement points. For a normal KSDS, the data set named by the DSN parameter is the KSDS. For an alternate index, the DSN refers to the path. The one exception is loading. A data set must be loaded via the base cluster.

When you are loading a VSAM data set, OUTPUT must be specified in the DECLARE statement, as in

```
DCL RECFLE FILE RECORD OUTPUT ENV (VSAM);
```

or named in the OPEN statement. If the data set is a KSDS, KEYED must also be coded. In writing the record,

```
WRITE FILE (RECFLE) FROM (OUTAREA);
```

would be coded for either an ESDS or RRDS. You might choose to code the KEYTO option. This means that the RBA of the record will be returned in the field named in the KEYTO option. Please remember that if you use this option when creating an RRDS, you must specify the KEYED parameter in the DECLARE statement.

When you are loading a KSDS, the KEYFROM option must be included in the WRITE statement, for example,

```
WRITE FILE (RECFLE) FROM (OUTAREA) KEYFROM (KEYFLD);
```

The records must be written in sequential order. The KEYFROM option may also be used in loading an RRDS, but if it is, you must specify the KEYED parameter in the DECLARE statement.

The job stream that loads the VSAM data set would include a DD statement such as

```
//RECFLE    DD DSN=VSAM.DATA,
              DISP=OLD
```

Please note that the ddname RECFLE ties back to the DECLARE statement in your PL/I program, and the DSN, VSAM.DATA, is the name you used in the DEFINE CLUSTER command. The same DD statement is used for ESDS, KSDS, or RRDS data sets.

Reading VSAM data sets requires that INPUT be included in either the DECLARE or OPEN statement. The DECLARE would be of the form

```
DCL RECFLE FILE RECORD INPUT ENV (VSAM);
```

Either of the following READ statements may be used to read the data set sequentially, starting with the first record in the data set:

```
READ FILE (RECFLE) INTO (INAREA);
```

or

```
READ FILE (RECFLE) SET (PTR);
```

depending on whether you are using the move mode or the locate mode. (The move mode actually moves the data into the area in your program named in the READ statement. The locate mode returns the address of the record which remains in the input buffer.) You might specify the KEYTO option in either form of the statement. For an ESDS, the RBA will be returned in the field named. For a KSDS, the named field will contain the key of the record just read.

If you want to read a particular record in a KSDS or in an ESDS that is accessible with a key via an alternate index, KEYED must be included in the DECLARE statement, for example,

```
DCL RECFLE FILE RECORD INPUT KEYED ENV (VSAM);
```

The READ statement must include the KEY option. Thus the READ statement could be coded as

```
READ FILE (RECFLE) INTO (INAREA) KEY (KEY_AREA);
```

or

```
READ FILE (RECFLE) SET (PTR) KEY (KEY_AREA);
```

VSAM AND HIGHER-LEVEL LANGUAGES

In either case, the field KEY_AREA must be set equal to the value of the key of the desired record. This is called random access.

You can read a particular record by specifying the value of the alternate key. If you do, you must include a DECLARE statement for the alternate index. The DECLARE statement could be similar to the one used for the base cluster, for example,

```
DCL ALTINDX FILE RECORD INPUT KEYED ENV (VSAM);
```

However, you must remember that the corresponding DD statement must reference the path, as in

```
//ALTINDX  DD DSN=VSAM.PATH,
//              DISP=SHR
```

Recall that alternate keys need not be unique. After reading a record using an alternate key, you can determine if there are additional records with the same key by testing the SAMEKEY built-in function. If the read was successful and there is an additional record with the same key, SAMEKEY (ALTINDX) is true; otherwise it is false.

If you wanted to read a VSAM data set accessible by a key sequentially starting with a particular record, the file declaration and first READ statement would be the same as for random access. Subsequent READ statements would not include the KEY option.

The DD statement used in reading differs from the one used in loading only in that you may specify a disposition of SHR. There is no reason not to permit multiple access of the data set during reading.

If you wish to update a VSAM data set, the file declaration must include the UPDATE option and, for KSDS and RRDS, the KEYED option. A typical DECLARE statement would be

```
DCL RECFLE FILE RECORD UPDATE KEYED ENV (VSAM);
```

Obviously, for ESDS the KEYED option need not be present.

Records may be changed by using the REWRITE statement. The principal restriction to keep in mind is that when you rewrite an ESDS record, the length must remain the same. You may code this statement in three ways:

```
REWRITE FILE (RECFLE);
```

or

```
REWRITE FILE (RECFLE) FROM (OUTAREA);
```

or

```
REWRITE FILE (RECFLE) FROM (OUTAREA) KEY (KEYAREA);
```

The first two examples presuppose that the record being changed was just read. In the first example the new record is taken from the input buffer. This statement presupposes that you read the record using locate mode and you made the changes to the record in the input buffer. The second example replaces the record read with the record to be found in the area named by the FROM option. In the above examples this area is OUTAREA. The third example differs from the first two in that the record to be changed need not have been read. The KEY option names the field that holds the key for a KSDS, the RBA for an ESDS, or the record number for an RRDS.

Records may be added randomly to a KSDS, but only to the end of an ESDS or RRDS. The DECLARE statement used here is the same as that used in record changing, and the WRITE statement is the same as that used in loading the data set. The DD statement should specify DISP=OLD to ensure that no one else tries to read the data set while you are in the process of changing it.

If you are updating or adding records to a data set with alternate indexes, it is critical that unique keys remain unique. If, for example, you are updating a KSDS via an alternate path, it is important that you do not change the base cluster key so that it is no longer unique.

There are certain error conditions that occur only with VSAM data sets. Your program should include ON-CONDITIONS for TRANSMIT and for KEY and, if you are processing the data set sequentially, for ENDFILE. The ONCODE built-in function will return a number that will indicate the nature of the problem. Refer to your PL/I textbook or the IBM manual for detailed information.

EXERCISES

1. Name the three types of VSAM data sets.

2. What are the components of each of the three VSAM data sets?

3. When the components are put together, what are they called?

EXERCISES

4. What is the unit of information brought into storage from a DASD as a result of an I/O operation?

5. What are the two parts of an index? Are there always two parts?

6. What information does each "record" of the index contain?

7. How does the system learn the length of a record in a VSAM data set?

8. With a keyed data set, how does the system know if there is sufficient space in a CI for a record to be added?

9. What happens if there is not enough space in the CI for the record?

10. In an ISAM data set, when a user deletes a record, it is only marked for deletion and remains in the data set until the data set is reorganized. What happens with a VSAM data set?

11. How does the system know that a DD statement refers to a VSAM data set?

12. Which of the following data sets definitely refer to a VSAM data set, which might refer to a VSAM data set, and which do not?

```
//DD1      DD DSN=DATASET1,
//            DISP=SHR,
//            DCB=DSORG=IS
//DD2      DD DSN=DATASET2,
//            DISP=OLD,
//            UNIT=SYSDA,
//            VOL=SER=DISK01,
//            AMP='AMORG'
//DD3      DD DSN=DATASET3,
//            DISP=OLD
//DD4      DD DSN=DATASET4,
//            DISP=SHR,
//            UNIT=SYSDA,
//            VOL=SER=VOL001
```

13. Write the command to reserve 10 cylinders on disk pack SCR001 in user catalog UCAT.

14. Code the command to define a KSDS cluster in the space defined in Exercise 13. The data to go into the data set comprise an assembler language program of approximately 1000 lines. Use the number field in columns 73 through 80 as the key.

15. Write the command to actually load the data in the VSAM data set.

16. Write the command to print, in character, the data set just loaded.

17. Write the command to list the contents of the user catalog MYCAT.

18. Write the command to delete the user catalog UCAT and everything that belongs to it.

19. Write the command to create a secondary index, using the operand in your assembler language program as the key. Assume the operand is in positions 10 through 15 in the record.

PROGRAMMING ASSIGNMENTS

1. If you are allowed to create a user catalog, execute a job that will create a user catalog.

2. If you are allowed to allocate space, execute a job that will allocate space on a volume.

3. Execute a job that will define a KSDS cluster. The cluster should use the space you allocated in Programming Assignment 2. If you are not allowed to allocate space, define the cluster as unique. The cluster should be cataloged in the user catalog you created in Programming Assignment 1. If you are not allowed to create a user catalog, catalog the cluster in the catalog your advisor tells you to use. The record size and key length and location should be compatible with the sequential data set you created in Chapter 3.

4. Execute a job that will load the KSDS you created in Programming Assignment 3 with data contained in the sequential data set you created in Chapter 3. In the same job print the data set.

5. Execute a job that will define an alternate index for the KSDS cluster you created in Programming Assignment 3. Choose any field you want as the ALTERNATE KEY field. (If you used the data in Appendix D to load the base cluster, you can use the student major field, bytes 40 and 41, as the ALTERNATE KEY field.) Execute a second job that will build the alternate index and define a path. Finally, execute a job that will print the base cluster in alternate key order.

6. Execute a job that will list the names of the clusters and spaces in the user catalog you used.

7. After Programming Assignments 1 through 5 are complete, execute a job that will delete the cluster, the alternate index, the path, the data space, and the user catalog.

SUMMARY

In this chapter you have learned

*   the three types of VSAM data sets: KSDS, ESDS, and RRDS

*   how VSAM data sets are organized into control intervals and control areas

*   how to use the utility program IDCAMS to

    create a VSAM cluster, an alternate index, a path, and a user catalog

    allocate VSAM space using the DEFINE command

    load a VSAM data set with data using the REPRO command

    build an alternate index using the BLDINDEX command

    print a VSAM data set using the PRINT command

    list the entries in a catalog using the LISTCAT command

    fix, using the VERIFY command, a VSAM data set that was improperly closed

    delete a VSAM cluster, an alternate index, a path, a user catalog, and VSAM space using the DELETE command

DATA SET UTILITIES

The first CREATE statement takes records from the SEQIN1 data set and modifies them as specified by the NAME parameter. The NAME parameter causes FLD1, which is defined in the first FD statement as a 6-byte field containing UVWXYZ, to overwrite the original data in the SEQIN1 record, starting at byte 10. Since the second CREATE statement does not contain a NAME parameter, records from SEQIN2 are written to the output data set without being modified.

In the above example, 10 records will be taken from the SEQIN1 data set and then 5 from the SEQIN2 data based upon the first two CREATE statements. These two CREATE statements will be executed 6 times. Our output to this point will contain 90 records, 60 from the SEQIN1 data set and 30 from the SEQIN2 data set. The last record will come from the data specified in the FD statement with the name FLD2. You will note that the third CREATE control statement is not repeated because the CREATE parameter in the REPEAT control statement specifies 2 and not 3.

The last and easiest control statement is the END statement, which terminates a group of control statements. It is illustrated in Figure 14.4.

Now that you have an understanding of how this utility program works, you will find it very useful.

IEBEDIT

The purpose of this utility program is to create a data set containing JCL selected from an input data set in accordance with instructions supplied by the control statement or statements. You probably will not find much use for this utility program, but you should be aware of its existence and what it does.

Figure 14.5 illustrates the use of IEBEDIT. The SYSUT1 DD statement points to the input data set. In the example, the input data set is on tape; it could have been on disk or card as well. If it had been on cards, SYSUT1 would have been coded as

```
//SYSUT1    DD DATA
```

since the input is JCL. The input cannot contain a /* statement because this would be interpreted as the end of the input data stream. If you want a /* statement, code two periods and an asterisk in columns 1, 2, and 3. When IEBEDIT finds this configuration, it produces a /* statement in the output.

CHAPTER 14 / UTILITIES

FIGURE 14.5

Sample IEBEDIT job

```
//JCLQB915 JOB ,'MENELAOS'
//STEPSLCT EXEC PGM=IEBEDIT
//SYSPRINT DD SYSOUT=A
//SYSUT1   DD DSN=TAPEJCL,
//             DISP=OLD
//SYSUT2   DD SYSOUT=B,
//             DCB=(RECFM=F,LRECL=80,BLKSIZE=80)
//SYSIN    DD *
 EDIT START=JOBTEST,TYPE=POSITION,STEPNAME=STEP3,NOPRINT
/*
//
```

The SYSUT2 DD statement defines the output data set. In the example in Figure 14.5, cards are used. The control statements are defined by the SYSIN DD statement.

IEBEDIT has only one control statement. All possible parameters are illustrated in Figure 14.5. The START parameter indicates the jobname, which is necessary if there is more than one job in the input data set. If there is only one job, this parameter is not required. The TYPE and STEPNAME parameters work together. When TYPE=POSITION is coded as in the example, the STEPNAME parameter identifies the first step to be selected from the named job in the SYSUT1 data set. The SYSUT1 data set will start with the step whose name is STEP3 in the job whose name is JOBTEST; any steps preceding STEP3 will be bypassed. STEP3 will be the first step in the output, and all the succeeding steps in job JOBTEST will be included in the output.

TYPE=POSITION is the default, so it was not necessary to explicitly code it. If TYPE=INCLUDE had been coded instead, the output would have contained only STEP3. Had TYPE=EXCLUDE been coded, all the steps in job JOBTEST except STEP3 would have been in the output.

You might want to include or exclude more than one step. The STEPNAME parameter may be coded as

```
TYPE=EXCLUDE,STEPNAME=(STEP2,STEP6-STEP8,STEP10)
```

In this example, STEP2 and STEP10 are explicitly excluded as are all the steps starting with STEP6 and ending with STEP8. If TYPE=INCLUDE had been coded, STEP2, STEP10, and the steps starting with STEP6 and ending with STEP8 would have been included.

DATA SET UTILITIES

The NOPRINT suppresses the listing of the output data set. Had it been omitted, the output would have been listed.

If the input data set contains a DD DATA statement, IEBEDIT will treat the JCL statements that follow it as data, not JCL. That might seem surprising, but after all that is what a DD DATA statement is supposed to do.

IEBGENER

IEBGENER deals with physical sequential data sets and libraries. IEBGENER may be used to make a back-up copy of a sequential data set or library member or to load a sequential data set as a library member. It may be used to change the blocking factor of a sequential data set or to expand a library. We have discussed IEBGENER so thoroughly in Chapters 2 through 5 that by now you are an expert on it.

IEBIMAGE

Stop! Before you read about IEBIMAGE, review Chapter 11 about the 3800 Printing Subsystem. In that section we discussed the six parameters (COPIES, BURST, FLASH, CHARS, MODIFY, and FCB) that apply to the 3800 Printing Subsystem. Three of these parameters (CHARS, MODIFY, and FCB) require entries in a library named SYS1.IMAGELIB. IEBIMAGE is the utility program that is used to create these entries.

Figure 14.6 illustrates a sample job that would be used to create a forms control buffer module. The SYSUT1 DD statement names the library in which the modules used by the 3800 Printing Subsystem are stored. If the modules

FIGURE 14.6

Creating an FCB using IEBIMAGE

```
//JCLQB920 JOB ,'PARIS'
//STEPFCB  EXEC PGM=IEBIMAGE
//SYSPRINT DD SYSOUT=A
//SYSUT1   DD DSN=SYS1.IMAGELIB,
//            DISP=OLD
//SYSIN    DD *
 FCB CH1=1,CH9=(7,13,20),                          *
            LPI=((6,1),(8,32),(12)),               *
            SIZE=110
 NAME FCB1
/*
//
```

are named in the DD statement as illustrated in Chapter 11, they must be stored in the library named SYS1.IMAGELIB. If the modules are invoked in your program, other libraries may be used. However, using other libraries is outside the scope of this book.

Every module created using IEBIMAGE is named using the NAME control statement. This statement obeys the same rules as the link edit control statement, with slight differences. The name supplied here must be one to four characters in length, and the first character need not be alphabetic — it may be a number. The reason is that IEBIMAGE will prefix the name you supply with a four-character value. What these four characters will be depends on what kind of module you are creating. In Figure 14.6, an FCB module is being created. For an FCB the prefix is FCB3. The name supplied in the example is FCB1. As a result, the module created by IEBIMAGE and stored in SYS1.IMAGELIB will have the name FCB3FCB1. The first four characters are generated by IEBIMAGE, and the next four are supplied by the user.

FCB CONTROL STATEMENT.   There is always only one FCB statement used to create an FCB module. The first parameter is CH=1, which means that there is to be a channel 1 code for line 1. The CH indicates that a channel code is being specified; the number that follows the CH indicates which channel code. Numbers from 1 through 12 are valid channel codes. The 1 on the other side of the equals sign is the line that the channel 1 code is associated with. When the programmer says the printer should advance to channel 1, the printer goes to line 1. The second parameter coded in Figure 14.6 is CH9=(7,13,20). This means that lines 7, 13, and 20 have channel 9 coded. When the programmer says the printer should advance to channel 9, the printer goes to line 7, 13, or 20, depending on which line is next. If the printer is currently at line 16, the printer will go to line 20. On the other hand, if it is currently at line 26, the printer will go to line 7 on the next page.

In this example, 1 and 9 codes are specified. Please remember that there are ten more channel codes that may be used.

The LPI parameter specifies the line spacing in lines per inch and specifies how many lines are to be printed at that line spacing. This is a new feature of the 3800 Printing Subsystem. Other printers permit changing the line spacing, but only the 3800 permits changing it within a document. In the example in Figure 14.6, the first line is to be printed at 6 lines per inch; that is, it will occupy one-sixth of an inch. The next 32 lines will be printed at 8 lines per inch, which means that the next 32 lines will require four inches. The rest of the page will be printed at 12 lines per inch. The only permitted line spacings are 6, 8, and 12 lines per inch. If the LPI parameter is omitted, a default of LPI=6 is used.

DATA SET UTILITIES

The last parameter in the FCB statement is the SIZE parameter. The value coded for the SIZE parameter is equal to the number of inches in the page multiplied by 10. If, for example, you are using seven-inch paper, SIZE will be equal to 70. If no SIZE is specified, the default is 110.

To use the FCB created with the job shown in Figure 14.6, you would code the DD statement as

```
//REPORT   DD SYSOUT=A,FCB=FCB1
```

COPYMOD CONTROL STATEMENT.   Figure 14.7 illustrates the JCL required to create a copy modification module. The EXEC and DD statements in the example are the same as those in Figure 14.6. The NAME specified in the NAME statement is SALE. This means that a module named MOD1SALE will be stored in the SYS1.IMAGELIB by IEBIMAGE. The DD statement to invoke this module would be coded

```
//REPORT   DD SYSOUT=A,COPIES=4,MODIFY=SALE
```

In the COPYMOD statement in Figure 14.7, the first parameter is the COPIES parameter. The first number indicates which copy and the second how

FIGURE 14.7

Creating a copy modification module

```
//JCLQB925 JOB ,'AJAX'
//STEPMOD  EXEC PGM=IEBIMAGE
//SYSPRINT DD SYSOUT=A
//SYSUT1   DD DSN=SYS1.IMAGELIB,
//            DISP=OLD
//SYSIN    DD *
 COPYMOD COPIES=(1,1),                                          *
            LINES=(1,1),                                        *
            POS=10,                                             *
            TEXT=(C,'CUSTOMER COPY')
 COPYMOD COPIES=(2,2),                                          *
            LINES=1,                                            *
            POS=10,                                             *
            TEXT=(C,'FILE COPY')
 COPYMOD COPIES=4,                                              *
            LINES=1,                                            *
            POS=10,                                             *
            TEXT=(C,'SALESMAN''S COPY')
 NAME SALE
/*
//
```

many copies this statement applies to. In the first COPYMOD statement, we are dealing with the first copy only. In the second, we start with the second copy and are dealing with two copies. Thus the second COPYMOD statement applies to the second and third copies. The third COPYMOD statement applies to the fourth copy. The COPIES parameter in this statement is different from the other two. There is only one number indicating which copy, but no number showing how many. When the second number is left out, it defaults to 1. Consequently, the second value could have been omitted in the first COPYMOD statement, but not in the second.

The next parameter used in the COPYMOD statement tells the system which lines are being modified by this copy modification module. The coding of the LINES parameter is very similar to that of the COPIES parameter. The first number indicates the starting line and the second number how many lines. In the second and third COPYMOD statements, only one number is specified with the LINES parameter. As with the COPIES parameter, when the second value is not coded, the parameter defaults to 1.

The third parameter in the COPYMOD statement indicates where in the line the text is to start printing. In all three statements, 10 is coded. As a result, the text to be inserted in the document will be inserted starting at position 10 of line 1.

The last parameter in the COPYMOD statement, the TEXT parameter, indicates what information is to be inserted in the document. You will notice that the letter C precedes the data, which are surrounded by apostrophes. The letter C indicates that the supplied data are in character form. If the supplied data were in hexadecimal form the letter X would have been coded. Why would you ever want to supply hexadecimal instead of character representation when you wished the data printed? One reason is that you might be coding these statements on a device that does not have the full character set to be found on the 3800. If, for example, the input device does not have an asterisk (*), you might code

```
TEXT=(X'5C5C5C')
```

to insert three asterisks in the output.

Look at the TEXT parameter in the last COPYMOD statement. SALESMAN'S COPY is to appear in the output. However, if it had been coded as it is written, an error would have resulted. The system would have been confused. When you want an apostrophe included in your text, it must be doubled as shown in Figure 14.7.

Let us summarize the results of using this copy modification module. On line 1 starting in position 10, additional information will be printed. The first copy will have CUSTOMER COPY; the second and third, FILE COPY; and the fourth, SALESMAN'S COPY.

IEBIMAGE is also used to create modules that contain different character sets. These modules are invoked with the CHARS parameter in the DD statement. We will not discuss how to do this here, since an application programmer would rarely perform this function.

More information about IEBIMAGE may be found in *IBM 3800 Printing Subsystem* (GC26-3846).

IEBISAM

IEBISAM deals exclusively with ISAM data sets. It can be used to copy an ISAM data set and to unload and load, as well as to print in either character or hexadecimal format. IEBISAM is discussed in detail in Chapter 12.

IEBPTPCH

IEBPTPCH is used to print or punch sequential data sets or members of partitioned data sets. The programmer may use control statements to print or punch parts of each record in an order different from the order in which the information appears in the original record. This utility program is discussed in detail in Chapters 4 and 5.

IEBTCRIN

IEBTCRIN is a utility program used to create a physical sequential data set from data produced on an IBM 2495 tape cartridge reader. The data may have been placed on the tape cartridge with an IBM magnetic tape Selectric typewriter or with an IBM 50 magnetic data inscriber. This utility program is not often used because it is rarely necessary to create physical sequential data sets from information on a tape cartridge. Consequently, we will not discuss how to use this utility.

IEBUPDAT

IEBUPDAT is a utility program that is no longer supported or distributed. It performed about the same function as IEBUPDTE, but it was much more difficult to use. You may come across it, however, since some installations never discard JCL.

IEBUPDTE

IEBUPDTE is used primarily to add source programs to a library or to change a source program in a library. IEBUPDTE may also be used to copy a member from one library to another. Please remember that IEBUPDTE can only be used to handle library members whose record length is 80 bytes or less. IEBUPDTE is discussed in detail in Chapter 5.

IEFBR14

IEFBR14 is not strictly speaking a utility program. It does nothing but permit the associated DD statements to be processed. Refer to Chapter 5 for more detailed information.

SYSTEM UTILITIES

IEHATLAS

When a program using DASD executes, a read or write error may occur because of a defective track on the disk pack. In this situation, your system programmer may choose to use the utility program IEHATLAS, which will find an alternate track to replace the bad track and transfer the usable data from the defective track. Replacement data for the error record may be supplied at the same time. (Remember that disk packs contain extra cylinders which supply alternates when a track currently in use becomes defective.)

Normally IEHATLAS is used by the system programmer, so an application programmer does not have to know exactly how to use this utility program. However, since, as application programmer, you probably know what information should be in the bad record that needs replacement, it is helpful if you have some knowledge of how this utility program works.

Figure 14.8 illustrates using IEHATLAS to assign an alternate track to replace a defective one and to replace the bad record. The SYSUT1 DD statement points to the data set that includes the defective track. Please note that a disposition of OLD is specified. This is required; it ensures that no other program will use the data set while it is being repaired. In the example

FIGURE 14.8

Sample IEHATLAS job

```
//JCLQB930 JOB ,'HEKTOR'
//STEPATL  EXEC PGM=IEHATLAS
//SYSPRINT DD SYSOUT=A
//SYSUT1   DD DSN=ERRDATA,
//            UNIT=SYSDA,
//            VOL=SER=WYL003,
//            DISP=OLD
//SYSIN    DD *
 TRACK=00000002000C00010008
F1F2F3F4F5F6F7F8F9C1C2C3
/*
//
```

in Figure 14.8, the defective track is in a data set, as opposed to unused space. The first control statement points to the defective track as well as the defective record. If the bad track were in the VTOC, VTOC would have been coded instead of TRACK. The exact details of the remainder of this statement are the responsibility of the system programmer. The next control statement contains the replacement data in hexadecimal format. It starts in column 1 and may extend to column 80. You may use as many 80-byte records as required. When all the replacement data have been coded, you stop and leave the rest of the statement blank.

IEHDASDR

Working under the operating system, IEHDASDR does what IBCDASDI and IBC-DMPRS do as independent utility programs. In fact, a disk pack dump created using IBCDMPRS may be restored by IEHDASDR. Figure 14.9 illustrates a DASDI operation using IEHDASDR; the function performed is almost the same as the one illustrated in the IBCDASDI example in Figure 14.1. Figure 14.10 illustrates an IEHDASDR dump and restore operation which corresponds to the IBCDMPRS example in Figure 14.2.

We will not go into detail on using this utility because the application programmer rarely uses it.

FIGURE 14.9

Sample IEHDASDR job

```
//JCLQB935 JOB ,'ODYSSEUS'
//STEPDASD EXEC PGM=IEHDASDR
//SYSPRINT DD SYSOUT=A
//DISKPACK DD UNIT=SYSDA,
//         DISP=OLD,
//         VOL=(PRIVATE,SER=111111)
//SYSIN    DD *
  FORMAT TODD=DISKPACK,
                VTOC=6,                      *
                EXTENT=5,                    *
                NEWVOLID=SCRATC,             *
                PURGE=YES                    *
/*
//
```

FIGURE 14.10

Sample dump and restore using IEHDASDR

```
//JCLQB940 JOB ,'NESTOR'
//DUMPREST EXEC PGM=IEHDASDR
//SYSPRINT DD SYSOUT=A
//DISKDUMP DD UNIT=SYSDA,
//            VOL=SER=111111,
//            DISP=OLD
//TAPEOUT   DD UNIT=TAPE9,
//            DSNAME=NEWTAPE
//DISKREST DD UNIT=SYSDA,
//            VOL=SER=DISK01,
//            DISP=OLD
//TAPEIN    DD DSNAME=OLDTAPE,
//            DISP=OLD,
//            UNIT=TAPE9,
//            VOL=SER=T12345
//SYSIN     DD *
  DUMP FROMDD=DISKDUMP,TODD=TAPEOUT
  RESTORE TODD=DISKREST,FROMDD=TAPEIN,PURGE=YES
/*
//
```

IEHINITT

The utility program IEHINITT is used by operations personnel or system programmers to write the volume label on a tape reel. Since this utility program will write a label on a tape regardless of security protection or expiration date, IEHINITT is often removed from SYS1.LINKLIB to prevent its unautho-

SYSTEM UTILITIES

rized use. When a scratch tape is mounted to be used as a standard labeled tape, the operator is requested to supply the volume serial number if one is not already written on the tape. Since the operator can supply the volume serial number when the tape reel is being used, why bother having a separate utility program to perform this function? One reason is efficiency. When a supply of new tapes arrives, IEHINITT may be used to write the volume label on the tapes as a group so that later jobs using these tape reels are not held up waiting for the operator's response.

FIGURE 14.11

Standard label tape organization

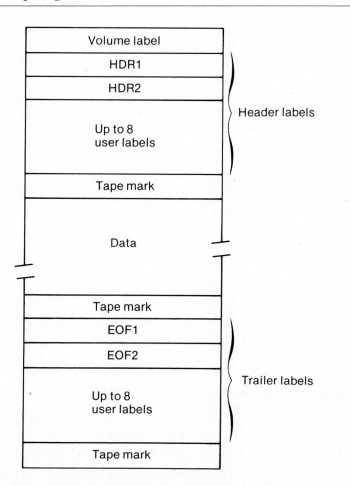

Figure 14.11 illustrates the layout of a normal standard labeled tape. The records that make up the labels are 80 bytes in length. The volume label contains the serial number that would be specified in the VOL parameter of the DD statement, e.g.,

```
//              VOL=SER=000106,
```

The HDR1 label contains system-type information, such as the expiration date, which you set with the DD statement LABEL parameter. The HDR2 label contains information that you specify with the DCB parameter when you create the data set. Not all installations have user labels, and they will be different in each installation. The trailer labels EOF1 and EOF2 contain virtually the same information as the header labels.

Obviously IEHINITT cannot supply all of this information. IEHINITT writes the volume label, containing the serial number supplied by a control statement, which we will discuss next, and a dummy HDR1 record followed by a tape mark.

Figure 14.12 illustrates JCL to use IEHINITT. The ANYNAME DD statement may actually have any valid ddname you want. The purpose of this statement is to supply one or more tape drives to be used. Only two parameters are coded, DCB and UNIT. In the DCB parameter, the subparameter DEN=3 means that the tape volume label is to be written at a density of 1600 BPI (bytes per inch). The values that may be coded for DEN and their meanings were discussed in Chapter 3. The UNIT parameter points to the physical device to be used. The coding TAPE9 specifies that this job can use any tape drive that can read and write nine-track tape. More than one tape drive could have been specified. Since, as we shall see when we discuss the control statements, 3 tapes are being initialized in this job, it would have been more efficient to do

FIGURE 14.12

Sample IEHINITT job

```
//JCLQB945 JOB ,'J.C.LEWIS'
//STEPLABL EXEC PGM=IEHINITT
//SYSPRINT DD SYSOUT=A
//ANYNAME  DD DCB=DEN=3,
//              UNIT=(TAPE9,,DEFER)
//SYSIN    DD *
ANYNAME INITT SER=000106,NUMTAPE=3
/*
//
```

SYSTEM UTILITIES

so. The DEFER subparameter included in the UNIT parameter permits the program to begin executing before the tape reels are mounted.

IEHINITT has only one control statement, INITT. The only required parameter on this statement is the serial number supplied with the SER parameter, as illustrated in Figure 14.12. Unlike other utility control statements, INITT requires the label. It must be the same as the ddname that points to the tape drive or drives to be used. The DISP parameter could have been coded as REWIND (which means that the tape is to be rewound after the label has been written) or UNLOAD (which means the tape is to be rewound and unloaded after the label has been written). In Figure 14.12, this parameter is not coded, so the default value of UNLOAD is taken. NUMTAPE=3 means that 3 tapes will be initialized. How is this possible when only one serial number is given? What happens here is that the first tape will have a serial number of 000106, the second 000107, and the third 000108. If you wish to initialize more than one reel of tape with one control statement, the serial number specified in the INITT control statement must be numeric. If, on the other hand, you do not want sequential serial numbers or you want an alphameric serial number, you must use a separate control statement for each volume. The NUMTAPE parameter would be omitted and the default value of 1 would be taken.

If your installation uses ASCII, you should specify LABTYPE=AL on the control statement. Without this parameter the label is written in EBCDIC.

IEHLIST

IEHLIST lists catalog, VTOC, and PDS directory entries. In Chapter 5 we discussed using the utility to list the names of the members in a PDS. It would be a good idea to go back to Chapter 5 now and review that material, paying particular attention to Figure 5.24.

You recall that the programmer invented for this book, J. C. Lewis, must begin all his data set names with the qualifiers WYL.QB.JCL, where QB stands for Queensborough Community College and JCL are Lewis's initials. Figure 14.13 shows a job that uses the LISTCTLG control statement to list the names of all cataloged data sets that belong to him.

On the control statement, coding

```
NODE=WYL.QB.JCL
```

limits the output to data set names that begin with WYL.QB.JCL. If

FIGURE 14.13

Using IEHLIST to list part of a catalog

```
//JCLQB948 JOB ,'J.C.LEWIS'
//LISTCTLG EXEC PGM=IEHLIST
//SYSPRINT DD SYSOUT=A
//ANYNAME  DD UNIT=SYSDA,
//              VOL=SER=WYL001,
//              DISP=OLD
//SYSIN    DD *
 LISTCTLG VOL=SYSDA=WYL001,
              NODE=WYL.QB.JCL
/*
//
```

```
    NODE=WYL.QB
```

had been coded, all cataloged Queensborough data sets would be listed. If NODE had been omitted, the whole catalog would be listed.

On the control statement, the VOL parameter must name the disk pack that contains the catalog. In the CUNY system, the catalog is on WYL001. Notice that the ANYNAME DD statement also points to this volume. As mentioned in Chapter 5, you can determine the serial number of the volume that contains the system catalog by reading the allocation messages from a job that uses the catalog. In Figure 4.7, for example, the messages

```
    IEF285I    SYSCTLG.VWYL001          KEPT
    IEF285I    VOL SER NOS= WYL001.
```

tell you that system catalog is on DASD volume WYL001.

In order to learn which data sets are stored on a volume, you can use the LISTVTOC control statement of IEHLIST. There are two parameters that may be used to specify the format of the output: DUMP and FORMAT. DUMP means the listing is to be unedited and hexadecimal. FORMAT means the listing is to be edited for easier reading. If you want to know which data sets are on disk pack WYL004, you code

```
    LISTVTOC VOL=SYSDA=WYL004
```

Since neither DUMP nor FORMAT is coded, a short edited form is produced.

If you code FORMAT, part of the output is labeled FORMAT 5 DSCB. This DSCB describes the freespace that is available on the volume.

SYSTEM UTILITIES

If you want to know which data sets will expire before a specified date—say, May 25, 1988, which corresponds to Julian date 14588—you code

```
LISTVTOC VOL=SYSDA=WYL004,DATE=14588
```

In the listing, all data sets with expiration dates before May 25, 1988, will be marked with an asterisk. This parameter cannot be used if you code either DUMP or FORMAT.

If you are only interested in verifying that certain data sets are on a particular volume, you use the DSNAME parameter to limit the listing. To check if data set WYL.QB.JCL.POLYFILE is on WYL004 requires the following coding:

```
LISTVTOC VOL=SYSDA=WYL004,DSNAME=WYL.QB.JCL.POLYFILE
```

To check on data sets TEST1 and TEST2 requires the coding

```
LISTVTOC VOL=SYSDA=WYL004,DSNAME=(TEST1,TEST2)
```

As a rule, you will find that the LISTVTOC and LISTCTLG control statements are of more use to the system programmer than to the application programmer. Nevertheless, there are times when an application programmer needs to find out what is on a disk pack.

IEHMOVE

IEHMOVE can be used to move or copy data sets, groups of data sets, catalogs, and entire volumes. IEHMOVE cannot handle either ISAM or VSAM data sets. We will not discuss using IEHMOVE to move or copy catalogs or volumes because these functions are normally performed by the system programmer. We will discuss using IEHMOVE to move data sets and groups of data sets. The IEHMOVE control statements and operands are summarized in Table 14.2

It is critical that you understand the difference between the copy operation and the move operation. Using the copy operation is like using the copier. When you are done, you have two: the original that you started with and a copy. Using the move operation is like having the moving men come in; the original is destroyed and only the new version exists. Please remember that with the copy operation the original version still exists, but with the move operation the original version is destroyed.

Figure 14.14 is a sample IEHMOVE job. Unlike most of the other utility programs that we have discussed, IEHMOVE requires DASD work space.

TABLE 14.2

Operands used with IEHMOVE control statements

Operand	DSGROUP Move	DSGROUP Copy	DSNAME Move	DSNAME Copy	PDS Move	PDS Copy	Remarks
TO=device=volser	R*	R	R	R	R	R	Specifies device type and volume serial number of receiving volume.
FROM=device=volser	N*	N	O*	O	O	O	Specifies device type and volume serial number of source volume. Used only for uncataloged data sets.
UNCATLG	O	O	O	O	O	O	For a copy operation the source data set is uncataloged. For a move operation output data set is not to be cataloged.
CATLG	N	O	N	O	N	O	The output data set should be cataloged. If the source data set is cataloged, then unless RENAME is coded, the source data set is uncataloged.
RENAME=newname	N	N	O	O	O	O	Specifies that the output data set should be renamed, and gives the new name.
FROMDD=ddname	N	N	O	O	O	O	Specifies the name of the DD statement from which DCB and LABEL information can be obtained for input data sets on tape.
TODD=ddname	O	O	O	O	O	O	Specifies the name of the DD statement from which DCB and LABEL information can be obtained for output data sets on tape.
UNLOAD	O	O	O	O	O	O	The data set is to be unloaded to the receiving volume.
EXPAND=nn	N	N	N	N	N	O	Specifies the number of directory blocks to be added to the PDS.

* R means required, O means optional, N means not applicable.

SYSTEM UTILITIES

FIGURE 14.14

Sample IEHMOVE job

```
//JCLQB950 JOB ,'J.C.LEWIS'
//STEPMOVE EXEC PGM=IEHMOVE
//SYSPRINT DD SYSOUT=A
//SYSUT1    DD UNIT=SYSDA,VOL=SER=SCR001,DISP=OLD
//DD1       DD UNIT=SYSDA,VOL=SER=WYL003,DISP=OLD
//DD2       DD UNIT=SYSDA,VOL=SER=WYL004,DISP=OLD
//DD3       DD UNIT=SYSDA,VOL=SER=WYL005,DISP=OLD
//SYSIN     DD *
 MOVE DSGROUP=A.B.C,TO=SYSDA=WYL005
 COPY DSGROUP=X.Y.Z,TO=SYSDA=WYL004,UNLOAD
 MOVE DSNAME=SAMPLE1,FROM=SYSDA=WYL005,TO=SYSDA=WYL004
 COPY DSNAME=SAMPL2,TO=SYSDA=WYL004,RENAME=SAMP2
 MOVE PDS=LIBRARY,FROM=SYSDA=WYL004,TO=SYSDA=WYL005,          *
           RENAME=NEWLIB,EXPAND=6
 COPY PDS=OLDLIB,FROM=SYSDA=WYL004,TO=SYSDA=WYL005
 COPY PDS=MYLIB,FROM=SYSDA=WYL004,TO=SYSDA=WYL005
  INCLUDE DSNAME=NEWLIB,MEMBER=ADDIT,FROM=SYSDA=WYL005
  EXCLUDE MEMBER=OMITIT
  REPLACE DSNAME=NEWLIB,MEMBER=REPIT,FROM=SYSDA=WYL005
 COPY PDS=STDLIB,RENAME=YOURLB,TO=SYSDA=WYL004
  SELECT MEMBER=(S1,(X2,S2),S3)
/*
//
```

IEHMOVE obtains this work space on the disk pack that you have made available with the SYSUT1 DD statement.

In the job shown in Figure 14.14, three disk packs, WYL003, WYL004, and WYL005, are made available to IEHMOVE with the DD statements DD1, DD2, and DD3. If additional DD statements had been provided, IEHMOVE would have had access to more disk packs. If, say, DD2 had been omitted, IEHMOVE would have had access only to WYL003 and WYL005. Any valid ddname (other than restricted names such as SYSABEND) could have been used in Figure 14.14.

DSGROUP PARAMETER. The first control statement uses the DSGROUP parameter. What is a DSGROUP? A DSGROUP is a group of data sets whose names are partially qualified by one or more identical names. For example, SYS1 is the system qualifier. We have discussed SYS1.PROCLIB, which contains procedures, and SYS1.LINKLIB, which contains executable code; they are part of a DSGROUP. The data sets belonging to user JCL form a DSGROUP because their names start with WYL.QB.JCL.

In Figure 14.14, the first control statement moves all cataloged data sets whose names start with A.B.C from WYL003 and WYL004 to WYL005. Remember that the data sets to be moved must be cataloged or they cannot be found; the control statement tells IEHMOVE where the data sets are to be placed, but not where they are to be found. With the move operation, after the data sets are written on WYL005, they are scratched from their source volume. The new versions of the data sets are cataloged to reflect their new location.

The second control statement in Figure 14.14 copies all cataloged data sets whose names begin with X.Y.Z from WYL003 and WYL005 to WYL004, where they will be written in unload format. Normally unload format is used to produce a back-up tape, but there is no technical reason why a disk pack cannot be used. As you recall, the copy operation does not cause the source data set to be scratched. If UNLOAD had not been coded, we would have two identical versions of these data sets. One group would be the original cataloged group; the other group, written on WYL004, would not be cataloged.

With a move operation, if the source data sets are cataloged, the new data sets are automatically cataloged. To prevent the new data sets from being cataloged, UNCATLG may be coded. When used with a copy operation, UNCATLG has a different meaning. In this case it means the source data sets should be uncataloged.

With a simple copy operation the new data sets are not cataloged. CATLG may be coded with a copy operation to catalog the new data sets. Since data set names of cataloged data sets must be unique, cataloging the new data sets requires that the source data sets be uncataloged, unless the new data sets are given a new name through the coding of RENAME. CATLG is the one parameter that applies only to the copy operation.

If

```
MOVE DSGROUP=P.Q.R,TO=SYSDA=WYL005,UNCATLG
```

is coded, the new data sets written on WYL005 will not be cataloged. If the operation had been COPY instead of MOVE, neither the original nor the new version would be cataloged.

If

```
COPY DSGROUP=P.Q.R,TO=SYSDA=WYL005,CATLG
```

is coded, the new data sets written on WYL005 will be cataloged, but the original data sets will be uncataloged.

Remember that you can have more than one data set with the same name in your system provided that only one is cataloged and that each data set is located on a different volume.

SYSTEM UTILITIES

With tape output instead of DASD, the TODD parameter can be added, e.g., TODD=TAPEOUT. In this case, IEHMOVE would use the DCB information provided in the TAPEOUT DD statement. Do not confuse the TO parameter, which tells IEHMOVE where to write the new version of the data set, with the TODD parameter, which tells IEHMOVE where DCB information may be found. If the output is nine-track tape with standard labels and default density, TODD may be omitted.
If

```
MOVE DSGROUP=P.Q.R.,TO=TAPE9=SCRATH,UNLOAD,TODD=TAPEOUT
```

is coded, a tape is created that may be used to transport the data sets to another system. Since the move operation is specified, the data sets will be scratched upon successful completion of the move itself. If COPY had been coded instead of MOVE, the tape created would have been a back-up tape. When partitioned or direct data sets are moved or copied to tape, they are automatically unloaded, because tape cannot support partitioned or direct organization. So this example did not require UNLOAD just to unload partitioned or direct data sets. Coding UNLOAD caused all the data sets to be unloaded, including physical sequential data sets. When a data set is unloaded, it is converted to 80-byte blocked records. If you later move or copy an unloaded data set back to disk, IEHMOVE will automatically reconstruct its original organization. The TODD parameter indicates for the unload operation where the IEHMOVE utility program will find DCB information.

There are three additional parameters that may be coded with a move or copy operation for a DSGROUP. Two parameters, PASSWORD and COPYAUTH, are related to security, which is outside the scope of this book, and the third deals with the case of multiple catalogs, which is a situation that a system programmer deals with.

Please review in your own mind the parameters CALTG, UNCATLG, UNLOAD, and TODD. If you do not understand them, review this section again. These parameters will be used in remaining move/copy operations that we will discuss.

DSNAME PARAMETER. The third control statement in Figure 14.14 illustrates using the DSNAME parameter to move a single data set. DSNAME may not be abbreviated as in the DD statement. This control statement differs from the MOVE DSGROUP control statement in that there is a FROM parameter which identifies the unit (SYSDA) and the disk pack (WYL005) where data set SAMPLE1 is to be found. The FROM parameter is only used for data sets that are not cataloged. The result of executing this command will be that data set SAMPLE1 will be written on WYL004 and scratched from WYL005.

The fourth control statement illustrates copying a cataloged data set onto WYL004 and giving the new version a new name. The original or source data set, SAMPLE2, must be cataloged because no FROM parameter is coded. The new version of the data set is renamed SAMP2 with the use of the RENAME parameter. After this command is executed, there will be a cataloged data set named SAMPLE2 and an uncataloged data set named SAMP2 located on WYL004. If

```
MOVE DSNAME=LOADIT,TO=SYSDA=WYL004,FROM=TAPE9=000104,          *
          FROMDD=TAPEDD
```

is coded, a data set from tape will be loaded back onto DASD. You are familiar with all the parameters in this control statement except FROMDD. FROMDD is related to the parameter TODD. When the unload tape is created, TODD points to a DD statement that contains the DCB information used in unloading the data set. FROMDD points to a DD statement that contains the DCB information used in loading the data set. FROMDD is not required if the tape that contains the unloaded data set is a standard label tape. The FROMDD parameter is needed only for unlabeled tapes.

The UNCATLG, TODD, and UNLOAD parameters are used with MOVE/COPY DSNAME in the same way as with MOVE/COPY DSGROUP. The CATLG parameter is used with COPY DSNAME in the same fashion as with COPY DSGROUP with one difference. Usually if CATLG is included on a COPY control statement, the new data set is cataloged and the old data set is uncataloged. However, if the data set is renamed, as in the previous example, coding CATLG causes the new data set to be cataloged, but the old data set is not uncataloged.

PDS PARAMETER. The MOVE/COPY PDS control statement is used with libraries or partitioned data sets. In its simple form it differs little from the MOVE/COPY DSNAME, which we studied earlier. The fifth control statement in Figure 14.14 illustrates a simple move operation including the one new parameter EXPAND. This parameter is used only when a new library is being created as a result of this control statement. It tells how many more directory blocks are to be created with the new library. If, in the example, the original library had 10 directory blocks, the new library will have 16. EXPAND refers only to the number of directory blocks to be added to the directory; the number of tracks in the new library will be the same as in the original library.

SYSTEM UTILITIES

To summarize, as a result of the fifth control statement in Figure 14.14, a new library named NEWLIB (see the RENAME parameter) will be created on WYL005 using a PDS named LIBRARY as input. After NEWLIB has been successfully created, LIBRARY will be scratched.

The MOVE/COPY PDS is not used just to create a new PDS, but may be used to merge members from other libraries into an existing library if the libraries have the same names. The sixth control statement in Figure 14.14 assumes that there are two versions of a PDS named OLDLIB, one on WYL004 and the other on WYL005. In this case all the members that have different names will be copied from PDS OLDLIB on WYL004 and written on PDS OLDLIB on WYL005. If a member with the same name exists in both PDSs, it is not copied. For example, if OLDLIB on WYL004 has members A, B, and C and initially OLDLIB on WYL005 has members C, D, and E, after this command is executed OLDLIB on WYL005 will have members A, B, C, D, and E. Member C, which existed in both libraries, will be the member that was originally on WYL005.

The next control statement looks like an ordinary COPY PDS, but its function is modified by the following INCLUDE, EXCLUDE, and REPLACE statements. Only one INCLUDE statement is coded, but there can be more. The INCLUDE statement permits a member from another library to be included in the copy or move operation. The DSNAME parameter names the library, and the MEMBER parameter names the member to be included in the new version of MYLIB. The FROM parameter is coded if the library named by the DSNAME parameter is not cataloged. The COPY and INCLUDE statements cause members in MYLIB on WYL004 to be copied to MYLIB on WYL005, and member ADDIT from library NEWLIB to be written to MYLIB on WYL005.

The next control statement is an EXCLUDE statement, which names a member (OMITIT) in the version of MYLIB on WYL004 that is not to be moved or copied. Only one EXCLUDE statement is coded in Figure 14.14, but you may code as many as there are members that you do not want copied or moved. The REPLACE control statement causes the specified member to be taken from a different library. In the example in Figure 14.14, member REPIT is being taken from library NEWLIB on WYL005 instead of MYLIB on WYL004. So all members from MYLIB on WYL004 except members OMITIT and REPIT are copied to MYLIB on WYL005. In addition, ADDIT and REPIT from NEWLIB on WYL005 are copied into MYLIB on WYL005.

The last two control statements in Figure 14.14 illustrate how the SELECT control statement is used to modify the action of a COPY statement. The COPY control statement contains nothing new. A cataloged PDS named STDLIB is to be copied onto WYL004 and then given the name YOURLIB. This straightforward operation is modified by the SELECT control statement. The SELECT control statement tells IEHMOVE that only the members named in the SELECT control statement are to be copied or moved. Only members S1, X2, and S3 are to be copied from STDLIB into the new PDS named YOURLIB. Furthermore, member X2 will be renamed S2. The result of executing these two control statements will be the creation of a PDS named YOURLIB on WYLO04. YOURLIB will contain three members, S1, S2, and S3. Remember that S2 is the same as member X2 in PDS STDLIB.

There are four control statements that may be used to modify the operation of a MOVE/COPY PDS: INCLUDE, EXCLUDE, REPLACE, and SELECT. The INCLUDE, EXCLUDE, and REPLACE control statements may be used together in any order and virtually any number. Only the INCLUDE statement may be used together with the SELECT control statement. None of these control statements may be used when data are loaded or unloaded.

You may have noticed that IEBCOPY and IEHMOVE may be used to perform many of the same operations. Nevertheless, each offers certain special features not found in the other. For example, when a tape version of a PDS is created using IEHMOVE, it is necessary to include all of the members of the PDS. However, when a tape version of a PDS is created using IEBCOPY, it is possible to copy selected members. On the other hand, IEHMOVE permits copying DSGROUPs, an operation that is not possible with IEBCOPY. Another advantage of IEHMOVE is that the space for the new data set does not have to be allocated in your JCL; IEHMOVE will allocate the space it needs.

IEHPROGM

IEHPROGM is a utility program that system programmers find extremely useful. Application programmers find a few of the functions of IEHPROGM helpful. We discussed SCRATCH and RENAME in Chapter 5 when we studied libraries. The control statements BLDG and DLTX were also discussed in Chapter 6 when we studied generation data groups. In this section we will discuss the CATLG and UNCATLG control statements. We will not discuss the remaining control statements, since application programmers rarely, if ever, use them.

Figure 14.15 illustrates a job to catalog one data set and uncatalog another. A separate step is coded for each function. This is not required or even desirable. It is done here to illustrate certain points about using IEHPROGM.

The first step in Figure 14.15 illustrates the use of the CATLG control statement. Please note that DSNAME cannot be abbreviated as in the DD statement. The VOL parameter is required in order to find the data set so that the

SYSTEM UTILITIES

FIGURE 14.15

Cataloging and uncataloging a data set using IEHPROGM

```
//JCLOB955 JOB ,'J.C.LEWIS'
//STEP1    EXEC PGM=IEHPROGM
//SYSPRINT DD SYSOUT=A
//DD1      DD UNIT=SYSDA,VOL=SER=DISK01,DISP=OLD
//SYSIN    DD *
  CATLG DSNAME=SAMPLE,VOL=SYSDA=DISK01
/*
//STEP2    EXEC  PGM=IEHPROGM
//SYSPRINT DD SYSOUT=A
//SYSIN    DD *
 UNCATLG DSNAME=SAMP2
/*
//
```

required information may be read from the data set label and written into
the system catalog. As you may recall, ISAM data sets cannot, for the most
part, be cataloged by specifying CATLG in the DISP parameter of the DD statement. IEHPROGM must be used.

If your data set is on more than one volume, the DD statement is coded
as

```
//DD1      DD UNIT=SYSDA,
//            VOL=SER=(DISK01,DISK02),
//            DISP=OLD
```

and the CATLG control statement as

```
CATLG DSNAME=SAMP,VOL=SYSDA=(DISK01,DISK02)
```

The second step in Figure 14.15 illustrates the uncatalog operation. The
UNCATLG control statement only supplies the name of the data set via the
DSNAME parameter. You will notice that there is no DD statement making
the volume on which the data set resides available and that the control
statement does not indicate where the data set resides. Since the data set is
cataloged (if it were not, why bother doing an uncatalog operation?), the
system already knows where it is. A more important point is that to uncatalog a data set, the system does not need access to the data set itself, but
only to the system catalog. Uncataloging a data set means removing information about the data set from the system catalog. In fact, the volume containing the data set need not even be mounted.

FIGURE 14.16

IFHSTATR example

```
//JCLQB960 JOB ,'J.C.LEWIS'
//STEPTAPE EXEC PGM=IFHSTATR
//SYSUT1    DD DSNAME=SYS1.MAN,
//             UNIT=TAPE9,
//             VOL=SER=SMF021,
//             DISP=OLD
//SYSUT2    DD SYSOUT=A
/*
//
```

IFHSTATR

The operating system gathers statistical information about jobs run and physical devices and media used, with a system called SMF. SMF can gather massive amounts of information about a system. In fact, the real problem is that SMF produces more information than can generally be used. When your system programmer generates your operating system, he or she generally reduces the amount of information that SMF will produce to a level that suits the needs of your environment. SMF creates different types of records, each type monitoring the performance of a different part of the computer system. For example, type 21 records monitor the performance of tape volumes. A type 21 record is written after a tape volume is used and indicates among other information how many I/O errors occurred during the time the tape was used.

IFHSTATR is a utility program that operations personnel use to evaluate how good the tape reels are. The input is the data created by SMF. IFHSTATR selects and prints type 21 records.

Figure 14.16 illustrates the JCL needed to run IFHSTATR. The SYSUT1 DD statement points to the SMF data and SYSUT2 to the output listing.

EXERCISES

1. What is an independent utility?

2. What function does the independent utility program IBCDASDI perform?

3. What function does the independent utility program IBCDMPRS perform?

523

4. What is the utility program IEBCOMPR used for?

5. What kind of data sets may be processed by IEBCOMPR?

6. Write a job stream to use IEBCOMPR to compare two cataloged data sets named SET1 and SET2.

7. What kind of data sets may be input to IEBCOPY?

8. What are the three control statements used by IEBCOPY?

9. What functions does IEBCOPY perform?

10. What function does IEBDG perform?

11. What type of data sets may be input to or output from IEBDG?

12. What would IEBEDIT be used for?

13. Write a job stream to use IEBEDIT to print selected JCL statements in a cataloged data set named JCLSET. Print only the JCL in the step named COMPARE in the job named NEWJOB.

14. What may IEBGENER be used for?

15. What is unique about IEBIMAGE?

16. What does IEBIMAGE do?

17. What does IEBISAM do?

18. What would you use IEBPTPCH for?

19. What function does IEBTCRIN provide?

20. What would you use IEBUPDTE for?

21. What restriction limits the usefulness of IEBUPDTE?

22. Why would IEHATLAS be used?

23. Which utility program could be used instead of IBCDASDI and IBCDMPRS?

24. Why should IEHINITT be used?

25. Write a job stream to use IEHINITT to write volume serial numbers ABC on one tape and XYZ on another.

26. If you wished to learn the volume on which a cataloged data set resides, which utility program would you use? Which control statement?

27. Name the utility program and control statement used to determine which data sets are on a disk pack.

28. Write a job stream to use IEHLIST to list the VTOC on volume DISK45 and to determine if a data set named MAYBE is on volume DISK63.

29. What is the difference between the move and copy operations of IEHMOVE?

30. What are the control statements that may be used to modify the IEHMOVE MOVE/COPY PDS control statement?

31. A computer center has five disk packs named DISK01 through DISK05. Write a job stream to use IEHMOVE to

    a. Move all the data sets whose names start with ACCTRECV to tape TAP100.

    b. Copy members A1 and A2 from a library named ALIB to a new library named BLIB on DISK04. The members should be renamed B1 and B2.

32. What functions would you as an application programmer use IEHPROGM for?

33. There are two versions of a data set named TWO. One version is on DISK90, and the other is on DISK10. The version on DISK90 is cataloged. Write a job stream to use IEHPROGM to uncatalog the version on DISK90 and catalog the version on DISK10.

34. Who would probably use IFHSTATR?

35. Who wrote the job in Figure 5.7?

PROGRAMMING ASSIGNMENTS

1. Use IEHMOVE to copy the data set you created in Chapter 3. The new data set should be renamed and cataloged.

2. Use IEBCOMPR to compare the data set you created in Programming Assignment 1 with the original data set it was copied from.

3. Perform an experiment to discover what the actions listed in Table 14.1 do. *Hints:* Define eight 5-byte fields, each containing a PICTURE defining a 5-byte pattern and each specifying a different action. When you wave (WV) or roll (RO), the results are more interesting if the fields have one or more blanks at the beginning and/or end. Create 20 records, and direct the output to the printer. You will have to add a DCB parameter to the

525

output DD statement to make the record length of the output data set equal to the record length implied in your CREATE statement.

4. Using IEBIMAGE, create an FCB for a six-inch page, where the first two inches are printed at 6 lines per inch, the next two inches at 8 lines per inch, and the remaining at 12 lines per inch. You need a channel 1 punch at line 1 and channel 7 punches where the line density changes. (Check with your advisor before running this job to learn if you are permitted to add members to SYS1.IMAGELIB. If you are not direct your output to FIRSTLIB. Remember this only applies to the 3800 printer.)

5. If you use a systematic naming convention at your computer center, use IEHMOVE to copy all your cataloged data sets to a back-up tape.

6. For this assignment you need a library containing at least three members, although the data in the three members is not significant. You may use the FIRSTLIB you created in Chapter 5. Your advisor may suggest a library. Or you may use IEBDG to create the library and members. In this case the members should be named MEMA, MEMB, and MEMC, and should consist of ten 50-byte records containing all As, Bs, or Cs. If you are clever, you can create all three members in one jobstep, using three sets of DSD-FD-CREATE-END control statements. Next use IEHMOVE to make a copy of the library. The new library should contain any two members from the original library. Finally, use IEBCOMPR to compare the two libraries.

7. Use IEHPROGM to uncatalog any one of your data sets. Then use IEHPROGM to recatalog it.

8. The utilities manual's discussion of IEBPTPCH says that if PZ is specified as the conversion in a FIELD parameter, a field of length L bytes will occupy $2 \times L$ characters in the printed output record. This is surprising, since a packed field of length L bytes contains $2 \times L - 1$ digits. You should discover what the extra character is used for. Create a data set that contains at least one packed field. You may create the data set any way you like, but perhaps the easiest way is to use IEBDG. Use IEBPTPCH to print this field, specifying a conversion of PZ.

9. The utilities manual's discussion of IEBPTPCH says that when STRTAFT=n is coded, n must not exceed 32767. However, if you code a value greater than 32767, you do not get a syntax error. To determine what happens when a value greater than 32767 is coded, create a data set containing 33,100 records. Each record should contain a field which contains the

526

record's sequence number, with numbers running from 00001 through 33100. Add 10 more bytes containing arbitrary data so that the record length is 15 bytes. Block the records so that the BLKSIZE is 1500 bytes. An easy way to create this data set is to use IEBDG. Use IEBPTPCH to list this data set using STRTAFT=33000 and STOPAFT=20. What happens?

SUMMARY

In this chapter virtually every utility program that may be used with the operating system has been at least mentioned. You should know what functions each utility program can perform. In addition, you should know how to use those utility programs that an application programmer is likely to use.

APPENDIX A

FLOWCHART SYMBOLS

Card file Document Process Magnetic tape Magnetic disk

Flowlines connect the data set symbols with the process symbols. Data set names are written within the data set symbols and ddnames are written on the flowlines.

Program names or functions are written within process symbols. When a job contains more than one step, flowlines connect the processing symbols to show the order in which they are executed.

527

APPENDIX B

FORMAT OF JCL STATEMENTS

This appendix gives the format of all the parameters of the JOB, EXEC, and DD statements. The first section is for VS1 systems, while the second section is for MVS systems.

APPENDIX B / FORMAT OF JCL STATEMENTS

VS1 SYSTEMS

The JOB Statement				
//Name	Operation	Operand	P/K	Comments
//jobname	JOB	([account number][,additional accounting information,...])	P	Can be made mandatory
		[programmer's name]	P	Can be made mandatory
		$\left[ADDRSPC=\begin{Bmatrix} VIRT \\ REAL \end{Bmatrix}\right]$	K	Requests storage type
		[CLASS=jobclass]	K	Assigns A–Z, 0–9
		[COND=((code, operator),...)]	K	Specifies a maximum of 8 tests
		[MPROFILE='profile string']	K	For ISSP only
		[MSGCLASS=output class]	K	Assigns A–Z, 0–9
		$\left[MSGLEVEL=(\begin{bmatrix}0\\1\\2\end{bmatrix}\begin{bmatrix},0\\,1\end{bmatrix})\right]$	K	
		[PROFILE='profile string']	K	For ISSP only
		[PRTY=priority]	K	Assigns 0–13
		$\left[RD=\begin{Bmatrix}R\\RNC\\NC\\NR\end{Bmatrix}\right]$	K	Restart definition
		[REGION=valueK]	K	Specifies amount of storage space
		$\left[RESTART=(\begin{Bmatrix}*\\stepname\\stepname.procstepname\end{Bmatrix}[,checkid])\right]$	K	For deferred restart
		$\left[TIME=\begin{Bmatrix}([minutes][,seconds])\\1440\end{Bmatrix}\right]$	K	Assigns job CPU time limit
		$\left[TYPRUN=\begin{Bmatrix}HOLD\\SCAN\end{Bmatrix}\right]$	K	Holds a job in job queue, or scans JCL for syntax errors

Legend:
P Positional parameter.
K Keyword parameter.
{ } Choose one.
[ ] Optional; if more than one line is enclosed, choose one or none.

Reprinted by permission from *OS/VS1 JCL Reference* (GC24-5099). © 1973 by International Business Machines Corporation.

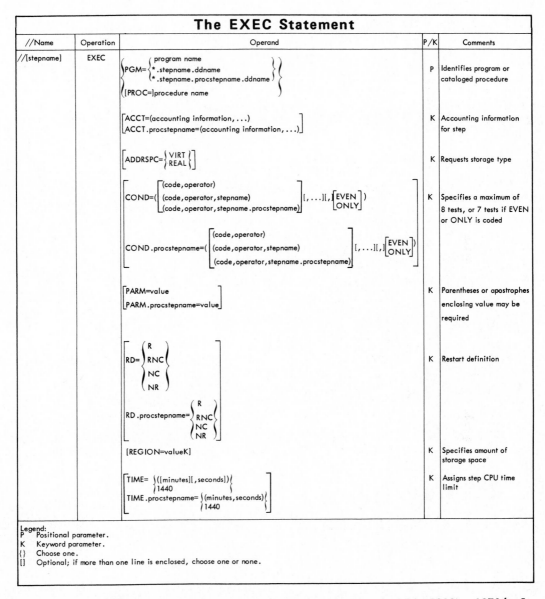

The EXEC Statement				
//Name	Operation	Operand	P/K	Comments
//[stepname]	EXEC	PGM= { program name / *.stepname.ddname / *.stepname.procstepname.ddname } [PROC=]procedure name	P	Identifies program or cataloged procedure
		[ACCT=(accounting information, ...) / ACCT.procstepname=(accounting information, ...)]	K	Accounting information for step
		[ADDRSPC= {VIRT / REAL}]	K	Requests storage type
		COND=([(code,operator) / (code,operator,stepname) / (code,operator,stepname.procstepname)] [,...][, [EVEN / ONLY]])	K	Specifies a maximum of 8 tests, or 7 tests if EVEN or ONLY is coded
		COND.procstepname=([(code,operator) / (code,operator,stepname) / (code,operator,stepname.procstepname)] [,...][,] [EVEN / ONLY])		
		PARM=value / PARM.procstepname=value	K	Parentheses or apostrophes enclosing value may be required
		RD= {R / RNC / NC / NR} RD.procstepname= {R / RNC / NC / NR}	K	Restart definition
		[REGION=valueK]	K	Specifies amount of storage space
		TIME= {([minutes][,seconds]) / 1440} TIME.procstepname= {(minutes,seconds) / 1440}	K	Assigns step CPU time limit

Legend:
P   Positional parameter.
K   Keyword parameter.
{}   Choose one.
[]   Optional; if more than one line is enclosed, choose one or none.

Reprinted by permission from *OS/VS1 JCL Reference* (GC24-5099). © 1973 by International Business Machines Corporation.

The DD Statement

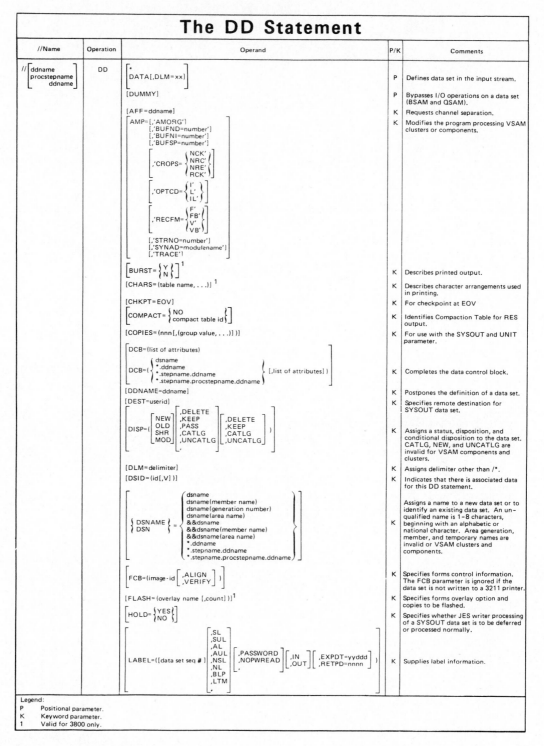

//Name	Operation	Operand	P/K	Comments
// [ddname / procstepname.ddname]	DD	*	P	Defines data set in the input stream.
		DATA[,DLM=xx]		
		[DUMMY]	P	Bypasses I/O operations on a data set (BSAM and QSAM).
		[AFF=ddname]	K	Requests channel separation.
		AMP=[,'AMORG'] [,'BUFND=number'] [,'BUFNI=number'] [,'BUFSP=number'] [,'CROPS= { NCK' / NRC' / NRE' / RCK' }] [,'OPTCD= { I' / L' / IL' }] [,'RECFM= { F' / FB' / V' / VB' }] [,'STRNO=number'] [,'SYNAD=modulename'] [,'TRACE']	K	Modifies the program processing VSAM clusters or components.
		[BURST= { Y / N }][1]	K	Describes printed output.
		[CHARS=(table name,...)][1]	K	Describes character arrangements used in printing.
		[CHKPT=EOV]	K	For checkpoint at EOV
		[COMPACT= { NO / compact table id }]	K	Identifies Compaction Table for RES output.
		[COPIES=(nnn[,(group value,...)])]	K	For use with the SYSOUT and UNIT parameter.
		DCB=(list of attributes) DCB=({ dsname / *.ddname / *.stepname.ddname / *.stepname.procstepname.ddname } [,list of attributes])	K	Completes the data control block.
		[DDNAME=ddname]	K	Postpones the definition of a data set.
		[DEST=userid]	K	Specifies remote destination for SYSOUT data set.
		DISP=([NEW / OLD / SHR / MOD] [,DELETE / ,KEEP / ,PASS / ,CATLG / ,UNCATLG / ,][,DELETE / ,KEEP / ,CATLG / ,UNCATLG])	K	Assigns a status, disposition, and conditional disposition to the data set. CATLG, NEW, and UNCATLG are invalid for VSAM components and clusters.
		[DLM=delimiter]	K	Assigns delimiter other than /*.
		[DSID=(id[,V])]	K	Indicates that there is associated data for this DD statement.
		{ DSNAME / DSN } = { dsname / dsname(member name) / dsname(generation number) / dsname(area name) / &&dsname / &&dsname(member name) / &&dsname(area name) / *.ddname / *.stepname.ddname / *.stepname.procstepname.ddname }	K	Assigns a name to a new data set or to identify an existing data set. An un-qualified name is 1–8 characters, beginning with an alphabetic or national character. Area generation, member, and temporary names are invalid or VSAM clusters and components.
		FCB=(image-id [,ALIGN / ,VERIFY])	K	Specifies forms control information. The FCB parameter is ignored if the data set is not written to a 3211 printer.
		[FLASH=(overlay name [,count])][1]	K	Specifies forms overlay option and copies to be flashed.
		HOLD= { YES / NO }	K	Specifies whether JES writer processing of a SYSOUT data set is to be deferred or processed normally.
		LABEL=([data set seq #] [,SL / ,SUL / ,AL / ,AUL / ,NSL / ,NL / ,BLP / ,LTM / ,][,PASSWORD / ,NOPWREAD][,IN / ,OUT][,EXPDT=yyddd / ,RETPD=nnnn])	K	Supplies label information.

Legend:
P   Positional parameter.
K   Keyword parameter.
1   Valid for 3800 only.

The DD Statement (con't)

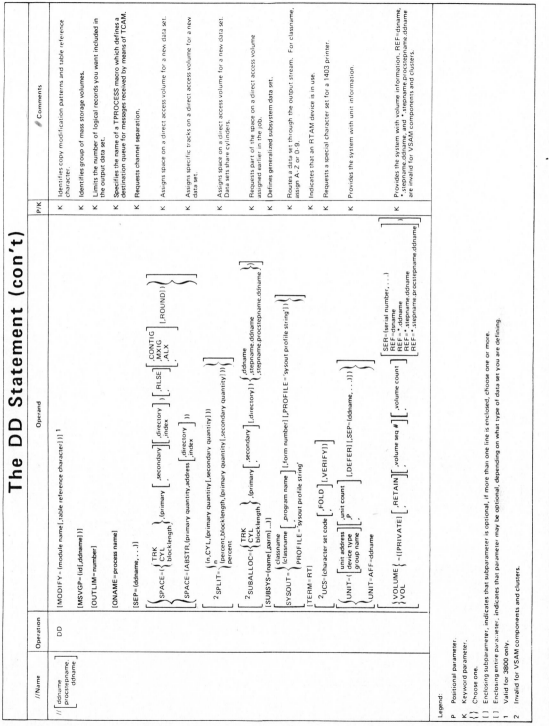

//Name	Operation	Operand	P/K	Comments

`// ddname`
`   [procstepname.`
`    ddname]`
	DD			

		`[MODIFY=(module name [,table reference character]) ]`¹	K	Identifies copy modification patterns and table reference character.
		`[MSVGP=(id[,ddname])]`	K	Identifies group of mass storage volumes.
		`[OUTLIM=number]`	K	Limits the number of logical records you want included in the output data set.
		`[QNAME=process name]`	K	Specifies the name of a TPROCESS macro which defines a destination queue for messages received by means of TCAM.
		`[SEP=(ddname,...)]`	K	Requests channel separation.
		`SPACE=({TRK / CYL / blocklength},({primary [,secondary][,directory / ,index]})[,RLSE][,{CONTIG / MXIG / ALX}][,ROUND])`	K	Assigns space on a direct access volume for a new data set.
		`SPACE=(ABSTR,(primary quantity,address[,{directory / index}]))`	K	Assigns specific tracks on a direct access volume for a new data set.
		`²SPLIT=({n / n,CYL,[primary quantity],[primary quantity[,secondary quantity]] / percent})`	K	Assigns space on a direct access volume for a new data set. Data sets share cylinders.
		`²SUBALLOC=({TRK / CYL / blocklength},({primary [,secondary][,directory]}),{ddname / stepname.ddname / stepname.procstepname.ddname})`	K	Requests part of the space on a direct access volume assigned earlier in the job.
		`[SUBSYS=(name[,parm]...)]`	K	Defines generalized subsystem data set.
		`SYSOUT=({classname / (classname[,{program name / (program name)}][,form number][,PROFILE='sysout profile string']) / PROFILE='sysout profile string'})`	K	Routes a data set through the output stream. For classname, assign A-Z or 0-9.
		`[TERM=RT]`	K	Indicates that an RTAM device is in use.
		`²UCS=(character set code [,FOLD][,VERIFY])`	K	Requests a special character set for a 1403 printer.
		`UNIT=({unit address / device type / group name}[,{unit count / P}][,DEFER][,SEP=(ddname,...)])` `UNIT=AFF=ddname`	K	Provides the system with unit information.
		`{VOLUME / VOL}=([PRIVATE][,RETAIN][,volume seq #][,volume count][,{SER=(serial number,...) / REF=dsname / REF=*.ddname / REF=*.stepname.ddname / REF=*.stepname.procstepname.ddname}])`	K	Provides the system with volume information. REF=dsname, *.stepname.ddname, and *.stepname.procstepname.ddname are invalid for VSAM components and clusters.

Legend:

P   Positional parameter.
K   Keyword parameter.
{}   Choose one.
[]   Enclosing subparameter, indicates that subparameter is optional, if more than one line is enclosed, choose one or more.
[ ] Enclosing entire parameter, indicates that parameter may be optional, depending on what type of data set you are defining.
1   Valid for 3800 only.
2   Invalid for VSAM components and clusters.

Reprinted by permission from *OS/VS1 JCL Reference* (GC24-5099). © 1973 by International Business Machines Corporation.

MVS SYSTEMS

		The JOB Statement		
//Name	Operation	Operand	P/K	Comments
//jobname	JOB	([account number] [,additional accounting information,...])	P	Identifies accounting information. Can be made mandatory.
		$\left[\text{ADDRSPC} = \left\{ \begin{array}{l} \text{VIRT} \\ \text{REAL} \end{array} \right\} \right]$	K	Requests storage type.
		[CLASS=jobclass]	K	Assigns a job class to each job.
		[COND=((code,operator),...)]	K	Specifies test for a return code.
		[GROUP=group name]	K	Specifies a group associated with a RACF-defined user.
		[MSGCLASS=output class]	K	Assigns an output class for the job.
		$\left[\text{MSGLEVEL=(} \left[\begin{array}{l} 0 \\ 1 \\ 2 \end{array} \right] \left[\begin{array}{l} ,0 \\ ,1 \end{array} \right]) \right]$	K	Specifies what job output is to be written.
		[NOTIFY=user identification]	K	Requests a message be sent to a time-sharing terminal.
		[PASSWORD=(password [,new password])]	K	Specifies a password for a RACF-defined user.
		[PERFORM=n]	K	Specifies the performance group a job belongs to.
		[programmer's name]	P	Identifies programmer. Can be made mandatory.
		[PRTY=priority]	K	Specifies a job's priority.
		$\left[\text{RD=} \left\{ \begin{array}{l} \text{R} \\ \text{RNC} \\ \text{NC} \\ \text{NR} \end{array} \right\} \right]$	K	Specifies restart facilities to be used.
		[REGION=valueK]	K	Specifies amount of storage space.
		$\left[\text{RESTART=(} \left\{ \begin{array}{l} * \\ \text{stepname} \\ \text{stepname.procstepname} \end{array} \right\} [,checkid]) \right]$	K	Specifies restart facilities for deferred restart.
		$\left[\text{TIME=} \left\{ \begin{array}{l} ([\text{minutes}] [,\text{seconds}]) \\ 1440 \end{array} \right\} \right]$	K	Assigns a job a CPU time limit.
		$\left[\text{TYPRUN=} \left\{ \begin{array}{l} \text{HOLD} \\ \text{JCLHOLD} \\ \text{SCAN} \\ \text{COPY} \end{array} \right\} \right]$	K	Holds a job in job queue, scans JCL for syntax errors, or copies the input deck to SYSOUT.
		[USER=userid]	K	Identifies a RACF-defined user.

Legend:

P   Positional parameter. (Positional parameters must precede keyword parameters)
K   Keyword parameter
{ } Choose one.
[ ] Optional; if more than one line is enclosed, choose one or none.

Reprinted by permission from *OS/VS2 MVS JCL* (GC28-0692). © 1974 by International Business Machines Corporation.

The EXEC Statement

//Name	Operation	Operand	P/K	Comments
// [stepname]	EXEC	[ACCT [.procstepname] = (accounting information, . . .)]	K	Accounting information for step.
		[ADDRSPC [.procstepname] = $\begin{Bmatrix} \text{VIRT} \\ \text{REAL} \end{Bmatrix}$]	K	Requests storage type.
		[COND [.procstepname] = ($\begin{Bmatrix} \text{(code,operator)} \\ \text{(code,operator,stepname)} \\ \text{(code,operator,stepname.procstepname)} \end{Bmatrix}$, . . . $\begin{bmatrix} ,\text{EVEN} \\ ,\text{ONLY} \end{bmatrix}$)]	K	Specifies a test for a return code.
		[DPRTY [.procstepname]=([value1][,value2])]	K	Specifies dispatching priority for a job step.
		[DYNAMNBR [.procstepname] =n]	K	Specifies dynamic allocation.
		[PARM [.procstepname] =value]	K	Passes variable information to a program at execution time.
		[PERFORM [.procstepname] =n]	K	Specifies a performance group for a job.
		[PGM= $\begin{Bmatrix} \text{program name} \\ *\text{.stepname.ddname} \\ *\text{.stepname.procstepname.ddname} \end{Bmatrix}$]	P	Identifies program.
		[[PROC=] procedure name]	P	Identifies a cataloged or instream procedure.
		[RD [.procstepname] = $\begin{Bmatrix} \text{R} \\ \text{RNC} \\ \text{NC} \\ \text{NR} \end{Bmatrix}$]	K	Specifies restart facilities to be used.
		[REGION [.procstepname] =valueK]	K	Specifies amount of storage space.
		[TIME [.procstepname] = $\begin{Bmatrix} ([\text{minutes}] [,\text{seconds}]) \\ 1440 \end{Bmatrix}$]	K	Assigns step CPU time limit.

Legend:

K   Keyword parameter.
P   Positional parameter. (Positional parameters must precede keyword parameters)
{} Choose one.
[] Optional; if more than one line is enclosed, choose one or none.

Reprinted by permission from *OS/VS2 MVS JCL* (GC28-0692). © 1974 by International Business Machines Corporation.

APPENDIX B / FORMAT OF JCL STATEMENTS

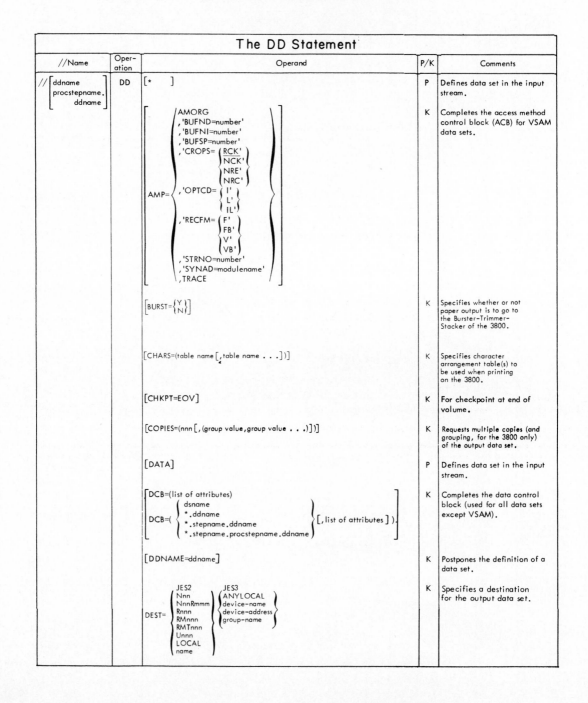

The DD Statement				
//Name	Oper-ation	Operand	P/K	Comments
// [ddname procstepname. ddname]	DD	[*]	P	Defines data set in the input stream.
		AMP= { AMORG ,'BUFND=number' ,'BUFNI=number' ,'BUFSP=number' ,'CROPS= (RCK' / NCK' / NRE' / NRC') ,'OPTCD= (I' / L' / IL') ,'RECFM= (F' / FB' / V' / VB') ,'STRNO=number' ,'SYNAD=modulename' ,TRACE }	K	Completes the access method control block (ACB) for VSAM data sets.
		[BURST= {Y / N}]	K	Specifies whether or not paper output is to go to the Burster-Trimmer-Stacker of the 3800.
		[CHARS=(table name [,table name . . .])]	K	Specifies character arrangement table(s) to be used when printing on the 3800.
		[CHKPT=EOV]	K	For checkpoint at end of volume.
		[COPIES=(nnn [,(group value,group value . . .)])]	K	Requests multiple copies (and grouping, for the 3800 only) of the output data set.
		[DATA]	P	Defines data set in the input stream.
		[DCB=(list of attributes) DCB=({dsname / *.ddname / *.stepname.ddname / *.stepname.procstepname.ddname} {,list of attributes}).]	K	Completes the data control block (used for all data sets except VSAM).
		[DDNAME=ddname]	K	Postpones the definition of a data set.
		DEST= {JES2 Nnn NnnRmmm Rnnn RMnnn RMTnnn Unnn LOCAL name} {JES3 ANYLOCAL device-name device-address group-name}	K	Specifies a destination for the output data set.

//Name	Oper-ation	Operand	P/K	Comments
// [ddname procstepname. ddname]	DD	DISP=([NEW OLD SHR MOD ,] [,DELETE ,KEEP ,PASS ,CATLG ,UNCATLG] [,DELETE ,KEEP ,CATLG ,UNCATLG])	K	Assigns a status, disposition, and conditional disposition to the data set.
		[DLM=delimiter]	K	Assigns delimiter other than /*.
		[DSID=(id[,V])]	K	Indicates to a diskette reader that data is to be merged into the JCL stream at this point or specifies the name to be given to a SYSOUT data set written on a diskette.
		{ DSNAME DSN } = { dsname dsname(member name) dsname(generation number) dsname(area name) &&dsname &&dsname(member name) &&dsname(area name) *.ddname *.stepname.ddname *.stepname.procstepname.ddname }	K	Assigns a name to a new data set or to identify an existing data set.
		[DUMMY]	P	Bypasses I/O operations on a data set (BSAM and QSAM).
		[DYNAM]	P	Specifies dynamic allocation.
		FCB=(image-id [,ALIGN ,VERIFY])	K	Specifies forms control information. The FCB parameter is ignored if the data set is not written to a 3211 or 1403 printer.
		[FLASH=(overlay name [,count])]	K	Identifies the forms overlay to be used on the 3800.
		[FREE= { END CLOSE }]	K	Specifies dynamic deallocation.
		[HOLD= { YES NO }]	K	Specifies whether output processing is to be deferred or processed normally.
		LABEL=([data set seq #] [,SL ,SUL ,AL ,AUL ,NSL ,NL ,BLP ,LTM ,] [,PASSWORD ,NOPWREAD ,] [,IN ,OUT] [,EXPDT=yyddd ,RETPD=nnnn])	K	Supplies label information.
		[MODIFY=(module name [,trc])]	K	Specifies a copy modification module that is to be loaded into the 3800.

The DD Statement (con't)

//Name	Oper-ation	Operand	P/K	Comments
// [ddname procstepname. ddname]	DD	[MSVGP=(id[,ddname])]	K	Identifies a mass storage group for a mass storage system (MSS) device.
		[OUTLIM=number]	K	Limits the number of logical records you want included in the output data set.
		[PROTECT=YES]	K	Requests RACF protection for tape volumes or for direct access data sets.
		[QNAME=process name]	K	Specifies the name of a TPROCESS macro which defines a destination queue for messages received by means of TCAM.
		SPACE=({TRK, CYL, blocklength}, (primary quantity [,secondary quantity][,directory / ,index]) [,RLSE][,CONTIG / ,MXIG / ,ALX][,ROUND])	K	Assigns space on a direct access volume for a new data set.
		SPACE=(ABSTR,(primary quantity,address [,directory / ,index]))	K	Assigns specific tracks on a direct access volume for a new data set.
		SUBSYS = (subsystem name [,parm1 [,parm2]...[,parm254]])	K	Specifies the subsystem that will process both the data set and the specified parameters.
		[SYSOUT=(class name [,program name][,form name / ,code name])]	K	Assigns an output class to an output data set.
		[TERM=TS]	K	Identifies a time-sharing user.
		UCS=(character set code [,FOLD][,VERIFY])	K	Requests a special character set for a 3211 or a 1403 printer.
		UNIT=({unit address / device type / user-assigned group name}[,unit count / ,P][,DEFER]) UNIT=AFF=ddname	K	Provides the system with unit information.
		{VOLUME / VOL}=([PRIVATE][,RETAIN][,volume seq number][,volume count][,] SER=(serial number,...) / REF=dsname / REF=*.ddname / REF=*.stepname.ddname / REF=*.stepname.procstepname.ddname)	K	Provides the system with volume information.

Legend:

P   Positional parameter. (Positional parameters must precede keyword parameters)
K   Keyword parameter.
‖   Choose one.

[ ]   Enclosing subparameter, indicates that subparameter is optional; if more than one line is enclosed, choose one or more.

Reprinted by permission from *OS/VS2 MVS JCL* (GC28-0692). © 1974 by International Business Machines Corporation.

APPENDIX C

DATA USED IN EXAMPLES

The following data are used in the examples throughout the text. The first thirty records are printed in Chapter 2 and used to create POLYFILE in Chapter 3. The last ten records are added to POLYFILE in Chapter 4.

The data represent records of an insurance policy data set. The fields, their positions, and their lengths are as shown in the table.

Field	Columns	Length
Policy number-key	1–5	5
Name	6–25	20
Type of policy: A = auto, H = home, L = life	29	1
Premium	30–35	6
Due date, MMDD	36–39	4
Year-to-date payments	40–45	6
Year policy started, YY	50–51	2

APPENDIX C / DATA USED IN EXAMPLES

```
----+----1----+----2----+----3----+----4----+----5----+----6
13009REED,TINA              A0842000426072100      74
15174HANDJANY,HAIDEH        H0229000220022900      71
17337BUTERO,MAURICE         H0501000434050100      63
19499LAFER,BRUCE            A0706000819050000      52
21661LEE,SUI                A0390170303030017      76
23821COOPER,LUCY            L0745000730070000      64
25980NELSON,LAWRENCE        L0513000217051300      78
28138KRUKIS,SONIA           A0346000510034600      59
30295CHEN,YIN               H0295000514010000      81
32451SIMPKINS,KEVIN         L0388000321038806      76
34605PORTER,MICHELE         A0627500128042700      65
36759DECICCO,RICHARD        A0255000619010000      71
38912ABREU,JUANITA          H0732001030070000      80
41063HIGH,CAROL             L0311000521031100      82
43214ENGLISH,REYNOLDS       A0443000228043300      82
45363LEE,BOHYON             A0515000214050000      79
47512THOMPSON,STANLEY       H0640750307064075      66
49659VALDEZ,FABIO           L0706000430070600      71
51805AMATO,ROBERT           A0466000417015000      63
53950RIZZUTO,JAMES          A0693000822000000      81
56094SCHWARTZ,MICHAEL       H1037000605050000      67
58238RUFINO,CARLOS          L0673000520047300      64
60380MORLEY,JOHN            A0786000514078600      71
62521BREVIL,JAMES           H0812000314081200      55
64660FALCONER,EDWARD        L1080000227008000      74
66799MARTIN,KATHLEEN        L0895000129089500      65
68937YEUNG,SUK              A0517000816050000      49
71074PAUL,MARINA            A0441000414034100      80
73210FRADIN,SHIRLEY         L0668000728066800      56
75344BURNS,JEFFREY          L0706000226070000      57

77478KATZ,HAL               A0485000406038500      64
79610WRIGHT,DONNA           H0926000901092000      75
81742CUOMO,DONNA            L0900000313090000      69
83872LOPEZ,ANNA             A0679000716010000      80
86002ALEXANDER,LISA         A0402000623030200      73
88130GOLDBERG,LORI          H0987000524095000      67
92057HOFMANN,PATRICA        H0737000315040000      77
92384PUGH,CLIFFORD          A0750000423075000      80
94509FERRIS,LAURA           A0135000815013500      73
96633BERGIN,MICHAEL         L1608000116100000      74
----+----1----+----2----+----3----+----4----+----5----+----6
```

APPENDIX D

DATA FOR PROGRAMMING ASSIGNMENTS

The following data may be used for the programming assignments. The data represent records of a student transcript data set. The fields, their positions, and their lengths are as shown in the table.

Field	Columns	Length
Student number-key	1–5	5
Name	6–25	20
Sex M/F	30	1
Year of birth, YY	31–32	2
Date of first admission, YYMM	33–36	4
Major	40–41	2
Credits attempted	45–47	3
Credits completed	48–50	3
Grade point average	51–53	3

APPENDIX D / DATA FOR PROGRAMMING ASSIGNMENTS

```
----+----1----+----2----+----3----+----4----+----5----+----6
13472ANDERSON,MARY            F638102    LA   064064342
18596BAKMAN,MICHAEL           M628102    DP   056034218
19623CARR,MICHELE             F607909    MT   076062254
20485CORNEJO,FRANK            M628209    LA   034032271
21849GORDON,BARBARA           F588202    LA   024024216
22468PERNA,JUDY               F478109    DP   048048400
28591KAPLAN,ANN               F638109    BT   064060341
34163LEHEY,JANETTE            F587702    LA   116042191
35926MARICIC,JAMES            M628109    DP   072060246
37482ROSENBERG,SCOTT          M598102    AT   036036301
38597SAGINARIO,LOUIE          M617909    CE   097097286
39432SCHNEYMAN,PAUL           M607809    DP   112112382
39582SCOTT,JOAN               F597702    DP   124120352
40613SIRACUSANO,COSMO         M638109    ME   086084275
41563YEE,MARY                 F608202    LA   046036200
42691WRIGHT,JAMAL             M527709    LA   054054256
43719VAZQUEZ,JAMES            M618109    DP   046030192
44827ROSENBERG,STEVE          M638202    AC   038034257
45927RICHARDS,RANDY           F618009    ET   077070284
46218KISAREWSKI,MICHAEL       M638302    DP   026026341
47526YEUNG,SUE                F628309    LA   029020284
49627VOLIKAS,PAUL             M648302    LA   034034261
49747RUBIO,EDGAR              M638009    DP   042032217
49982REEKSTIN,ROBIN           F628002    DP   076076381
50621NOBLESALA,FERNANDO       M547209    ET   137042201
51276MURRY,RITA               F648202    LA   027025284
51384MOLINA,ANGELA            F588102    AC   047045252
51486SALERNO,ROBERT           M608209    LA   038030147
52924LYNCH,PATRICIA           F558302    DP   032032352
54621LEW,SUK YI               F628009    MT   047040259

55609BERGAMASCO,MARGARET      F457909    DP   062062384
57842CAVE,REBECCA             F638009    AT   037030199
59027FRANKLIN,CARL            M658209    DP   042042259
61347GOYA,WINSTON             M638102    MT   036026204
62427JEREZ,PATRICIA           F607909    LA   044029218
64983MANOZA,SILVIA            F627902    DP   046044337
66717FISHER,STEVEN            M648006    ET   026026261
67849GREENE,DAVID             M627909    LA   046040289
70316HARRISON,MARIE           F648109    ET   026020214
74926POWELL,JOHN              M618002    DP   060060259
----+----1----+----2----+----3----+----4----+----5----+----6
```

APPENDIX E

MAGNETIC TAPE AND DISK— ADVANCED CONCEPTS

RECORD FORMATS

In Chapter 3 you learned that data may be stored on magnetic tape and disk as fixed-length records and as fixed-length blocked records. These two record formats are shown in Figure 3.1. There are several other record formats that are used with sequential data sets and entirely different record formats that are used with ISAM data sets. These record formats are discussed in this appendix.

Sequential Data Sets

VARIABLE-LENGTH RECORDS.   Chapter 3 assumed that all the records were the same length. This does not have to be the case; records may also have variable lengths. Suppose, for example, a dentist keeps a data set which contains patient information. Each record might contain identifying information about the patient and information about each visit. Patients with few visits would have short records, while patients with many visits would have long records.

Figure E.1a shows unblocked variable-length records. When variable-length records are written, the system adds four bytes, called the record descriptor word (RDW), to the beginning of each record. The system stores the logical record length in the record descriptor word. The system also adds an additional four bytes, called the block descriptor word (BDW), to the beginning of each block. The system stores the blocksize in the block descriptor word. The block descriptor word is not really necessary, since for unblocked records the blocksize is equal to the record length, but nevertheless the system adds the block descriptor word to each record.

Like fixed-length records, variable-length records are frequently blocked. As shown in Figure E.1b, when blocked variable-length records are written, the system automatically adds a record descriptor word to each record and a block descriptor word to each block.

When variable-length blocked records are written, the system puts as many records into a block as will fit without causing the block to exceed the specified blocksize. If a record cannot fit in a block, a new block is started.

For variable-length records, LRECL must be equal to the length of the largest record plus 4. So if the largest record has a length of 150 bytes, LRECL would be set equal to 154. Also, for variable-length records, the BLKSIZE must be at least equal to LRECL plus 4. So for this example, BLKSIZE could be as small as 158, but larger values would be valid, too.

SPANNED RECORDS. Variable-length records may also be spanned. With spanned records, the record length may be larger than the blocksize. As Figure E.1c shows, if the record length is larger than the blocksize, a record may occupy more than one block. Another way to say this is that the record spans more than one block, which is where the name spanned records comes from.

The system adds 4 bytes, called the segment descriptor word (SDW), to the start of each segment. The segment descriptor word contains the length of the segment and a code which indicates whether the segment is a complete record, the first segment, an intermediate segment, or the last segment of a record.

When spanned records are blocked, the system fills each block. If adding a record to a block will cause the block to exceed the specified blocksize, the record is split into segments. The first segment is put into the incomplete block to bring it up to size, and the second segment is put into the next block. If the second segment is too large to fit into the next block, it is split into two segments. This splitting is repeated as many times as necessary to get the segments to fit into blocks.

FIGURE E.1

Record formats used with sequential data sets

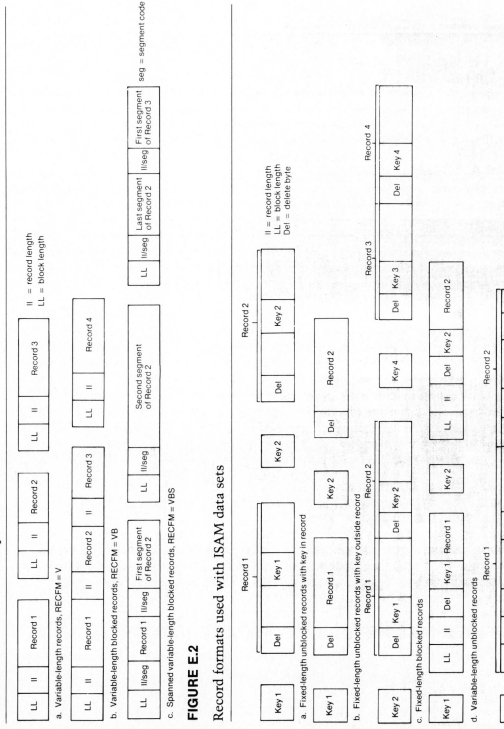

a. Variable-length records, RECFM = V

ll = record length
LL = block length

b. Variable-length blocked records, RECFM = VB

c. Spanned variable-length blocked records, RECFM = VBS

seg = segment code

FIGURE E.2

Record formats used with ISAM data sets

a. Fixed-length unblocked records with key in record

b. Fixed-length unblocked records with key outside record

c. Fixed-length blocked records

d. Variable-length unblocked records

e. Variable-length blocked records

ll = record length
LL = block length
Del = delete byte

UNDEFINED FORMAT RECORDS. Records may also have an undefined format. With undefined format records, each block is treated as a record. The blocks may have a variable size. An undefined record format is specified by coding RECFM=U.

ISAM Data Sets

Let us examine the various record formats that may be used with an ISAM data set. They are illustrated in Figure E.2. The first difference from the other record formats we studied is that the key field is outside the record. Since the key is available outside the record, it is not necessary to examine the record itself to learn if this is the record being sought.

Figure E.2a shows the layout of the fixed-length unblocked record. You will notice that the first field in the record is labeled "Del." This is the delete byte and is in position 0 of the record. (The first byte of the record is position 0, the second is position 1, and so forth.) When the delete byte contains the hexadecimal value FF, this record is a dummy record or is marked for deletion. The record is actually deleted when the data set is reorganized. A dummy record is written to the data set to reserve space for future record additions. You will notice that the key itself resides somewhere in the middle of the record. In general, if the key occupies the first byte of the record (position 0), records cannot be deleted because there is no way to mark them for deletion.

Figure E.2b shows a fixed-length unblocked record in which the key is in position 0. In this case, the key is stored only outside the record and is not repeated within the record.

Figure E.2c shows a fixed-length blocked record; the key field contains the highest key in the block.

Figures E.2d and e show the record layout of variable-length records. In this case, the first 4 bytes are reserved for system use. If you want to be able to delete records, you must save the fifth byte for use as the delete byte. The key in this situation can start in the sixth byte or position 5.

MAGNETIC DISK—SPACE REQUIREMENTS

When a job requests that a data set be created on a particular disk pack, the system checks to see that there is sufficient free space on the pack to contain the data set. If there is not sufficient space available, the job will not run.

MAGNETIC DISK—SPACE REQUIREMENTS

To know beforehand whether your data set will fit on a disk pack, you have to know how much free space there is on the pack and how much space your data set requires. In Chapter 14, you learned how to use the utility IEHLIST to find out how much free space there is on a disk pack. To find out how much space your data set requires, you can use a table such as Table E.1.

Table E.1 refers to a 3336 Disk Pack; IBM publishes similar tables for other disk packs. Table E.1 shows how the capacity of a disk pack depends on the size of the record and whether the data set contains keys.

Table E.1 shows that for records without keys the largest block that can fit on a track is 13,030 bytes. Since a block must fit on one track, 13,030 is the largest blocksize that may be used with a 3336 Disk Pack. For records with keys Table E.1 shows that the largest blocksize is 12,974 bytes.

To illustrate how Table E.1 is used, assume you have a sequential data set which contains 100,000 records and whose record length is 300 bytes. Since sequential data sets do not contain keys, you will use the columns headed "Without Keys." If you wanted to perform similar calculations for indexed or direct data sets, you would use the columns headed "With Keys."

Let us first assume that the records are unblocked. Therefore, each block contains one record and the blocksize is 300 bytes. The columns for records without keys in Table E.1 show that if the blocksize is between 290 bytes and 303 bytes, 30 blocks will fit on a track. Since each block contains one record, this means that 30 records will fit on a track. The whole data set requires 100,000 records divided by 30 records per track or 3,333.33 tracks. Since space is allocated in full tracks, this is rounded up to 3,334 tracks.

If the records are blocked using a blocking factor of 10, the blocksize will be 3,000 bytes. Table E.1 shows that 4 such blocks will fit on a track, but since each block contains 10 records, this is equivalent to 40 records on a track. The 100,000 records would require only 100,000/40 = 2,500 tracks. In this case, blocking the records reduced the space requirements by 834 tracks, a 25 percent reduction.

You must not think that larger blocking factors always reduce the space requirements. For example, with a blocking factor of 15, the blocksize would be 4,500 bytes. Table E.1 shows that only 2 such blocks will fit on a track. Since each block contains 15 records, this is equivalent to 30 records on a track, which is exactly what the track held when the records were not blocked.

To calculate the largest blocking factor that could be used with these records, simply divide the maximum blocksize, 13,030 bytes, by the logical record length, 300 bytes. The answer is 43.43, but since the blocking factor must be an integer, you discard the fractional part of the answer and conclude that the maximum blocking factor is 43.

TABLE E.1

Track capacity of 3336 Disk Pack

Bytes per Block Without Keys		With Keys		Blocks per Track	Bytes per Block Without Keys		With Keys		Blocks per Track
Min	Max	Min	Max		Min	Max	Min	Max	
6448	13030	6392	12974	1	277	289	221	233	31
4254	6447	4198	6391	2	264	276	208	220	32
3157	4253	3101	4197	3	253	263	197	207	33
2499	3156	2443	3100	4	242	252	186	196	34
2060	2498	2004	2442	5	231	241	175	185	35
1746	2059	1690	2003	6	221	230	165	174	36
1611	1745	1455	1689	7	212	220	156	164	37
1328	1510	1272	1454	8	203	211	147	155	38
1182	1327	1126	1271	9	195	202	139	146	39
1062	1181	1006	1125	10	187	194	131	138	40
963	1061	907	1005	11	179	186	123	130	41
878	962	822	906	12	172	178	116	122	42
806	877	750	821	13	165	171	109	115	43
743	805	687	749	14	158	164	102	108	44
688	742	632	686	15	152	157	96	101	45
640	687	584	631	16	146	151	90	95	46
597	639	541	583	17	140	145	84	89	47
558	596	502	540	18	134	139	78	83	48
524	557	468	501	19	129	133	73	77	49
492	523	436	467	20	124	128	68	72	50
464	491	408	435	21	119	123	63	67	51
438	463	382	407	22	114	118	58	62	52
414	437	358	381	23	109	113	53	57	53
392	413	336	357	24	105	108	49	52	54
372	391	316	335	25	101	104	45	48	55
353	371	297	315	26	96	100	40	44	56
336	352	280	296	27	92	95	36	39	57
319	335	263	279	28	89	91	33	35	58
304	318	248	262	29	85	88	29	32	59
290	303	234	247	30	81	84	25	28	60

MAGNETIC DISK—SPACE REQUIREMENTS

TABLE E.1 (cont.)

Track capacity of 3336 Disk Pack

Bytes per Block Without Keys		Bytes per Block With Keys		Blocks per Track	Bytes per Block Without Keys		Bytes per Block With Keys		Blocks per Track
Min	Max	Min	Max		Min	Max	Min	Max	
78	80	22	24	61	26	27			81
74	77	18	21	62	24	25			82
71	73	15	17	63	22	23			83
68	70	12	14	64	20	21			84
65	67	9	11	65	19	19			85
62	64	6	8	66	17	18			86
59	61	3	5	67	15	16			87
56	58	2	2	68	13	14			88
54	55			69	12	12			89
51	53			70	10	11			90
48	50			71	9	9			91
46	47			72	7	8			92
43	45			73	6	6			93
41	42			74	4	5			94
39	40			75	3	3			95
36	38			76	1	2			96
34	35			77					
32	33			78					
30	31			79					
28	29			80					

Reprinted by permission from "IBM 3330 Series Disk Storage" (GX20-1920-1), November 1973, by International Business Machine Corporation.

For data sets on disk, it is common to choose blocking factors such that two or four blocks fit on a track. This is called half-track or quarter-track blocking.

EXERCISES

Suppose a data set that you want to store on a 3336 Disk Pack contains 60,000 records, and that each record has a length of 400 bytes. Use Table E.1 to answer the following questions:

1. If the data set is unblocked, how many records will fit on a track, and how many tracks will be required to store the data set?

2. If a blocking factor of 10 is used, how many records will fit on a track, and how many tracks will be required to store the data set?

3. What is the maximum blocking factor that could be used with these records?

GLOSSARY

Positional parameter is recognized by the operating system by its position in the operand field. These parameters must be coded before any of the keyword parameters. (2)

Prime area is that part of the ISAM data set that contains the data. It is always required. (12)

Prime key is the original key in a KSDS. (13)

Procedure is precoded JCL. (8)

PROC statement, if used, is the first statement in a procedure. It is required for instream procedures, but is optional for cataloged procedures. It is used to set default values for symbolic parameters. (8)

Procstep is an abbreviation for procedure step. (8)

Queue is a waiting list or line. (1)

Random access refers to the ability to directly read a particular record and add a record in the middle of a data set without re-creating the data set. (12)

Real storage in a virtual system is main storage as opposed to auxiliary storage. (1)

Record definition field contains the length of the corresponding record in the control interval and the number of records that are of that length. (13)

Recording density is the number of bytes recorded per inch of tape. Common values currently are 800, 1600, and 6250. (3)

Relative byte address (RBA) is the byte count starting from the beginning of the storage space used to locate a particular record. (13)

Relative key position (RKP) specifies the location of the key in the record. The first byte is 0, the second is 1, and so forth. (12)

Relative record data set (RRDS) is a VSAM data set in which each record is uniquely identified by its position in the data set or its record number. (13)

Remote job entry (RJE) refers to job entry devices (such as a card reader) located away from the central computer but connected by communication lines, which frequently are supplied by the telephone company. (1)

Reorganization (ISAM) recovers space by eliminating records marked for deletion and places records from the overflow areas in their proper place in the prime area. (12)

Reorganization (PDS) reclaims unused space in a library or PDS. (5)

Return code—see **Condition code**. (2)

SDS stands for sequential data set. (4)

GLOSSARY

Segment is a piece of a load module created when overlay structure is used. (8)

Sequence set is the lowest level index in the index portion of the KSDS. (13)

Sequential access method (SAM) means that records are processed in the order in which they physically occur in the data set. (1)

Serial number consists of one to six alphameric characters and is used to identify a reel of tape or a disk pack. (3)

Sorting puts data set records into a specified order. (10)

Source code is the high-level-language program. (8)

Source module is the assembler or a high-level-language program. (8)

Special characters are characters other than letters, digits, and the three national characters. (2)

Spooling writes the input job stream to DASD and writes the printer or card punch output to DASD instead of the printer or card punch. Spooling isolates the CPU from the slow unit record devices. Spool is an acronym for simultaneous peripheral operations online. (1)

Staging is the process of taking data from a mass storage volume and placing it on a 3336 Disk Pack, where it is accessible through an application program. (7)

STEPLIB is the ddname of a DD statement that points to the library or libraries in which the executable load modules used in a step are found. (8)

Stepname is the name field coded on the EXEC statement. (2)

Symbolic parameter starts with an ampersand and represents a parameter or subparameter in a procedure. (8)

Syntax is the structure of expressions in the language. (1)

Syntax error is an error that violates a JCL rule. In English, such an error is called a grammatical error. (2)

Sysgen is the process by which a system is created or generated to meet the individual requirements of an installation. (1)

Task is an executable program and associated data. It is the basic unit of work performed by a computer. (1)

Temporary data set is a data set whose name starts with two ampersands. These data sets do not exist when the job starts or after the job ends; they only exist for the life of the job. (8)

Terminal consists of a typewriter device or typewriter-like keyboard and TV-like display screen connected by a communications line to a computer at a central site. (1)

GLOSSARY

Time sharing is having many terminal users employ a computer simultaneously. (1)

Track is a circle on the recording surface of a disk pack upon which data are recorded. (3)

Transparent means that the user is not aware of a process. For example, in a virtual system paging is transparent to the user. (1)

Unit record device is a card reader, card punch, or printer. (1)

Unpacking converts packed decimal data to character format, usually for printing. (1)

Utility program performs commonly required tasks. See Chapter 14. (1)

Virtual storage treats auxiliary storage as if it were main storage. Programs are divided into small sections called pages. (1)

Virtual storage access method (VSAM) is an access method especially designed for use with virtual systems. (1)

Virtual storage operating system, VS1, is a virtual version of MFT. (1)

Volume is a reel of tape or a removable disk pack. (3)

Volume label is the first record on a reel of tape. It contains the serial number of the volume. (3)

VTOC stands for volume table of contents. There is a VTOC on each disk pack which is used to keep track of the data sets stored on each volume as well as the space still available for use. (3)

Workstation is an RJE station or terminal. Workstation may be written as either one or two words. (1)

BIBLIOGRAPHY

OS/VS1 JCL Reference, GC24-5099
MVS JCL, GC28-1300

OS/VS1 Utilities, GC26-3901
OS/VS2 MVS Utilities, GC26-3902

OS/VS1 System Messages, GC38-1001
OS/VS Message Library, VS2 System Messages, GC38-1002

OS/VS1 System Codes, GC38-1003
OS/VS Message Library, VS2 System Codes, GC38-1008

OS/VS MSS Services Reference Information, GC35-0017

IBM OS/VS COBOL Compiler and Library Programmer's Guide, SC28-6483
OS PL/I Optimizing Compiler Programmer's Guide, SC33-0006
OS/VS-VM/370 Assembler Programmer's Guide, GC33-4021
IBM OS FORTRAN IV Compiler Programmer's Guide, SC28-6852

OS/VS Linkage Editor and Loader, GC26-3813

OS/VS Sort/Merge Programmer's Guide, SC33-4035

IBM 3800 Printing Subsystem Programmer's Guide, GC26-3846

OS/VS1 Access Method Services, GC26-3840
OS/VS2 Access Method Services, GC26-3841

OS/VS1 Checkpoint/Restart, GC26-3876
OS/VS2 MVS Checkpoint/Restart, GC26-3877

INDEX

INDEX

INDEX

INDEX

INDEX

INDEX

COMMON ABEND CODES AND THEIR CAUSES

001 CHECK,GET,PUT—I/O error.

An I/O error occurred during the reading or writing of a data file. Your DCB did not contain the address of an error handling routine; therefore, your program was terminated. Specify an error handling routine address. Other conditions causing this abend: the logical record length and blocksize specified in the DCB or DD statement differ from the logical record length and blocksize indicated in the data set.

0C1   Operation exception.

An operation code is not assigned or the assigned operation is not available on the particular model. In this instance the machine did not recognize the instruction or operation used. Possible reasons include a clobbered core or a subscript error. This error could be caused by an attempt to read a file that was not opened, a misspelled ddname, or a missing DD statement.

0C4   Protection exception.

In high-level languages this means that a subscript was out of range or a computed GOTO type statement took a wild branch.

0C5   Addressing exception.

An address specifies any part of data, an instruction, or a control word outside the available real storage for the particular model. A subscript error also usually causes this error (see 0C1 and 0C4).

0C7   Data exception.

With a high-level language, this code usually results from attempting a "decimal" operation on properly defined fields with invalid contents (garbage, not initialized, overwritten, etc.). The equivalent of decimal in COBOL is COMPUTATIONAL-3 and in PL/I is FIXED DECIMAL. Note that converting a zoned decimal (character) format to binary involves a decimal operation.

122   Normal operator-issued cancel and dump.

The job may have been cancelled because of an endless loop or because resources were not available. Consult your operator to find out why the job was cancelled and resubmit it. There may be nothing wrong with your job.

213 OPEN—I/O error.

The error occurred during execution of an OPEN macro instruction for a direct access device. In the case of disk reads, this usually means that the data set